Contents

PART II
PLANNING FOR, DESIGNING, AND IMPLEMENTING THE MIS

PART III
ADVANCED CONCEPTS

PART IV
CASE STUDIES

Management theory and practice have undergone radical changes in the past two decades; these changes will inevitably continue and even accelerate. It is no longer enough that managers be skilled in a functional specialty such as engineering or marketing and that they understand the traditional functions of planning, organizing, and controlling. Something more is needed: the systems approach to management, coupled with the ability to participate in the design and utilization of computer-based information systems. Indeed, the systems approach is the new philosophy of managerial life. We are now in the "age of systems."

There are a number of books available on the individual topics of (a) management and organization, (b) computers, (c) information, and (d) the systems approach. However, none have combined and blended these topics into a set of related concepts, a unified body of knowledge and practice. This is the ambitious aim of our book. We hope it will provide a more up-to-date and integrated treatment of organization and management, as well as emphasize the utilization of management information systems to improve the art of managing.

One objective is to get practicing managers and students of management to "think systems." If we can take the mystery out of computer-based information systems for them, they should be better prepared to become involved in the effective design and use of those systems. Such involvement is essential for the manager of the 1980s!

For the computer specialist, the information-systems specialist, or the student of computer systems, the objective is to improve the utility of the systems they design. We make the unequivocal point that such systems must always be designed from the point of view of the manager-user and not that of the specialist. In order to achieve this perspective, the information-systems specialist must understand management, management decision making, and the role of systems design in improving the management process.

An additional objective of the book is to help close the communication gap that separates the manager from the computer specialist. This gap undeniably exists and is the direct cause of the gross underutilization of the vast majority of computer installations. The reasons are readily apparent. Managers either are too busy, uninterested, or unwilling to take the time to raise their understanding to a level necessary for direct involvement. This book should bring them to that minimum level. Information-systems specialists, on the other hand, are more often engrossed in the special nature of the system. That it should be designed for the requirements of the manager-user is not necessarily uppermost in their minds. In other words, if left to their own devices, they design a system that ignores reality. This book can direct them to new and vastly more profitable areas of application.

NEW ORGANIZATION

This third edition has been prepared for two reasons. First, we wanted to take advantage of the valuable feedback received from students, professors, and managers who have used this book. Second, we needed to reflect the changed relationship between the firm and the computer. A few years ago, only large companies could afford computerized management information systems. Now, solutions employing small computers are within the reach of every business (and will soon touch the lives of every individual).

The organization of this third edition has been directed toward capturing and holding the attention of both the practitioner and pragmatic student. Additional practical and specific material has been provided. Part I presents the underlying concepts for understanding management, systems, the computer and databases, and management information systems. Part II discusses strategic and project planning for management information systems, followed by an operational approach to design, implementation, evaluation, and maintenance of an MIS. There is also a review of potholes to avoid on the MIS development highway. Part III offers conceptual and theoretical ideas on systems, control, information feedback and feedforward, and modeling. Instructors may wish to omit this part for an undergraduate course.

While keeping the best of the case studies from the second edition, a couple of new ones have been added. The "Johnson Enterprises" case study accompanies the student through several chapters, applying the concepts learned in each chapter. This case culminates in a decision problem: choose a small computer solution to the firm's management information system needs.

As before, we realize that any attempt to cover all aspects of MIS in less than several dozen volumes leads to criticisms of superficiality. Our object, however, is to provide a range of introductory *practical* and *conceptual* material which is suitable to the heterogeneous MIS courses taught in collegiate schools of business.

ACKNOWLEDGMENTS

We are grateful to our colleagues who provided many helpful suggestions and to Robert M. Manente of IBM, who made this revision possible by his support of

James Claggett during the critical phases of this project. We also wish to thank the companies and their representatives who so kindly allowed us to reprint their material.

The authors' wives, Emily Murdick, Carol Ross, and Sue Ellen Claggett, deserve special mention for their production assistance and support during the preparation of the manuscript. In addition, Geri Ekeroth cheerfully provided typing assistance whenever needed.

Robert G. Murdick
Joel E. Ross

Boca Raton, Florida

James R. Claggett

Armonk, New York

Information Systems
for Modern Management

1

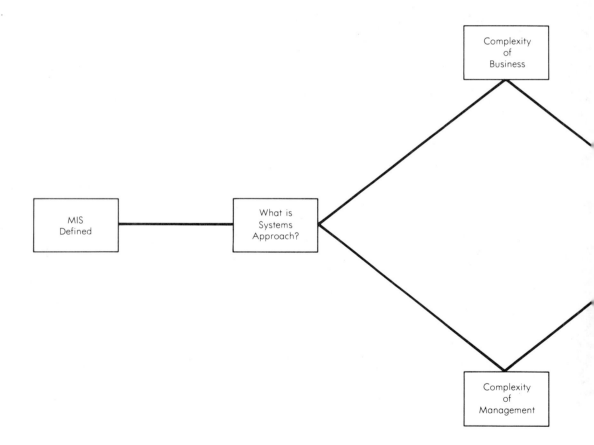

MIS Defined

What is Systems Approach?

Complexity of Business

Complexity of Management

The Meaning and Role of Management Information Systems

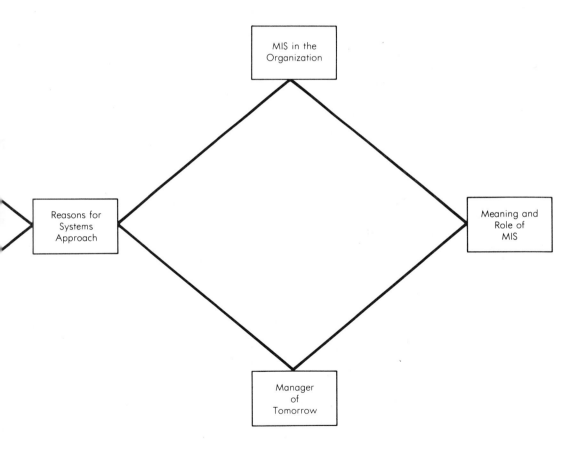

MIS in the Organization

Reasons for Systems Approach

Meaning and Role of MIS

Manager of Tomorrow

Item: In 1983 over 80 percent of colleges of business accredited by the American Association of Collegiate Schools of Business offered a degree program or major emphasis in information systems or planned to implement such a program within the next three years.

Item: More than half of all employed Americans now earn their living as "knowledge workers," exchanging various kinds of information.

Item: In 1982 alone more than 100 companies sold almost 3 million personal computers.

Item: Some 16,000 software programs are available for the Apple personal computer.

These headlines are interesting and fairly descriptive of the explosion in computer use during the very recent past. But what does it mean in terms of today's student of management information systems and today's practicing manager? Very simply, it probably means that managers who do not have the ability to use the computer will become organizationally dysfunctional, or worse, useless as decision makers.

Several years ago the consulting firm of Booz, Allen, and Hamilton conducted a comprehensive study surrounding computer usage and concluded that modern-generation equipment was being used for first-generation systems design. At about the same time another respected consulting organization, McKinsey & Company, concluded that "In terms of technical achievement, the computer revolution in the U.S. has been outrunning all expectations. In terms of economic payoff on new applications, it has rapidly lost momentum."

These conclusions reflect the fact that for decades the focus on computer use has been on the machine itself rather than on the vastly more important dimension of application and software—the systems design capability—the "brainware" if you like. It is the purpose of this book to fill this gap by concentrating on the managerial applications of computer use—*management information systems.*

WHAT IS A MANAGEMENT INFORMATION SYSTEM?

Despite the fact that the computer is nothing more than a tool for processing data, many managers view it as *the* central element in an information system. This attitude tends to overrate and distort the role of the computer. Its real role is to provide information for decisions and for planning and controlling operations.

Judging from the business press, the brave new world of *management information systems* (*MIS*) is upon us. There is hardly a business magazine today that does not contain articles on information systems, data banks, and related subjects. Despite this proliferation of books, articles, seminars, and courses surrounding this area, few efforts have managed to synthesize the separate subjects of *management, information, and systems* and to show how these are related to computers. This synthesis is a major goal of this book. Let us begin by defining the concept.

A Management Information System Defined

Because this book is largely devoted to the design and utilization of computer-based information systems, it is appropriate to define clearly the term MIS.

MIS is not new; only its computerization is new. Before computers, MIS techniques existed to supply managers with the information that would permit them to plan and control operations. The computer has added one or more dimensions, such as speed, accuracy, and increased volumes of data, that permit the consideration of more alternatives in a decision.

The scope and purpose of MIS is better understood if each part of the term is defined. Thus,

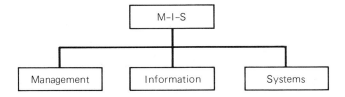

Management

Management has been defined in a variety of ways, but for our purposes it comprises the processes or activities that describe what managers do in the operation of their organization: plan, organize, initiate, and control operations. They *plan* by setting strategies and goals and selecting the best course of action to achieve the plan. They *organize* the tasks necessary for the operational plan, set these tasks up into homogeneous groups, and assign authority delegation. They *control* the performance of the work by setting performance standards and avoiding deviations from standard.

Because *decision making* is such a fundamental prerequisite to each of the foregoing processes, the job of an MIS becomes that of *facilitating decisions* necessary for planning, organizing, and controlling the work and functions of the business.

Information

Data must be distinguished from *information*, and this distinction is clear and important for our purposes. Data are facts and figures that are not currently being used in a decision process and usually take the form of historical records that are recorded and filed without immediate intent to retrieve for decision making. An example would be any one of the supporting documents, ledgers, and so on that comprise the source material for profit and loss statements. Such material would only be of historical interest to an external auditor.

Information consists of data that have been retrieved, processed, or otherwise used for informative or inference purposes, argument, or as a basis for forecasting or decision making. An example here would also be any one of the supporting documents already mentioned, but in this case the data could be used by an internal auditor, the management services department of an external auditor, or internal management for profit planning and control or for other decision-making purposes.

Systems

A *system* can be described simply as a set of elements joined together for a common objective. A subsystem is part of a larger system with which we are concerned. *All* systems are parts of larger systems. For our purposes the organization is the system, and the parts (divisions, departments, functions, units, etc.) are the subsystems.

Whereas we have achieved a very high degree of automation and joining together of subsystems in scientific, mechanical, and factory manufacturing operations, we have barely scratched the surface of applying systems principles to organizational or business systems. The concept of synergism has not generally been applied to the business organization, particularly as it applies to the integration of the subsystems through information interchange. Marketing, operations, and finance are frequently on diverse paths and working at cross purposes. The systems concept of MIS is therefore one of optimizing the output of the organization by *connecting the operating subsystems through the medium of information exchange.*

> *The objective of an MIS is to provide information for decision making on planning, initiating, organizing, and controlling the operations of the subsystems of the firm and to provide a synergistic organization in the process.*

In summary, we are concerned with three systems: (1) that social system called *the organization*, (2) a *system of management* that is used in practice to improve the operations and productivity of the organization and its subsystems, and (3) the *management information system*, which provides the information for making decisions regarding the integration of the organization through the process of management.

NOTE ON DECISION SUPPORT SYSTEMS

Recently, the phrase *decision support systems* (DSS) has become popular. It is sometimes described as the next evolutionary step after management information systems (MIS). For this description to be valid, MIS must be defined narrowly as the automating of routine and structured tasks to support decision making. Although this is certainly one definition of the term MIS, we use a much broader definition in this book, one that encompasses current thought on DSS.

- MIS support decision making in both structured and unstructured problem environments.
- MIS support decision making at all levels of the organization.
- MIS are intended to be woven into the fabric of the organization, not standing alone.
- MIS support all aspects of the decision making process.
- MIS are made of people, computers, procedures, databases, interactive query facilities, and so on. They are intended to be evolutionary/adaptive and easy for people to use.

In other words, although we use the older term MIS, we have defined it broadly and it is a superset of current ideas on DSS.

WHAT IS THE SYSTEMS APPROACH?

The systems approach can be explained by describing *what it is not*. As one chief executive recently commented, "Marketing seems to be selling what can't be designed and what manufacturing can't produce and to customers that finance wouldn't approve anyway!" Imagine also these hypothetical but typical questions in a manufacturing organization that reflect nonintegration:

What has purchasing done with the parts for the rush order?
Why wasn't production notified of the changed sales forecast?
What is the impact on my operations of the change in prime rate?
Why is assembly working half-time while other departments are working overtime?

The systems approach in business was an idea born in the decade of the 1960s. The notion was one of *synergism*—the sum of the parts is greater than the whole—2 + 2 = 5—the output of the total organization can be enhanced if the component parts can be integrated. This concept was the rationale for the conglomerate form of organization—a concept that subsequently fell into disrepute because of widespread conglomerate near failure.

For our purposes the systems approach to management is designed to utilize scientific analysis in complex organizations for (1) developing and managing operating systems (e.g., money flows, personnel systems), and (2) designing information systems for decision making. The link between these two is obvious because the reason for *information systems* design is to assist in decision making regarding the management of *operating systems*.

A basic and fundamental notion of the systems approach to organization and management is the interrelationship of the parts or subsystems of the organization. The starting point of the approach is a set of objectives, and the focus is on the design of the whole as distinct from the design of components or subsystems. The *synergistic* characteristic of the systems approach cannot be overemphasized. In organizational and information systems design we want to achieve *synergism*, which is the simultaneous action of separate but interrelated parts that together produce a total effect greater than the sum of the individual parts. The result obtained by a team of 11 well-coached football players is greater than that achieved by 11 individual players "doing their own thing." The analogy for the business organization is clear. The MIS can go a long way toward achieving the integration we seek.

In the past, the effectiveness of business organizations has been somewhat less than optimum because managers failed to relate the parts or functions of the systems to each other and to the whole. The sales function was performed without a great deal of integration with design or production; production control was frequently not coordinated with financial or personnel planning; and the classic management information system was concerned largely with variance reporting on an historical basis and was constructed around the chart of accounts without too much regard for organizational information needs.

A basic tenet of systems theory is that every system is held together by information exchange. This is certainly true of the business system or the organizational system. Yet information systems and computers have not focused in on this essential characteristic or need for integration. The need, and the potential, for such integration through information can be demonstrated conceptually in Figure 1-1. The heavy solid line indicates classical authority relationships and the hierarchical structure of the typical organization. The dashed lines show the same organizational structure but with the parts joined together in a system by means of information flow.

Students of management, and business people, frequently express some criticism of an overemphasis on the systems approach. They say that it is nothing new, that managers have intuitively known of synergism and reckoned

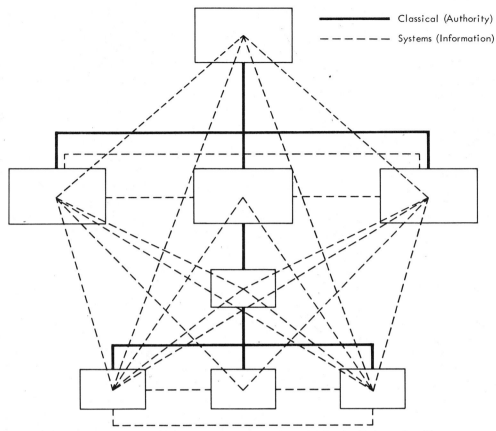

FIGURE 1-1 The Classical and Systems Approach to Organization and Information Flow

with it in the past. While this is a valid comment, it becomes necessary to point out two shortcomings of "systems thinking" in the past. First, we have been unable to design very many MIS that facilitate organizational integration, and second, the absolute need for the systems approach will continue to accelerate in the 1980s. There are two major reasons for this acceleration: (1) the increased complexity of business and (2) the increased complexity of management.

The Increased Complexity of Business

This complexity can be attributed to four primary causes: (1) the technological revolution, (2) research and development, (3) product changes, and (4) the information explosion.

The Technological Revolution

We need only look around the home and workplace to witness the fantastic changes wrought by the technological revolution of the past 20 to 25 years. We have walked on the moon and returned. Time and space have been dwarfed. Transportation, communications, agriculture, and manufacturing are among the many industries undergoing vast changes in products, techniques, output, and productivity. The "technological revolution" is not a continuation of the Industrial Revolution; it is a vast and fundamental change in its own right, as advanced mechanization and automation techniques are adopted and improved across a broad range of industries. The future of this revolution is not entirely clear, but two things are quite certain: change will continue at an accelerated pace, and this change will demand giant steps in improved management. It is fundamental that in order to cope with these changes, the manager of the future will require large amounts of selective information for the complex tasks and decisions ahead. Thus *the technological revolution will require a managerial revolution.*

Research and Development

The breathtaking rate of the technological change racing through all types of industry is due in large part to increasing expenditures for research and development. Despite the fact that relatively few firms engage in research and development and that these concentrate in a few areas, the impact of these expenditures is felt by all. Not only are products and supporting operations becoming more complex but the life cycle of products is being shortened. For example, consider how the DC-6, a reciprocating engine airplane, was made obsolete in less than five years by the pure jets.

Charles Kettering, a General Motors executive, once commented, "By its very nature research is a gamble...but the only risk that is greater than doing research is not doing it." This comment was not intended to imply that all companies should perform research. However, all should be aware of its impact on their operations and should provide for better planning, better management, and better information to accommodate the effects.

Product Changes

Technological advances resulting partly from research and development, partly from growing customer sophistication, have resulted in the third cause of complexity—product changes. Whereas the manager of the past could depend upon a high percentage of his or her product ideas becoming marketable, today's manager must deal with an enormously high product mortality rate. Moreover, the modern organization is faced with the necessity to optimize return from a given product in a much shorter time. The Model T Ford may have been good for a product life span of 10 years, but today's automobile manufacturer must offer more than a thousand combinations of model, color, and power selections.

DuPont's nylon, invented in the 1930s, had no competition for many years. Today the head start of many chemical fabrics is measured in months. It is a point of pride with many companies that over half their income today is derived from products that did not exist 5 to 10 years ago. New industries are being born overnight. The computer and electronics industries provide dramatic examples.

These factors contributing to complexity combine to form another element that calls for better management and the systems approach—the lengthening time span required between decisions and realization of commitments. These commitments are for such large amounts of money and for such long periods of time that the manager cannot afford to make mistakes. Major oil companies plan 20 years ahead for acquisition sources. Consider also the complexity of decisions required by airlines, heavy equipment manufacturing, and other industries that cannot afford to guess wrong.

The implication emerges that today's manager must keep abreast of the factors influencing his or her firm's products and future operations. This requirement demonstrates once again the need for a properly designed management information system, particularly with regard to environment–an environment that includes competitors who are themselves using up-to-date methods.

The Information Explosion

Finally, the information explosion has profound impacts upon the complexity of management and organizations. As a decision maker, the manager is essentially a processor of information. The modern manager knows that the ability to obtain, store, process, retrieve, and display the right information for the right decision is vital. This is, after all, the basic reason for an information system —better decisions.

Various estimates have been made concerning the information explosion. It is said, for example, that people's knowledge is doubling in each 5- to 10-year period and that this rate of knowledge accumulation is accelerating. It is estimated that 85 to 90 percent of the scientists of all time are now living, an indication of the accelerated growth of knowledge and information in recent years. Here we are interested not so much in the precise degree to which information is expanding as in the knowledge that information available to and required by today's manager is expanding enormously. To remain ahead of competitors and to keep pace with the technological revolution and its impact on the firm's products or services, the manager must keep abreast of selected information and organize it for decision making.

Increased Complexity of Management

What new techniques have become available that make the 1980s the era of the systems approach? There have been four developments that, when integrated with what we already know about managing, may give us a breakthrough in improving the management process. Essentially, these four developments are (1) the theory of information feedback systems, (2) a better understanding of the decision making process, (3) operations research or management science techniques that permit an experimental or simulation approach to complex problems, and (4) the electronic computer.

Information Feedback Systems

Basic to the understanding of the systems approach and to the design of management information systems is the concept of information feedback systems. This concept or theory is something more than our old exception principle. It explains the goal-seeking, self-correcting interplay between the parts of a system, whether the system is business, mechanical, or otherwise. Essentially, feedback systems are concerned with the way information is used for the purpose of control, and they apply not only to business or management systems but to engineering, biological, and many other types of systems. Examples of information feedback systems include the thermostat-furnace-temperature system, as well as the subsystems comprising the missile, the automobile, the body, the economic system, the inventory control system, and countless others. All have a vital trait in common: *the output of the system leads to a decision resulting in some type of action that corrects the output, which in turn leads to another decision.* Although the theory of information feedback systems is not entirely new (the speed governor for steam engines dates back to about 1780), it has only recently become available to and applied in business applications. Later chapters explore this theory more fully.

Decision Making

A development of extraordinary importance to building a foundation for the systems approach is the recent notion of *automating* or *programming* decisions. Indeed, this concept is at the very core of systems design, as we shall discover later.

Some attribute this improved understanding of automatic decisions and the decision-making process to the military. Prior to 1950, the commander, using "tactical judgment and experience," made such on-the-spot decisions as threat evaluation, weapon selection, enemy identification, alerting of forces, and target assignment. Subsequently, these and similar decisions were "automated" by formal rule and procedure, thus leading to the proposition that formal rules may yield better decisions for routine problems than those based solely on human judgment, given the constraints under which humans must make decisions.

The notion of *programming* decisions by *decision rule* is now a basic consideration of management and information systems design. If decisions can be based upon a policy, a procedure, or a rule, they are likely to be made better and more economically. Moreover, if the decision rule can be programmed for computer application, the potential exists for faster, more accurate, and more economical operations. Examples of common decision rules that have been programmed for computer solution are payroll, inventory control, customer billing, and purchasing.

Later chapters explain in detail decision rules in information systems design and the use of management science in designing these rules.

Management Science

Closely allied to programmed decisions and decision rules are the techniques of management science. Indeed, one of the primary purposes of these techniques is the design of programmed decision rules. Another purpose, often overlooked, is that of assisting managers to make complex decisions. The techniques of management science combine with the computational ability of the computer to provide problem solutions that were not practical heretofore.

Linear programming, system simulation, the Monte Carlo technique, queuing, gambling, probability theory, and other quantitative approaches are available to the management scientist. However, we are interested not so much in specific tools or techniques as in the management science approach to problem solving.

A powerful tool of management science is *simulation*. Although this technique was used relatively infrequently prior to 1970, it offers great potential breakthroughs for applications of the systems approach. The technique involves construction of a mathematical model of the system (e.g., business or function) under study. The behavior of the model under manipulation simulates the behavior of the real system to the extent that the consequences of different management policies, marketing assumptions, or resource alternatives can be forecast prior to final decision.

The Electronic Computer

The fourth major development making the systems approach to management possible is the electronic digital computer. Without it, the vast amount of data handling connected with storage, processing, and retrieval of information would not be possible, nor could the arithmetic computations required in many problem-solving situations be economically undertaken.

Despite the fact that the computer is nothing more than a tool for processing data or making computations, many managers view it as *the* central element in an information system. This attitude tends to overrate and distort the role of the computer. The vital element in an information system is the human one; it is the managerial talent that designs and operates the system!

The computer's capability to process and store information has outraced man's ability to design systems that adequately utilize this capability. "Brainware" has fallen woefully behind "hardware." Unfortunately, it appears that the human talent available for the design of managerial applications will lag behind the technology of the computer for many years to come.

In the past, managers sought information from miscellaneous—haphazard —sources and processed the information on a personal basis. Too often they failed to ask for information concerning the impact of a decision in one area on other areas of the company.

Three changes are now occurring in progressive companies:

1. *Management* has become systems oriented and more sophisticated in management techniques.
2. *Information* is planned for and made available to managers as needed.
3. A *system* of information ties planning and control by managers to operational systems of implementation.

The combined result of these concepts is the management information system. The purpose of an MIS is to raise managing from the level of piecemeal spotty information, intuitive guesswork, and isolated problem solving to the level of systems insights, systems information, sophisticated data processing, and systems problem solving. Managers have always had "sources" of information; the MIS provides a *system* of information. It thus is a powerful method for aiding managers in solving problems and making decisions.

THE SYSTEMS VIEW OF BUSINESS

In the past, managers have tended to solve problems as isolated situations, independent of other operations of the company. For example, if a shoe manufacturer noted a sales decline and traced it to lack of aggressive effort by sales representatives, the problem was assumed to be a sales management problem. Solutions were sought through better training or replacement of their salespeople. The thought that there are many contributing factors to increasing sales was simply not brought to the surface. Better advertising, better management of sales representatives' routes, better quality control in the factory, better design, fewer styles, more sizes, prompt and *correct* shipment of orders, better credit arrangements, and better market strategy all may be part of the problem. Partial substandard performance in several areas may have caused salespeople to regard their task as hopeless. These activities are related in a "system" of which the business is comprised.

Further Development of the Nature
and Meaning of "System"

Our previous elementary definition of "system" is illustrated by examples of some very diverse types of systems:

System	Elements	Basic Goal
Human body	Organs, connective tissue, bone structure, nerve network	Homeostasis
Social club	Members	Recreation for members
Factory	People, machines, buildings, materials	Production of goods
Missile system	People, missiles and launch sites, detection and communication networks	Counterattack
Police	People, equipment, buildings, communication networks	Control of crime
Computer	Physical components and connections	Processing of data
Philosophy	Ideas	Understanding
Accounting	Journals, ledgers, computers, people	Report of financial operations and the value of the firm and document transactions

This list of examples shows that systems vary greatly in elements, appearance, size, attributes, and basic goals. A carefully worded definition is therefore needed to identify their common features.

A system is a set of elements forming an activity or a processing procedure / scheme seeking a common goal or goals by operating on data and / or energy and / or matter in a time reference to yield information and / or energy and / or matter.

Some specific cases illustrate the somewhat abstract definition:

1. *Manufacturing system.* A group of people, machines, and facilities (*a set of elements*) work to produce a specified number and type of products (*seek a common goal*) by operating on product specifications, schedules, raw materials, subassemblies, and electrical power converted to mechanical power (*operate on data, matter, and energy*) to yield the specified products and information by the date the customer wants them (*to yield matter in a time reference*).

2. *Management information system.* A group of people, a set of manuals, and data processing equipment (*a set of elements*) select, store, process, and retrieve data (*operate on data and matter*) to reduce the uncertainty in decision-making (*seek a common goal*) by yielding information for managers at the time they can most efficiently use it (*yield information in a time reference*).

3. *Business organization system.* A group of people (*set of elements*) gathers and processes material and informational resources (*form an activity*) toward a set of multiple common goals including an economic profit for the business (*seek common goals*) by performing financing, design, production, and marketing (*operate on data, energy, and matter*) to achieve finished products and their sale at a specified minimum rate per year (*yield matter in a time reference*).

The synthesis of large, complex systems and the development of the concept of systems have also focused attention on the need for a systems approach to science and to man's problems. The term "large and complex" does not necessarily refer to size alone, but rather to the number of parts that make up the system and to their multiple interrelationships. The human organism and the microbiological systems are not large in physical size, but they are very complex when measured by number of parts and by processes in which the parts engage.

If we are to understand the complexities of nature and if we must design complex systems such as the modern management information system, we must develop the science of systems. That is, we must look more closely at what constitutes a system, at what the characteristics of systems are, what distinguishes classes of systems, and what comprises the systems approach. The methods of science require more precision than commonsense, intuitive methods. Science requires a thorough study of structure and processes. Therefore, although such careful inquiry may seem dry to the practice-minded reader, it is necessary for the design of effective, complex, practical systems.

MIS ORGANIZATION WITHIN THE COMPANY

If the MIS is to assist managerial decision making at all levels of the company, then low organizational level information systems must be integrated in broader MIS until one companywide MIS is available for top management. The design, redesign, modification, and maintenance of the company's total MIS must be headed by a top management figure. The question is, "Where should the head of this MIS be located in the organization?"

Organization Within the Company Structure

The most common place for MIS is under the vice president of finance. In many companies, the finance/accounting organization gained early control over the computer center. As a result, information systems were conceived of as control decision aids rather than planning decision aids. An example of a large successful company where the MIS evolved from the control concept is Xerox Corporation. Originally, a manager of Corporate Systems and Data Processing was responsible for the computer equipment and data processing. Now the MIS is centralized at the corporate level under the director of Corporate Information Services. Figure 1-2 shows the placement of MIS in Xerox now and for the future.

Besides locating the MIS organization with the financial/accounting control organization, or in the corporate planning organization, two other practices are followed. The most desirable practice is to have the MIS function report to

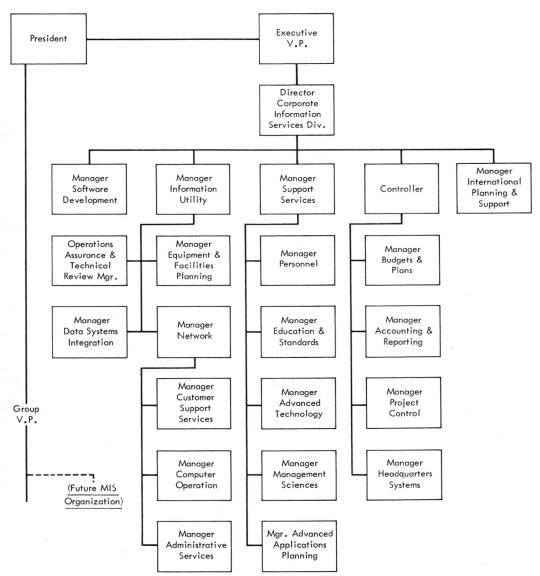

FIGURE 1-2 Placement of MIS Organization in Xerox Corporation

Source: Courtesy of Xerox Corporation.

the president so that it can supply information without distortion. Perhaps the worst practice is to make the MIS function report to the corporate head of computer facilities.

Organization Within the MIS Function

For a major first-time MIS effort, a company steering committee consisting of the MIS manager, the sales manager, production manager, finance manager, and engineering manager may guide the systems effort. A special project team

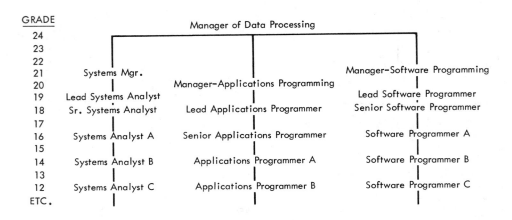

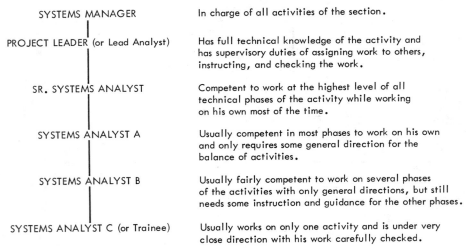

FIGURE 1-3 Organization Structure and Relative Salary Level

composed of representatives from each of the functional areas plus the technical systems people would carry out the design effort with heavy managerial involvement. Once the first MIS has been installed, there must be an organization which monitors it, keeps it running smoothly, and redesigns it from time to time.

The permanent MIS organization must include systems analysts (designers), computer and data communications specialists, and, sometimes, management scientists. The latter develop mathematical relationships for processing raw data into useful information such as sales forecasts, inventory reorder levels, and capital expenditure evaluations.

Figure 1-3 shows both organization structure and relative salary level of a typical organization.

SUMMARY: THE MANAGER OF TOMORROW

Very simply, a system is a set of elements, such as people, things, and concepts, that are related to achieve a mutual goal.

The business manager of tomorrow will be working with the same basic resources as the manager of today—people, physical systems operated by people, and conceptual systems. Changes in behavior of people and our understanding of how to motivate people in the work environment have progressed quite slowly despite many promised gimmicks. It is very likely that progress will continue to be slow in this highly important area of knowledge.

Changes in physical systems such as the factory production system, the physical distribution system, the data processing system, or the engineering development and test system are occurring rapidly with the accelerating progress in technology. The manager of tomorrow will live and work in a pushbutton world of color video surrounded by automatically controlled physical operations —in many cases, self-repairing systems. These changes will be the *visible* changes, which will provide a completely new façade for managing.

The really great change in managing, however, will be the change in the conceptual framework that underlies all organization and physical operations. This change will be in the development of system concepts. That is, all aspects of the total business including people, their activities, the physical parts of the business, and suppliers, customers, government, and public will be integrated by management far beyond today's primitive level. Perhaps the future manager will put it this way: "The synergistic/symbiotic relationship of a business and society will be optimized through a sophisticated total systems approach."

Why will such great changes in the conceptual framework of business occur? How will managers be able to handle the increasing complexity of business? Why will the manager be able to make better decisions that will lead to better total business system results? The answer is that the information utilized by the manager will be of far better quality, more timely, more selective, and more available. The "better quality" means that the information will be more nearly complete, more reliable, and processed to be available in many arrangements. The manager will be able to think rapidly through many approaches and solutions to complex problems because of such information. Providing this information will be a system of scanning the environment, an internal data bank and model bank, and computers beyond the imagination of today's lay public.

The major themes that run throughout this book are

1. A systems approach to managing is necessary to compete in business today.
2. The systems approach to management must precede the design and use of an MIS.
3. The computer is only a component, a tool, in the MIS, *not* the MIS or the central focus of the MIS.
4. Management must take an active part in the design of the MIS as the principal user. Technical knowledge of the computer is not necessary for the manager to perform his role in the design.
5. *Integrated*, *planned systems* are the essence of MIS, not "islands of mechanization" or data processing systems.

This book is about managing, it is *not* about the computer. It is *not* a book on "data processing" or programming. It *is* concerned with the systems approach to managing by the development of improved decision making through MIS. It *is* a book for managers and system design generalists.

PROBLEMS AND QUESTIONS

1. What are the political and social consequences of implementing the systems approach? For example, how can we implement government planning of airport facilities when unbridled competition is permitted? Is it reasonable for five different airlines to fly only half-filled planes to the same destination at about the same time?

2. What impact would (a) the technological revolution, (b) research and development, (c) product changes, and (d) the information explosion have on the need for information by management in an automobile manufacturing company? A hospital? A university?

3. Four advances in management development have been described: (a) the theory of information feedback systems, (b) a better understanding of the decision-making process, (c) management science, and (d) the electronic computer. Compare the use of these developments, by an organization of your choice, in the 1930s and in the 1980s. Possible selections are a manufacturing firm, a retail chain, a railroad system, an airlines company, a bank, and an insurance firm.

4. The president of one of the nation's largest food manufacturers and packagers recently declared, "Our information system gives us the edge we need over our competitors." Describe ways in which an information system could provide a competitive edge for this company.

5. Show how the systems approach would be useful in attacking the ecology problems of a large city. How might an industrial organization cooperate with the government in these problems?

6. Show how the components of a management information system (management, information, system) are interrelated. Show also how an MIS can facilitate the general functions of management (plan, organize, control).

7. Give two examples of data and demonstrate how these data can be made into information for decision making.

8. Give three functions of a manufacturing firm (e.g., marketing, production, finance) and show how an MIS could help integrate these functions. Do the same for a bank. A retail store.

9. For the three functions just given, how could the combined output of the three be greater than the output of each taken separately?

SELECTED REFERENCES

ALLEN, BRANDT. "An Unmanaged Computer System Can Stop You Dead," *Harvard Business Review*, November–December 1982.

AULGUR, JERETTA. "Computer Information Systems: A Vital Component of the Business Curriculum," *Collegiate News & Views*, Winter 1982–83.

BUSS, MARTIN D. "How to Rank Computer Projects," *Harvard Business Review*, January–February 1983.

McFARLAN, F. WARREN, JAMES L. McKENNEY, AND PHILIP PYBURN. "The Information Archipelago—Plotting a Course," *Harvard Business Review*, January–February 1983.

NOLAN, RICHARD L. "Managing Information Systems by Committee," *Harvard Business Review*, July–August 1982.

WEINBERG, GERALD M. *An Introduction to General Systems Thinking*. New York: John Wiley & Sons, 1975.

Recommended Journals

Info Systems. Hitchcock Publishing Company, Wheaton, Illinois.

Journal of Systems Management. Association for Systems Management, Cleveland, Ohio.

MIS Interrupt. The University of Calgary, Calgary, Alberta, Canada.

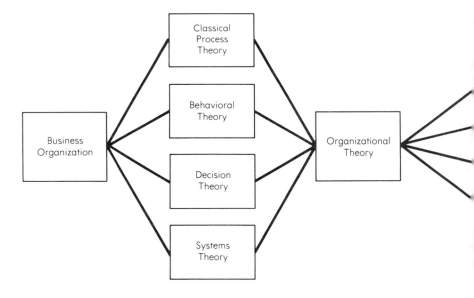

2

Management, Organizational Theory and the Systems Approach

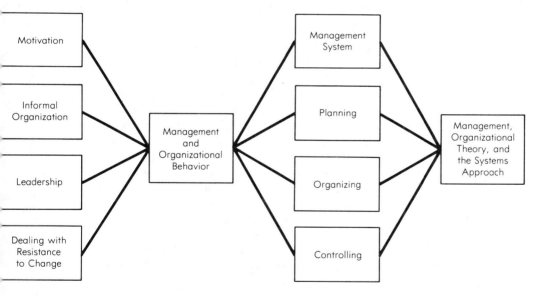

Future organizations will be based upon information and decision systems rather than upon static hierarchical authority / responsibility structure. The mark of a good manager will be the ability to arrange organizational patterns for problem solving and to develop technical systems that facilitate problem solving and implementation.

"Management" has existed since people first realized that a cooperative society was necessary to accomplish their goals. The approaches to management of societal groups has paralleled the economic development and value systems of society throughout time. With the rapid expansion of science in the last five centuries, with the highly developed complexities of modern business organizations in the twentieth century, it is not surprising that many scholars and practitioners have been investigating the management process.

Institutions attempt to accomplish their purposes by structuring their organizations so that problems may be solved quickly and efficiently. This requires a class of workers, called managers, to perform this structuring function. In addition, managers must influence the organization (individuals and work groups) to work cooperatively to achieve organizational objectives. As organizations have grown larger since the beginning of the Industrial Revolution, the necessity for formalized systems of information flow has risen in parallel. The information requirements for managers must be satisfied by a management information system. This MIS must be designed on the basis of management tasks, management principles, individual managers' styles and behaviors, and organizational structure and behavior. Further, the nature of the MIS design and the method of its implementation are reflected back by the members of the organization to impact managers and the functioning of the organization. A discussion of MIS therefore requires a foundation knowledge of management, organizational theory, and the systems approach.

DEVELOPMENT OF ORGANIZATIONAL THEORY

Overview

Organization theory and management theory differ in two ways. First, the former is concerned with the structure of interpersonal relations and the organization as a mechanism for promoting human collaboration. Management, on the other hand, sees the organization largely as a vehicle for achieving an output or an objective. Second, modern organization theory is a relatively new discipline, a development of the past few years, based heavily on scientific research.[1]

Among the more prevalent models of organization theory are the decision-making, bureaucracy, social systems, and systems models. The foremost proponent of the decision-making approach is Herbert Simon, who views organization members as "decision makers and problem solvers" and concludes that "administrative processes are decisional processes."[2] The bureaucracy model had its beginnings in the writings of Max Weber. It is still a valuable approach to organizations despite the widespread popularity of such satirical, antibureaucratic interpretations as *Parkinson's law*[3] and the *Peter principle*.[4] Weber's delineation of the structural and procedural characteristics of bureaucracy, the hierarchical structure of authority, and the notion of discipline based on formal positions are all concepts widely in use today and provided a foundation for construction of subsequent theories. The social systems model, derived from sociology, states that organizations are social systems.[5] A major proponent of this model is Talcott Parsons, who maintains that today's bureaucratic organizations came into existence as a result of complex modern society and its functional specialization and differentiation.[6] Moreover, it is the "primacy of orientation to

[1]Although modern organization theory is a development of the past few years, the brilliant Max Weber designed his bureaucratic model around the turn of the century, and it is largely unchanged today. Weber's analysis of bureaucracy is contained in Chapter VIII, "Bureaucracy," in H. H. Gerth and C. Wright Mills, eds. and trans., *Max Weber: Essays in Sociology* (New York: Oxford University Press, 1946).

[2]Herbert A. Simon, *The New Science of Decision Making* (New York: Harper & Row, 1960), p. 66.

[3]C. N. Parkinson, *Parkinson's Law* (Boston: Houghton Mifflin, 1957). Among Parkinson's antibureaucratic statements are "Work expands to fill the time available" and "An official wants to multiply subordinates, not rivals."

[4]Laurence J. Peter and Raymond Hull, *The Peter Principle—Why Things Always Go Wrong* (New York: William Morrow, 1969). Peter's principle asserts that "in a hierarchy every employee tends to rise to his level of incompetence."

[5]Dwight Waldo and Martin Landau, *The Study of Organizational Behavior: Status, Problems, and Trends* (Washington, D.C.: American Society for Public Administration, 1966), p. 11.

[6]Talcott Parsons, *Structure and Process in Modern Societies* (New York: The Free Press, 1963), pp. 16–58.

the attainment of a specific goal" that is the "defining characteristic of an organization which distinguishes it from other types of social systems."[7]

Two additional theories of organization—behavioral and decision theories—have influenced the development of modern organization and management theories. We will examine these in some detail, which in turn will bring us naturally to the systems approach to organization theory. A fundamental premise of this book is that the systems approach better fits the needs of a manager in today's organizations.

Classical Process Theory

The basic tenets attributed to classical theorists such as Henri Fayol,[8] Frederick W. Taylor,[9] L. Gulick and Lyndall Urwick,[10] and J. D. Mooney[11] are

1. *Clear lines of authority.* Every individual should be related through a chain of command to the top manager (scalar chain).
2. *Specialization of labor.* Breaking work down into small tasks that are easily learned leads to greater productivity. The company can then be departmentalized on the basis of grouping of similar tasks.
3. *Unity of command.* No person should report to more than one manager or supervisor.
4. *Span of control.* The number of people reporting to a manager should be limited by the nature of the tasks. Many articles argued whether span should be broad or narrow and tried to establish an ideal number.
5. *Clear separation of line and staff.* The staff members (or managers) are to act as *advisors* to line managers and not to influence other organizational members directly.

Classical theory achieved its momentum in the 1930s when the popular formal approach was developed by Gulick and Urwick[12] and by Mooney when his book, *Principles of Organization*, was first published.[13] Mooney popularized the *process* of managing, POSDCORB (planning, organizing, staffing, directing, coordinating, reporting, budgeting). Mooney also identified four methods of organizing: by major purpose, by process, by clientele, and by place. Mooney and his

---

[7]Ibid., p. 17.

[8]Henri Fayol, *Administration Industrielle et Generale* (1916), translated (London: Sir Isaac Pitman, 1949).

[9]Frederick W. Taylor, *Scientific Management* (New York: Harper & Row, 1947).

[10]L. Gulick and Lyndall Urwick, eds., *Papers on the Science of Administration* (New York: Institute of Public Administration, 1937).

[11]J. D. Mooney and A. C. Riley, *The Principles of Organization*, (New York: Harper & Row, 1943).

[12]Gulick and Urwick, *Papers on the Science of Administration*.

[13]Mooney and Riley, *The Principles of Organization*.

contemporaries discussed organization in terms of the coordinative, scalar, functional, and line-and-staff principles.

The basic premise of the classical school is that organizing is a logical, rational process. Given the objective, what you want accomplished, you determine the work to be done, group this work into logical units and define positions within these units in terms of a structure of accountability. Out of this comes the chart of organization and the position description of duties—a symmetrical picture of design. Emotional, illogical behavior is pathological; the work will be done if everyone follows the organization structure. The classical theory assumed that workers were rational and logical and would perform as expected. Moreover, workers prefer to have their job limits clearly defined. The activities of a group should be viewed on an objective and impersonal basis without regard to personal problems and characteristics. To the classicist, organizing relates to formal relationships between jobs to be done and positions; behavioral characteristics are treated, but as a separate matter. Hence, organization has a more limited meaning to classicists than to some of the more modern theorists.

In summary, the classical theory is valuable and is widely used today. It is limited by its concentration on the *formal anatomy* and structure of organizations and its insistence that human problems will take care of themselves if tasks are assigned and duties are organized. This somewhat narrow view overlooks such important factors as the informal organization, human interactions within work groups, and the contributions of the behavioral sciences. However, classical theory is still very much alive, is widely utilized, and is probably the approach taken by the preponderance of practicing managers.

Behaviorial Theory

The shortcomings of the classical model of organization and management were uncovered by the Hawthorne experiments of 1927 to 1932. At the Western Electric Company plant there, Elton Mayo, F. J. Roethlisberger, and their associates found that employee attitudes could be more important to productivity than the technical and physical environment. This discovery opened the way for a flood of research on organizational behavior, leadership, and motivation. The results are so important for an understanding of the systems approach and MIS that we will review the current theory farther on in this chapter.

Decision Theory

Decision making is the most important task of managers; many scholars believe that decision making and the process leading up to it account for most of what executives do. Among those who place great importance on the process is Herbert Simon, who states, "I shall find it convenient to take mild liberties with the English language by using 'decision making' as though it were synonymous with 'managing.'" Decision-making in its broadest context includes among the activities preceding the decision: (1) finding occasions for making a decision, (2) finding possible courses of action, and (3) choosing among courses of action.[14]

Viewed in the foregoing context, decision making becomes the "keyhole" look at management. Moreover, if we accept the thesis of the pure decision theorists, the entire process of management can be explained in terms of decision making. We take the position in this book that decision making is a fundamental aspect of management. Indeed, the systems approach to management would use the decision as its central focus. However, to say, as some decision theorists do, that the entire body of management theory can be based on the structure of decision making is to oversimplify the matter. Although decisions may be a major result of managing, other approaches, schools, disciplines, and processes provide the manager with the total body of knowledge he or she requires.

An additional doubt about whether decision theory has the total answer is raised by the question, "Does the decision complete the action sought or commence the action?" In other words, once the decision is made, it must be implemented, and the processes of implementation may require more than the answers provided by decision theory—particularly if we are concerned with only the quantitative aspects of decision theory.

According to Forrester, "Investigation of the nature of decision making in the context of modern military tactics forms a basis for understanding the place of decision making in industry."[15] At any rate, the armed forces were largely responsible for promoting a structured approach to decision making. Cyert, March, and Simon[16] are among those who have advanced the notion of adapting these decision-making methodologies to administration and opening a new era in which organization members are viewed as "decision makers and problem solvers." This idea is one of the key concepts of organization and management theory and a vital one in the design of management information systems.

Systems Theory of Organization and Management

We may synthesize the functions of management and the separate approaches to the study of organization and management to obtain a *system* of organization and management. The task is to construct a conceptual model through which we can understand how to *manage* the transformation of *resource flows* through the *organization* by means of a systems approach. Such an approach must also include as essential components the functions of the management process, mod-

---

[14]Simon, *The New Science of Decision Making*, p. 1.

[15]Jay W. Forester, *Industrial Dynamics* (Cambridge, Mass.: M.I.T. Press, 1961), p. vii.

[16]Richard M. Cyert and James G. March, *A Behavioral Theory of the Firm* (Englewood Cliffs, N.J.: Prentice-Hall, 1963). See also Simon, *The New Science of Decision Making*.

ern organization theory, and the techniques of the various "schools" of management.

Because our model will utilize the basic functions of management and the techniques of other approaches as the foundation, it is first desirable to indicate how these can be integrated. Figure 2-1 shows these interrelationships for selected illustrations. We have added an additional systems technique to show how this approach might also be useful in combining functions and techniques. The purpose of Figure 2-1 is to demonstrate how the functions of management utilize the techniques and approaches of other disciplines and that these approaches are of little value unless used to perform a function of management.

In actual practice the functions of management are interwoven and interrelated; the performance of one does not cease before the next commences, nor are the functions carried out in sequence. For example, a manager may perform controlling at the same time that he or she is planning and directing. Although there are times when some functions must be performed before others can be put into action (e.g., directing requires that persons have been assigned activities), generally speaking, there is no sequence to the operation of these functions or to the utilization of the techniques of management. However, none of them can be performed in a vacuum. As a matter of fact, planning is involved in the work of organizing, controlling is performed in the work of staffing, decision theory is used in the function of organizing, and management information systems are utilized in all functions and all disciplines. Each function and technique affects the others, and all are intimately interrelated in a system to form the major components of the system of management.

Given the foregoing integration of functions and techniques, we can now construct a conceptual model (Figure 2-2) of the system of organization and management—*a system that integrates the parts: resource flows, functions of management, organization theory, and the various techniques.* Notice that a vital additional component has been added, *a management information system.* This is the component of the system that provides information for planning, activates plans, and furnishes the essential feedback information necessary to achieve stability through control.

Figure 2-2 has taken the functions of management as the basic platform from which the system is constructed. These functions explain what managers do, how they manage resources to accomplish objectives. In doing this they depend upon the behavioral science knowledge of organization theory and the techniques of the other approaches to management. In performing the functions of management, managers call upon these techniques for use in the systems approach to management. To illustrate, we can examine the function of planning and its relationship to other functions and techniques. It is clear that in developing a plan, managers would want to utilize one or more of the techniques available to them. For example, the disciplines of the decision theorists as well as the techniques of mathematics would be most helpful if applicable to the particular situation. The past experience of the firm as well as that of other firms might also

	PLAN	ORGANIZE	STAFF	DIRECT	CONTROL	COMMUNICATE
PLAN	M	Implement plan through organization	Train for planning	Gain acceptance of plans	Recognize as a standard for achievement	Plan procedures for communications throughout the organization
ORGANIZE	Develop plan through organization	A	Assign tasks per organization	Communicate through organization	Recognize as a control vehicle	Organize resources to provide for communication
STAFF	Recruit and place for plans	View personnel requirements as a function of organization	N	Delegate by job description	Develop performance standard for recruiting	Formalize communication system
DIRECT	Direct with policies	Establish an organization structure for direction	Motivate through training	A	Participate in setting standards	Keep communications flowing freely at all stages and for all processes
CONTROL	Control plan	Recognize that control depends on organization	View requirements as a function of standards	Accept controls	G	Control the communication of standards; control the communication performance for corrective action
COMMUNICATE	Communicate plans in the proper detail to each person in the company	Communicate through organization charts, manuals, and reports: the distribution of resources	Communicate personnel needs and specifications	Communicate to initiate action at the proper time	Communicate standards of performance; communicate performance to responsible individuals for corrective action	E
CLASSICAL RATIONAL	Select objectives: develop plans	Develop work structure hierarchy departmentalization	Develop position guides, job specs	Assign authority rewards, sanctions	Develop plans, budgets, schedules, standards, reports	Establish a hierarchy of reports
BEHAVIORAL THEORY	Predict organization acceptance	Consider human needs in organizing	Encourage group participation in job standards	Assess leadership and motivation of workers	Gain acceptance of standards	Communicate on an interpersonal and two-way basis
DECISION THEORY	Evaluate alternatives	Engage in organization modeling	Establish selection and promotion policies	Assess alternatives in labor relations	Establish rules for control	Determine information flow for decision process
SYSTEMS	Consider stakeholder demands, system goals, and optimization	Relate organization to objectives, tasks, decision centers, and information flow	Develop personnel inventory and job database	Develop information systems and interpersonal two-way agreement	Develop trade-offs in cost and time	Optimize database and reporting

(Left margin labels: Functions — PLAN through COMMUNICATE; Tools — CLASSICAL RATIONAL through SYSTEMS)

FIGURE 2-1   Selected Illustrations Showing Interrelationships Among Functions and Concepts of Management

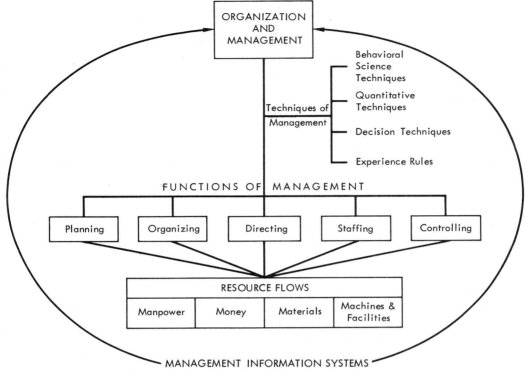

FIGURE 2-2 Organization and Management — A System

be of assistance. The behavioral science knowledge of modern organization theory is invaluable in implementing the plan.

The final component of the system is the envelope called *management information systems*, which encloses the entire model. This system collects, analyzes, stores, and displays data to management decision makers at all levels for the management of the resource flows of materials, personnel, money, and facilities and machines. This component is also vital to the practice of the functions of management.

MANAGEMENT AND ORGANIZATIONAL BEHAVIOR

Managing and Organizational Theory

For managers to implement the managerial functions and organizational plans and processes, they must have a motivated and supportive work force. The way that management organizes its resources, particularly the human resources, the

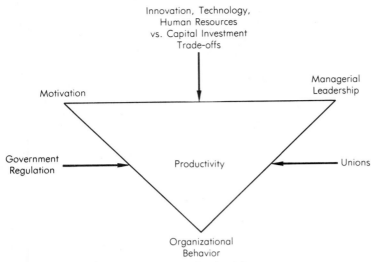

FIGURE 2-3   Major Factors Affecting Productivity

way it structures the work, the degree to which it seeks involvement of workers in these activities, and the degree and style of communication established in the organization have a tremendous impact on the type of organization that emerges. A knowledge of motivation, organizational behavior, and leadership is important to the designer of an MIS so that information systems will match actual organization requirements and increase productivity. Figure 2-3 shows the major factors affecting productivity with emphasis on all three.

Motivation

If we could utilize as much as half of the potential of human beings for productive work, the productivity increase would far exceed that possible from available technology. Why do people behave the way they do? What inner mechanism motivates people to give their all in certain situations but not in others? It is well worth a great effort by management to seek answers to these questions. Social scientists have provided some hypotheses about such behavior that can guide managers. Several of these, expressed in simplified fashion, follow.

Differentiation

The one law about human behavior that we can be certain of is that all people are different. The often-heard phrase, "All people are equal but some are more equal than others," has tremendous implications for the busy manager who tends to treat all subordinates alike, or for the more sophisticated manager who attempts to structure them into two or three classes.

Behavior differences between individuals are produced by physical differences, mental capabilities, life experiences, culture, and perceptions of a situation.

With age often comes a reinforcement of experiences and interpretations, which leads to resistance to new methods and concepts. Not only do behavior patterns vary among individuals, but individual behavior changes over time.

We point out this important fact of *differences* among individuals at this early stage because we are now going to present some characteristics of human behavior that appear to be shared by most people. We first wished to sweep out of the way the fallacy of stereotypes that entraps the insensitive leader.

Needs Models of Motivation

Needs are internal to the individual, and managers cannot impose them in the minds of their subordinates by edict, policy, or regulation. Managers may, however, provide *incentives* with the hope that needs will arise. The incentive pay system in the factory shows that incentives are often blocked by other factors in an individual's environment. Relatively few workers are motivated to become "rate-busters" by externally offered rewards. A second important implication for managers is that *a satisfied need is not a motivator*. The "human relations" concept of organizational behavior floundered on the assumption that the happy worker would be a highly productive worker. The proponents of this earlier theory failed to recognize that dissatisfaction (tension) is the cause of goal-directed activity.

Needs may generally be categorized as biological needs for maintenance of life and acquired (or learned) needs arising from experience. The strength of a need depends upon expectancy and availability. Expectancy is the degree of belief that a need can be satisfied. The proposition for the manager is, "Set goals and rewards within the capabilities of each individual." Availability of need satisfaction is also under the control of the manager in many cases. The management may make possible such goals as increased income, security through vesting in a pension plan, vacation time, personal fulfillment in work, or status achievement.

A number of "needs" theories of motivation appear plausible but lack rigorous research verification. As we shall show at the end of the discussion on motivation, all are in agreement with more validated models on what actions managers should take to increase worker motivation.

One of the best known but least substantiated models is the "hierarchy of needs" classification developed by the psychologist, A. H. Maslow.[17] The five categories, from highest priority to more acquired needs, are

1. Physiological needs
2. Safety, stability, and security
3. Affiliation, belonging to a group, love
4. Self-esteem (ego need) and the esteem of others (social recognition)
5. Self actualization—fulfillment of the person's potential and interests.

This classification with specific illustrations is shown in Figure 2-4.

---

[17]A. H. Maslow, *Motivation and Personality* (New York: Harper & Row, 1954).

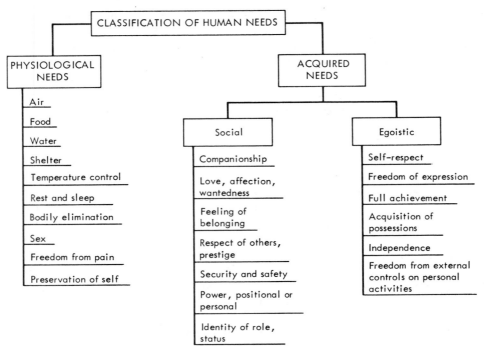

FIGURE 2-4 Basic Human Needs

In our society, the basic physiological needs are usually satisfied through the medium of money. We might expect therefore, as managers, that constant increments of money decrease in importance once the physiological needs are satisfied. Money remains important only to the extent that it can contribute to social or ego-need fulfillment, and then we may begin to substitute specific rewards or sanctions of the social or ego-need type.

In the case of people with whom security is a high-priority need, we can place them in stable organizations, provide security against layoffs and firing, offer steady growth, and provide comfortable medical, health, and pension benefits. Affiliation need may be closely associated with security. Those individuals desiring security feel safer in a group to which they belong and in which their roles and the roles of the others are clearly defined—that is, where they are "accepted."

The affiliation need develops just as strongly, or more so, in groups under pressure, in groups dissatisfied with working conditions, or in groups who find the work boring and trivial. This is discussed further in the section on informal organization.

The need for the esteem of others can be a very strong motivator in many instances. People who have an unconscious feeling of inadequacy may overcompensate by striving hard and by repeatedly seeking new successes. This need often appears characteristic of successful managers who seek prestige, status, power, and symbolically large salaries.

Self-esteem may be fulfilled in many ways, making it difficult for management to develop incentives based on this need. One individual may find self-esteem because he can outperform other managers in this activity. Another finds that self-esteem is lost if she participates, and she seeks a transfer or quits. Self-esteem is essentially a matching of a person's performance with his or her values and of those values held by the individuals in the organization. Each manager or supervisor is best prepared to use this motivator on an individual basis with his or her immediate subordinates.

The highest need in the hierarchy is the need for self-fulfillment, the need to achieve all that the individual is capable of, and to achieve it in a kind of work that the individual enjoys. Many people do not find enough independence of action and breadth of responsibility within the confines of the division of work developed through classical organizational precepts. Modern managements are now taking this learned need into account. Job enrichment through vertical and horizontal expansion of duties, increased participation of individuals in setting their own goals and in decision making, and a more careful search for the interest and capabilities of each employee are being carried out by the more progressive companies. In other words, the potential for performance, good and bad, of the individual in any system of the organization must be recognized by managers and systems designers.

Another "needs" theory that has received considerable attention is Frederick Herzberg's two-factor theory.[18] Herzberg's studies led him to conclude that there are two different categories of motivating factors. He discovered that poor *environment* factors—such as working conditions, policies and administration, money, and reshuffling of tasks—may make workers dissatisfied, but improving these conditions—what he calls *hygiene* factors—does not motivate workers to greater productivity. On the other hand, the *positive* motivators, Herzberg says, are stimulated by

1. Removing controls over the worker but holding the worker accountable for results
2. Giving a person a complete, natural module of work, not just adding and subtracting tasks
3. Granting the worker additional authority and job freedom
4. Making periodic reports available to the employee so that he or she may initiate corrective action instead of being directed to take it
5. Introducing new and more difficult assignments so that the employee may learn and grow

Other investigators using Herzberg's research methods have confirmed his results for various types of workers. Positive motivators have been found to be

---

[18]Frederick Herzberg, "One More Time: How Do You Motivate Employees?" *Harvard Business Review*, January–February, 1968.

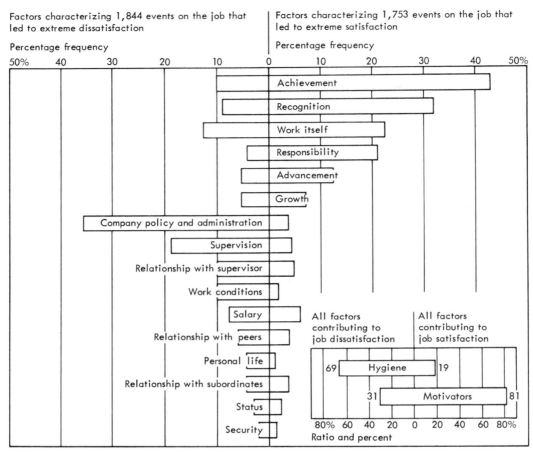

FIGURE 2-5   Factors Affecting Job Attitudes

Source: Frederick Herzberg, "One More Time: How Do You Motivate Employees?" *Harvard Business Review,* January – February 1968, p. 57.

the needs for achievement, recognition, the work itself, responsibility, advancement, and growth. A summary of hygiene factors and positive motivators is given in Figure 2-5.

The implications of Herzberg's research are clear. Management must provide a satisfactory level for work factors such as salary, work conditions, and others indicated in Figure 2-5. Paying very large salaries will not motivate workers, however. Management must seek the positive work motivators, such as opportunity for growth and recognition. These factors appear to be different for different classes of workers.

One of the most extensively researched models of motivation is the "achievement" model of D. C. McClelland and J. W. Atkinson.[19] They identified

[19] David C. McClelland, *The Achieving Society* (New York: Van Nostrand Reinhold, 1961), and J. W. Atkinson, *An Introduction to Motivation* (New York: Van Nostrand Reinhold, 1964).

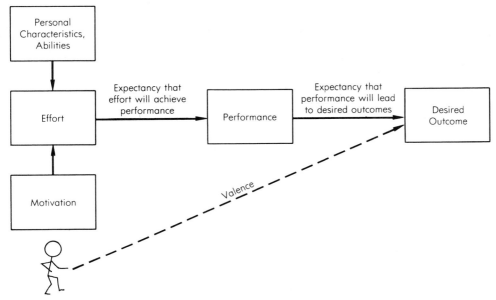

FIGURE 2-6 Expectancy Model of Motivation

three needs of people as

Need	Definition
Achievement	The need to set high attainable goals and be measured against them
Affiliation	The need for warm friendly interpersonal relationships
Power	The need to control and manipulate the individual's environment

McClelland found that achievement needs were relatively stable and developed over a person's childhood. For this reason, the selection process is very important in staffing. Managers must be supplied with high-quality and adequate information to make good choices.

Expectancy Models of Motivation

Expectancy models of motivation have been developed by Victor H. Vroom and by co-researchers Lyman Porter and Edward Lawler.[20,21] They view motivation as dependent on the strength of an individual's desire for a set of goals and

[20] Victor H. Vroom, *Work and Motivation* (New York: John Wiley, 1964).

[21] Lyman W. Porter and Edward Lawler III, *Managerial Attitudes and Performance* (Homewood, Ill.: Richard D. Irwin, 1968).

the likelihood that a specific type of behavior will lead to the achievement of the individual's goal. A simple representation of these ideas is shown in Figure 2-6. As can be seen, an individual starts with some desired outcome or goal in mind. He then constructs a bridge of likely happenings in terms of effort and performance to reach his particular goals. Motivation depends upon the certainty of the bridge's holding up.

Five terms used in the model of Fig. 2-6 are

Effort: how hard and how persistently an individual works.

Performance: behavior that directly promotes organizational goals. When a supervisor asks an employee to perform a work-related task, the doing of the task is "performance."

Expectancy: likelihood that a potential outcome will occur.

Outcomes: individual's feelings derived directly from the person's work, organizational rewards such as pay, and the social and physical environment in which the work is performed. Other terms used for job satisfaction are "satisfactions" and "rewards."

Valence: the strength of an individual's desire for a particular outcome.

Operant Conditioning Model

B. F. Skinner is the outstanding proponent of the human being as a system. Skinner rejects the explanations that humans initiate behavior; rather, the human is a passive processor of inputs. Behavior is determined by the individual in the light of its consequences. Management may therefore control the behavior of workers by prompt reinforcement of desirable behavior.[22] Skinner identifies four basic types of conditioning consequences:

1. Specify objectives and desired standard of performance.
2. Provide immediate feedback to the worker on his or her performance.
3. Provide positive reinforcement when performance meets standards by praise, incentive payments, and the like. Provide encouragement when performance does not meet standards but the worker has tried hard.
4. Do nothing when the worker has loafed or gone off in the wrong direction.

The concept of operant conditioning has been criticized on such grounds as that it ignores social processes, neglects conflicting stimuli, manipulates the individual, and is a technology rather than a theory. Its success under other names has been impressive, however. Wage incentive systems, commission plans, and MBO are examples.

---

[22] B. F. Skinner, *Beyond Freedom and Dignity* (New York: Knopf, 1971). See also David K. Hart and William G. Scott, "The Optimal Image of Man for Systems Theory," *Academy of Management Journal*, December 1972.

Implications of Motivation
Theories for Managers

Despite the differences among the theories of motivation, the common message for managers is: Determine what each worker wants, construct tasks, and present an environment that will permit the worker to achieve his or her goals. Develop a reward system for achievement of goals that matches organizational goals.

The Informal Organization
as a Social System

The formal organization and the informal organization within a company are inseparable in terms of interaction, but the characteristics of each may be discussed separately. Here we focus on informal relationships so that their influence on formally designed management systems such as the MIS may be taken into account.

Nature and Formation
of Informal Groups

Social organizations arise and persist because of our need for interaction with other humans. Two or more people who share activities, sentiments, or interactions form a social system. People gather into groups to satisfy needs of affiliation, security, identity, and power. The term *group dynamics* was popularized by Kurt Lewin, a social psychologist, to designate the forces and behavior that occur within a group. The linking groups and subgroups of members of a business organization form the *information organization*. "The informal organization is the total of member-initiated institutions existing without the sanction of formal authority."[23] The informal and the formal organizations modify, supplement, and reinforce or weaken each other.

Sociologists have identified six types of informal groups:

1. The *total organization* consists of all the many interlocking groups or subsystems in the entire organization.
2. *Large groups* form over some issue of internal politics. Typical of these groups might be production versus marketing factions, one aggressive young executive and his followers versus an old-line executive and his followers, or nonunion groups versus union groups.
3. *Primary cliques* form when workers are located together for work purposes or when employees have similar jobs and hence common interests. The workers in a maintenance crew, the top executives who work together and dine together in the executive dining room, and the professional accountants dispersed throughout the company are examples of primary cliques.

[23]Albert H. Rubenstein and Chadwick J. Haberstroh, eds., *Some Theories of Organization* (Homewood, Ill.: The Dorsey Press, 1960), p. 63.

4. *Cliques* include any small group that forms to gain some special power or social advantage.

5. *Friendship-kinship groups* form in many companies in which generation after generation of the same families become employees. Kinship groups form from relatives. Friendship groups form because of close social and neighborhood ties.

6. *Isolates* are the individuals who are loners and do not attach themselves to any group, or shift from group to group.

Cliques are composed of people who share the same values or norms. Acceptance in the clique is achieved only through acceptance by all members of the clique, not by just a single individual. Subcliques are linked partially to cliques in certain activities or by some common members. Isolates, not actually groups, are the "loners" who have weak connections with other people and groups. They do interact with other people and thus have some effect on the total social organization.

Determinants underlying the appearance of informal groups are

1. *Location*: the physical location in plant or office that provides face-to-face contact
2. *Occupation*: the tendency for people performing similar jobs to group together
3. *Interests*: people with like interests form small, informal groups
4. *Special issues*: the joining together for a common cause to form an informal group that usually disbands when the issue is resolved

FIGURE 2-7 Organization Stucture

Source: Reproduced from the Professional Systems Course, copyrighted by Leslie H. Matthies. Published by Systemation, Inc., P.O. Box 730, Colorado Spring, Colo.

Informal organizations assume certain characteristics that are different from those of formal, structured organizations; these must be taken into account when managing in a climate of informal groups.

1. *Informal organizations* act as agents of *social control*, generating a culture that demands conformity from group members.
2. *Human interactions* are quite different from those in the formal organization and different techniques of analysis are required.
3. *Status and communication* systems exist quite apart from the formal structure.
4. Informal organizations *resist change*.
5. The group has an *informal leader* who is not necessarily the formally appointed one.

Because organizations are made up of people, not boxes on organization charts, managers and systems designers must not isolate themselves from the actual organizational dynamics. Management must utilize information about social groups in the design of systems and must acknowledge the realities of organization as indicated in Figure 2-7.

Communication

One of the major functions of the informal organization is to provide for communication outside of the lengthy, rigid, formal chain of responsibility. Employees communicate with each other both laterally and vertically as necessary to get their jobs done, but this occurs according to the informal contacts they have in different parts of the organization. Such communication makes possible much more rapid response to job and situation requirements.

When official channels fail to provide full information about events, the informal organization often constructs its own messages. These messages, called "rumors," appear to spread through the informal organization with the speed of light. When a leak of official information occurs or when official information begins to work its way through the formal channels, the informal "grapevine" takes over in the same way.

Group Standards and Norms

The informal organization exerts strong pressures for conformity through social control methods. Implicitly, a new member in a social group accepts the norms and standards of the group, which are communicated to him or her by example, anecdote, expressions of attitude, and other behavior. Pressure for conformity of attitude and of action are brought to bear upon group initiates.

Group norms may restrict work output or increase it. If management wishes to change group norms, it must find people who are accepted by the group or who are influential within the group and change their attitudes. Obviously, this is not easy.

Group discipline can be very severe. The first signs of individual deviation from group norms may be greeted by kidding or sarcastic remarks. Refusal to provide work assistance and to communicate may follow. Heated arguments, physical violence, or covert damage to the person's property, such as tools, lunch, automobile, or home, may occur.

Within an informal group, each member achieves identity through his or her role, a role determined by the behavior expectations of others in the group. Informal leadership is assumed by those who exert more influence on the group than other individuals do, since role and status within the organization are closely related. Further on, we will discuss these topics in terms of power and accommodation.

Nature and Sources of Power and Authority

Power and authority are derived from both the formal and informal organizations in complex ways. To understand how these influences are related, we will discuss some basic concepts, admitting at the start that scholars are in disagreement among themselves with respect to the meaning of authority and power and their relationship to acceptance, responsibility, accountability, and control.

Authority may be considered, roughly, the "legitimate" right to command and to apply sanctions. Thus authority is derived from the formal organization. But how much authority does a person have if his or her subordinates refuse to obey? A number of explanations concern the source of authority. Some of the most commonly accepted are

1. Institutional approach
2. Subordinate approach
3. Organizational relationship
4. Legal decree
5. Personal acceptance or consultative authority
6. Identification
7. Sanctions
8. Authority of the situation

In the institutional theory, authority is derived from accepted cultural institutions—traditional, legal, or theological. Thus the concept of private ownership of property bestows upon the owners the authority to use the property as they see fit within general constraints imposed by society.

The subordinate acceptance school of thought states that managers have authority to the degree that their subordinates accept their decisions. Authority thus flows from the bottom of the organization upward and is gained by managers through their leadership and ability to win support from their subordinates.

Authority is often considered to be based upon the organizational position or organizational relationships that have been established. Here the individual receives his or her authority by virtue of the authority of the position.

Authority by legal decree is commonly found in the government. The law grants authority so that enforcement of the statutes may be carried out.

Personal acceptance or consultative authority arises because of recognition of the leader. Recognition may be due to the leader's popularity, past achievements, integrity, or skill and knowledge. In an organization, such a person may not have any formal authority (authority by position), but his or her recommendations may carry such weight that he or she appears to have extensive authority. Max Weber's charisma classification of authority would fall under this heading. Charismatic legitimacy is based upon irrational faith in the values and goals of the leaders.

One view holds that authority is derived from group "belongingness." According to this view, people will accept decisions that have been agreed upon by the group to which they belong, thereby delegating authority to the group. People who are strongly associated with the group making the decision will more readily accept the authority of the group. Therefore, the society in which we live is a source of authority, and society may thus be defined as the most comprehensive group to which an individual feels he "belongs." At the other end of the scale is the ad hoc committee that a manager appoints to develop a recommendation or make a decision where there is likely to be considerable resistance to any recommendation or decision. The committee participants, by taking part in the decision making, identify themselves with this group and accept its authority.

Authority is often identified with possession of sanctions, the rewards or punishment that one person may mete out to another.

The concept of the "authority of the situation" represents an attempt to integrate the goals of the organization with the goals of the individuals involved. As Mary Parker Follett describes it,

> *True authority springs from only the intrinsic competence, worthiness, and strength of one in a place of authority. To be called authority, it must be spontaneously and tacitly acquiesced to by the workers. Authority does not leap forth from the commands of those at the top simply because the organization charts say so. It arises out of "the law of the situation."*[24]

In application, the manager and his or her subordinate get together, assemble the facts of the situation, discuss alternate solutions to the problem at hand, and weigh the pros and cons. Through full discussion and mutual understanding, it is believed, one preferable course of action will be seen to be called for by the situation. The views of the manager (organization's goals) and of the subordinate (individual's goals) are thus integrated into a single course of action.

In all the situations except the last, authority is limited. Application of authority may lead to direct rebellion, reluctant acceptance, eager participation, or habitual acceptance such as occurs for routine instructions.

[24]H. C. Metcalf and L. Urwick, eds., *Dynamic Administration: The Collected Papers of Mary Parker Follett* (New York: Harper & Row, 1940).

Power and authority are considered by many theorists to be closely allied but frequently distinct. Power implies the capacity to exercise coercion—the hangman's rope, the police officer's club, the threat of firing from the job, or the threat of demotion. To the extent that authority involves some degree of sanctions, the ability to hurt the other person or group, it contains some element of power. Authority is separate from power when members of a group accept willingly the leadership of various members.

Conflict occurs within groups and between groups in both the formal and informal organization. Conflict is related to both power and cooperation: conflict brings shifts in power and is often resolved by power (influence); cooperation is often the end result of conflict.

Cooperation is a stronger need for individuals with greater needs for affiliation and stability. However, for those who covertly seek power, cooperation is necessitated by mutual goals.

In the past, conflict was often considered harmful and destructive of organizational goals. Modern administrative thought takes the view that there is much constructive potential in conflict. In business, this is achieved through "controlled competition" among individuals and groups.

Solutions of conflict, other than integration and cooperation, are (1) victory/defeat, (2) compromise, (3) avoidance of the subject, and (4) deadlock with varying ultimate consequences. Because the design and implementation of new systems often face group pressures against change, the designer and manager should be aware of methods for handling constructively the conflict of organizational and informal group goals.

Leadership for Managers

The essence of managing is effective and efficient utilization of resources, including human resources. In the organizational system, management must endeavor to stimulate the human components to achieve as much of their potential as possible. What behavior patterns should managers learn so that they may lead their subordinates toward achievement on basic organizational goals? In this section we discuss such managerial behavior in the light of the motivation and organizational behavior factors that we have just covered.

Nature of Leadership

Leadership has been defined in many ways. In general, leadership means providing the values and focus of action for other members of a group. Leadership is the process of influencing others to act so as to accomplish certain goals. Leadership may be distinguished by the different role that the leader plays relative to followers. Figure 2-8 depicts the various characteristics of leadership.

Many writers divide leadership into two categories, informal and formal, because of the importance of each within an organization. Amitai Etzioni carries

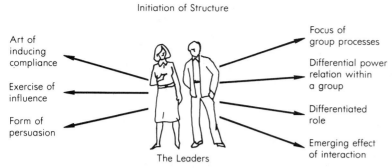

FIGURE 2-8 Leadership Definitions

this further and makes the following distinction:

1. *Official*: one whose power (influence) is derived chiefly from his organizational position
2. *Informal leader*: one whose ability to control others is due chiefly to personal attributes, such as knowledge, personality, persuasiveness, identification with the informal group, charisma, or courage to speak out
3. *Formal leader*: one who commands both positional power and personal influence[25]

This last classification actually represents the ideal leadership style of a *manager*. The problem of systems design is to recognize all three types of leadership and their limitations so that the system becomes workable in terms of the current human components and susceptible to revision as these human components change.

Situational Model of Leadership

For many years, companies sought to identify leaders by means of personality and mental traits. Although some minimum levels of certain traits appear desirable, research, as well as experience, has proved this to be a sterile approach. With the development of organizational behavior research, behavioral theories of leadership were developed.

At first, research concentrated on leadership style. Leadership style was considered to vary along a continuum from task oriented to person oriented. Keith Davis defined four leadership styles along this continuum as autocratic, custodial, supportive, and collegial as defined in Table 2-1. Note that the supportive and collegial models reflect the goals of Herzberg's positive motivators. Notice also how the continuum of leadership styles affects the vital variables of employee needs and performance.

[25]Amitai Etzioni, *Modern Organizations* (Englewood Cliffs, N.J.: Prentice-Hall, 1964), p. 61.

TABLE 2-1 Four Leadership Styles and Organizational Behavior

	Autocratic	Custodial	Supportive	Collegial
Depends on:	Power	Economic resources	Leadership	Mutual contribution
Managerial orientation:	Authority	Material rewards	Support	Integration and teamwork
Employee orientation:	Obedience	Security	Performance	Responsibility
Employee psychological result:	Personal dependence	Organizational dependence	Participation	Self-discipline
Employee needs met:	Subsistence	Maintenance	Higher order	Self-realization
Performance result:	Minimum	Passive cooperation	Awakened drives	Enthusiasm
Morale measure:	Compliance	Satisfaction	Motivation	Commitment to task and team

Source: Keith Davis, "Evolving Models of Organizational Behavior," *Academy of Management Journal,* March 1968, p. 29.

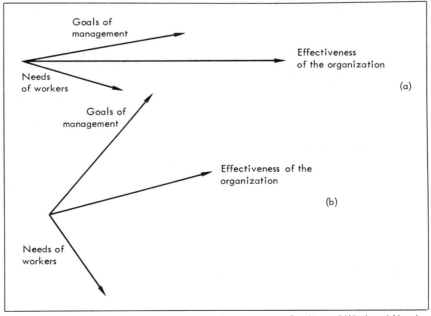

FIGURE 2-9 Organizational Effectiveness, Management Goals, and Workers' Needs

There are two implications of this task-work orientation continuum. The first is that it is not possible for a leader to be both task oriented and person oriented. The second is that by concentrating on people, rather than on tasks, task achievement will be high. Recent research has indicated that task concerns and people concerns are not mutually exclusive. Suppose, for example, that organizational tasks and the needs of workers are closely related as shown in Figure 2-9(a). The leadership that focuses on both people and tasks will be very effective. Where goals of management and goals of workers diverge, as shown in Figure 2-9(b), focus purely on tasks or purely on workers' needs will be ineffective. In these cases (1) the goals of management must be changed, (2) employees with different needs must be hired to replace the present ones, or (3) managers must influence the workers to work toward organizational goals.

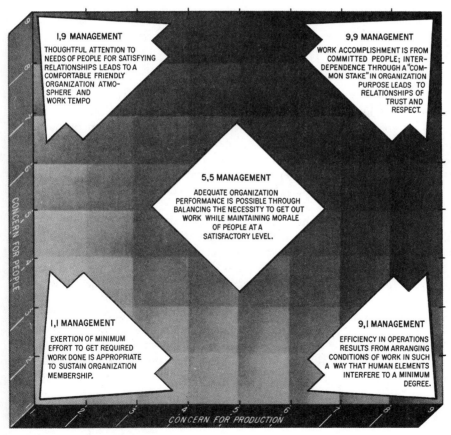

FIGURE 2-10　The Managerial Grid

Source: Robert R. Blake et al., ''Breakthrough in Organizational Development,'' *Havard Business Review*, November – December 1965, p. 136.

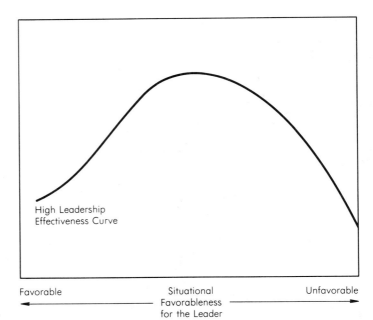

People-oriented
style matched with
high rating on LPC* scale

High Leadership
Effectiveness Curve

Task-oriented style
matched with low rating
on LPC scale

Favorable   Situational   Unfavorable
Favorableness
for the Leader

*Least Preferred Coworker

FIGURE 2-11   Leader Effectiveness

    Robert R. Blake and Jane S. Mouton developed and tested the concept that organizational goals and satisfaction of workers' needs are not incompatible.[26] They have been successful in analyzing or evaluating managers' styles in terms of these concepts. To do this, they developed a managerial grid for rating, as indicated in Figure 2-10. A manager may be evaluated and his or her style located on the grid. Then he or she may be retrained to move toward the ideal (9, 9) position.

    The behavioral approaches have gradually led to the modern theory of leadership—the situational approach. In essence, this theory says that effective leadership depends upon such factors as the nature of the work, the characteristics of the workers, the relationship between the leader and the workers, and the leader's style. For very favorable and very unfavorable situations, the leader is most effective if he is task oriented in style and is rated as low as a desired co-worker by members of his group.[27] Fred Fiedler's model may be sketched in extremely condensed form in Figure 2-11. The curve represents conditions of high leadership effectiveness for various combinations of style matched with co-worker preference versus situational favorableness. Note that people-oriented leadership style and preferred leader produces the most effective leadership only when the

    [26]Robert R. Blake et al., "Breakthrough in Organization Development," *Harvard Business Review*, November–December 1964.

    [27]The least preferred co-worker (LPC) questionnaire developed by Fred Fiedler measures feelings of the worker about the leader.

situation of position power, task structure, and the leader member relations provide medium "situational favorableness." Otherwise, task-oriented and "least preferred co-worker" leader yields the most effective leadership.

Application of Organization Behavioral Concepts to the Design and Operation of the MIS

Without proper consideration of the behavior of people in the business organization setting, the best *technically* designed system is likely to fail. The key factors from the previous part of this chapter that bear upon MIS design are (1) social organization with its norms, roles, relationships, and communications networks and (2) the psychological needs of the individuals for esteem, self-actualization, and freedom from repressive control. The introduction of a new MIS represents a threat to the individual in terms of his organizational relationships and psychological needs. Management must do more than involve everyone concerned in the development of the MIS; it must take into account the newly emerging organizational patterns which may arise. *Resistance* to the new MIS must be *avoided* rather than *defeated* by sheer power. The latter is virtually impossible because organizations can find many subtle ways to gum up operations.

Nature of Resistance to MIS

Contrary to popular belief, people do not have an innate resistance to change simply because it is change. We see people at work every day making self-initiated changes to make their work simpler, better, or more pleasant. An important concept for the manager is that change has two facets: *technological* and *social*. We find that it is not the technological change of a new MIS, but the *social* change which people resist.

A new system, when introduced, produces newly emerging behavioral patterns which are not likely to match the theoretically *required* organizational patterns. These emerging behavioral patterns are the ones that translate system inputs into system outputs, however. Therefore, the "required" organizational patterns must be modified to build upon the positive potential of the behavioral aspects. People must see in the MIS features that support their social and psychological needs.

A number of common specific reasons result in resistance of the MIS:

1. *Threat to status*: A supervisor is downgraded below a technician in his organization.
2. *Threat to ego*: A key skilled clerical job is performed by an unskilled computer operator.
3. *Economic threat*: A supervisor fears loss of job.
4. *Job complexity*: A new computer input terminal is to be installed, which requires some knowledge of computer input language.

5. *Isolation*: A top manager, deprived of "personal" information, is made dependent on computer output.
6. *Superior-subordinate relationships changed*: New information flow produces new balances between superior and subordinate.
7. *Job ambiguity and loss of control*: Production planning and control are performed largely by the MIS except for special situations that occur randomly.
8. *Time rigidity*: The total system requires "programmed" coordinated action similar to a mass-production assembly line.
9. *Interpersonal relationships changed*: Former informal work groups and working relationships are broken up.

Procedure for Effecting Change Without Resistance

There are three positive steps for effecting change based upon our knowledge of organizational behavior:

1. Create a climate for change.
2. Develop effective agents of change.
3. Modify the required organizational system in the light of anticipated emergent behavior.

Create a Climate for Change

A climate for change may be obtained by getting managers and workers to feel dissatisfied with the present system. One company achieved this successfully by holding a series of seminars, first for small groups of managers and then for small groups of workers. Discussions were focused on what was wrong with the present system and ways for revising the present system. A record of suggestions was kept, but evaluations and commitments were not made. Thus the participants were left with a feeling that changes were needed, that changes of some kind would be made, and that their views were taken into account before any specific changes were considered.

Develop Effective Agents of Change

Within any organization there are informal leaders and technical leaders to whom other members of the group look for protection and security. Management and the systems designer must identify such leaders and win their support. One company took a group of such individuals and sent them to brief seminars and workshops away from the company to stimulate new ideas. One at a time, each was encouraged to work with the systems designer to develop portions of a new MIS. In turn, they developed the support of other workers for changes and at the same time reflected the desires of the workers with regard to the changes.

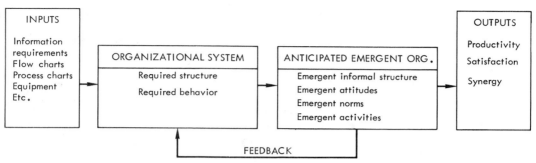

FIGURE 2-12   Organization Modified by Feedback of Anticipated Emergent Behavior

Modify the "Required" Organization

The "required" organization is that required to fit the technical side of the system. It is a mechanistic technical organizational design. However, rearrangement of the organization into one that is not technically ideal may be made to achieve working relationships that are far more productive. As the technical side of the MIS is developed, the organizational requirements must be made as anticipated emergent organizational behavior dictates. Figure 2-12 represents the feedback that will yield a more highly productive organization for operation and utilization of the MIS.

MANAGEMENT, INFORMATION, AND THE SYSTEMS APPROACH

In Chapter 1 we discussed the characteristics of the systems approach. We will now look at the systems approach to the management of organizations. We emphasize again that the systems model incorporates all other approaches and validated principles; it is not just a technical model of management and the organization. We state this because the technical representation of the model receives more attention as the approximate structure of the management and organizational system.

Tasks and Functions of Management

There are three important tasks of management and hence goals of the organization:

1. Match the capabilities of the institution (business enterprise, university, public agency, etc.) to various needs of the environment and select specific missions from among these opportunities.

2. Establish a work environment and allocation of resources for maximum productivity of the total (organizational) system.

3. Manage responsibilities to, and impact on, *stake*holders of the institution. (This includes responsibilities to the public, society, as stakeholder.)

The functions that management performs to guide the organization in developing and implementing these three tasks are planning, organizing, staffing, initiating (or directing), and controlling. *Staffing* is behaviorally related to organizing, and *initiating* is behaviorally oriented, as discussed previously. We will, therefore, focus on management's functions of *planning, organizing,* and *controlling* from systems and information perspectives.

The General Management System

The functions of management are not performed sequentially. Planning is involved in organizing and controlling. Similarly, organizing is required for planning and controlling. Each function interacts with the others to form the

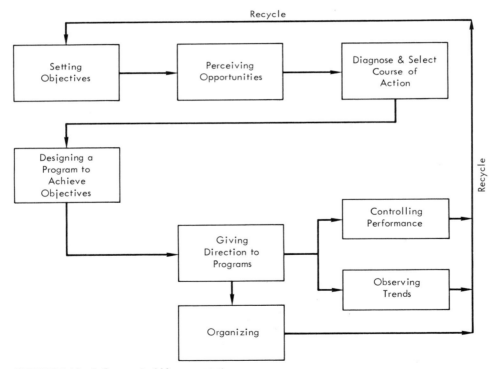

FIGURE 2-13 A Concept of Management

management process. The general model of managing is shown in Figure 2-13 and can be described as follows:

Planning

1. Setting of objectives for the manager's area of activity
2. Perception of opportunities, problems, and alternatives surrounding the achievement of the objective
3. Diagnosis of opportunities, analysis of objectives, and selection of a course of action
4. Design of a program of action to achieve the objective

Directing

5. Leadership in the necessary organizational action required to achieve the program, including communication and motivation of subordinates

Organizing

6. Supervision of the action plan through an organization whose task relationships are defined and understood

Controlling

7. Observation and measurement of performance against standards for achieving the plan and correction of performance deviations if required
8. Observation of significant trends within and without the manager's activity so that goals and programs may be modified as necessary

Feedback

9. Recycling of information concerning plans, actions, and progress at different stages of the management process to insure that proper programming to achieve the objective is being accomplished

Thus, the management process is *iterative*.

Many organizations and managers make the basic mistake of believing that a management *information* system can be designed or made operational without the backup of an adequate *management* system. An adequate management system includes organizational arrangements, structure and procedures for adequate planning and control, clear establishment of objectives, and all the other manifestations of good organization and management. Given this management structure, this framework of good management practices, an information system can be designed upon its foundation. Only then can the information system provide the manager with the information needed in the form, place, and time to perform the job according to the specifications of the *management* system.

The purpose of the management system is to develop plans for achieving objectives, to organize for implementing plans, and to control performance so that plans and actions occur on schedule. The place of information in performing these three basic processes is shown in Figure 2-14. The first step, recognition of a problem or an opportunity, is usually prompted by information from the control process concerning a deviation from standard or by search and evaluation of those systems (environmental, competitive, internal) affecting the planning process. Definition of the problem, determination and evaluation of alternative courses of action, and selection of a course of action are fundamentally steps in the planning and decision-making process. Information needs for this process are those indicated in Figure 2-14. Finally, once a decision is made or a plan developed, it is necessary to *implement* and *control* the solution. Implementation becomes a matter of organizing the necessary resources and directing them in the performance of the plan. Control involves the measurement of performance and

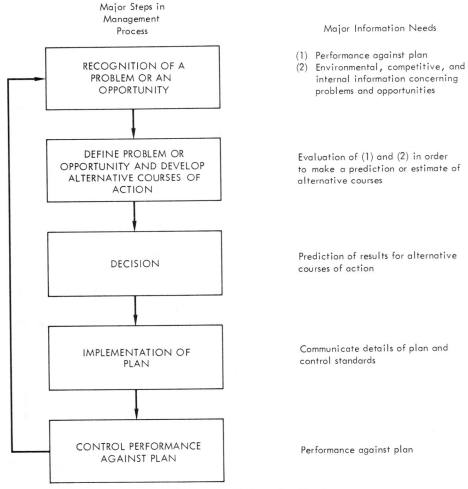

FIGURE 2-14   The Management Process and Information Needs

correction of deviations. The process starts over again either by a recognition of the need for planning or by the appearance of a new problem arising from the control process.

In the remainder of this chapter we will want to examine three aspects of the major managerial functions of planning, organizing, and controlling. First, a definition and description of the process will be advanced so that the reader will have an understanding of how it is performed. Second, we will want to ask, "How does the *systems* approach to the managerial function differ from the more traditional approach?" Finally, because *management* is the real reason for having information systems, we will want to set the stage for MIS by describing how planning, organizing, and controlling are facilitated by the storage and retrieval of *information*.

Planning

The most basic and pervasive management function is planning. All managers at all levels plan, and the success of the performance of the other management functions depends upon this activity. Planning is deciding in advance what has to be done, who has to do it, when it has to be done, and how it is to be done. It bridges the gap from where we are to where we want to go. Managers plan for the allocation of resources and the work of other people, in contrast to the non-manager, who plans only his or her own activities.

The growth of planning has shown a tremendous surge due to

1. Recognition by companies that they must prepare for, not react to, increasingly rapid changes in the environment
2. Growing competition from both domestic and foreign business
3. The rapid growth of computer-based information systems as computer power goes up while computing costs go down
4. Increased complexity of managing because of the growth in size, diversity of businesses, and increasing demands of a broad range of stakeholders (groups impacted by the business)
5. High risk and high investment requirements of modern business
6. Developments of planning theory, techniques, and tools

Dimensions of Plans

Table 2-2 shows the classification of plans by key characteristic. Every plan may be described in terms of each of these characteristics.

Table 2-2 provides an integration of plans by relating dimensions to characteristics according to the time horizons of the plans. The matrix of this table thus provides a structure for the total plan of a company. Such integration is necessary to establish a *unified set of objectives* for a company. Without such a unified set of objectives, managers and other employees may be seeking conflicting objectives without realizing it. There was a time when the company president would say, "My objective is a 20 percent return on investment and a profit of 15 percent of sales." Table 2-2 shows that a company has many objectives, both long term and short term. Objectives will include those such as market share, innovation, productivity, deployment of resources, employee attitudes, managerial performance, and public responsibility.[28] Here we are defining the overall objectives of the company and not those of the divisions, departments, or other subgroups. Later we will discuss how a hierarchy of organizational objectives integrates the firm's activities.

Policies are statements that attempt to inform and guide employees so that the totality of actions by individuals are consistent with the sense of direction of the company. Policies are of two types. In the first instance they provide limits for discretionary action by specified individuals. In the second case, they specify a procedure or action to be taken in specific circumstances. Policies represent both a method for implementing plans and a method for controlling such implementation.

Policies are often classified according to functions in a firm and examples might be as follows:

Function	Policy	Example
Marketing	Advertising and promotion	Advertising budget will be at least 2% of sales.
	Channels of distribution	Distribute through manufacturer's representatives.
	Pricing	Offer 10% discount for carload lots.
	Sales	Do not sell direct.
Production	Inventory	Do not exceed 30 days' finished goods.
	Make or buy	Make when price difference exceeds cost of capital.
	Product stabilization	Operate within 70–90% of capacity.
	Size of run	Run economic lot size for nonpriority items.
Financial	Capital distributions	Maintain quarterly dividend at 50% of net earnings.
	Capital procurement	Finance growth from retained earnings.
	Depreciation	Use method with greatest tax benefit.
	Working capital	Maintain 2-to-1 "acid-test" ratio.
Personnel	Compensation	Meet local rates.
	Benefits	Offer all benefits recommended by industry association.
	Selection and training	Subsidize tuition reimbursement plan.
General	Competitive actions	Do not collude in any way with competitors to establish prices or divide markets.

[28] Peter F. Drucker, *The Practice of Management* (New York: Harper & Row, 1954), p. 63.

TABLE 2-2 Dimensions of Plans

Dimension / Time	Illustrations		
	Long Range	Medium Range	Short Range
Level	Corporate	Division	Operational profit plan
Function	General management	Marketing	Production schedule
Purpose	Strategy	Product line	Training program
Scope	Companywide	Business / functional	Business / departmental

The Strategic Planning Process

The systems approach to planning starts with the strategic plan as the framework. The strategic plan is specific but not detailed, because although specific goals may be established for the distant future, detailed methods for achieving these goals must be related to current environmental (including competitive) conditions. The long-term goals of the strategic plan provide the constraints for setting intermediate- and short-term goals. Therefore, as shown in Figure 2-15, the strategic plan ties together the development plan (short-range plan). The development plan focuses on the growth of the company through internal or external expansion. The operations plan is the one-year plan that links together in full detail the functional plans with project or program plans.

The first step in any planning is "needs research" to determine the relationship of the system to its environment. "Whom does the organization serve?" is the question that must be answered first. The "stakeholders" may provide both threats and support to the continued viability of the firm. The stakeholders will likely have conflicting interests with each other so that the company must establish trade-offs among its basic missions and objectives according to power relationships among the stakeholders.[29] In essence, stakeholders provide strong constraints on companies.

Typical stakeholder groups are

1. *The stockholders and directors.* The stockholders have the "legitimate" property claim to the corporation, which they presumably exercise through the board of directors that represents them. However, the directors are often far removed from the dispersed stockholders; besides, different stockholders want different things—such as dividends versus reinvestment, safety versus risk, or stability versus growth.

2. *The government.* The federal government affects the direction of a business through legislation and taxation. As a partner who takes about 50 percent of the profits, it is often at odds with the interests of other claimants. State and local governments also regulate, tax, and influence the direction of a company.

3. *The public.* The public feels that corporations should not exist just for profit, that they should also act in the public interest. Noise, pollution, and beautification of factory sites are considered subjects for public action.

[29]See, for example, Henry Mitzberg, "Organizational Power and Goals: A Skeletal Theory," in Dan E. Schendel and Charles W. Hofer, eds., *Strategic Management* (Boston: Little, Brown, 1979).

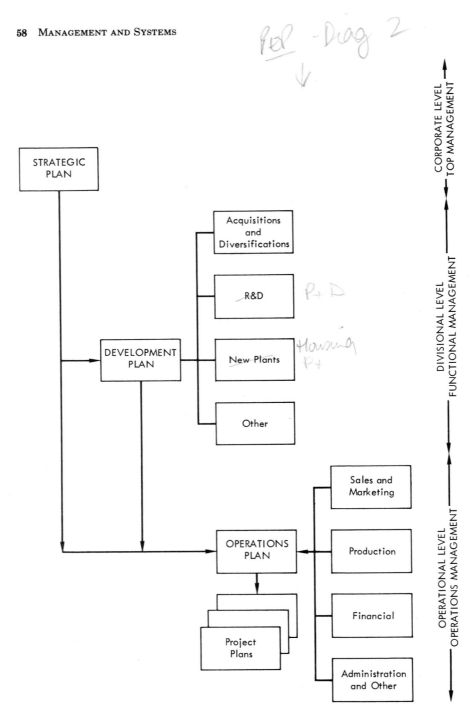

FIGURE 2-15   Systems Approach to Planning

4. *Customers and vendors.* The customers are tugging on the firm for better service, better products, and lower costs. At the other end, the vendors are trying to obtain higher prices and to sell more standardized supplies.

5. *Special interest groups.* The trade associations, consumer groups, conservationists, and individuals owning large blocks of stock in the company all pursue their own special and different interests.

6. *The management of the company.* Different managements of similar companies in an industry may pursue different ends. It is also natural that management wishes to avoid taking large risks for large profits and prefers to simply do well enough to stay in power. The management seeks special remuneration that may or may not exceed its contribution.

7. *The employees of the company.* Both as individuals and as a group, employees frequently find that their goals do not jibe with those of management. Worse yet, employees may engage in a constant struggle against management without regard to their own long-term interests. Some companies, in the face of this, have simply liquidated.

The problems that confront managers are how to identify the objectives and goals of the company and how to manage its resources in such a way as to integrate these varied interests, many of which are in apparent conflict. For example, stockholders may believe that salaries of managers and key employees are too high and are resulting in low dividends. At the same time, the managers and employees may feel that salaries are too low, so that they are not motivated to perform to their utmost. The problem might be resolved by convincing stockholders that profits will decline if managers leave to be replaced by less capable people. At the same time, managers may be given some status rewards that are not as costly as large salary increases (e.g., company cars or country club memberships). Although this hypothetical example is extremely simplified, it does indicate the process of integrating apparently diverse interests.

The strategic planning process consists of two steps: (1) developing the *strategy* and (2) formulating the steps, timing, and costs required to achieve the strategy. The expression of these steps, timing, and costs is called the strategic plan (or, often, the long-range plan).

Strategy is the desired configuration of the firm *at a future specified date.* This configuration, identity, or posture of the firm may be described in terms of

1. *Scope*: products, customers, markets, price-quality relationships of products, and product characteristics

2. *Competitive edge*: special market position or supply position, unique product advantages, special financial strength or credit lines, unique management or technical talents, or capacity for rapid response to competitive moves

3. *Specifications of targets*: quantitative statements of acceptable and desired goals such as size of the company, market share, profitability return on investment, assets, and trade-off between risk and reward

4. *Assignment of resources*: allocation of long-term capital, investment and disinvestment, emphasis on particular activities such as marketing, engineering, production, management development, geographic regions, and market segments[30]

[30] Robert L. Katz, *Management of the Total Enterprise* (Englewood Cliffs, N.J.: Prentice-Hall, 1970); see also J. Thomas Cannon, *Business Strategy and Policy* (New York: Harcourt Brace, 1968).

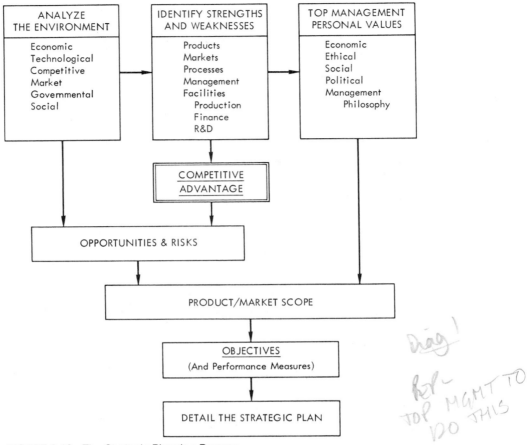

FIGURE 2-16 The Strategic Planning Process

The *strategic planning process* consists of the following steps, shown schematically in Figure 2-16.

1. *Analyze the environment.*[31] Identify those existing and future conditions in the environment that have an influence on the company. The objective in performing this step is to identify *new opportunities* for existing and new products and services and to identify major future *risks* to market position and profit margins. Conditions of primary interest would include economic, competitive, technological, governmental, and market.

2. *Identify company strengths, weaknesses.* After an analysis of the conditions in step 1 and an orderly review of products, markets, processes, personnel, and facilities, certain strengths and weaknesses will emerge. Such resource analysis will not only

[31]For a comprehensive treatment of this step in the strategic planning process, see Francis J. Aguilar, *Scanning the Business Environment* (New York: Macmillan, 1967).

serve to highlight possible competitive advantages available to the company but will also tend to focus on opportunities and risks.

3. *Consider personal values of top management.* The aesthetic, social, religious, and personal values of top management and influential stockholders exert a significant influence on strategy. Additionally, the emerging constraints of social responsibility and consumerism are factors to consider. Personal values represent both guides and constraints upon the direction of the business.

4. *Identify opportunities and risks.* The company should, at this point, be able to identify opportunities in the environment to fill a unique niche. These opportunities occur when there are specific needs for products (or services) that the firm is uniquely able to supply because of its resources.

5. *Define product/market scope.* This involves the explicit definition of the future scope of the company's activities. The main idea is to concentrate on a very limited number of carefully defined product/market segments. These depend upon the analysis resulting from steps 1 to 4 above.

   Careful identification of the product/market scope is advantageous because it (a) reduces time and complexity of decisions regarding acquisitions, new investments, and other elements of the development plan, (b) promotes integration of divisions and other organizational entities by providing a basis for their plans, and (c) allows the company to focus on decisions and actions that take advantage of their competitive edge.

6. *Define the competitive edge.* This requires a careful evaluation of unique company skills, position, market advantages, and other competitive factors.

7. *Establish objectives and measures of performance.* Quantitative specifications are required to describe many characteristics of the firm and to provide a clear definition of strategy. Quantitative goals may be established for such parameters as annual rate of growth of sales, profits, return on investment; market share; number of employees; value of assets; debt; standing in the industry; and so on.[32]

8. *Determine deployment of resources.* Should resources be applied to growth from within or to acquisitions? What areas should the company focus its resources upon? Readjustment of application of resources is thus established in a manner similar to the grand-scale shifts of men and materiel in military conflicts. Conversion from one type of resource to another as changing from labor-intensive to capital-intensive manufacturing is also a part of such deployment.

Short-Range Planning

Short-range planning (frequently called operational or annual planning) is almost always heavily financial in nature; it states objectives and standards of performance in terms of financial results. The basic notion is to decentralize profit responsibility to "profit centers" where the profit determinants of sales, turnover, and cost of sales are established. These determinants in turn are broken down into measurable and controllable elements such as investment (fixed assets, inventory, accounts receivable, cash, etc.) and cost of sales (direct labor, overhead, selling, transportation, and administration).

---

[32]See, for example, Katz, *Management of the Total Enterprise;* see also Edward P. Learned, C. R. Christensen, and K. R. Andrews, *Business Policy* (Homewood, Ill.: Richard D. Irwin, 1972), and Steiner, *Top Management Planning.*

Information and Planning

It is evident that the first and second steps in the planning process—developing external and internal planning constraints depend heavily upon the availability and utilization of critical information. It is hard to imagine the manager trying to develop any of the three major types of plans without first gathering the necessary planning premises that permit adequate evaluation of alternative courses of action to achieve the plan.

The planning information needs of an organization can be classified into three broad types: (1) environmental, (2) competitive, and (3) internal. Because these are so important in the planning process and in the design of an information system for planning, it is desirable that each category be considered in some detail. Conceptually, planning premises can be viewed as shown in Figure 2-17.

Environmental Information. Environmental information needs can be classified and described as follows:

1. *Political and governmental considerations.* Some information on political stability, at whatever level of government, is important for forecasting plans. Additionally, the nature and extent of government controls and their effect on the organization must be taken into account. A third factor is the important role played by government financial and tax policies; they have a very significant effect on many planning decisions.
2. *Demographic and social trends.* The products, services, or outputs of most firms and organizations are affected by the totals, composition, or location of the population. Social trends and consumer buying behavior are important. It is necessary therefore to forecast trends for both the short and long run in this critical area.

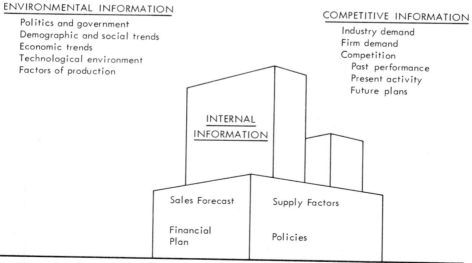

ENVIRONMENTAL INFORMATION

Politics and government
Demographic and social trends
Economic trends
Technological environment
Factors of production

COMPETITIVE INFORMATION

Industry demand
Firm demand
Competition
   Past performance
   Present activity
   Future plans

INTERNAL INFORMATION

Sales Forecast

Financial Plan

Supply Factors

Policies

FIGURE 2-17 Planning Premises

3. *Economic trends.* Included herein would be (a) the GNP level and trend and consumer disposable income, which are significant for almost all organizations; (b) employment, productivity, capital investment, and numerous other economic indicators that provide valuable planning information for those firms whose output is a function of these important variables; and (c) price and wage levels, whose effects are vital to almost all organizations regardless of product or service.

4. *Technological environment.* Because of accelerating technical changes and their effect on new products and processes, it becomes necessary or desirable for many firms to forecast the technological changes in their industry and the probable effect on the firm. Firms such as TRW, Inc., forecast key technological advances in all fields for a period of 20 years.

5. *Factors of production.* These include source, cost, location, availability, accessibility, and productivity of the major production factors of (a) labor, (b) materials and parts, and (c) capital.

Competitive Information. Information concerning factors that affect the operation of the firm within an industry includes data concerning industry and firm demand as well as data on the competitors. Three types to consider are

1. *Industry demand.* Because the sales and the corresponding level of operations for any single firm are largely a function of the level of demand for the given industry it is a part of, the firm must forecast the demand for that area or industry.

2. *Firm demand.* The demand for products of an individual firm is a function of the industry demand and the capabilities and activities of the individual firm relative to the capabilities and actions of competing firms.

3. *The competition.* Data on competing firms are very important for forecasting individual demands and making decisions and plans to achieve the forecast. This information generally falls into three types:
   a. *Past performance*—profitability, return on investment, share of the market and similar data help to identify competitors and may also provide a yardstick for setting performance objectives for the individual firm.
   b. *Present activity*—developments concerning the competition that will affect the planning process. Such developments may include price strategy, advertising campaigns, new product introductions, changes in distribution channels, and so on.
   c. *Future plans*—information concerning new products, acquisitions, R & D efforts, and other plans that affect the individual firm's future.

Internal Information. Because internal premises affect the planning decisions of so many levels in the organization, in some respects they are more important than the external information. Although the business environment and premises surrounding competition are no doubt very important, these categories of information are, after all, considered necessary for decision making by relatively few managers in a firm, mainly top managers and marketing managers. However, internal planning premises are vital for subsidiary planning at all levels in the organization. A budget or a sales forecast, once adopted, becomes essential planning data for a variety of subsequent and connecting plans.

As they relate to the total planning process, internal data are aimed at an identification of the organization's strengths and weaknesses—the external constraints that, when viewed in the perspective of external information, are vital decision-making premises that help managers shape future plans. It is useful to think of internal premises as being of the following types:

1. *Sales forecast.* This is perhaps the single most important planning document in the organization, because the allocation of the entire company's resources is a function of the sales plan. It sets the framework on which most other internal plans are constructed and can therefore be regarded as the dominant planning premise internal to the firm.

2. *The financial plan.* This plan, frequently called the budget, is second only to the sales forecast in importance. In many ways, the financial plan preempts the sales forecast because it represents a quantitative and time commitment of the allocation of the *total resources* of the company (workers, plant, capital, materials, overhead, and general and administrative expenses). Properly constructed, the financial plan involves the entire organization and, when completed, provides subsidiary planning information for a variety of subplans throughout the company. It is a system that links all activities of the company together.

3. *Supply factors.* Labor, capital, plant and equipment, organization, and other supply factors are vital planning premises that provide constraints or boundaries within which planning takes place. These factors are controllable to a large extent by the firm, but their availability and limitations must be taken into account in developing the financial plan and subsidiary plans for achieving objectives.

4. *Policies.* Basic policies are relatively fixed for long-run purposes and cannot readily be changed to permit flexibility in developing alternative courses of action in the short run. To the extent that product, marketing, financial, personnel, and other basic policies are unchangeable in the short run, they provide constraints to planning in much the same way as do supply factors.

Organizing

Organizing is required of managers because it is the method by which effective group action is obtained. A structure of roles must be designed and maintained for people to work together in carrying out plans and accomplishing objectives. This is the task of organizing. It involves the grouping of tasks necessary to accomplish plans, the assignment of activities to departments, and the provision for coordination through authority delegation.

Organization Systems

1. *The formal organizational system as described in charts, policies, and procedures.* This is the "legal" structural system, which defines levels of authority and responsibility. It is the mechanistic system for relating tasks, positions, and methods of operation. It is the system that is most visible, because of its basis in logic (apart from behavioral considerations) and because of its thorough documentation. Its main weakness is that it is a static system model representing a dynamic system.

2. *The informal organization.* The informal organization is a dynamic social system model. If it were properly set down on paper, it would show attachment relationships among individuals, communications networks as they actually exist, and numerous factors that affect the operation of this social system. A disadvantage of

studying this system alone is that it is difficult to set down the relationships and behavior of people and groups, particularly because they are constantly changing.

3. *The individual as a system.* The psychological makeup of people as individuals describes the individual person as a subsystem. The total business system comprises the aggregate of these subsystems. The weakness of this model is that the needs and behavior of people in cooperative groups extend beyond those of each individual independently. The interactions and the behavior of those around him affect the values, attitudes, and behavior of the individual.

4. *The management information system.* Every organization must have means for gathering and transmitting information to the major decision makers to control present and future activities. The information system and the management group are similar to the nervous system and brain of the human being. If sensing or reporting is faulty, incomplete, or cut at some major juncture, the entire organism will become disoriented. The study of the management information system of a business organization requires consideration of every behavioral and mechanistic aspect of the organization, and therefore this is an excellent system to study.

5. *The organizational communications system.* Communication within a company depends upon the formal and informal organizations that have been established and upon the framework imposed by the management information system. Communication is a function of the behavior of people, of the formal procedures established by management, and of the equipment available. Communication is a vital system, but only a part of other, larger systems.

6. *The power system.* Besides the "legal" power system set forth by the formal organization, there is a network of sponsor-protégé relationships and informal conversions of activities into control over other people in the organizations. For example, either individuals in the accounting area or secretaries to managers may exert and develop power through the blocking or delaying of communications. A production manager may achieve power by gaining the support of the sales manager, who cannot afford to have shipments delayed. Managers who socialize together outside of work may form a power group or clique. The power system is difficult to define and describe, although the sociologist Melville Dalton has presented excellent studies of it in three plants.[33] The power system is an important part of organization processes.

7. *The functional systems.* The processing of a customer need from its identification through conversion of raw materials into finished goods and the distribution of these goods is carried out by a sequence of fairly distinct activities. These activities, sometimes known as the technical subsystems, consist of marketing, engineering, production, finance, logistics, and sometimes others. Many people visualize the entire business system as the integration of these subsystems. Information needs with respect to the operation of all the systems represent one approach to the construction of a management information system.

8. *The management process systems.* The system for management planning, the system for organizing, the system for initiating, and the system for measuring and controlling may, taken together, represent the organizational system. As indicated, these systems are not independent. They are so closely interwoven that their study on an individual basis does not offer a good "systems" approach to the study of organization and management.

---

[33] Melville Dalton, *Men Who Manage* (New York: John Wiley, 1959).

9. *The material logistics system.* It may be considered that the entire firm is essentially a logistics system, a processor of materials into finished goods that are shipped to customers. In such a case, the focus is on the operational aspects and systems. Little attention is given to the behavioral and managerial subsystems.

Systems Approach to Organizing

The complexity of the total organization system requires that we use the iterative and phased steps typical of the systems approach. This means that we block out the organization roughly from several perspectives and then attempt to weld these systems into a unified concept. Next we refine the design until it is finished *and implemented*. The managerial function of organizing thus is directed to objectives of structure and processes for achieving coordination and decision making. This concept is shown in Figure 2-18.

The phases of organizing are

1. Develop a technical (classical) organization based on the traditional methods of *departmentation*.
2. Start with total company objectives and develop a *hierarchy* or network *of systems* required. Such systems sometimes match portions of the technical organization structure and sometimes cut across the classical lines of authority.
3. Involve key managers and specialists in developing a matrix, team, or system type of organization as influenced by the desires and special skills of these people. An analysis of decisions and information requirements must be carried out during this process.

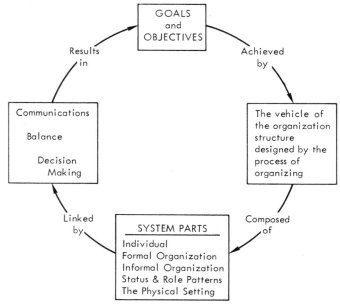

FIGURE 2-18 Integration of the Organizational System Through the Organizing Process

We will touch upon the first two phases briefly. The first part of the third phase is beyond the scope of this book. The second part of the third phase is dealt with in detail in Part II of this book.

Classical Organization Structuring: Departmentation. The classical hierarchical organization structure is the most influential structural rationale of the modern corporation. It provides the foundation upon which adaptations and modifications are constructed.

The key words are *structure* and *formal.* The basic tenets are specialization of work (departmentation), span of management (supervision of a limited number of subordinates), chain of command (authority delegation), and unity of command (no subordinate has more than one superior). The structure takes on the shape of a pyramid. The manager determines work activities to get the job done, writes job descriptions, organizes people into groups, and assigns them to superiors. He or she then establishes objectives and deadlines and determines standards of performance. Operations are controlled through a reporting system.

Because the classical format is so prevalent, we will examine the basic tenets of this form of organization.

Departmentation deals with the formation of organizational units. Among the first components of an organization structure is the manner in which work is divided into homogeneous groups of activities. The activities form departments. Methods of departmentation that experience has proved logical and useful are by function, by product, by territory, by customer, by process, and by project. An example of each of these is illustrated in Figure 2-19. For example, departmentation by *function* is shown at the top level by the common functions of marketing, personnel, operations, R & D, and finance. The breakdown of operations into the furniture division, the metal products division, and the floor-covering division is an example of *product* organization. The sales department is organized into eastern and western districts to establish a *territory* departmentation, and these territories are further departmented by the *customer* breakdown of retail, government, institutions, and manufacturers' representatives. The manufacturing operation in the metal products division depicts both *process* (assembly, welding, stamping) and *function* (maintenance, power, shipping). Finally, a special *project* team, organized for new product development, reports to the president.

Functional departmentation is by far the oldest and most widely used form of grouping activities. In almost every organization there are three fundamental activities of producing, selling, and financing to be performed. These are the basic functions. As organizations grow, additional staff or service functions are added. Almost all organizations show some functional division of labor.

Product departmentation is common for enterprises with several products or services. The method is easily understood and takes advantage of specialized knowledge. Common examples are department stores (e.g., appliances, furniture, cosmetics) and banks (commercial, personal).

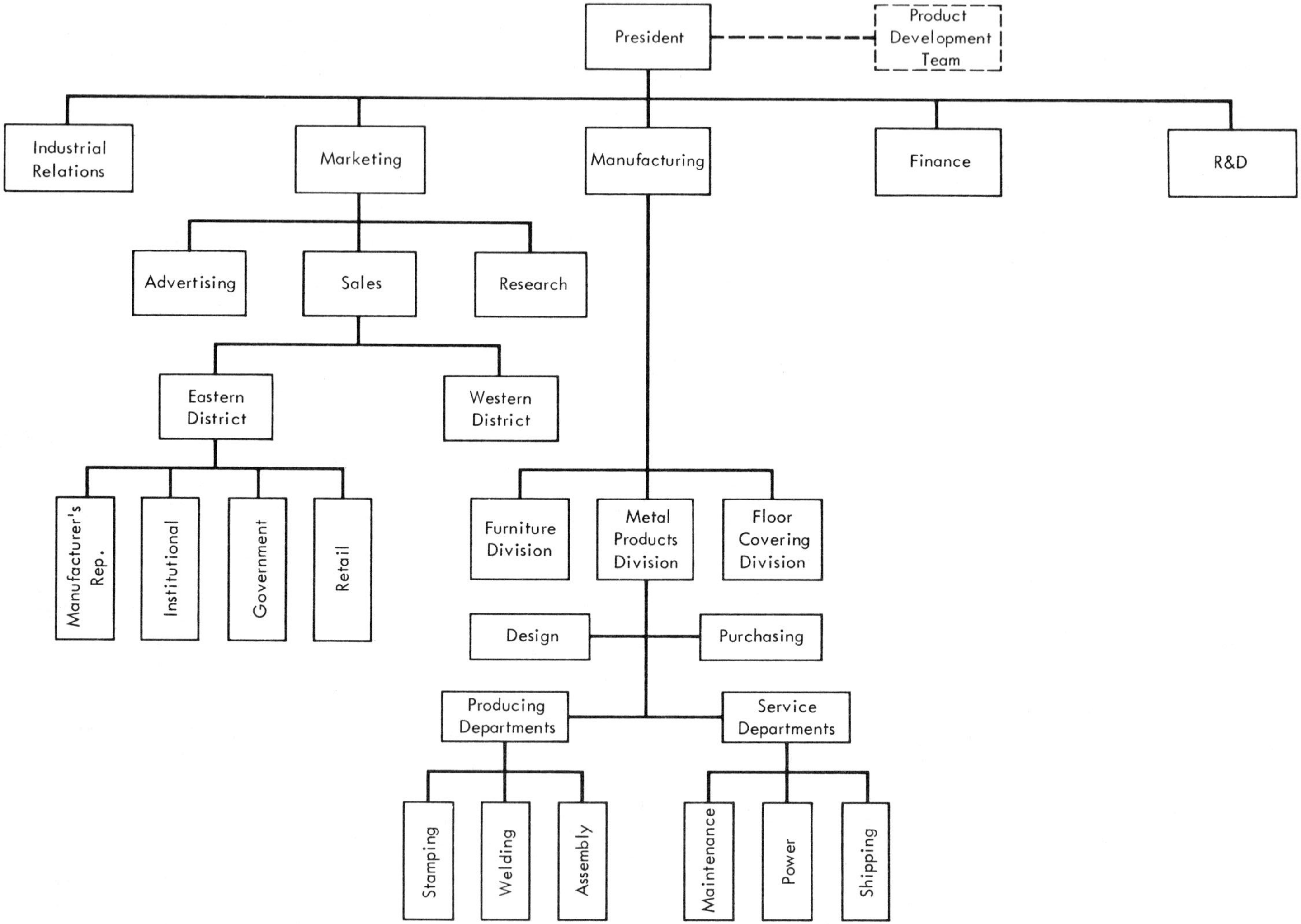

FIGURE 2-19 Methods of Departmentation

Territory departmentation is frequently used by organizations that are physically dispersed. The rationale is that activities in a given area should be grouped and assigned to a manager. Such an approach takes advantage of economies of localized operation. The most frequent use of this method is in the sales force, where division by geographical region favors recruitment and training. Manufacturing and distribution may be organized by territory for similar reasons.

Customer departmentation may be used when the major emphasis is upon service to the customer or where it permits taking advantage of specialized knowledge. Sex, age, and income are common yardsticks for identifying customers. Examples of this type of organization include banks (loans to retailers, wholesalers, manufacturers), department stores (men's shop, teen shop, bridal salon), and aircraft manufacturers (government, foreign, domestic).

Process departmentation, most frequently used in manufacturing enterprises and at the lowest level of organization, is a logical method whereby maximum use can be obtained from equipment and special skills. Frequently the process matches an occupational classification, such as welding, painting, or plumbing.

The number of levels of subdepartments in the hierarchy is related to the span of management at each level, the number of subordinates that the manager can supervise (Figure 2-20). Generally speaking, research to identify the specific number or range of skilled subordinates has resulted in identifying only impacting factors. The obvious reason is that besides these objective factors, a particular manager's style and skills have significant influence. For example, President Dwight Eisenhower was noted for his span of management of one—his chief of staff. At the other extreme, 750 Roman Catholic bishops report directly to the pope.

In classical organizations, authority is delegated down the hierarchy. It does no good to set up a hierarchy of activities unless authority is delegated to units within the structure.

Absolute centralization in one person and absolute decentralization of authority are the two extremes of delegation. Obviously, the tendency is to settle somewhere along the continuum. The major determinant of a manager's ability to delegate authority is his or her temperament and personality, but other determinants are beyond the individual's control. Some of these are (1) cost—the more costly the decision, the more likely it is to be centralized; (2) uniformity of policy—the more uniform and centralized a policy (price, personnel) the less need there is to delegate authority surrounding it; (3) complexity of the organization—the more complex, the greater the need for coordination and centralization of authority; (4) custom of the business—frequently the delegation philosophy and character of top management determine authority delegation; and (5) environment for good management—the availability in the company of managers and good management practices (including control techniques) that would encourage delegation.

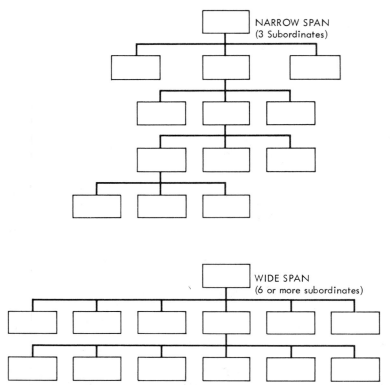

FIGURE 2-20 Two Approaches to Span of Management

System Structuring. Until we introduce the behavioral, decision, and information concepts, we are still dealing with the rational aspects of organizing. We will cover various such rational system structures here.

Early attempts at systems structures were matrix organizations typically found in technical development organizations. It gets its name because it is a *two-way* structure relating project managers and functional managers. Project managers exert planning, scheduling, and cost control authority over people who are permanently assigned to functional units. Thus, workers report to two managers, a violation of a classical principle. Similarly, in large consumer product companies, *product* managers have responsibilities for their products, whereas functional managers are responsible for the functional activities for all products. Workers report to both product managers and their functional managers.

The introduction of teams and task forces has been an attempt to formalize lateral and network information flows required to solve system problems. One trend has been to partition the firm along several dimensions and to place responsibility with managers for each dimension. For example, William C. Goggin, chief executive officer of Dow Corning Corporation, presented a four-

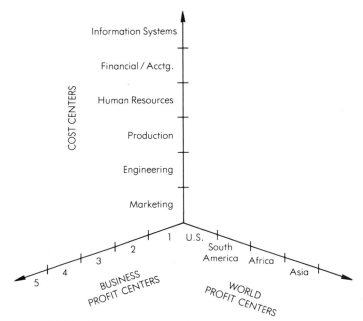

FIGURE 2-21   Three-Dimensional Organization

dimensional design of organization at Dow Corning. Three dimensions, shown in Figure 2-21, are

1. Business profit centers—the different businesses in which the company is engaged. The businesses are product lines that serve a related group of industries, markets, or customers.
2. Cost centers, such as functional activities of marketing, manufacturing, and finance. Support cost centers such as corporate planning, corporate communications, and legal services are also included here.
3. Geographical area.

The fourth dimension is *time*, in which the organization changes form.[34]

An example of first establishing subsystems of the total organization system may be seen by inspecting Figure 2-22. In this case, the hierarchy for delegation of authority could be established by combining groups of systems and then combining these groups further as the top of the hierarchy is approached.

Another system approach is the venture team. More and more multinational, multidivisional, multiproduct companies are beginning to realize that the

[34] William C. Goggin, "How the Multidimensional Structure Works at Dow Corning," *Harvard Business Review*, January–February 1974.

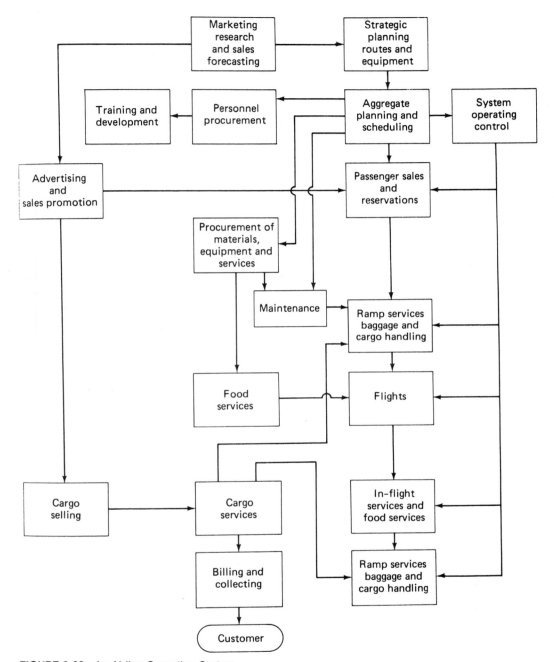

FIGURE 2-22 An Airline Operating System

Source: Robert G. Murdick, *MIS: Concepts and Design* (Englewood Cliffs, N.J.: Prentice-Hall, 1980), p. 123. Reprinted by permission.

traditional departmentalized structure cannot accommodate risk, innovation, and new ventures or products. They are turning to the venture team, a recent organizational innovation that resulted from the need to meet the demand for a breakthrough in product marketing.

The venture team resembles the project manager approach in that its resources and personnel are obtained from the functional departments. Other similarities include organizational separation of team members, multidisciplinary composition of personnel, and the goal-directed effort of a single project, in this case the development and introduction of a new product.

Information and Organizing

Organization structure and information needs are inextricably interwoven. In an analogy between an organization and the human body, the organization *structure* can be compared with the human anatomy and the *information* to the nervous system.

The systems view of the organization takes into account the integrative nature of information flows. This concept is demonstrated in Figure 2-23, where each organizational entity is seen as an information system with the components of input, processor, and output. Each is connected to the others through information and communication channels and each organizational entity becomes a decision point.

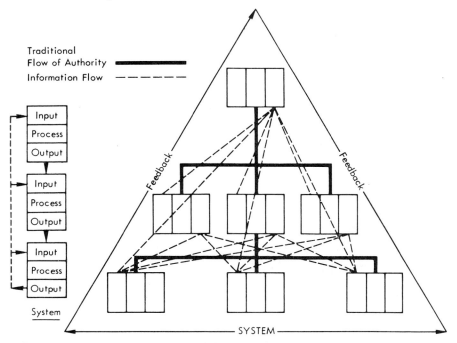

FIGURE 2-23 The Organization as an Information System

Information also affects organizing by the manner in which information systems are designed. These should conform to the organizational structure and the delegation of authority within the company. Only then can each organizational unit's objective be established and its contribution to companywide goals be measured. This means that organizations must be designed around information flow and those factors of information chosen to plan and control performance. Frequently organizational structure and performance reporting do not coincide. In these cases information systems cannot truly reflect plans and results of operations.

Another major cause of organizational and information mismatch is the lag between organizational changes and information systems to facilitate them. As needs, structure, and managers change, the information system should be changed to support them. Rarely does one find a change in informational systems matching a change in organizational responsibilities and the needs of managers. The result is often an "information lag."

Controlling

If the manager could depend upon the flawless execution of plans by a perfectly balanced organization, there would be no need for control because results would invariably be as expected. However, plans and operations rarely remain on course, and control is needed to obtain desired results.

The most common process consists of three steps: (1) setting standards of performance, (2) measuring performance against these standards, and (3) correcting deviations from standards and plans.

Setting Standards of Performance

Setting standards of performance involves defining for personnel in all levels of the organization what is expected of them in terms of job performance. Hence, standards are criteria against which results can be measured. These criteria can be quantitative (e.g., 10 percent increase in sales) or qualitative (e.g., maintain high level of morale). A frequently used definition of standards of performance is *a statement of conditions existing when a job is performed satisfactorily.*

Measuring Performance

Once standards have been established, it is necessary to measure performance against the expectation of the standards. The statement of measurement, and of any differences, is usually in the form of a personal observation or some type of report—oral or written.

The oldest and most prevalent means of measuring performance is by personal observation. The shop supervisor is on the scene and can personally check the time, cost, and quality of product. Sales managers visit sales offices or make calls with their sales representatives to observe performance personally. Advantages include the benefits of immediacy, personal direct contact, and firsthand observation of intangibles such as personnel development or customer reaction. Disadvantages are those associated with the time-consuming nature of the method and the lack of precision in measurement.

Oral reports of performance may take the form of interviews, informal reports, or group and committee meetings. Measuring performance in this way has many of the advantages and drawbacks of the personal observation method. Additionally, oral reporting usually does not result in any permanent record of performance.

Increasingly, control and performance reporting is in written or video form, owing in part to the accelerating use of computer-based information systems and related reporting. The written report has the advantage of providing a permanent record, subject to periodic review by the manager and subordinates.

Correcting Deviations

It does little good to set standards of performance and measure deviations from standard unless corrections are made to get the plan back on course to achieve the objective. Methods and techniques for correcting deviations can be described in terms of the functions of management:

Plan: Recycle the management process—review the plan, modify the goal, or change the standard.

Organize: Examine the organization structure to determine whether it is reflected in standards, make sure that duties are well understood, reassign people if necessary.

Staff: Improve selection of subordinates, improve training, reassign duties.

Direct: Provide better leadership, improve motivation, explain the job better, manage by objective, make sure that there is manager-subordinate agreement on standard.

Chapter 11 deals in some depth with control in general and information systems as tools for controlling. As the reader will see after further study, control systems, no matter how complex, consist of the three processes just described.

SUMMARY

The development of an MIS must be based on an understanding of organizations, their managers, and information systems. This chapter deals with the development of organizational and management theory with special attention to the behavioral model. The systems approach to management and organization is then presented as a unified blending of classical, behavioral, and information concepts.

Development of Organization and Management (O & M) Theory

The major stages of O & M development were classical theory, behavioral theory, decision theory, and modern systems theory.

Classical theory is primarily a rational technical view of O & M. Five tenets are (1) clear lines of authority, (2) specialization of labor, (3) unity of command, (4) proper span of control, (5) clear separation of line and staff. The processes or functions of management were identified as planning, organizing, staffing, directing, and controlling. Behavioral theory uncovered the fact that worker attitudes and behavior played a larger part in productivity than the technical aspects of O & M. The combination of both classical and behavioral concepts led to a neoclassical view.

Other researchers found that decision making played a very important part in the success of organizations. They studied the firm as a decision-making system, looking at both individual and group decision making.

The systems theory of O & M combined all these previous approaches and other specialized descriptions such as sociology, operations research, information and control theory, political science, and so on to yield an integrated prescription for O & M. This chapter is limited to showing a general systems approach that ties together the classical and behavioral concepts and information needs.

Management and Organizational Behavior

The "behavior" of an organization is the combined behavior of individuals and groups in the organization. Such behavior *emerges* as a result of technical organization structures and procedures, psychological characteristics of the individuals, sociopsychological characteristics of work groups, sociological and cultural characteristics of the organization, and nature of the work tasks. From a management view, the three most important factors to be understood in managing organizations are motivation, organizational behavior, and leadership.

"Needs" motivation models most commonly applied are Maslow's needs model, Herzberg's two-factor model, and McClelland's achievement model. The "expectancy" model of motivation has received the greatest acceptance by behavioral researchers. B. F. Skinner has made a strong, but highly controversial case for the operant conditioning model. All these models lead to the identical prescription for managers to obtain highly motivated employees. The prescription is (1) identify the personal goals of individual workers, (2) develop a work situation that will allow workers to achieve their goals while accomplishing organizational objectives, and (3) provide fair compensation related to the work.

The informal organization also affects behavior. The types of informal groups, determinants, and characteristics are discussed. Communication, group norms, and power are key characteristics that are expanded on.

Leadership also shapes the emergent organization and is an important attribute of a manager. Leading essentially means influencing others. The degree to which a leader is effective is described by the situational model of Fred Fiedler. In very favorable and unfavorable situations, a task-oriented leadership style correlated with a low co-worker preference index value is most effective. In moderately favorable situations, a people-oriented style combined with a high co-worker preference index value yields the most effective leadership.

Behavioral concepts are especially important to the implementation of the MIS. They provide methods for avoiding and overcoming resistance to change.

Management, Information, and the Systems Approach

The systems approach starts with the tasks of management in terms of capabilities of the firm, the allocation of resources, and the stakeholders of the firm. The missions and objectives of the firms are established by applying the main managerial functions, planning, organizing, and controlling to these tasks.

These functions are described from a systems and information requirements perspective to provide a systems model of O & M.

PROBLEMS AND QUESTIONS

1. Check under the proper column to indicate whether the concept is most directly related to a particular management / organization model.

	Concept	Classical	Behavioral	Decision	System
			Model		
a.	"Needs" theory	_____	_____	_____	_____
b.	Unity of command	_____	_____	_____	_____
c.	Synthesis of disciplines	_____	_____	_____	_____
d.	Operations research	_____	_____	_____	_____
e.	Probability trees	_____	_____	_____	_____
f.	Expectancy theory	_____	_____	_____	_____
g.	Span of control theory	_____	_____	_____	_____
h.	Trade-offs to optimize the effectiveness of the organization	_____	_____	_____	_____
i.	Situational leadership	_____	_____	_____	_____
j.	Rational-economic approach	_____	_____	_____	_____

2. Companies are dependent on information from or about external sources. Match the following:

a.	EPA guidelines	1.	Foreign	_____
b.	Ecology demonstration in front of company headquarters	2.	Competitors	_____
c.	Late deliveries of major product component	3.	Vendors	_____
d.	Increase in sales returns	4.	Banks	_____
e.	Credit line extended	5.	Customers	_____
f.	Market share is diminishing	6.	Public	_____
g.	Unfavorable editorials about the company	7.	Special interest groups	_____
h.	Tariffs raised on products sold to Japan	8.	Government	_____

3. Put in block headings according to Figure 2-6, expectancy model. Place the letters following in the appropriate blocks and on the proper arrows for Ms. Gonzalez, senior systems analyst.

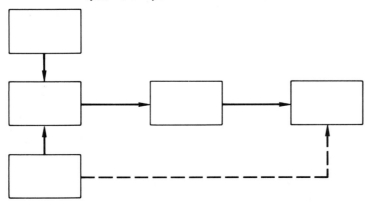

a. Works overtime and attends night classes at college
b. Wastes practically no time at work
c. Is friendly
d. Believes there is a 90 percent probability that if she goes all out, her design of the MIS will be excellent
e. Has strong desire to exert maximum effort

f. Has good analytical ability and strong work experience
g. Wants promotion to satisfy ego need
h. Desire for promotion and increased salary is 9 on a scale of 10
i. Design of MIS within time limits but below cost objective
j. Is skilled in software and hardware evaluation
k. Involves people from all functional areas

4. Match the following to sources of authority.

a. _____ Manager of MIS directs a systems analyst to make a cost-benefit analysis of a new system.
b. _____ A vice president of marketing demands from a systems analyst that a computer terminal be removed from her office.
c. _____ A conference on some failures of a new MIS leads to clear-cut corrective action.
d. _____ An outside consultant recommends that the company install 15 computer terminals.
e. _____ The MIS manager calls his staff of 23 systems people together and tells them that a new project must be completed within six months.
f. _____ A new low-level analyst just graduated at the top of his class with strong MIS, hardware, and software specialties recommends an MIS configuration (design).
g. _____ The company president approves a $100,000 MIS study.

1. Institutional approach
2. Subordinate approach
3. Organizational relationship
4. Personal acceptance
5. Sanctions
6. Authority of the situation

5. Identify the characteristic of the following information by checking the appropriate column.

Information	Strategic	Medium Range	Short Range
a. Facts about a company being considered for acquisition	_____	_____	_____
b. Monthly backorders	_____	_____	_____
c. Working capital	_____	_____	_____
d. Product development of a new automobile	_____	_____	_____
e. Robotization of a production plant	_____	_____	_____
f. World oil reserves	_____	_____	_____
g. New greatly improved product of competitor	_____	_____	_____
h. Number of computer systems people required	_____	_____	_____

6. Place the appropriate letters in the blocks for the following inventory control systems.

a. Demand history
b. Vendor action
c. Lead-time forecast model

d. Inventory control processor
e. Lead-time history
f. Demand forecast model

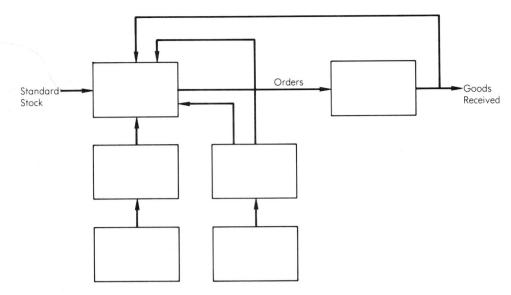

Standard Stock

Orders

Goods Received

7. The classical theory is said to be bureaucratic and structured. Of what concern would the formal organization structure be to an information systems designer?

8. Defend the statement that "management is synonymous with decision making." What part would MIS play in decision making?

9. In view of the fact that the world made progress for thousands of years prior to the advent of management as we know it today, what justification is there for Peter Drucker's statement that management is the most important activity in our society?

10. How would you relate the formal organization, the informal organization, and the management information system in a systems description of business organizations? Draw a block diagram, using solid and dashed lines to indicate relationships and information flows.

11. Some authorities consider an organization to be a problem-solving, decision-making system. Discuss this concept in terms of organizational behavior and company objectives and problems.

12. Should systems be designed to fit the people in the organization or should the people be required to adapt to the systems? What inferences can you draw from your conclusion?

13. Search the literature and describe the effect of group cohesion on organizational behavior and as a system factor.

14. A certain division of a large company employs about 2000 people, of whom approximately 800 are engineers and scientists. It follows an unwritten policy of dropping off (by transfer or squeezing out) approximately 10 percent of its lowest-performance people each year. These individuals are usually given assistance in relocating and about six months notice in which to find new jobs. Analyze the effect of this policy on employee motivation and leadership style.

15. In a manufacturing company of 2000 employees, a new systems group of four professionals started work on a complete marketing, forecasting, production, and personnel MIS. They worked closely with the managers for nearly a year on the design

of the MIS. The changeover to the new computerized system was carried out over a two-week period so that workers could be shifted to their new jobs and trained for the new operations. Within a month, confusion was rampant. Sales orders were misplaced, production was jammed up, and the personnel update file was a mixture of obsolete and new update cards. Both the systems designers and managers felt that the MIS design was an efficient one, well within the capabilities of the employees to implement.

  a. Define the problem and its cause as you see it.
  b. Suggest several alternative solutions.

16. Classify the financial plan as to time, function, level, and purpose. Do the same for the strategic plan, the personnel plan, and the sales plan.

17. The manager of manufacturing for the Triad Pump Co., Mr. Ives, at age 60 was appointed manager of the new MIS function. Triad had over $100 million in annual sales, serviced over 2300 customer accounts, and employed over 3000 people. Mr. Ives knew all operations of the company well. He and two assistants analyzed information needs by examining position guides, developed a system for processing data, and with the approval of top management, purchased computer hardware.

  When the new MIS was being installed, transfers to new jobs were made and new forms and procedures were revealed. Workers grew confused and angry. Within a week, conditions were chaotic despite Mr. Ives' carefully planned installation.

  a. What did Mr. Ives fail to do?
  b. How should Mr. Ives proceed at this point?

18. Obtain an organization chart of the following:

A city   A hospital
A bank   An oil company
A large department store   One of the "Big Eight" accounting firms

  a. Discuss similarities and differences.
  b. Identify line and staff managers.
  c. Can you identify matrix management and organization?
  d. Where do MIS and computer operations appear on the charts? Why?

19. A principle of control is segregation of duties. That is, any employee who has access to assets and also access to records of these assets is in a position to embezzle from the firm. Give an example of possible lack of segregation of duties for the following:

  a. The computer operator in a bank
  b. The petty cash clerk
  c. The inventory control clerk
  d. The store managers of government employee stores operated by the accounting office

20. Make a list of management reports that the MIS might provide to ensure control throughout for

  a. A manufacturing company
  b. A bank
  c. A hospital
  d. A chain of department stores

SELECTED REFERENCES

ANDERSEN (ARTHUR) & CO. *A Guide for Studying and Evaluating Internal Accounting Controls*. New York: Arthur Andersen & Co., January 1978.

ARGYRIS, CHRIS. "Management Information Systems: The Challenge of Rationality and Emotionality," *Management Science*, February 1971.

BARROW, JEFFREY C. "The Variables of Leadership: A Review and Conceptual Framework," *Academy of Management Review*, April 1977.

BASS, BERNARD. *Stogdill's Handbook of Leadership*, rev. New York: The Free Press, 1982.

BLAKE, ROBERT R., AND JANE S. MOUTON. *The Managerial Grid*. Houston: Gulf, 1964.

BYARS, LLOYD L. "Solutions to Productivity Problems." *Journal of Systems Management*, January 1982.

DRUCKER, PETER F. *Management: Tasks, Responsibilities, Practices*. New York: Harper & Row, 1974.

GALBRAITH, JAY R. *Organization Design*. Reading, Mass.: Addison-Wesley, 1977.

GREEN, STEPHEN G., ET AL. "Personality and Situational Effects on Leader Behavior." *Academy of Management Journal*, June 1976.

GREGERMAN, IRA B. *Knowledge Worker Productivity*. New York: AMACOM, 1981.

HARE, A. PAUL. *Handbook of Small Group Research*. New York: The Free Press, 1976.

HART, DAVID K., AND WILLIAM G. SCOTT. "The Optimal Image of Man for Systems Theory." *Academy of Management Journal*, December 1972.

HERSEY, PAUL, AND KENNETH H. BLANCHARD. *Management of Organizational Behavior*, 2nd ed. Englewood Cliffs, N.J.: Prentice-Hall, 1972.

JAGO, ARTHUR G. "Leadership: Perspectives in Theory and Research." *Management Science*, March 1982.

KAST, FREMONT E., AND JAMES E. ROSENZWEIG. *Organization and Management: A Systems Approach*. New York: McGraw-Hill, 1970.

LAWLER, EDWARD E. III, AND JOHN GRANT RHODE. *Information and Control in Organizations*. Pacific Palisades, Calif.: Goodyear, 1976.

LEE, JAMES A. *The Gold and the Garbage in Management Theories and Prescriptions*. Athens: Ohio University Press, 1980.

LEVINSON, HARRY. "Executive Development: What You Need to Know." *Training and Development Journal*, September 1981.

MACAROV, DAVID. *Worker Productivity: Myths and Reality*. Beverly Hills, Calif.: Sage, 1982.

MINTZBERG, HENRY. *The Structuring of Organizations*. Englewood Cliffs, N.J.: Prentice-Hall, 1979.

OWENS, JAMES. "A Reappraisal of Leadership Theory and Training." *Personnel Administrator*, November 1981.

REDDIN, WILLIAM J. "The 3-D Management Style Theory." *Training and Development Journal*, April 1967.

TOSI, HENRY L., AND STEPHEN J. CARROLL. *Management: Contingencies, Structure, and Process*. Chicago: St. Clair Press, 1976.

VROOM, VICTOR, AND PHILIP YETTON. *Leadership and Decision Making.* Pittsburgh: University of Pittsburgh Press, 1973.

WREN, DANIEL A. *The Evolution of Management Thought*, 2nd ed. New York: John Wiley, 1979.

ZALTMAN, GERALD, ROBERT DUNCAN, AND JONNY HOLBEK. *Innovation and Organizations.* New York: John Wiley, 1973.

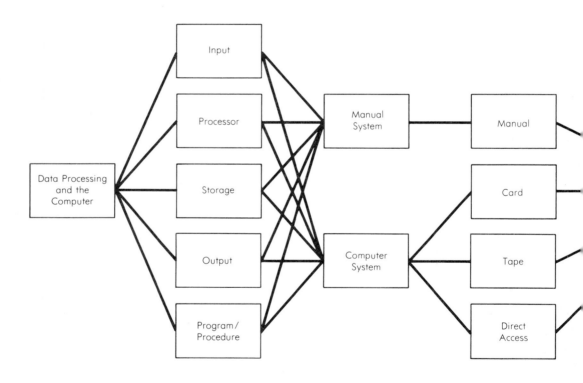

What the Manager Should Know About Computer Systems

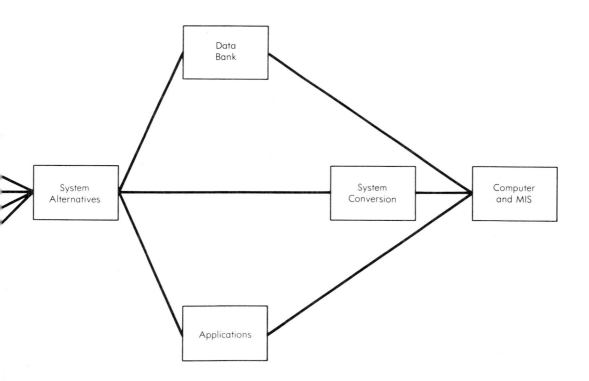

When we review the factors contributing to complexity in organizations and the advances in management that permit the application of the systems approach, it becomes clear that vital changes lie ahead for the manager. First, we know that the future will bring changes and that the changes will occur at an accelerated rate. Second, these changes will require more information—more knowledge about our product, our customer, and about alternative ways to improve our effectiveness. And third, the requirement for more information will necessitate new methods and new procedures for gathering, retrieving, and evaluating this information for making vital decisions.

It is not the purpose of this chapter to provide either a technical discussion or an in-depth treatment of the hardware or the operation of a computer. We believe that such an exposure is not essential for the manager-user. Just as the driver of an automobile can operate the vehicle without a sophisticated engineering knowledge of its engine, the manager can be quite closely involved in MIS design without a technical background in computer operation.

However, some familiarity with the computer and its role in the processing of information is desirable. The objective of this chapter is to explain the elements and operation of the computer sufficiently so that the manager-user can participate in systems design. To do this, the manager should be able to understand and evaluate the potential and performance of the computer in the accomplishment of his or her operational effectiveness. A secondary purpose is to help close the understanding and appreciation "gap" between managers and computer professionals. The approach will be by analogy, making the transition from the commonplace and easily understood manual system to the more complex computer application.

DATA PROCESSING
AND THE COMPUTER

Not since the advent of the automobile and the introduction of the telephone has an invention had such widespread impact on our society as the computer. Consider that in 1982, more than 100 companies sold 2.8 million units for almost

$5 billion. Prior to 1980, the total installed base of *all* computers was smaller than this. By the end of 1985, at least 10 million small computers will be installed. This process is likely to accelerate due to falling costs: $30,000 of computing power in 1960 cost $1000 in 1980; by 1985, it will cost $100.[1]

As previously suggested, there are several prerequisites for a modern, effective computer-based management information system. The *first* of these is a *management* system—the organizational arrangements, the structure and procedures for adequate planning and control, and the many other manifestations of good organization and administration. Indeed, such a system is a prerequisite for progress in any endeavor. *Second*, there must exist data and information—information about the company's goals, resources, environment, policies, operations, plans, and performance against plans. These types of information represent knowledge about the company's plans and its managerial and operational processes. *Third*, to process these data, it is necessary to have appropriate equipment that will (a) provide the capability for economic, rapid access to large-scale storage of retrievable data, (b) process these data economically and at high speed, and (c) enter information into the system and retrieve and display it. These three activities are now often performed by special electronic communication devices and by today's computer and related hardware.

A final prerequisite to an effective computer-based management information system is *information management*, an organization for designing, maintaining, and managing the required systems and procedures.

We shall be concerned in subsequent chapters with information management and systems design. In this chapter we want to examine first how information is stored, processed, and retrieved by means of the electronic computer and related devices. The objective is to understand how the computer operates as the fundamental information processor and the essential element of a management information system.

Components and Operation of a Data Processing System

An information system is composed of five basic components, as shown in Figure 3-1. In a manual system, human beings perform the five basic functions; in a computer-based system, the functions are performed by equipment. In either type of system the basic functions are (1) entering data into the system; (2) processing the data (rearranging input data and processing files); (3) maintaining files and records; (4) developing procedures that tell what data are needed and when, where they are obtained, and how they are used, as well as providing instruction routines for the processor to follow; and (5) preparing report output.

People's knowledge and store of information is what can be acquired and stored in their memory or some peripheral source. The information must then be

---

[1] "Integrated Information Systems: The Microcomputer Explosion," *Forbes*, April 26, 1982, p. 74.

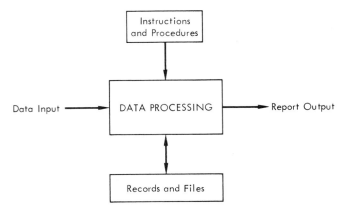

FIGURE 3-1   Basic Components of an
Information System

retrieved and manipulated to be useful. To augment memory, people use a variety of devices, including books, forms, and records. We are concerned here with the two major sources of storage and manipulation for information systems: records and the computer.

If it were not for records, the size and reliability of data storage would be restricted to what people could remember. Records were the earliest device for assisting in the data processing task. Consisting first of pictures and marks, writing later relied on alphabets and numerals.[2] The "alphabet" for processing business data consists of 10 numerals, 26 letters, and 25 special characters. This "alphabet" may be represented by punched holes in cards (Figure 3-2), by positive and negative charges on magnetizable material, by electrical impulses over wires and cables, and by radio signals. This encoding is necessary to provide a scheme that is efficient for processing purposes.

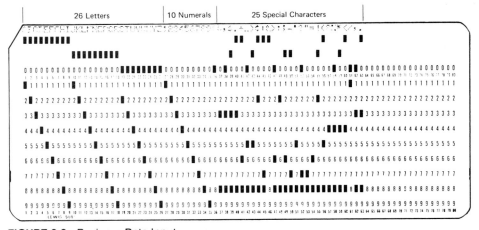

FIGURE 3-2   Business Data Input

[2]To appreciate the value of writing as a memory device, try to multiply two three-digit numbers without the aid of pencil and paper.

Both manual and computer-based information systems have the elements and attributes of systems in general and can be described in terms of these elements: input, output, and processor. Our examination of computer systems in this chapter will proceed by analogy to make the transition from the easily understood manual system to a slightly more complex computer-based system. The transition and analogy will accomplish two purposes. First, we will be able to see how a computer-based data processing system can become a vital adjunct to management planning and control. Second, by examining the system through its components (input, output, processor), we will be better able to understand how these components of an information system provide the framework for MIS design.

OPERATION OF A MANUAL INFORMATION SYSTEM

The human being is the earliest and still the most prevalent form of data processor. Despite the fantastic growth of computer applications, manual information systems still outnumber them in quantity of systems and information handled.

People receive input data by seeing or hearing them. These data are then stored in the brain, which also acts as a control and logic unit. The outputs from this type of information processing are oral or written reports and in some cases a variety of physical actions. The human mind, acting as a control and logic unit, can perform many operations on data: adding, subtracting, multiplying, and dividing; storing results; repeating the operations on different sets of data; comparing two items; outputting results in a prearranged manner; and revising the processing operations as a result of changed instructions.

Despite an ability to perform the foregoing processing tasks, the human remains an unreliable processor. The human mind is slow in performing the arithmetical computations required and is rather erratic in applying rules of logic. Fatigue and boredom are among human frailties that cause from 1 to 10 percent of human error in computation and clerical tasks. On the other hand, where judgment is required, the human mind is indispensable. Judgment is needed to make decisions in data processing systems because of the difficulty of planning to handle all eventualities. In summary, human beings alone are inefficient data processors, but they become a vital element of all data processing systems because of the need for decisions and judgment.

All the many information systems in the typical company (e.g., payroll, accounts receivable, billing, inventory, production scheduling, shipping) are fundamentally similar in that they possess the basic components of any system: input, processor, and output. Examining a typical manual system will make the understanding of such a system easier and facilitate the transition to a computer-based system. Figure 3-3 shows an inventory clerk operating a manual inventory accounting system. The fundamental elements of data processing, *manual or computer*, may be described in terms of this illustration.

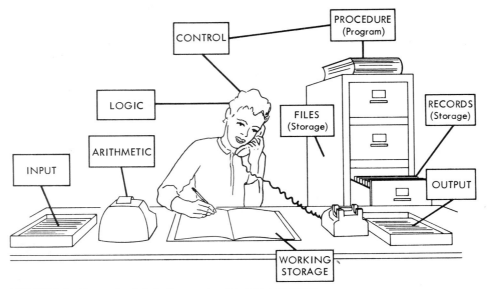

FIGURE 3-3 Elements of Data Processing (Inventory System)

Note that the components of this manual inventory accounting system are the same as those of an information system, illustrated in Figure 3-1. They are also the same components we will use to describe a computer-based information system:

1. Input
2. Processor
   Arithmetic
   Control
   Logic
3. Storage
   Internal
      Memory
      Working storage
   External
      Records and files
4. Procedure or program for instructing the processor
5. Output

Generally speaking, there are two types of inventory control systems, whether manual or computer. The first is the elementary inventory accounting system, which merely adds receipts and subtracts issues from inventory to produce an up-to-date inventory of all items. The second, and more sophisticated type of system, computes demand based on prior sales or issues and calculates economic order quantities and reorder points. This application will be discussed in Chapter 5. In this chapter we will utilize the first type of inventory accounting system to illustrate both the manual information system and the conversion from manual to computer based. Refer to Figure 3-3 for the following discussion of manual system components.

Input

We see that the *input device* for the manual inventory processing system is the inbasket of the inventory clerk. This device receives the *input data* to the system, which may be in various forms and media and is related to information surrounding inventory receipts and issues. Inventory records are updated with receipts on the one hand and reduced with orders for the item on the other. Receipts and issues may be recorded in writing by a storekeeper, stamped on an invoice by a mechanical device, or punched into a card. The resulting cards, invoices, receipt documents, issue papers, shipping documents, and a variety of other *input* information affecting the inventory system are entered into the inbasket for processing and ultimate preparation of output. *Output* can take the form of (1) updated inventory records, (2) an inventory status report, or (3) other reports and documents related to inventory. Note that the input component will accept a variety of information formats.

Processor

From the standpoint of manipulating or processing the data, the *processor* of the manual system is the most important component. It is made up of a control element (contained in the inventory clerk's brain), which keeps the proper relationship among the components of input, processor, storage, and output. An additional element of the *processor* is the calculator or the *arithmetic* element, which performs the four mathematical functions of add, subtract, multiply, and divide. The logic element of the processor, also in the clerk's brain, compares two quantities to see if one is equal to, greater than, or less than the other. It is surprising to most people to discover that these five operations (add, subtract, multiply, divide, compare) comprise the entire processing ability of the computer. However, this ability is a fantastic one, as we shall see.

The three elements of the *processor* component in the manual inventory accounting system can be summarized and illustrated:

Element	Processing Task
Control	Decides sequence and extent of processing among data contained in input, storage, and output
Arithmetic	Multiplies units issued by unit price and deducts from on-hand balance
Logic	Compares on-hand balance with minimum inventory level and prepares status report

Storage

The third element depicted in Figure 3-3 is the *storage*. There are two parts to the storage: the *internal* (internal to the processor) and the *external*. The internal storage in this manual system is the working storage represented by the pencil and whatever temporary record the processor (clerk) is working on. This internal storage is sometimes called *memory* because it is stored in and is immediately available to the processor (clerk).

External storage is represented by the individual *records* for an item of inventory. When these individual records are combined they make up a *file*. Prior to performing any processing or calculation upon external storage, the processor (clerk) would have to retrieve the applicable records from the appropriate file. The classification, structuring, and organization of this external storage is very important to the design and operation of any information system, manual or computer based. In the illustration of inventory accounting, the inventory records may be organized by customer, class, project, or a variety of ways. As a general rule, the costs of classification vary inversely with the costs of using and retrieving the information.

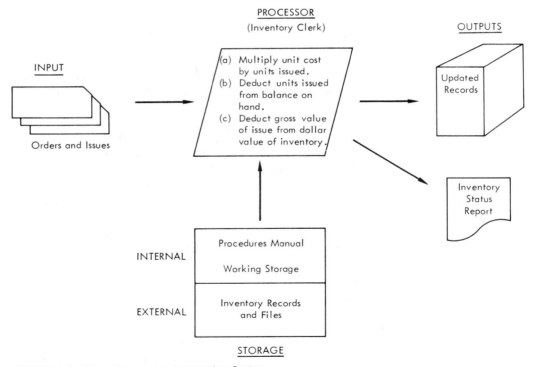

FIGURE 3-4 Manual Inventory Accounting System

Program / Procedure

Another essential element of this manual system is the *procedure*, which instructs the processor (clerk) on how calculations are to be performed or information processed. This is analogous to the *program* of the computer. The procedures manual may, for example, instruct the processor to "(1) multiply unit cost by units issued, (2) deduct units issued from balance on hand, and (3) deduct gross value of issue from dollar value of inventory." The clerk would then perform this processing on the input information, update the inventory balance (external storage), and prepare the required *output* report to go in the outbasket. Preparation of the *output* is the final step of the information processing system.

Output

The reason we design and operate systems is to achieve some *output*. In the case of the inventory accounting system, the outputs are two: (1) an updated inventory master file record and (2) an inventory status report. In the manual system of Figure 3-3, these outputs would be updated files and an inventory status report placed in the outbasket.

A schematic diagram of the foregoing manual information system is depicted in Figure 3-4.

COMPONENTS OF A COMPUTER SYSTEM

Although many managers are awed and sometimes confused by the computer, its operation is essentially no more complex than that of the manual system just described. Indeed, if we make the transition from manual to computer-based system by drawing an analogy between them, there should be no difficulty in understanding the functions and operation of the computer.

We saw in Figure 3-3 the elements of data processing as done manually by a clerk. The field of computers is called *electronic data processing*, and the computer is nothing more than an electronic data processor, with its components the same as those of the manual system described. However, it accepts data in the form of alphanumeric (alphabetic and numerical) characters, as demonstrated in Figure 3-2. If we wish to convert our manual inventory system to computer, the input data would be the same for both systems; only its input *form* would be different. The computer *processes* these data. For example, it adds items received and deducts items issued to update the inventory record, but it does all this *electronically*. The alphabetic and numerical characters, normally received as

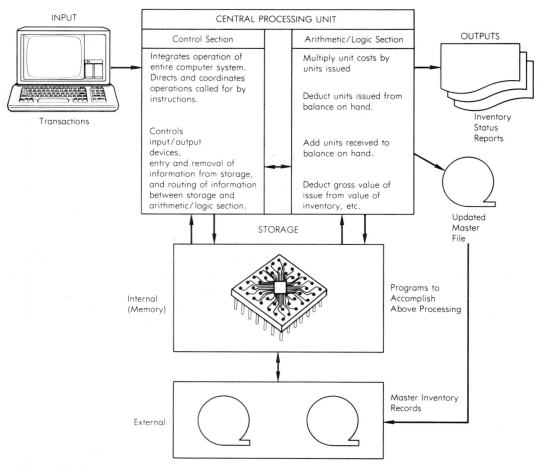

INPUT

Transactions

CENTRAL PROCESSING UNIT

Control Section	Arithmetic/Logic Section
Integrates operation of entire computer system. Directs and coordinates operations called for by instructions.	Multiply unit costs by units issued

Deduct units issued from balance on hand. |
| Controls input/output devices, entry and removal of information from storage, and routing of information between storage and arithmetic/logic section. | Add units received to balance on hand.

Deduct gross value of issue from value of inventory, etc. |

OUTPUTS

Inventory Status Reports

Updated Master File

STORAGE

Internal (Memory)

Programs to Accomplish Above Processing

External

Master Inventory Records

FIGURE 3-5   Computer-Based Inventory Accounting System

electrical impulses sent from a terminal,[3] are sensed and are represented in electronic form within the computer. The subsequent arithmetic or processing operations are accomplished electronically; hence the computer can be described as an *electronic data processor*.

The manual inventory control system previously discussed, when converted to computer application, might appear schematically as in Figure 3-5, which

---

[3] Input to the computer can come in many forms: punched cards, positive and negative charges on magnetic media, electrical impulses over a wire from a terminal, and radio signals. Historically, punched cards and paper tape were predominant. Although cards are still used today, input usually comes from a terminal (a television screen with a typewriter keyboard). Cards will continue to be used in the examples because they are easy to visualize.   .

(a)

(b)

FIGURE 3-6a Components of a Large Computer System (IBM 3081 Model Group K)

Source: Photo courtesy of IBM.

FIGURE 3-6b Components of a Medium-Sized Computer System (DEC VAX 11 / 750)

Source: Photo courtesy of Digital Equipment Corporation.

FIGURE 3-6c Components of a Small Computer System (Apple II Plus)

Source: Photo courtesy of Apple Computer, Inc.

(c)

illustrates the basic components of the computer system. Figure 3-6 shows the actual hardware components of modern generation computer systems. A discussion of the components follows.

Input

The function of entering data into the computer system is performed by an input device. Unlike the manual system with its human processor, the input to the computer must be in machine-acceptable form. Normally this input takes the form of punched cards, magnetic media (tape, disk, diskette), and direct input from terminal keyboards. Typical computer input/output devices are shown in Figure 3-7.

The input devices read or sense these coded data and make them available in a form acceptable to the computer. Whatever device is used, the data must generally be coded in a form compatible with the characters of Figure 3-2. In the

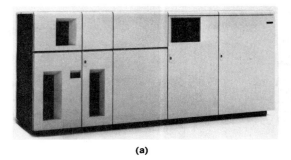

(a)

(c)

(b)

FIGURE 3-7a   Input / Output Device (IBM 3800 Printing Subsystem)

Source: Photo courtesy of IBM.

FIGURE 3-7b   Input / Output Devices (Apple II Plus terminal, two Disk II floppy disk drives, and a Silentype thermal printer)

Source: Photo courtesy of Apple Computer, Inc.

FIGURE 3-7c   Input / Output Device (IBM 3279 Color Display)

Source: Photo courtesy of IBM.

case of our illustration of the inventory accounting system of Figure 3-5, the input would most likely be in the form of transactions from a terminal where the clerk enters information about receipts and issues.

The Central Processor

The central processor is the most significant component of the computer. As in the case of our inventory control clerk in the manual system, it consists of a *control* section, which coordinates the system components, and the *arithmetic/logic* unit, which performs the same functions (add, subtract, multiply, divide, compare, shift, move, store) as the clerk-calculator combination of the manual system. However, the CPU (central processing unit) of the computer accomplishes these tasks at fantastically increased speed and accuracy. This meager processing logic, accompanied by the five simple functions, accounts for the almost infinite variety of tasks the computer can perform. Figure 3-6 illustrates central processing units.

The control section of the CPU directs and coordinates all operations called for by the instructions (programs) to the system. It controls the input/output units and the arithmetic/logic unit, transferring data to and from storage and routing information between storage and the arithmetic/logic unit. It is by means of the control section that automatic, integrated operation of the entire computer system is achieved.

The arithmetic/logic section performs the arithmetic and logic operations. The former portion calculates, shifts numbers, sets the algebraic sign of results, rounds, compares, and performs the other tasks of calculation. The logic section carries out the decision-making operations to change the sequence of instruction execution, and it is capable of testing various conditions encountered during processing.

Storage

Storage is somewhat like a huge electronic filing cabinet, completely indexed and accessible instantly to the computer. All data must be placed in storage before being processed by the computer. Storage consists of *internal*, which is a part of the processing component, and *external*.

Note the similarity between manual and computer systems. Internal storage, frequently referred to as *memory*, is the characteristic that permits the computer to store, in electronic form, data from input devices as well as long series of instructions called *programs* that tell the machine what to do. These programs are similar to the procedures manual of the manual system. It is this memory facility that distinguishes the computer from devices such as calculators and bookkeeping machines, which, although they have input, output, and processing capabilities, cannot store programs internally within the processing unit. The program enables the computer to perform complex and lengthy calculations in order to process specific input data.

To understand how programs of instructions permit the computer to process data, we must examine the concept of *computer memory* to see how information and instructions can be stored within the computer. The information can be (1) instructions (programs) to direct the processing unit, (2) data (input, in process, or output), and (3) reference data associated with processing (tables, code charts, constant factors, etc.). Because the computer memory is the storehouse of this information, it is important to understand how it is represented in memory.

Integrated circuits are the technological base for most processor memory today. The physical details of how semiconductor memory works are beyond the scope of this book.[4] Very likely the current technology will be obsolete in 5 to 10

---

[4]For an excellent discussion of both internal and external storage, see *Computer Storage Systems and Technology* by Richard E. Matick (New York: John Wiley, 1977).

years, replaced by something faster, cheaper, and denser. However, the intuitive explanation of how memory works will probably survive. Consider a simple light switch: it must be on or off and there are no other states. In computer jargon, these states are referred to as 1 and 0, and this representation is called *binary*. Because each "light switch" can represent only two states, more "switches" are needed to represent information of any reasonable complexity.

Unlike the decimal number system, where each position in a number represents a power of 10, the binary system of numbering represents each position by a power of 2. Moreover, in the binary numbering system we can use only 1s and 0s. Hence the binary number 1001 is $1 \times 2^3 + 0 \times 2^2 + 0 \times 2^1 + 1 \times 2^0 = 9$. This is the manner in which numbers and characters are represented in the *computer memory*. Binary numbers from 0 to 9 can be represented by the following table:

Binary	Decimal
0000	0
0001	1
0010	2
0011	3
0100	4
0101	5
0110	6
0111	7
1000	8
1001	9

Computer memory is made of fixed units comprising a certain number of "light switches." We want to be able to represent in memory 10 decimal digits, 26 alphabetic characters, and 25 special symbols (comma, dollar sign, etc.) (see Figure 3-2). Binary schemes for representing these data vary, but all utilize a prearranged assignment of bits and groups of bits. This system of representation is important because of the need to arrange storage and locate it by address.

Storage of computer memory is divided into locations, each with an assigned address. Each location holds a specific unit of data, which may be a character, a digit, an entire record, or a word. When a data item is desired, it is obtained from its known location in addressable storage units that are organized to provide data when wanted. There are several schemes for using the processor to assist the programmer in keeping track of the storage locations. These schemes provide *data names*, such as "update inventory" or "calculate net pay," to refer automatically to sections in the program designed to perform these calculations. Notice the similarity between these programs and the procedures manual of the manual inventory system described previously.

(a)

(b)

FIGURE 3-8a Storage Device (IBM 3380 Direct Access Storage)

Source: Photo courtesy of IBM.

FIGURE 3-8b Storage Device (IBM 3850 MSS-Honeycomb)

Source: Photo courtesy of IBM.

FIGURE 3-8c Storage Device (IBM 3420 Magnetic Tape Unit)

(c)

External storage (consisting of records and files, reference data, and other programs) is of two types:

1. *Direct access.* Disk, diskette, magnetic drum, and data cell devices providing random-order mass data storage that can be accessed randomly, without having to read from the beginning of the file to find the desired data. Figure 3-8 shows some of these devices that stand apart from the processing unit.
2. *Sequential.* Magnetic tape that is sequentially ordered and that must be read from the beginning in order to read or write a desired record.[5]

Output

Output devices produce the final results of the data processing. They *record* information from the computer on a variety of media, such as cards and magnetic media. They *print* information on paper. Additionally, output devices may generate signals for transmission over teleprocessing networks, produce graphic displays, microfilm images, and take a variety of special forms. For the most part, basic business applications take the output form of a paper printout. As indicated in Figure 3-5, the output from the inventory accounting system would be (1) a printout containing an inventory status report and (2) an updated inventory master file. Figure 3-7 shows some typical output devices that are linked directly to the computer system.

System Alternatives

The particular configuration of any computer system for a given use is a function of a number of variables such as transactions, storage, desired speed, cost constraints, and design sophistication, just to name a few.

TABLE 3-1   General Characteristics of Three Alternative Hardware Systems

Characteristic	Punched Card	Tape	Direct Access
Processing	Sequential	Sequential	Optional
Sorting	High	High	Reduced
Files per run	One	One	Multiple
Type processing	Batch	Batch	Optional
Input cost (cards, etc.)	High	Less	Less
Errors	Significant	Less	Less
Inquiry capability	Very difficult	Poor	Great
Versatility	Poor	Better	Best

[5]Magnetic tape storage can be compared with a home tape recorder because the tape media of each are physically almost alike. If we wish to play song number 5 of the tape, we must play through songs 1, 2, 3, and 4 to reach it. So it is with tape storage for the computer. Conversely, random-order storage can be compared with the phonograph. Information is recorded on grooves in a disk, and if we wish to play song number 5, we can place the needle in the proper groove immediately. So it is with disk storage for the computer.

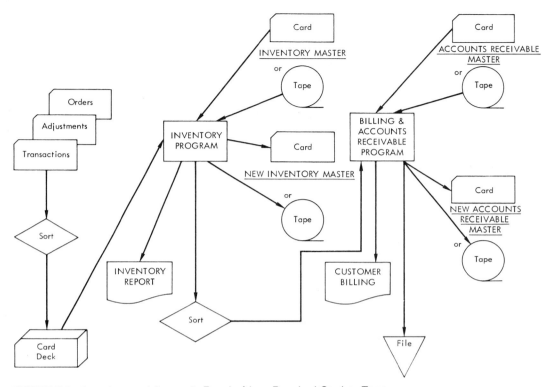

FIGURE 3-9   Inventory and Accounts Receivable — Punched Card or Tape

To give the reader a "feel" for his or her own needs, we can very briefly examine the characteristics of three alternatives: a card system, a tape system, and a direct access system. The general configuration of these systems is indicated in Figures 3-9 and 3-10 for two applications: inventory and accounts receivable. The general characteristics of the three systems are shown in Table 3-1.

Data Communications

No discussion of computer utilization would be complete without mention of data communication—the marriage of data processing and data transmission. A very few years ago, data communications was an obscure subject studied by only a few specialists. The airline reservations system was the best known example of actually using data communications. Today the field is a technological maze, with hardware products and software applications proliferating rapidly. Many more people are involved with data communications today, and most large applications have substantial data communications requirements. Major users of data communications are listed in Table 3-2.

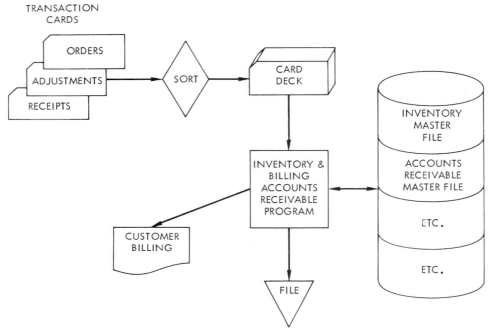

FIGURE 3-10   Inventory and Accounts Receivable — Direct Access

The data communications process generally requires at least five parts:

1. *A transmitter or source of information.* This is usually some type of input/output device such as a typewriter, keyboard, or display. These were shown in Figures 3-6 and 3-7.
2. *A converter on the transmitting end.* This converts the digital signals of the data transmission into analog signals for transmission over the network. Historically, converters were almost always supplied by "common carriers," such as AT & T or Western Union. A variety of manufacturers offer a wide range of these products today.
3. *A transmission channel or carrier.* The telephone companies and other commercial service enterprises offer private-line service at different speeds. TWX is the U.S. and Canadian exchange teletypewriter service, and TELEX is a worldwide exchange service offered by Western Union. Other line facilities are WATS (Wide Area Telephone Service) and COMSAT satellite communications.
4. *A converter on the receiving end.* This converts the analog signal of the data link (transmission channel) back into a digital signal for computer use.
5. *A receiver of transmitted information.* This is the computer and a variety of input/output devices.

Pictorially, one arrangement of these five parts might look like that shown in Figure 3-11. Data can be sent from the terminal to the computer and also from the computer to the terminal.

TABLE 3-2 Major Users of Data Communications

Industry	Type Organization	Types of Applications
Transportation	Airlines, rail, truck, and bus	Reservation system, traffic control and dispatching, MIS, maintenance systems
Utilities	Public utilities, common carriers	Communications facilities, MIS
Manufacturing	All manufacturing	Shipping, order processing, internal time-sharing, MIS
Industrial	Natural resources, metals, chemicals, machines, textiles, etc.	Warehouse control, shipping, process control, MIS
Retailing	All retailers	Point-of-sale systems, credit authorization, warehouse control, MIS
Service	Banks, S & Ls, financial, information services, warehousing, time-sharing, insurance	Branch banking, money and securities transfers, time-sharing, automated clerical operations, credit authorization, warehousing, quotation services
Government	Military and public administration	Communications, command and control, MIS, law enforcement, logistics, public health and education, postal automation

Although the possible arrangements of terminals, converters, transmission channels, and computers are virtually limitless, there are only a few key ideas that the manager needs to understand. The first of these concepts is shown in Figure 3-12. The main computer in this situation communicates with the terminals. The terminals can vary in their "intelligence" levels (how much processing capability resides inside the terminal versus relying entirely on the computer for processing). Input and output are performed via the terminals and most processing occurs in the computer. The transmission channels may be local lines (wires within a building) or remote lines (often telephone lines that can link up to any place we can reach via telephone). The converters are generally left out of data communications diagrams to simplify understanding; however, they are usually required to make the system work. If the terminals are capable of some process-

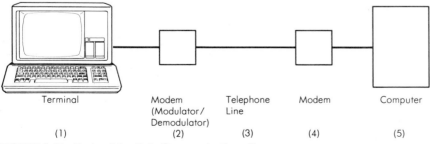

Terminal	Modem (Modulator/ Demodulator)	Telephone Line	Modem	Computer
(1)	(2)	(3)	(4)	(5)

FIGURE 3-11 Parts of the Data Communications Process

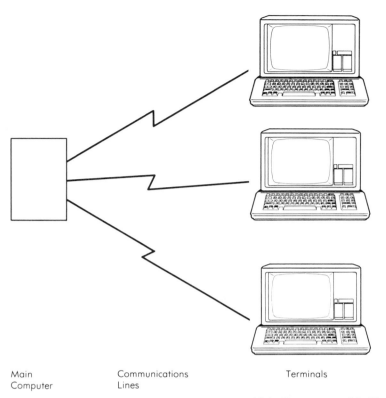

Main	Communications	Terminals
Computer	Lines	

FIGURE 3-12 Data Communications Between a Main Computer and Its Terminals

ing on their own, Figure 3-12 is a minimal example of *distributed data processing*; that is, the total processing that the system does is *distributed* over multiple hardware units.

A second key possibility is shown in Figure 3-13. This is clearly an example of distributed data processing because the main computer and the other computers share processing responsibilities regardless of the intelligence of the terminals. Figures 3-12 and 3-13 are both referred to as "master-slave" relationships because there is a main computer driving the system as a whole.

The third concept a manager should be familiar with is called a "peer-to-peer" relationship and is shown in Figure 3-14. Again, this is a clear example of distributed data processing because each of the computers in the ring shares in the processing load of the whole system. However, there is no main or host computer that is master of the situation, hence peer to peer. Sometimes the computers are assigned entirely different tasks, for example, payroll on one and temperature control on another. In this case, the data communications between them may be very sparse. On the other hand, they may be assigned highly related tasks such as billing and accounts receivable. In this case, they need to share data

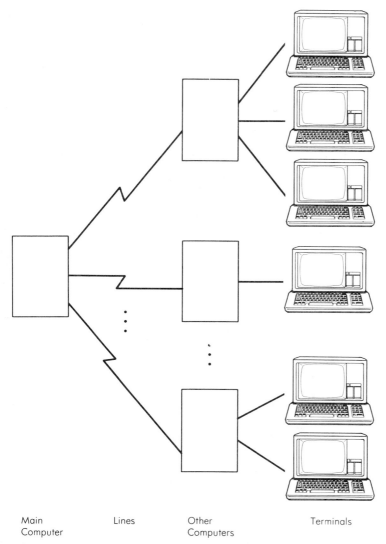

Main   Lines   Other   Terminals
Computer   Computers

FIGURE 3-13   Data Communications Among a Main Computer, Other
Computers, and Their Terminals

and communicate continuously. This topic will be considered in greater depth in
Chapter 4, Database Management.

To summarize, one of the most important business applications of data
communications and the computer is distributed data processing. This allows the
processing required of a computer system to be distributed to the most convenient and logical place in the business; that is, computer support can be aligned
with business needs and organization. For example, a central warehouse may

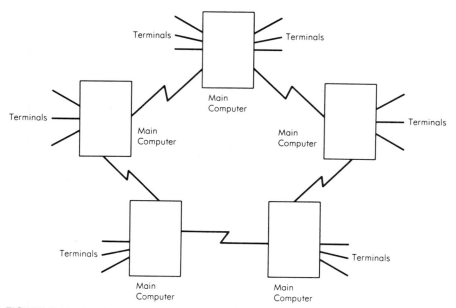

FIGURE 3-14   Data Communications Among Several Main Computers and Their Terminals

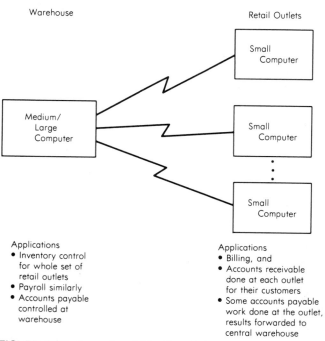

FIGURE 3-15   Example of Distributed Data Processing and Data Communications Used in Business

TABLE 3-3 Comparison of Manual and Computer-Based Inventory Accounting Systems

Component	Manual System	Computer System
Input	Various manual transaction documents	Punched cards or input from terminal
Processor	Inventory control clerk with calculating machine and human logic	Central processing unit
Storage		
Internal	Working storage of inventory clerk	Memory of central processing unit
External	Manual inventory records and files	Master inventory file maintained on magnetic media
Procedure	Processing instructions contained in procedures manual	Program for processing data contained in memory of internal storage
Output	Manually prepared status report and updated master file	Automatic preparation of status report and updating of master file

support multiple retail outlets. Inventory control must be done at the warehouse to prevent multiple outlets from selling the same item twice. Billing and accounts receivable can be done at the retail outlets. Communications links would be set up between the outlets and the warehouse (see Figure 3-15).

Summary

We have chosen the illustration of the inventory control system to make the transition by analogy from a manual to a computer-based system.

There is nothing very complex about the computer components, a greater understanding of which can be obtained by comparing the components of the manual and computer systems as in Table 3-3. Both have the basic components: input, processor, storage (internal and external), programs or procedures for processing data, and outputs. A major consideration of the computer system is the structure of data storage in computer memory so that this information can be accessed.

CONVERSION OF MANUAL TO COMPUTER-BASED SYSTEMS

To increase our understanding of computer-based management information systems, we continue our transition from manual to computer system by describing the steps involved in making a conversion or changeover from the inventory accounting system of Figure 3-4, assuming as we do so that a feasibility study has been made and that the system conversion is economical and feasible. The steps involved in the conversion are preparations of

1. System description (overview)
2. Input documents
3. Output documents
4. File design
5. Program logic (detail)
6. Computer program
7. System verification
8. Documentation

System Description

The system description is usually prepared after preliminary investigation and definition of the problem. The description is essentially a statement of the major inputs, outputs, processing operations, and files needed. The purpose is to show the logical flow of information and the logical operations necessary to carry out the particular design alternative chosen. Systems descriptions are in both *narrative* and *pictorial* form.

Narrative

The narrative description is an English language depiction of the operation of the system. It should describe inputs, outputs, files, and operations. It should be in that degree of detail that will allow users and computer technicians to understand the operation of the system and to utilize the narrative as a starting point for more detailed design. The narrative form of our simple inventory accounting system might run as follows:

> *The activity is concerned with an inventory control accounting system for finished goods inventory. Transactions (receipts and issues) are read from terminals, the relevant master record is found on disk and updated, and the new inventory status report is printed.*

Pictorial

A picture allows us to condense greatly the narrative version of our system description. This symbolic form facilitates a quick analysis of the job being performed and provides a visual overview of the entire operation. Although there are numerous methods of depicting the system description, *flowcharting* is one of the most popular techniques still in use.

The flowchart for the narrative description of our inventory accounting system appears as Figure 3-16. The flowchart for a more sophisticated inventory control system is shown in Figure 3-22. The symbols used for program and system flowcharting are illustrated in Figure 3-21.

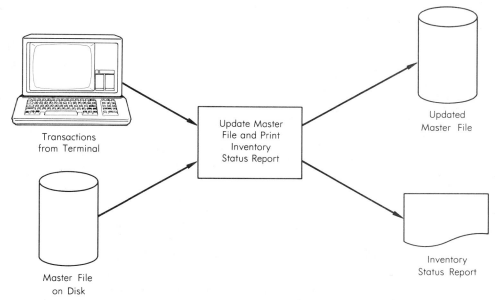

FIGURE 3-16   Systems Flowchart, Inventory Accounting System

Input Documents

After the system description is completed, it is necessary to specify how the information will be put into a form that is acceptable to the computer. Volume of information, frequency, accuracy and verification requirements, and the handling of the information are considerations in the selection of input format. Sometimes inputs have to be accepted in the form in which they are received from the outside. In this case, the task of conversion is merely one of preparing input in machine-usable form.

The exact layout of input documents is necessary because the computer program is an exact and precise sequence of steps that operates only when data are located in prescribed positions. In our example, the input comes from terminals. The electronic impulses sent by the terminal are in computer-readable form. The computer stores this information in its memory for future processing.

The terminal screen layout shown in Figure 3-17 is for our inventory accounting example. The item number of inventory is represented by an eight-digit numeric field. For each transaction, the terminal screen is completely filled in. In addition to the item number, a five-digit quantity field tells how many units are involved in this transaction. The nature of the transaction (price, territory, customer, etc.) is entered in the third field, which is an eight-character code.

Examination of the input document reveals that it provides all the relevant information contained in the system description. The typical *item description*

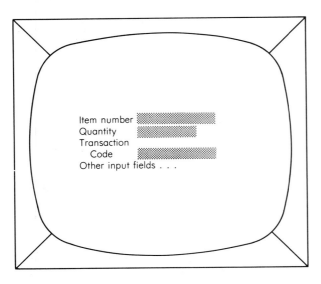

Item number
Quantity
Transaction
 Code
Other input fields . . .

FIGURE 3-17 Layout for Input Transaction from Terminal

normally associated with inventory is not contained in the input document because it is already filed in storage.

Output Documents

Outputs are subject to much the same considerations as input documents, but the output format should be treated with additional care because it represents the purpose or objective of the entire operation. It is the output document with which management is almost exclusively concerned, and because of its critical nature, care should be taken in its design.

The output layout in our example is shown in Figure 3-18. Although the computer is capable of printing much more complex reports than our example, we show the minimum information required to meet the specifications of our system description and output requirements.

STATUS OF INVENTORY REPORT

Item Number   Item Description   Balance
Positions 1-8   Positions 9-24   Positions 25-32

FIGURE 3-18 Output Report Format

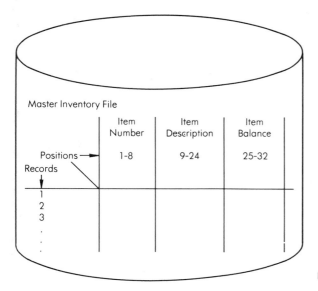

FIGURE 3-19 Layout of Disk Records

File Design

The logic required to control the flow of data through the system is a part of systems design, and the flow is in turn dependent upon the design of data files. These two steps are closely associated and should be considered in conjunction with considerations of type of equipment, storage capacity, input and output media, and format.

The character-by-character contents of every record are specified by the file record layouts. Since disk files are already specified for our example, we are concerned with the disk record layout. This is shown in Figure 3-19.

The item number is an 8-digit field, the same as that on the input terminal screen. The item description consists of two 8-digit fields making up 16 alphabetic characters. This description is an integral part of the inventory file maintained on disk; there is no reason to include it on the input screen representing individual transactions. The file design of the disk is completed by the 8-digit item balance field. For the sake of simplicity we have not included several other elements of file design, such as price, unit costs, weight, minimum and maximum inventory limits, and so on.

We will consider this topic further in Chapter 4.

Program Logic

Although there are numerous means of thinking through and documenting program logic, we will use flowcharts because they have been historically dominant and they are easy to depict and understand.

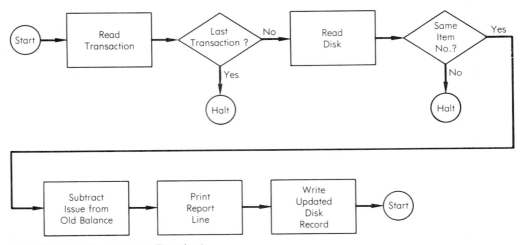

FIGURE 3-20 The Program Flowchart

The program flowchart is the programmer's logic of the detailed, step-by-step representation of how the computer program will accomplish the job. It is the "blueprint" of a program and is used to marshal and organize the facts for examination on paper; to outline problems, logic, and solutions; and to deal with the whole problem in systematic steps. A rough flowchart of conversion from manual to computer inventory accounting might appear as shown in Figure 3-20.

The flowchart symbols for both programming and system flowcharting are shown in Figure 3-21. By comparing these symbols with the decisions and actions depicted in our flowchart for the inventory accounting system, we can see how the computer will perform the logic of the application. After the program writes

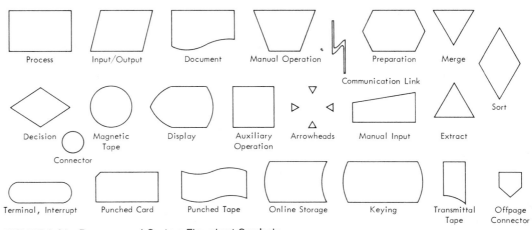

FIGURE 3-21 Program and System Flowchart Symbols

out a new, updated master record on disk (Figure 3-19), it loops back to read another transaction, and so on, until all transactions are processed.

After the programmer has decided the exact flow of the program, he or she must then take steps to explain the logic used in a language the computer understands. Stated another way, the flowchart of Figure 3-20 must be written as a sequence of instructions that can be compiled (translated from a programming language to binary notation) into machine-readable format.

A sequence of instructions that works together to perform a task is called a program. The program is stored internally, and the processor has access to the instructions as required.

TABLE 3-4   Commonly Used Computer Programming Languages for Business Applications

Acronym	Language	Description
APL	A Programming Language	A general language with complex notation and unusual but powerful operations. Notation is exceptionally compact.
BASIC	Beginner's All-purpose Symbolic Instruction Code	A very simple language for use in solving numeric problems developed in on-line systems. Frequently used by nontechnical users.
COBOL	Common Business-Oriented Language	This is an English-like language that is the most widespread in use for business data processing problems. It is problem oriented and is characterized by such key words with common meaning as "IF____IS LESS THAN____GO TO____."
DYNAMO		An early discrete simulation language used for "industrial dynamics" simulations.
FORTRAN	FORmula TRANslator	Developed about 1957, this was the first language to be widely used for solving numeric problems. It is perhaps the most widely used language prior to 1970 and has been implemented on almost all computers. It is oriented to specific kinds of problems. For example, the solution to the problem: area of a circle = πr^2 was written PI*R**2.
PASCAL		An excellent language for teaching language constructs and clear programming thought.
PL/1		In extremely wide use. Generally limited to IBM equipment. For scientific, business, on line, real time.
RPG	Report Program Generator	A language to generate programs to prepare reports (usually only once) from existing data in the system.
SIMSCRIPT		Another language for doing discrete simulation problems. Based on FORTRAN.

TABLE 3-5   Types of Application Program Packages Available for Purchase

Database management	Graphics
Project control	Purchasing decisions
Electronic mail	Estate tax planning
Badge control security	Federal tax preparation
General accounting	Tariff analysis
Accounts receivable	Investment analysis
Accounts payable	Medical management
Payroll	Dental management
General personnel	Life insurance administration
Forecasting	Mailing list control
Estimating	Sales forecasting
Financial modeling	Wholesale distribution
Word processing	Inventory management
Text processing	Bar code reading
Model testing and	Bill-of-materials
evaluation	processing

The details of computer programming are complex and specific and beyond the scope of this brief investigation. We are concerned only with the general nature of how the processor is instructed to perform its operation on the input data to produce the output data in the desired format. In simplified form, an instruction to the processor consists of two parts: an operation code and operands. The operation code simply says, "Perform a READ operation," "Perform an ADD operation," and so on. The operands give additional information to the processor. For example, being told to add is not enough; we must know what two things to add and where to put the answer. These last three pieces of information are called operands. All computer programs, no matter how large or complex, are really made up of lots of relatively primitive instructions like those just discussed.

Computer programming has made giant strides since the old days of "one-for-one" languages such as Easy Coder, Auto Coder, and Auto Tran. Today a large assortment of operator-machine languages is available. The most popular of these are described in Table 3-4. Until we are able to communicate with the computer in the English language (a day that will surely arrive), most of our needs can be met from those programming languages listed.

It is proper to digress here and note that many everyday business problems can be solved by *purchasing* a standard package of programs (rather than by writing the application program(s) yourself). Table 3-5 lists several of the program packages available.

System Verification

After the program has been written and run through the compilation process, it is placed in memory in binary or "machine-readable" form and is ready to process the terminal input, update the master file on disk, and print the required report. The computer will execute the instructions of the program in sequence until the program comes to a halt.

Lest this step seem trivial, note that the probability of all programs working correctly the first time approaches zero. Test cases must be run against each program and all errors corrected. Then more test cases must be run against the whole system (all the programs put together) and any additional errors fixed. Only then is it reasonable to put the customers' actual transactions and the firm's real inventory files under control of the automated system.

Documentation

Based on war story after war story, one might conclude that more systems fail for lack of adequate documentation than for any other single reason. Three types of documentation are needed:

1. For those providing input, a simple overview of the system, a clear description of exactly what input is expected, and a note about what input is not acceptable
2. For those running and maintaining the system, all the technical documentation generated during the development process
3. For those using the output, a simple overview of the system, a clear description of what the output means, and a note about its limitations

This documentation will make the automated inventory system understandable to everyone involved.

Summary

We have gone through the complete cycle of converting a manual inventory accounting system to a computer-based system. Included were the eight steps in making the conversion, the steps that described the operation of the components of the computer system.

The reader should now have a very good idea of how information needs are translated into the language and operation of the computer. However, we have taken the simplest form of inventory accounting system to illustrate this conversion. Few, if any, applications are as simple and straightforward as the one we have demonstrated by way of illustration. The reader may wish to take the more complicated inventory control system of Figure 3-22 and speculate on the steps involved in bringing this system through the conversion process just described. Steps in the evolution of a program are shown in Figure 3-23.

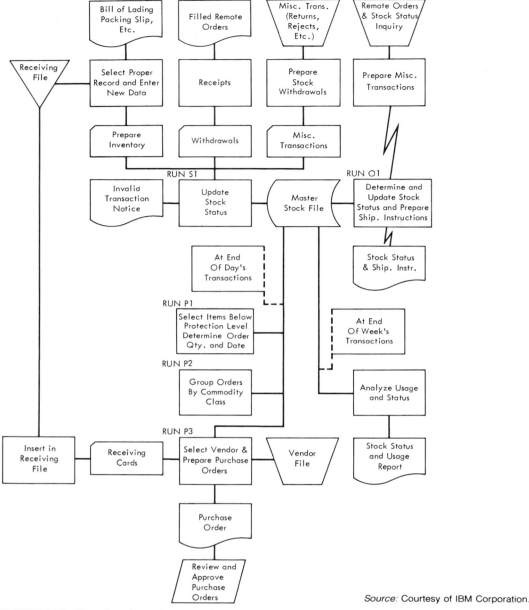

FIGURE 3-22 Flowchart for an Inventory Control System

Source: Courtesy of IBM Corporation.

NOTE: A typical system flowchart description of an inventory control application, this chart uses specific symbols for certain processing functions and input / output. The application involves a multiple-warehouse system: items are stocked in a central warehouse for distribution to remote warehouses; all customer orders are received by remotely located warehouses and transmitted by teletype (communication link symbol) to the central data processing installation. The system provides four major groups of operations: (1) updating stock status [run S1], based on actual transactions; (2) response to inquiries [run O1] from auxiliary warehouses and central warehouse; (3) reorder analysis [runs P1, P2, P3], including purchase order preparation; and (4) weekly analysis reports [run S2] to show slow-moving items, major changes in usage rates, behind-schedule deliveries, economic lot sizes, and so on.

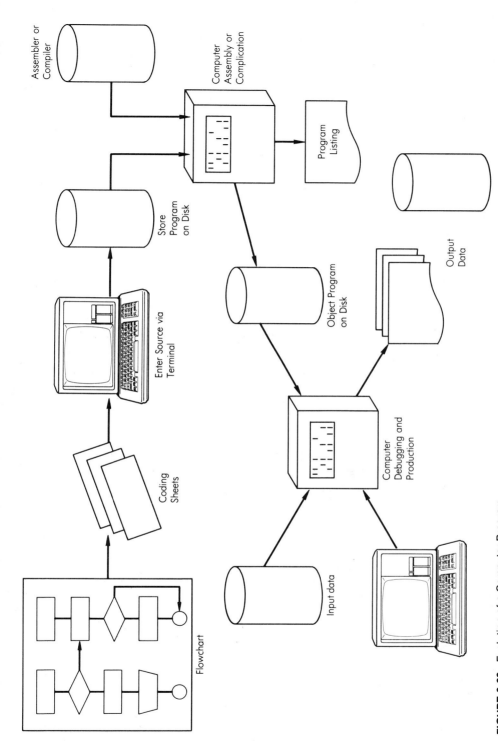

FIGURE 3-23 Evolution of a Computer Program

117

THE DATA BANK CONCEPT

The point has been made repeatedly that the most basic element of a management information system, and indeed the element vital to the management process, is knowledge—information about the goals and objectives of the organization, its policies, resources, operations, and environment. An individual's personal knowledge is only what can be acquired and stored in his or her memory and then retrieved and manipulated as necessary, and although many managers insist on operating with only the information stored in personal memory, it is essential nowadays to augment this capacity with other storage media. Books, magazines, forms, records, and a variety of other media assist us in storing information until it is needed. However, in today's complex managerial environment it is becoming more and more necessary that the organization turn to the computer for storing, processing, and retrieving information. In developing an information system to serve the diverse needs of today's organization, knowledge and information relative to the organization's management and operations can be stored in the memory of the computer. This knowledge can be described and labeled as a data bank. Conceptually, Figure 3-24 shows the transfer of information from human memory and other media to the memory of a computer. To understand and appreciate the concept of central storage and the acquisition of information from a data bank, it is helpful to review an elementary sample of storage under a manual system.

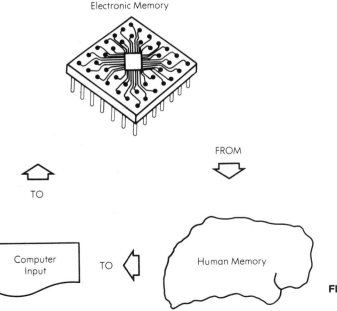

FIGURE 3-24 Transfer of Information to Computer Memory

Information Storage — Manual System

Today's complex organizations are burdened with a combination of problems, not the least of which is information handling. The ratio of clerical workers to production workers continues to rise, and there appears to be no end in sight to the increasing volume of clerical operations performed in modern companies today. Yet despite the increase in clerical workers and clerical operations, one out of four production workers in manufacturing is handling paperwork, and the percentage is much higher in nonmanufacturing industries.

Managers embroiled in paperwork have no time for planning and evaluation, and their working hours become more crisis oriented when most of their time is spent searching for information with which to handle crises that arise in addition to the normal work flow. Add this cost of underutilization of management personnel to the rising cost and complexity of information handling, and the conclusion emerges that the gathering and dissemination of information is usually the company's most difficult problem. Information is voluminous, scattered, and often difficult to obtain.

Generally, dissemination of information falls within one or more of five categories: (1) replies to inquiries, (2) standard routine reports, (3) exception reports, (4) shop or operational paper, and (5) special reports. Costs and complexities of maintaining manual information systems for these types of reports usually result from two factors: duplication of conventional record files in two or more departments and problems associated with *integration* of decentralized planning and operating departments.

The natural inclination of people to hoard duplicate information relating to their jobs, plus the tendency of departments to overlook some of the costs associated with information, results in duplication of record files in many departments. This is not to say that in a manual information system some duplication is not necessary; indeed, it is. An information *input* of a single transaction (customer purchase order) results in action within a number of other files, each separately maintained. Record files affected are, first, the customer file (for credit checking, preparation of shipping instructions, preparation of an invoice, etc.); second, the accounts receivable records; third, inventory adjustment; and fourth, updating of production scheduling and other production statistics. Depending upon the nature of the company and the organization of its information system, several additional files may be affected by this one transaction.

The integration of planning, operating, and controlling between departments through the medium of information is a problem of even greater importance. Departments tend to recognize only some of the costs and information important to them and frequently fail to recognize the interaction of their operations with other departments in the company. The sales department is well aware of customer service and the need for substantial inventories of finished goods, yet is unaware of the planning and resources involved in maintaining optimum inventory levels. The production department is concerned with utilization of employment, overhead, and facilities, yet it is not fully aware of how these actions influence the marketing effort. Finance, on the other hand, watches over excessive inventory and carrying costs, fearful of cash drains and their effect on profits. It is essential that the efforts of these decentralized departments be integrated.

How can today's managers possibly digest all the pertinent detail in a dynamic company? How can they maintain their information files at a minimum and at the same time ensure that the many departments within the company are integrated into a total system? The answer in both cases appears to lie in the proper design and implementation of a management information system. Yet this is difficult if not impossible to accomplish with a manual information system. Experience has shown that if today's company wishes to improve its operations, it can do so with (1) a central information system and (2) a framework to facilitate mechanization. These two attributes are part of the data bank concept.

Information Storage and Retrieval — Data Bank

The corporate or organization data bank can overcome the two primary objections to the manual system mentioned. The accumulation of information in an information center where "one set of books" is maintained avoids the mainte-

Owner & Sons — Purchase Order			
Quantity	Stock Number	Unit Cost	Total
120	74B 34916-z	3.60	432.00

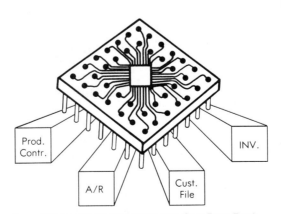

FIGURE 3-25 Integration of Separate Record Files into One Data Bank

nance of separate record files and also tends to *integrate* the separate functions and departments of the company.

The data bank, or the *central database*, as it is sometimes called, is constructed to store and retrieve the information used in common by the various subsystems of the company. Using modern information processing technology, a high-speed, random access, mass storage device is used to store large volumes of data concerning the various aspects of the firm and its environment. All relevant information about the company's operation is contained in one readily accessible file, arranged so that duplication and redundancy are avoided. Moreover, because only one set of records is necessary, it will be easier to maintain their accuracy.

Taking the example of the customer purchase order used to demonstrate our manual system, Figure 3-25 shows how the four separate files maintained in four departments can now be combined into one central data bank. Data are captured once, validated, and placed in the appropriate location in the database.

Figure 3-26 is a more comprehensive illustration of the data bank concept and illustrates how more, but by no means all, of a typical manufacturing

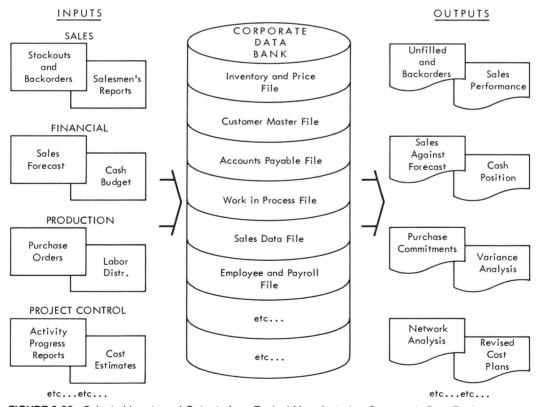

FIGURE 3-26 Selected Inputs and Outputs from Typical Manufacturing Company's Data Bank

company's information files can be integrated into the central database. In the usual case, the database is organized around the major information subsystems required to run the business: (1) general accounting files, (2) inventory file, (3) customer and sales file, (4) vendor file, and (5) personnel file.

It is essential that the database satisfy the requirements of the user; otherwise he or she will continue to maintain his or her own system and thereby defeat the purpose of the central database. The key element in this concept is that each subsystem utilize the same database in the satisfaction of its information needs. This will yield an additional significant advantage—the integration of departments and functions. Each organizational entity, integrated into a whole through its access and interface with the total information resources of the company, gains a greater understanding and appreciation of how its actions and plans affect others throughout the organization. This integration is demonstrated conceptually in Figure 3-27.

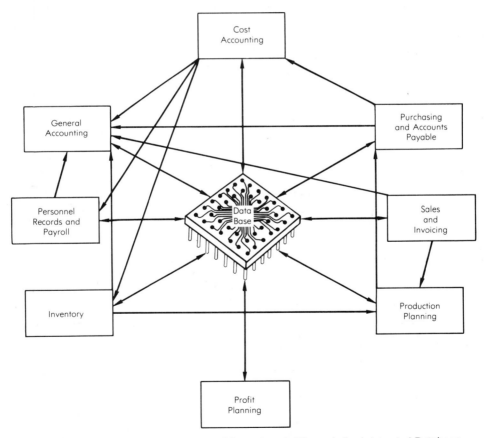

FIGURE 3-27 Integration of Functions and Departments Through the Integrated Database

A major side benefit of a central database is the simultaneous review of company structure, information needs, and management that naturally accompanies the comprehensive review required. The development of the data may act as a catalyst in highlighting such problems as communication, organization, planning, and control.

Potential problems surrounding database construction are generally those connected with interdepartmental coordination and agreement. These might include (1) the possibility of invalid input of information by a unit wishing to maintain *information security*; (2) the "multiplier effect" of erroneously entered data, which has an immediate influence on other departments utilizing the data; (3) the *time dimension* of input data, which requires that user departments agree on the time during which a transaction should be reflected by data input; and (4) the interdepartment agreement required concerning the degree of detail to be included in data elements of the database. Unless some common ground for agreement and solution of these problems is found, organizational units tend to maintain their own system for their peculiar needs. This, of course, defeats the purpose of the central database.

TYPES OF COMPUTER-BASED APPLICATIONS

An insight into the design of management information systems can be gained by considering three types or classifications of application. We are not concerned with the many classifications by function or process (e.g., payroll, purchasing, inventory control), but rather with those where batch (cyclical) processing is used —applications that utilize the on-line or real-time capability of modern equipment, and applications designed primarily for making or aiding decisions.

The state of the art in these applications and the effectiveness of each in providing management assistance for planning, operating, and controlling are important factors to consider when designing or modifying a management information system. The characteristics of the three types of application can be compared:

Type of Application	Degree of Implementation	Greatest Use	Orientation	Integration of Database	Decision Making
Batch	Greatest	Integration of subsystems	Historical and accounting	Limited	Limited
Real time	Few	Control	Remote	Integrated	"Preset" decision rules
Decision making	Very limited	Planning	Decision assistance	Moderate	Poor

Batch Processing Applications

Batch processing is the classical method of processing data and is far and away the most frequently used MIS application. It entails the cyclical processing of input information in "batches." The time it takes to process the data and receive an output is known as "turnaround" time.

The batch processing of checking accounts in commercial banks is a good illustration of this type of application. The turnaround time, or the minimum unit of time in processing checks, is one business day, since a depositor's account is considered satisfactory if it has a positive balance at the close of the business day. Thus, checks received from all sources are proved and sorted for processing against customers' accounts. The checks are "paid" by posting to accounts after they are sorted to the accounts on which they are drawn. Any checks that cause an overdraft by reasons of insufficient funds may be charged back to the source from which it was received.

Most applications in the batch processing category involve the automation of routine functions, deal primarily with the data of the accounting system, and are oriented to record keeping and historical information. Most, but by no means all, of these systems are used for (1) payroll, (2) accounts payable, (3) customer billing, (4) general ledger, and (5) accounts receivable.

Because most of the cost of maintaining information in a company is for the batch processing type of application, these systems offer perhaps the greatest potential for reduction of *information handling costs*. Because of the relatively larger amount of experience with these applications, considerable advances have been made in such large-volume, self-contained applications as payrolls, inventory control, accounts payable, and customer billing.

Some of the more advanced work on improving batch processing applications involves the integration of such separate but related applications as the integration of inventory control and purchasing. Additionally, considerable advance has been made in the database concept of these applications whereby multiple applications are obtained from single-source, single-file integrated databases.

One consideration to keep in mind when developing batch processing applications is the subsequent difficulty involved in integrating a database from a variety of batch processing systems that were independently developed.

Real-Time Applications

Compared with batch processing, the real-time applications are very few, but they are highly publicized because of their exciting nature and their great potential for the future. These applications feature the computer's exciting capability for direct and instant access in which a dialogue is carried on between computer and user.

Most current real-time applications are little more than on-line versions of previous systems, and most are primarily one-application oriented, with little integration between subsystems. Characteristically, this type of application features remote terminal access with data transmission through telephone lines or some other means. Illustrative of real-time applications are those systems for airline reservations, room reservations, work-in-progress control in plants, inventory status ordering and reporting of geographically dispersed distributors, and credit status interrogation for a variety of users.

Real-time operation can be defined as data processing in parallel with a physical process so that the results of the data processing are immediately useful to the physical operation. This definition causes some difficulty because of the varying elapsed times required to *complete a transaction* and the varying time required for data processing to be *immediately useful*. To illustrate, we can say that real time in the case of an airline reservation system involves the processing of an answer while the customer is on the phone. On the other hand we have systems that scan and match workers' identification badges and job tickets on a real-time basis but wait days or weeks to process paychecks.

Generally speaking, real-time systems have these three characteristics: (1) data will be maintained "on-line," (2) data will be updated as events occur, and (3) the computer can be interrogated from remote terminals or other devices. There is some doubt whether managers really need this capability in more than a small fraction of their daily information needs. As a practical matter, more systems with real-time capability utilize both the batch processing and real-time modes for their operations. Such a system is illustrated in Figure 3-28, a conceptual design of the U.S. Bureau of Employment Security management information system. Note the organization of the central data bank and the capability of the system to service many remote users by terminal. Users can "interrogate" the system as desired. Perhaps the best known real-time application is the airline reservation system.

Decision Applications

Although spectacular breakthroughs have been made in computer applications for command and control decisions, similar uses for management problems are few and quite limited. Nothing approaching decision systems such as the SAGE (Semi-Automatic Ground Environment) air defense system or the ones that guided Apollo's flight to the moon and the Columbia space shuttle flights have yet been designed for business use.

Computer applications that make and execute low-level, routine decisions are relatively frequent. Examples are inventory reordering and certain types of production scheduling. However, for higher-order top-management decisions, available applications involve much interaction of the decision maker with the computer. This type of operator-machine interface may be called *computer-assisted decision making*.

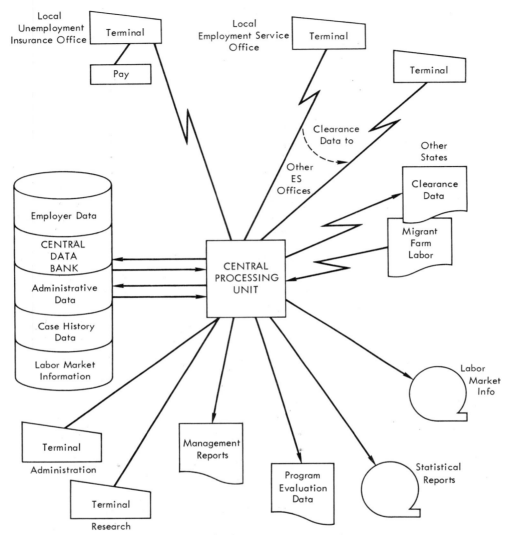

FIGURE 3-28 U.S. Bureau of Employment Security Management Information System Conceptual Design

The primary reason for lack of progress in higher-level decision making by management information systems is the difficulty of defining decision rules for business problems. Although management science techniques have been successfully applied to discrete parts of business activity, their application to higher-management decision processes is still an item for further research. Indeed, applications at higher levels are the forthcoming frontier of computer applications.

With regard to *computer-assisted decision making*, several surveys indicate that the effectiveness of current and near-term applications in assisting management is, at best, below average. However, the majority of firms plan to devote a major share of computer effort to computer-assisted decision making for management in the future.

One of the most rapidly growing applications for computer-assisted decision making is the simulation or model. The corporate model enables management to (1) reduce the time required to react to change, (2) evaluate alternative courses of action with a full knowledge of all pertinent factors, and (3) make longer-range plans by taking longer looks into the future. By posing "what if" questions to the model, the decision maker can explore different alternatives and weigh the consequences of each. In other words, he can simulate the effects of many decisions without having to wait for the results of the decisions in "real life."

Figure 3-29 demonstrates a simulation utilized very effectively by Moore-McCormack Lines, Inc., for scheduling and routing cargo vessels. Two alternative means of varying inputs will illustrate the model. Assuming that some parameters are fixed (i.e., current fleet, freight rates, commodity volumes, origin and destination patterns, operating costs), the following inputs can be varied to determine their effect upon operations: schedule patterns, vessel assignments, and decision rules. On the other hand, the decision maker can assume that modes of operation are fixed and can then vary the following inputs to determine their effects: freight rates, annual volumes, operations costs, and origin and destination patterns. Under each of the foregoing assumptions and variations of fixed parameters and inputs, one valuable output from the model is a financial statement indicating the performance of each individual vessel based on the assumptions put into the model.

SUMMARY

In this chapter we have made the transition by analogy from a manual information system to one that is computer based. With the example of the inventory accounting system, it was shown that the components of both systems are the same: input, processor, storage, output, and procedure. In the manual system, the operations are performed manually or with minimum mechanical assistance, but the computer system processes data electronically; hence, we call it an electronic data processor.

In first establishing a computer information system or modifying a manual one for computer use, the programmer and designer go through the steps of system description, design of input document, output documents, file design, flowcharting the program, writing the computer program, and making the program operational.

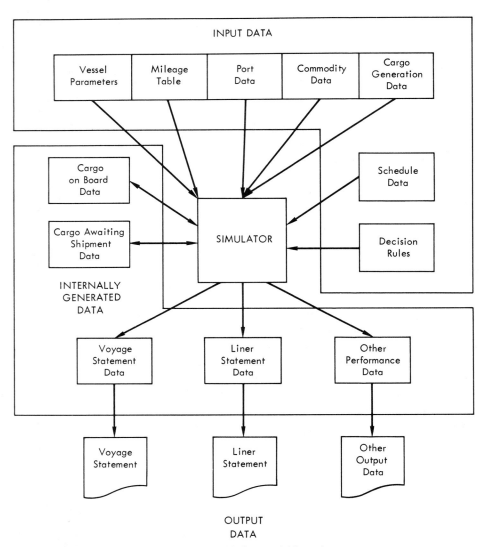

FIGURE 3-29 Simulation Model — Moore-McCormack Lines, Inc.

The concept of a central database has several advantages over the notion of individual departmental files. The data bank is constructed to store and retrieve information used in common by various subsystems of the company. This centralization avoids the duplication costs involved in maintaining separate record files, but more important, an integrated database tends to integrate the functions and subsystems of the organization.

Of the three types of applications (batch processing, real-time, and decision), batch processing is far and away the most numerous and advanced in degree of implementation. Operational real-time systems are few in number but of great potential for advancing the boundaries of managerial decision making and control. Applications for top management decision making are practically nonexistent, although systems designed for computer-assisted decision making are growing in number and degree of sophistication. Modeling appears to offer the greatest potential for decision assistance in the future.

PROBLEMS AND QUESTIONS

1. Case 4, Johnson Enterprises, discusses the value of the computer to a business. This case is continued for each chapter through Chapter 9, each section dealing with the main topics of the chapter. Read the background material for Case 4 and work the section entitled Johnson Enterprises (A).

2. The components of a data processing system are listed below along with those of a manual information system and of a computer system. Match column A with columns B and C.

(A) Data Processing System	(B) Manual Information System (Shipping)	(C) Computer System
a. Input	_____ Shipping clerk	_____ Central processor
b. Processor	_____ Records and files	_____ Program
c. Storage	_____ Procedures manual	_____ Printer
d. Instructions	_____ Customer's invoice	_____ Disk
e. Output	_____ Shipping document	_____ Terminal

3. Examine the flowcharts in Figures 3-A and 3-B. These are order entry and purchasing, respectively, for the International Medical Instruments case (Case 1). Now match the symbol number with the title shown below.

a. Order entry:

Symbol Number	Title
1. _____	a. Prepare sales order and confirm customer order
2. _____	b. Received orders log
3. _____	c. Verify product ID and number
4. _____	d. Customer credit file
5. _____	e. To salesperson
6. _____	f. From salesperson
7. _____	g. From order follow-up
8. _____	h. From order entry (new customer)
9. _____	i. Price list
10. _____	j. Verify billing and shipping address

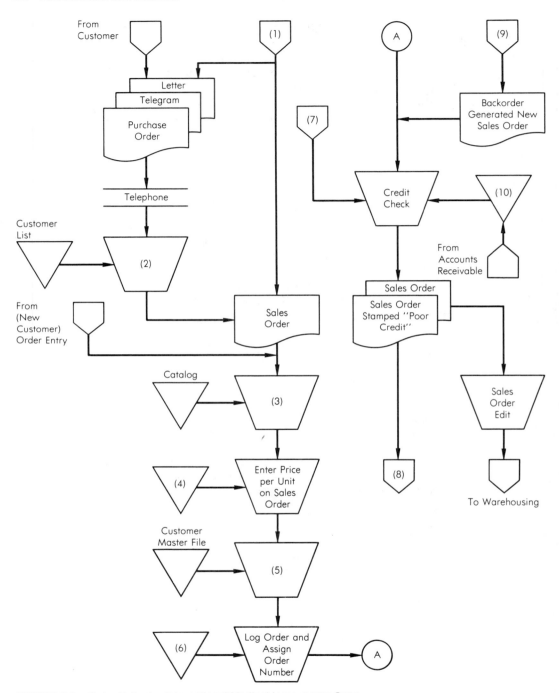

FIGURE 3-A Order Entry for International Medical Instruments Case

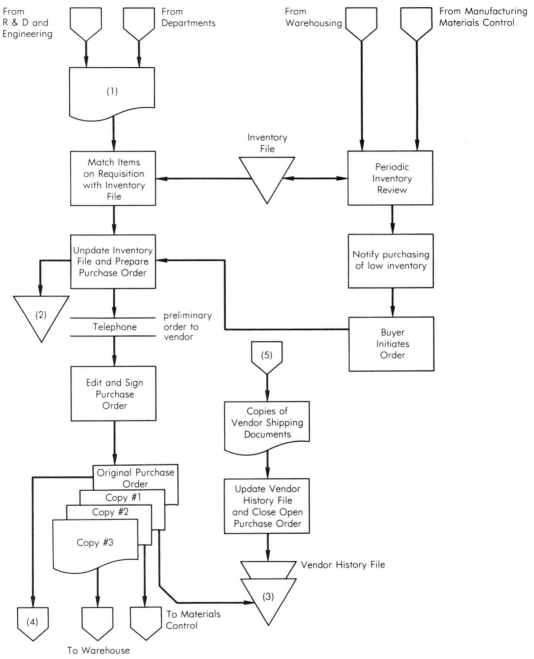

FIGURE 3-B   Purchasing for International Medical Instruments Case

b. Purchasing:

Symbol Number		Title
1. _____	a.	Purchasing Department open order file
2. _____	b.	From Receiving
3. _____	c.	Purchasing requisition
4. _____	d.	To vendor
5. _____	e.	Inventory file

4. What are the five parts of the data communications process?

_____

_____

_____

_____

_____

Illustrate by explaining a normal telephone call from one person to another.

5. **a.** One computer is clearly in control of other computers and terminals. This relationship is called _____ .
   b. Several computers are sharing a work load on the basis of "equal authority." This relationship is called _____ .

6. List the eight steps involved in converting a manual system to a computer-based system.

_____

_____

_____

_____

_____

_____

_____

_____

Do any of these logically precede others?

7. For the International Medical Instruments case,

   a. Weigh the advantages and disadvantages of a card system versus a tape system versus a direct access system and recommend a configuration for the order processing subsystem.
   b. Choose one or more applications (billing, material status reporting, warehousing, etc.) and perform the conversion steps listed in this chapter (system description, input documents, etc.).
   c. Draw a general design of a proposed data bank for company use.
   d. Would real-time application be justifiable for any of the company's computer applications? Justify your answer.

8. To what extent should the manager-user be familiar with the details of system conversion? With programming the computer? With systems analysis? With systems design? With the work of the programmer and analyst?

9. What are the advantages of having a companywide data bank? What typical items are contained in a data bank and how are they structured? Show how different functions (e.g., cost accounting, sales, inventory) can be integrated with a data bank.

10. Differentiate between batch processing and real-time applications. In what type of application would each be utilized?

SELECTED REFERENCES

BRABB, GEORGE J. *Computers and Information Systems in Business*, 2nd ed. Boston: Houghton Mifflin, 1980.

ELIASON, ALAN L., AND KENT D. KITTS. *Business Computer Systems and Applications*, 2nd ed. Chicago: Science Research Associates, 1979.

FUORI, WILLIAM M. *Introduction to the Computer: The Tool of Business.* Englewood Cliffs, N.J.: Prentice-Hall, 1981.

KRAUSS, LEONARD I., AND AILEEN MACGAHAN. *Computer Fraud and Countermeasures.* Englewood Cliffs, N.J.: Prentice-Hall, 1979.

KROENKE, DAVID M. *Business Computer Systems.* Santa Cruz, Calif.: Mitchell, 1981.

MURACH, MIKE. *Business Data Processing*, 3rd ed. Chicago: Science Research Associates, 1980.

O'BRIEN, JAMES A. *Computers in Business Management.* Homewood, Ill.: Richard D. Irwin, 1982.

SKELLY, GARY B., AND THOMAS J. CASHMAN. *Introduction to Computers and Data Processing.* Long Beach, Calif.: Anaheim, 1980.

4

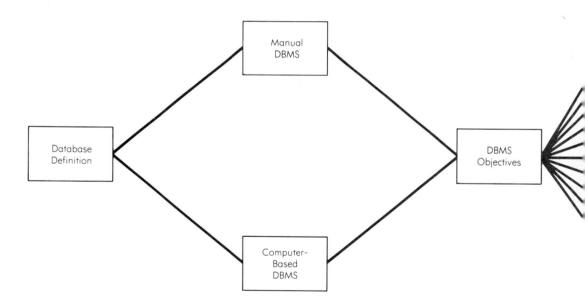

Database Management

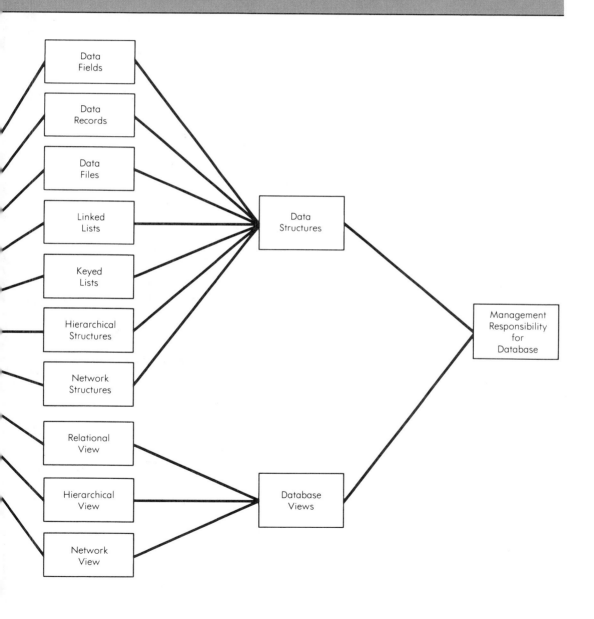

Let us refresh our memory on the key components of any computer system (as discussed in Chapter 3):

- Input
- The processor
- Storage
- Output
- Data communications

There are two items missing that will give life to the computer system and allow it to become a management information system: data and information. The computer system may well be independent of the data it handles. For example, an inventory control system will work equally well for Sears' clothing department data and for Chevrolet division's auto parts data. However, until *some* meaningful data are put into the computer system, it is not useful for management.

The subject of the database was touched on previously, but because of its critical role in giving life to the computer system and transforming it to an MIS, a closer look must be taken. Consistent with the approach taken throughout this text, we will look at database management from the viewpoint of the manager.

THE BUSINESS SETTING

Business has been conducted for thousands of years, and there have always been databases associated with these business activities. Before writing was invented, the databases were completely within the brains of the people as they bartered. Some of the earliest known writings were lists of business transactions (databases). Databases of thoughts, in the form of books or scrolls, were commonplace by the time of Plato and Aristotle. The Romans kept huge databases of laws, of who paid taxes, and so forth. As time passed, businesses grew more complex, and the data associated with them became more extensive. Today it threatens to overwhelm us.

Data and Information

Before we pursue the topic of databases further, a distinction must be made between data and information. *Data* will be used to mean *a set of symbols or experience-stimuli that has no meaning or no value by itself. Information,* as distinct from data, will be used to mean *data that has been processed according to some set of rules and now has meaning and value.* An example:

> *. . . 170, 164, 135, 190, 153, 142, 120, 121, 189, . . .*

The list of numbers has no meaning and no value as it stands—it is just data. Now we add to that the following assertion:

> *The numbers are the weights of each person, in sequence, who stepped onto the elevator at 101 Park Avenue, New York City.*

We are now somewhere between "just data" and information. We have given the data some meaning, but it still has no value in the sense that it will affect behavior or that management decisions can be influenced by it. But now let us process the data to answer the following management questions:

- What is the average weight of the people who used the elevator at 101 Park Avenue?
- What is the weight of the heaviest individual who used the elevator?

We can now process the original data, using the extra assertion and the two management questions, to produce meaningful and valuable new data—information. Management can now decide on elevator lifting capacities and other related questions.

Databases contain data, not information. This is extremely important and will be repeated. *Databases contain data, not information.* By itself, the database is meaningless and worthless. With some assertions about the meaning of the data and some rules for processing the data, we are able to produce information from the database. Management can act upon information. Thus, through proper design and use of the database, it can be an essential tool for producing information for making management decisions.

What Is a Database?

When an organization has a centrally controlled, integrated collection of logically organized data, it has a *database.* The idea of a database being centrally controlled is important. If the collection of data does not respond to commands and queries from a central control point, it is not a single database; similarly for the part of the definition that calls for integration. The various pieces of data within the database must have some logical connections or relationships among themselves for the database to be integrated. For example, inventory control and production planning data are closely related and when put into one database, are a prime example of integration. And, finally, logical organization is required; that is, the data elements must be in specific places and bear specific relationships to each other for the collection of data to be a database.

Databases are the following:

1. The Library of Congress is a database, although an extremely large and diverse one. It is centrally controlled, integrated, and logically organized.
2. The secretary's filing cabinet contains personnel records on all of the firm's employees. That set of personnel records is centrally controlled, integrated, and logically organized; hence, it constitutes a database.
3. The telephone book is also a database by our definition.

Note however, that these examples comprise *data*, not necessarily *information*.

One bypath should be explored before we leave the question, "What is a database?" Consider a banking system in which the customer accounts database is distributed across the various bank branch offices. This means that the physical location of the customer records is spread out over several different physical locations. However, this is still a single database because it is centrally controlled, integrated, and logically organized. This is an example of a *distributed database*. Distributed databases are extremely important and valuable in some situations. However, we will not consider them further since they will add very little to the manager's understanding of databases.

A Database Management System

Around each database has been defined (or has evolved) a system for operating the database. This system, or set of rules and methods, allows for the *definition, creation, updating, reading, maintenance*, and *protection* of the database. In short, this system is a database management system (DBMS).

There are several components to a DBMS:

1. At least one person who "owns" and is responsible for the database
2. A set of rules and relationships that defines and governs the interactions among elements of the database
3. People who put data into the database
4. People who get data out of the database
5. The database itself

It will be helpful to see how these five components of a DBMS actually work on a real database. Let us look at our Library of Congress example:

General DBMS	*Library of Congress DBMS*
1. At least one person who "owns" and is responsible for the database.	1. The librarians (and staff) are responsible for looking after the operation of the Library of Congress.

2. A set of rules and relationships that defines and governs the interactions among elements of the database.

2. There is a long list of rules on who is allowed to use various materials, which items can be checked out, etc. There are also rules that prevent mixing the books with the microfiche and so on.

3. People who put data into the database.

3. Authors, publishers, and librarians contribute material to the Library of Congress.

4. People who get data out of the database.

4. Professors, students, and congress-members get data from the Library of Congress.

5. The database itself.

5. The Library of Congress itself, made up of its books, manuscripts, archives, and newspapers, constitutes a database.

Management and the Database

The process of management takes information as input to decision making. Managers have always been critically dependent on being able to retrieve data from their databases, process those data, and come up with useful information. Because of this special dependence upon information (which in turn depends on data), good managers have always paid special attention to their databases. One sign of impending disaster is a manager who cannot find a needed record and no one on his staff can find it either.

Although the secretary may "own" and be responsible for the personnel files, it is management's responsibility to define the types of questions those files will be used to answer. Unless management specifies such questions, there is no basis for saving one piece of data in preference to another.

Once the manager decides what kinds of questions the files will be used to answer, the manager and secretary can work together to decide which data should be kept, what rules will govern the using of the data, who can add to them, and who can take from them.

We repeat and emphasize: although the manager does not administer the database at the operational level, the manager is the key to defining, organizing, and using the database management system correctly.

ENTER: THE COMPUTER

Speed is one of the most valuable of the computer's attributes. A second feature is accuracy in handling large quantities of data. And, finally, the computer does not become fatigued or bored with repetitive work. All these characteristics are important in database management:

Speed, because a modern business must process many transactions in a short time
Accuracy, because many firms require the data they store and use to be correct.
Good at repetitive work, because databases are by their nature repetitive (at least in
   format and type of content)

Hence, the computer has had a radical impact on database management systems.

The Electronic Database

When an organization has a centrally controlled, integrated collection of logically organized data, it has a database. Now let us study what happens when we add the computer. Consider the example of the personnel records for a small firm. All the files were kept in a filing cabinet and properly met the criteria for a database. When we introduce a computer system to automate the database,

1. The records are now stored on disk rather than in a filing cabinet
2. The records are electrical charges rather than writing on paper
3. The records are added, modified, and deleted by typing requests on the display rather than writing on paper

However, the idea of the database has not changed one bit. It is still a centrally controlled, integrated collection of logically organized data. The key difference now is that the computer does the processing that defines, creates, modifies, and maintains the database. It also does the processing that turns the data into useful information.

To summarize the idea of an *electronic database*, it is a database that has been automated by using a computer system.

DBMS Revisited

Electronic databases require close management to an even greater degree than other databases. There are a number of reasons:

- Computing equipment is expensive (as are computer experts), so efficient and effective use should be made of these resources.
- Electrical charges on a disk that are incorrect are harder to detect than are errors on paper. Also they are more likely to represent unrecoverable errors. (For example, to destroy paper from a filing cabinet takes real physical effort, whereas destroying the contents of computer storage only takes a misthought and/or an ill-planned keystroke.)
- Computers execute requests quickly, which tempts people to print volumes of unnecessary reports, save anything that might be handy someday, and carry "record keeping" to new depths of excess.
- The database experts, like the other computer specialists, will build a system that is an end in itself.

These and more reasons indicate the need for special management attention focused on electronic databases and their attendant problems.

Five components were listed for any nonelectronic database management system. These five components carry over into the electronic database arena. However, in the case of the electronic database management system, we must introduce some variations on the human interaction component:

Nonelectronic DBMS	*Electronic DBMS*
1. At least one person who "owns" and is responsible for the database.	1. *Database administrator* responsible for the database schema.
2. A set of rules and relationships that defines and governs the interactions among elements of the database.	2. *Schema* that describes the nature of logical and physical relationships among records in the database.
3. **and 4.** People who put data into and take data out of the database.	3. **and 4.** equivalent: a. *Data management programs* that control all activities related to the physical database b. *Database programs* that manipulate the database (from a "logical" record vantage point) to produce information. c. *Programmers* to provide the correct incantations d. *Query and report programs* that allow the manager or final user to inspect the database in ordinary language.
5. The database itself	5. Same, except in physical representation

The key difference between nonelectronic and electronic databases, as described in the table, lies in the methods for getting data into and out of the database. In the nonelectronic database, people physically add, modify, and delete records. In the electronic system, programmers design programs to (1) handle the physical data manipulations, (2) work on the database from a "logical" record viewpoint, and (3) allow managers and other final users to inspect the database's contents in a language they understand. There is nothing conceptually different in the two types of database management systems. However, *substantial additional technical expertise* is required to define, design, implement, operate, and maintain successfully an electronic database management system. Management will require some technical education, programmers will be needed, and the clerical staff must be trained to use the electronic DBMS.

The User

As with any management information system, and especially a computerized MIS, the key person to be considered is the user. Too often systems designers are not attuned to this critical factor. If the system is not built with the user foremost in mind, it has missed its point. Common errors are to build it to the computer technician's desires or the latest state of the art.

Let us look at a simple example: the personnel records filing system. These records were kept in a file cabinet and were accessed by the manager or by the secretary upon management request. When this DBMS is automated, *the users of the system do not change.* The interjection of programmers and other computer specialists has not changed the purpose of the database or its users. It has only changed *how* the DBMS works. The lesson here is that the DBMS must still be easy for the manager and secretary to use. It must hold and produce the same type of information for the manager and secretary except that

- Response must be faster.
- Putting records into the database must be at least as easy.
- The output must be better formatted and more readable.
- Less space should be occupied.
- Requests for information should be just as easy to make.
- No special magic should be required to keep the database healthy.

In summary, although database systems are an important and fascinating technical topic, they exist in the business environment solely to support the firm's management in executing the company's main business. Always consider the database user first.

Impact on Management

There can be no question that electronic database systems are a significant factor in our business world. They will become more important as time passes. However, the DBMS represents some serious problems for management:

1. How to manage the technical experts required to use large and sophisticated databases
2. How to keep these systems from taking on a life of their own and sapping the life from the main line of business
3. How to get information rather than mountains of data from the database
4. How to protect human freedom, given the potential of databases to "remember" our every move
5. How to integrate DBMS gracefully into the larger organization.

On the other side of the coin, management can derive some great benefits from proper use of a good DBMS:

1. Much more data can be considered when producing information for management decision making.
2. Information can be made available to management more quickly.

3. Business can be transacted more effectively and efficiently (e.g., when customer data are available instantly and, in the case of banks, in whatever branch the customer patronizes).

4. Databases from sources outside the company are available to assist management in decision making (e.g., stock information).

We could extend both the list of positive aspects and the list of negative points. Managers need to recognize that a powerful tool is available for their use. If properly managed, it will increase their effectiveness substantially.

OBJECTIVES OF A DBMS

Before we take a closer look at databases, let us consider what objectives management should keep in mind as they design and organize their database management system(s).

1. Provide for mass storage of relevant data.
2. Make access to the data easy for the user.
3. Provide prompt response to user requests for data.
4. Make the latest modifications to the database available immediately.
5. Eliminate redundant data.
6. Allow multiple users to be active at one time.
7. Allow for growth in the database system.
8. Protect the data from physical harm and unauthorized access.

Various database management systems, both electronic and nonelectronic, succeed in meeting these objectives to varying degrees. However, they are the goals that a DBMS should strive to fulfill.

DATABASE TECHNICAL OVERVIEW

Managers hire experts in various fields (accountants, economists, engineers, programmers, medical doctors) so that complex problems can be solved by the organization. Managers are supposed to plan, organize, control, and communicate, not be expert in solving all the technical problems. So the question arises, "Why should I, as a manager, learn any of the details about databases?" The question carries some weight. We buy the office buildings we use without even rudimentary knowledge of electricity or plumbing. We buy the company automobile without any attempt to become mechanically proficient. And then we trust the experts completely to fix our plumbing, electricity, and automobile. So why not our computer database?

The question comes down to one of degree. The buildings and the automobile are important and expensive, but they are not the heart of the business. With the database(s), we are committing the life blood of the organization. Our customer account records, our product plans, our personnel files are all in electronic databases. These are vital to the survival of the business. Management cannot casually treat this as just another technical question to be handled by the computer technicians. The success of the business depends on management involvement; hence the need for management to understand the major technical concepts related to database systems.

Data Aggregates

The database can be subdivided into levels as follows:

Database—aggregate of files to meet MIS requirements.

File—related records or blocks.

Block—two or more records retained in a particular storage medium such as a file cabinet or computer tape.

Record—a collection of data elements related to a common identifier such as a person, machine, place, or operation.

Group—two or more data elements that are logically related and must appear together to form a complete unit of meaning (street number and name, first and last name of a person).

Data element—sometimes called *words*, *fields*, or *data items*, is the lowest level of the data structure and the only one with which a specific value may be associated. For example, age, part number, or department number are data elements, as are names or descriptions.

Let us look at these in reverse order.

Data Fields (Elements)

All a computer can do is read one character at a time. Similarly, it can print one character at a time. It is the responsibility of someone else to ensure that characters are logically grouped and presented to a computer in a sensible fashion. When characters are grouped together in this fashion, they constitute a data aggregate called a *field*.

Fields are usually composed of a fixed number of characters. For example, a field might be established to contain a telephone number (with an area code), making this field 10 characters long. However, fields need not be fixed in length. If they are not of fixed length, some indicator must be used to know where the field ends. One common method is to reserve the first couple units of space in the field for a length value. Fixed and variable length fields are demonstrated in Figure 4-1.

In addition to a length property, a field also has an attribute dimension. That is, only a certain type of character may be put in a particular field. Consider

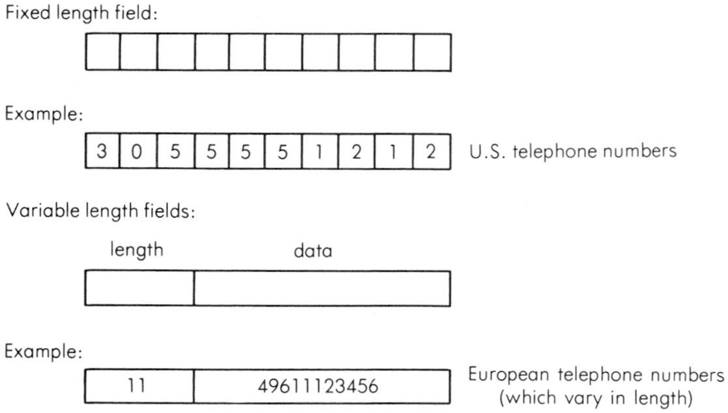

Fixed length field:

Example:

3	0	5	5	5	5	1	2	1	2

U.S. telephone numbers

Variable length fields:

length   data

Example:

11	49611123456

European telephone numbers
(which vary in length)

FIGURE 4-1   Fixed and Variable Length Fields

a field set aside to contain social security numbers. It should be long enough to contain the full nine characters of a social security number. There will never be letters or even special characters in this field; it will only have numbers in it—hence, it is called a *numeric* field. On the other hand, it may be useful to set up a field containing only letters—an *alphabetic* field. If the field can contain either alphabetic or numeric characters, it is called *alphanumeric*. These are but three types of fields. As our discussion progresses, we will see the need for other types of fields.

As it turns out, there is actually another attribute dimension to the concept of fields. Exactly two types of characters may be put in any field: correct ones and incorrect ones. There are two ways in which incorrect characters may be put in fields. To return to the example of the field containing social security numbers, it occasionally happens that well-intentioned computer users put dashes as characters between the third and fourth digits and the sixth and seventh digits of their social security numbers in what should have been a strictly numeric field. This constitutes an error in type and should be trapped as part of the input edit function. Another error, which ultimately causes greater anguish to data processing people, is logical error. In this case the user records the wrong social security number. This is a very costly error because it cannot be so readily diagnosed. Typically, it will be found only when Mr. 123456789 does not receive his monthly social security check because it has been sent to Mr. 123456788. Errors of this kind create a very special type of grief in database systems, as will become apparent.

Data Records

Fields may be grouped together to constitute the next type of data aggregate, which is a *record*. A record is simply a collection of related fields. Clearly, the fields must be ordered in some fashion so that a given field may always be

TABLE 4-1 Payroll Logical Record

Field Name	Field Format
SS-NO	9-character numeric
NAME	40-character alphabetic
HOURS-WORKED	
MON	3-character numeric
TUES	3-character numeric
WED	3-character numeric
THUR	3-character numeric
FRI	3-character numeric

found in the same place in each record. The physical organization of a record is called a *record layout*. A typical record layout for a time card application may be seen in Table 4-1. From this example we can see that a record is composed of three fields: the social security field of numeric characters, the name field of alphabetic characters, and the hours-worked field, which in turn is composed of five subfields for each day of the week. It is the programmer's function to prepare such a record layout for each type of record with which he will be working. For the programmer's purposes this will be called a *logical record*.

Extremely important with respect to understanding database concepts is the notion that a programmer is doing much more than simply listing fields when he is preparing a record layout. He or she is forming a logical association among the fields of the record. This process is called *binding*. Thus, a programmer creates the fields SS-NO, NAME, and HOURS-WORKED, orders them, and thus binds them together into a larger data aggregate called a record. This record is given a name, probably PAYROLL, which will later serve to identify a set of employee records, all of type PAYROLL.

The record layout of Table 4-1 serves to describe a logical record of type PAYROLL. Sooner or later, there will have to be a physical representation of this record that the computer can read. Next the programmer will have to choose the appropriate medium for this type of record. He or she may choose to place these records on magnetic tape, on disk, on drum, and even on computer cards. When the appropriate choice has been made, the logical record description is transformed into a physical record description. Let us suppose that the programmer wishes to place these records on data cards. He or she must take a description of the card in terms of its physical composition (a computer card is 80 characters long) and transform the record layout to the physical layout. An example of this physical record layout for the record PAYROLL can be seen in Figure 4-2.

Thus we find that there are two types of records. First, there is the logical record, which describes the fields of the record and their relationship one to another. Second, there is the physical record, which shows how the logical record will be represented, depending on the particular medium chosen to store that kind of record. In the case of a logical record of type PAYROLL, it can be seen

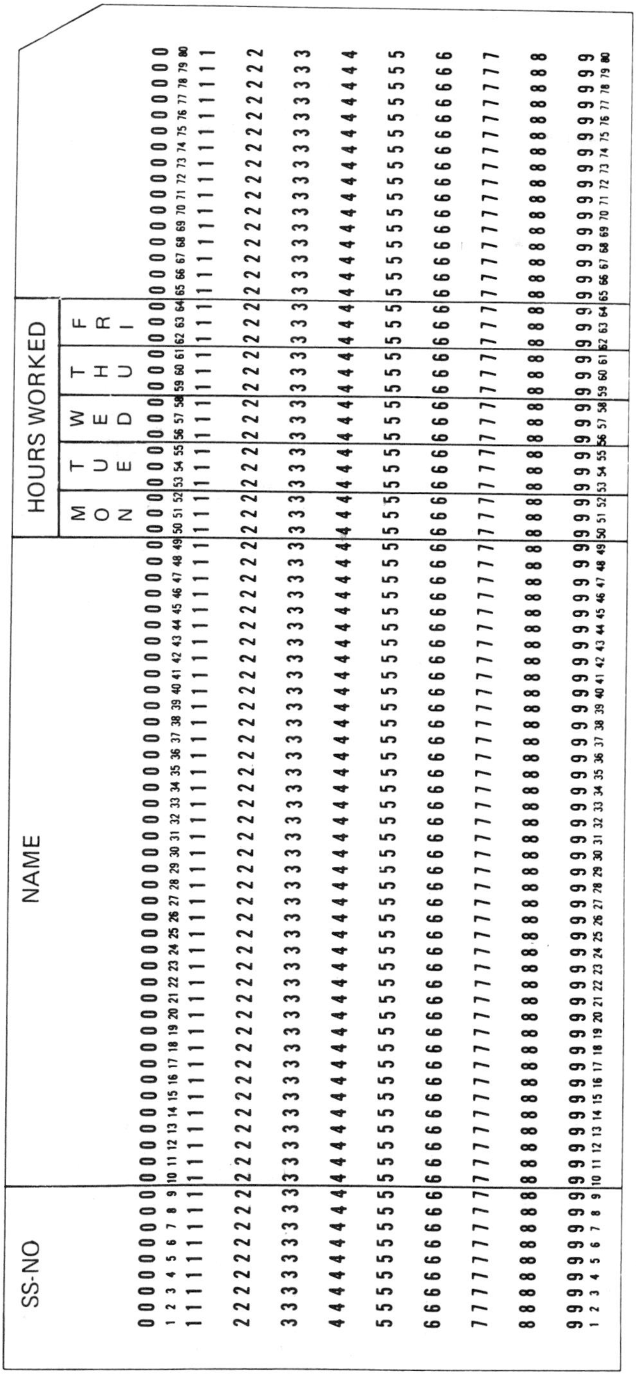

FIGURE 4-2 Physical Payroll Record

that the total record length is 64 characters. On the other hand, the physical record will be 80 characters long.

The PAYROLL records could just as well have been put on disk. If so, each logical record would still be 64 characters long, and each physical record's length would depend on the actual disk device. More than one logical record could perhaps be grouped into a physical record, yielding a *block*. For example, if the physical record size was 128 characters long, two logical records could be *blocked* into that physical record. Where there is a one-to-one correspondence between the logical and the physical records, the logical records are said to be *unblocked*.

Data Files

After the computer programmer has created the concept of a record, he or she then sets about to construct a computer program that will read a record organized according to the designated record layout. Presumably, there will be more than one record of the type specified in the record layout. That is, the programer will write the program in such a fashion as to read a group of cards of the type PAYROLL from a card reader. This group of cards will be stacked one on top of another, placed into the card reader, and read one at a time by the card reader under control of the computer program. These cards will be presented to the computer program in a strictly sequential order.

This ordered collection of records is called a *sequential file*. Thus, a file is a group of records having the same format. In the case of the PAYROLL records, they are stored on the card medium. As such, they constitute a *card file*. These records could just as easily have been stored on magnetic tape or on disk. It is possible to construct sequential files on both magnetic tape and disk.

One of the principal virtues of files constructed on disk units is that the records do not have to be placed in them in a strictly sequential order. Rather, records may be placed in disk files in a random order. This type of file would be called a random access file. Each record in a random access file has associated with it a relative index number. Whenever a record is to be read from a random access file, a computer program must produce a relative index number for this record to locate the record in the file. One of the principal virtues of a file organized this way is that, to obtain record number 100, we merely produce the number and use it directly to read the necessary record. Hence, the term *direct access file* is sometimes used interchangeably with the term random access file.

Consider now the problem of reading record number 100 from a file which has a sequential organization. We must read record number 1, read record number 2, read record number 3, and so forth until the necessary record is obtained. Thus to obtain one record, we must read 100 records. This would seem to suggest that we immediately abandon all magnetic tape files, card files, and sequential disk files in favor of a clearly superior random access file organization. This would be an extremely expensive suggestion. Disk storage is one of the most expensive storage media available. Magnetic tape, on the other hand, is relatively inexpensive. Large volumes of data can be stored on sequential files on magnetic tape at the least possible cost.

This direct cost associated with storing records on disk files is not the entire problem associated with their use. With the introduction of later generations of computer hardware and software, the task of writing computer programs to be read directly from the various input/output devices associated with this new generation of computers becomes far too complex for even the more sophisticated programmers to manage. Consequently, most computer vendors supply a set of programs to people who purchase their machines that handles all the input and output activities for each type of computer peripheral. When a programmer wishes to either read or write a record to an input/output device, the computer program will format the request in a particular manner and present it to the appropriate program supplied by the vendor. The vendor's program then performs the action indicated by the user's program.

The set of programs provided by a computer manufacturer defines a set of *access methods* that serves to define the way in which records will be written or read from peripheral devices. The typical program provided by the vendor to perform a *sequential file access* is fairly simple and uncomplicated. The typical program provided by the vendor to perform a *random file access* is fairly complex and lengthy. Thus, if a file is organized as a random access file, every attempt to read from or write into this file causes the execution of a rather lengthy program. While the computer is executing this access program, it is not directly performing useful work for the user. Thus the user has increased the *overhead* associated with a given program activity by using random access file methods. This overhead might at first glance lead us to the conclusion that we should forgo the use of direct access methods and disk files. The fact is that there is a need for an intelligent mix of sequential and direct access files, of magnetic tapes, and of disks and diskettes.

Physical and Logical Storage Structures

Consider Figure 4-3. This makes clear the distinction among the user, the database management system, the computer program(s) called the access method, and the database itself. Between each of these entities is a well-structured interface. The user makes his or her wishes known to the DBMS via a query language and update and report requests. The DBMS translates these user commands into database manipulation requests couched in terms of the logical records in the database. The access method takes the requests and further translates them into data manipulation instructions for the physical database. Finally, answers are sent back through this set of interfaces.

We turn now to some sample storage structures, both the logical and physical representations.

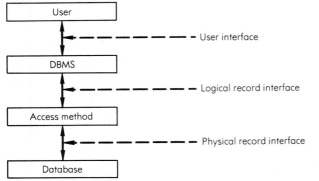

FIGURE 4-3 Levels of Interface in a Database System

Linked-List Structure

We will use the records of the type SALARY from Table 4-2 to illustrate the linked-list structure. We will assume that each of these records is in a direct access file. To process this file as it is, we will have to write a program that will systematically produce relative record numbers so that the appropriate access method can secure the appropriate record for us. Every time the program processes the file, it will have to produce the relative record number in precisely the same sequence. To relieve the program and the programmer of this function, let us create a new file with the record layout described in Table 4-3. The principal difference between the record SALARY in Table 4-2 and the new record SALARY of Table 4-3 is that the new record contains an additional field called NEXT-RECORD. In this field will be stored the relative record number of the

TABLE 4-2 Salary Logical Record

Field Name	Field Format
EMPLOYEE-NO	5-character alphanumeric
OFFICE-NO	3-character alphanumeric
WK-SALARY	5-character alphanumeric
NO-DEDUCT	2-character alphanumeric
JOB-CLASSIFICATION	3-character alphanumeric

TABLE 4-3 Linked Salary Logical Record

Field Name	Field Format
EMPLOYEE-NO	5-character alphanumeric
OFFICE-NO	3-character alphanumeric
WK-SALARY	5-character alphanumeric
NO-DEDUCT	2-character alphanumeric
JOB-CLASSIFICATION	3-character alphanumeric
NEXT-RECORD	5-character numeric

next record. To process this file we will simply need to read the first record. From this first record we can obtain the next logical record from the field NEXT-RE-CORD. Hence, the logical or sequential relationship among the records of this file is built into the file structure. Records organized in this manner are said to form a *linked list*.

Figure 4-4(a) gives a graphical representation of records in a linked list. Figure 4-4(b) shows how the records would be organized if the order were to be based upon EMPLOYEE-NO.

The linked list with its serial searching for retrieval of data has an advantage over other methods. Suppose that we have a list of records that are linked by names of individuals in alphabetical order. Now assume that a query comes in asking if we have a record on Moore. We search the file serially until we come to Moore or until we come to a name that would follow Moore. In the latter case, we know that Moore is not in the file. In other record structures, we would have to search the entire file before we could be sure that Moore was not there.

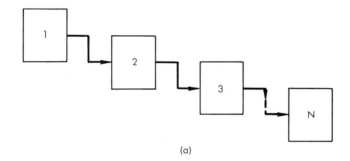

(a)

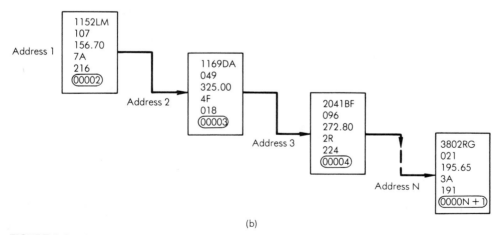

(b)

FIGURE 4-4 Linked List of Physical Records

TABLE 4-4 Keyed Employee Logical Record

Field Name	Field Format
EMPLOYEE-NO	5-character alphanumeric
.	.
.	.
.	.
NEXT-RECORD	5-character numeric
NEXT-JOB	5-character numeric

Keyed-List or Indexed-List Structure

Let us now suppose that we wish to read the SALARY file of records such as in Table 4-2 and print a report in the order of the JOB-CLASSIFICATION field. To do this we cannot use the linked structure by NEXT-RECORD, because it would present the records to us in order of EMPLOYEE-NO. Consequently, we would have to write a program to sort these records and present them in order of JOB-CLASSIFICATION. It is possible, assuming that the job classification order will occur rather frequently, for us to add yet another field to records of type SALARY. Let us call this new record field NEXT-JOB. The new record layout will be seen in Table 4-4.

After reading the first record of this new type SALARY, we can get the next record by employee number by using the field NEXT-RECORD, or we can get the next record by job classification by using the contents of the field NEXT-JOB. A graphical representation of this new record structure can be seen in Figure 4-5. This new structure of records is called a *keyed list* or *indexed list*. (Some writers distinguish between a key and an index. We will treat them as meaning the same thing.)

These new fields do not contain any data that directly relate to the employees whose record they occupy. Rather they serve to locate or point to the *next* record where "next" is a logical relationship established when the record was created. These new fields are called *pointer fields*. It is the function of these pointer fields to allow us to order in some logical fashion the records of a file without having to use a computer program or computer programmer to do this ordering function.

Hierarchical Structure

The hierarchical data structure is shown from a conceptual viewpoint in Figure 4-6. In this type of data arrangement, data records are organized into *echelons* or levels. To obtain a particular record from, say, the third echelon, we would first identify the appropriate *parent* or *owner* record at the second echelon, which would in turn be identified by the choice of a particular pointer from

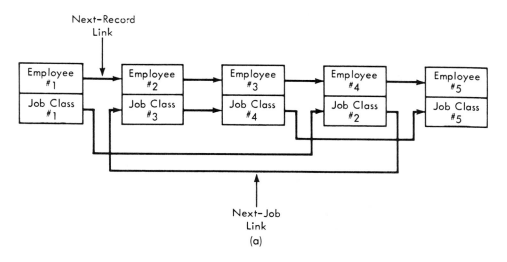

FIGURE 4-5 List of Physical Records Linked with Different Keys: (a) two keys, (b) three keys

echelon 1. For example, Figure 4-6 shows a tree structure for an inventory system file. If we wish to search records of trunk lids to find a particular year and model, we must first specify the warehouse. Then we search "mechanical parts" until we reach "trunk lids." Finally we search the "trunk lid" file. The physical represen-

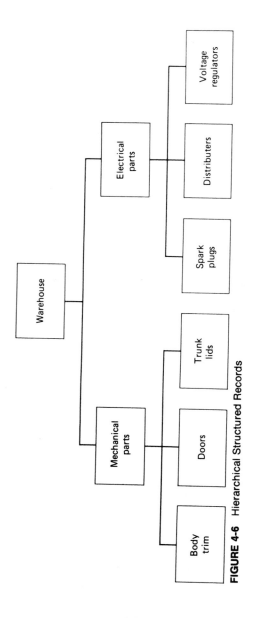

FIGURE 4-6 Hierarchical Structured Records

154

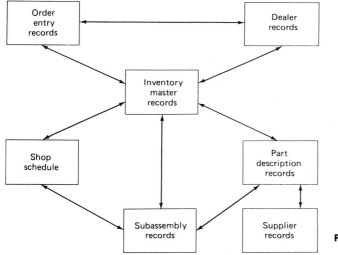

FIGURE 4-7 Network Structured Records

tation of this example would be complex and would not enhance the reader's understanding of the hierarchical storage structure.

Network Structure

In a network, complex associations can be formed among the related groups of records. Figure 4-7 illustrates a network structure for an inventory system. Suppose that an order entry clerk wishes to know the parts list for a specified subassembly on an order. She will request a search of the inventory master records to find the pointer that will locate the subassembly description in the subassembly records. Once the subassembly is located here, the parts list can be read out of the record. Again, only a conceptual viewpoint is provided. The physical representation takes us beyond the technical depth desired here.

Relational View of a Database

The three best known approaches to defining a database are

- The relational approach
- The hierarchical approach
- The network approach

We will look at each of these in turn from a management perspective.

Consider the tables in Figure 4-8. The student table contains rows representing three students. Each row has the student number, name, age, and sex.

Student table:

ST#	STNAME	AGE	SEX
S1	Jack	21	M
S2	Jill	20	F
S3	Jess	21	M

Course table:

C#	CNAME	PROF
C1	Finance	P1
C2	Math	P2
C3	English	P2
C4	Literature	P3
C5	Economics	P1

Enrollment table:

C#	ST#	CREDITS
C1	S1	3
C2	S1	4
C3	S2	3
C5	S2	3
C5	S3	5

FIGURE 4-8 University Database Example

The course table similarly lists five courses by number, name, and professor teaching the course. Finally, the enrollment table tells us which students are enrolled in which courses for how many credits. Each of these tables is called a *relation*. The rows are called *tuples*, and the columns are called *attributes*. We will continue to use the terms table, row, and column.

One of the key tests in evaluating a database is whether it can be used easily. Let us test it.

- To add a new student, append a new row to the student table.
- For a student to drop a course, delete a row from the enrollment table.
- To modify the professor field for English, find the English course row and modify the professor.
- To ask the database a question, for example, "What are the names of the students professor P2 is teaching?"

    1. Make a temporary table from the course table, picking all rows involving P2.

C#	CNAME	PROF
C2	Math	P2
C3	English	P2

2. Use the course number(s) as an index into the enrollment table and create a new temporary table from this source.

C#	ST#	CREDITS
C2	S1	4
C3	S2	3

3. Use the student number(s) as an index into the student table and create a new temporary table from this source.

ST#	STNAME	AGE	SEX
S1	Jack	21	M
S2	Jill	20	F

4. Use the attribute STNAME to overlay the temporary table just created. This gives the names of professor P2's students: Jack and Jill. The answer comes in table (relation) format:

STNAME
Jack
Jill

The internal workings of the DBMS are not of interest here, other than to note that procedural tasks, like the ones just considered, are what computers do best. The example illustrates that adding, deleting, and modifying records in a relational database are conceptually straightforward. Asking questions of the database is also fairly easy. The actual user commands can be expressed in brief and readable format. Real management questions can be addressed without in-depth knowledge of the physical properties of the database, only knowledge of what kinds of data are in which tables. This relational approach has a number of positive features:

- Few basic concepts (tables, rows, columns)
- Symmetry (we could equally well have handled the question, "Which professors teach Jill?")
- Powerful database operations (for the user)

The drawbacks should also be considered. Some users feel that the relational approach is still too state-of-the-art. Others point out the large amounts of computing resources required to support a relational system. It has even been asserted that no really large, pure, relational databases are operational today. If any of these drawbacks has merit today, the arguments will weaken as relational databases become more common and computing prices fall.

Hierarchical View of a Database

We touched on the hierarchical storage structure earlier. The hierarchical database is just an extension of that idea. Figure 4-9 shows the general form of an hierarchical database. One serious concern will no doubt be apparent at this point. If we try to do the same tasks that we did in the relational case, we immediately hit problems (see Figures 4-10 and 4-11):

Action	If COURSE is the parent and STUDENT the child (Figure 4-10)	If STUDENT is the parent and COURSE the child (Figure 4-11)
• Add a new student	• Cannot do this until the student signs up for a course (parents are required)	• Add the student as a new parent
• Student drops a course	• Delete the student record	• Delete the course record
• Modify Literature professor	• Modify the professor field in the parent C4	• 1. Look at each student record to see if he or she is taking Literature 2. No one is, so this request cannot really be honored (in the sense that the database remembers the new Literature professor)
• Name the students that a professor is teaching	• 1. Look at each root to see if the professor is teaching the course 2. If so, see which students are listed	• For each student, see if one of their courses is being taught by the professor

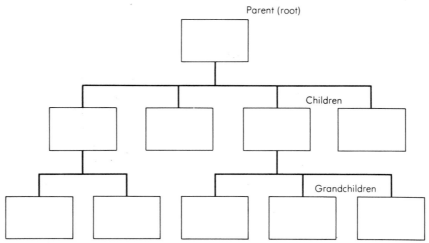

FIGURE 4-9 Hierarchical Database

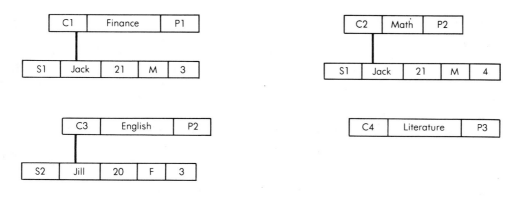

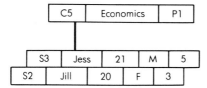

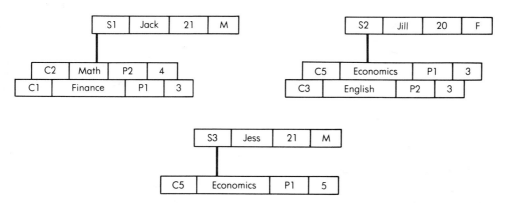

FIGURE 4-10 Hierarchical Database for Student Example (Alternative 1 with "Course" as Parent)

The manager should note the following drawbacks to the hierarchical database relative to the relational database:

- There are more basic concepts.
- Symmetry is generally missing.

The positive points are that hierarchical databases have been around for quite a while and are well understood. They work very well for inherently hierarchical data and certain types of questions related to them.

FIGURE 4-11 Hierarchical Database for Student Example (Alternative 2 with "Student" as Parent)

Network View of a Database

We will not dwell on the network approach. It takes the same data as the relational and hierarchical databases, but rather than putting them in tables or tree (hierarchical) structures, it appends pointers (links) to each record. There can be as many pointers as desired. Hence any relation can be found and analyzed quickly by following the appropriate chain of pointers. Adding, modifying, and deleting records is a bit tedious for the programmer because of the need to put the links of the chain back together.

The positive points of this approach are the same as those for relational databases. The large number of pointers to and from records is a source of overhead and confusion, hence a drawback. Finally, the computing power required to process a request may be less than for relational databases, but the storage taken up by the database may be greater.

MANAGEMENT RESPONSIBILITY

As mentioned earlier, the manager cannot take the risk of leaving key database management system decisions to the computer technicians. The critical operational systems of the firm depend on the company database(s). For this reason, managers must understand some of the terms related to database systems, understand some of the data storage concepts, and be able to discuss the most common database approaches. All these factors have been covered in sufficient detail to allow the manager to participate intelligently in key decisions regarding database management systems. Where answers are of the form,

It depends on what you want to do with your database,

the important decision-making criteria have been provided.

One final note is required on management responsibility in the database context. The user needs a facility for asking the DBMS for information and reports. The facility must be understandable to the user, not couched in arcane computer gibberish. The productivity of the organization depends on this user interface. The success of the database system also rests on user acceptance of the interface. Management alone can influence the user interface to meet the user's needs.

SUMMARY

We have looked at the general idea of a database and its impact on the business environment. We have extended this view to take in the whole database management system. The computer provided a major step forward in database handling, with electronic database systems replacing previous nonelectronic ones. Although management always needed to be involved in defining the DBMS, with the advent of the electronic database, it has become imperative that management make the key DBMS decisions.

Finally, we reviewed some of the technical aspects of database systems:

- Data aggregates
- Storage structures
- Relational databases
- Hierarchical databases
- Network databases

The manager must have a working knowledge in these areas to participate competently in DBMS decision making.

PROBLEMS AND QUESTIONS

1. Work Case 4, Johnson Enterprises (B).
2. It is important to be clear on the key terms used in database systems:

   a. Distinguish between information and data.

   data_____

   _____

   information_____

   _____

   b. What three ideas make up the concept of a database?

   _____

   _____

   _____

3. What are the five components of a DBMS?

   _____

   _____

   _____

   _____

   _____

4. Column A lists the key components of an electronic database management system. Match the items in column A with the actions in column B.

A	B
_____ database administrator	1. controls physical access to database
_____ schema	2. provides computer expertise on databases
_____ data management programs	3. is responsible for database schema
_____ database programs	4. is a centrally controlled, integrated, collection of logically organized data
_____ programmer	5. describes logical relationships among records
_____ query programs	6. manipulates database from logical perspective
_____ database	7. allows managers to talk to database

5. What are six objectives of a DBMS?

_____

_____

_____

_____

_____

_____

6. Match the terms in column A with the definitions in column B.

A	B
_____ data element / field	1. collection of related records or blocks
_____ group	2. basic unit of meaningful characters
_____ record	3. collection of data elements
_____ block	4. multiple data elements that must appear together to be meaningful
_____ file	5. packaged multiple of records

7. Give examples of natural applications for these types of files:
   sequential_____
   direct access_____

8. Consider the following table:

NAME	AGE	SEX	SOC. SEC. #
Cindy	21	F	123456789
Margo	20	F	123472481
Jason	23	M	132400022
Frank	27	M	214712345

Put these records into a linked-list storage structure, ordered from youngest to oldest (ignore the fields defined by the dashed lines).

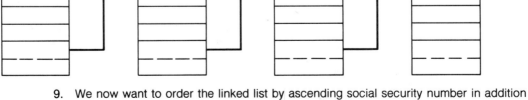

9. We now want to order the linked list by ascending social security number in addition to age. Use the linked list to produce a keyed list or indexed list. The social security number is the key or index. Use the fields defined by the dashed lines as the index field (problem 8).

10. What are the three best known approaches to defining a database?

_____

_____

_____

11. Compare the positive and negative aspects of the three approaches listed.

SELECTED REFERENCES

BOND, RUSS. "Clearing a path Through the Data Maze." *Data Management*, September 1981.

CARDENES, ALFONSO F. *Data Base Management Systems*. Boston: Allyn & Bacon, 1979.

DATE, C. J. *An Introduction to Database Systems*, 3rd ed. Reading, Mass: Addison-Wesley, 1981.

MARTIN, JAMES. *Principles of Data-Base Management*. Englewood Cliffs, N.J.: Prentice-Hall, 1976.

MOLINA, FRANCISCO WALTER. "A Practical Data Base Design Method." *Data Base*, Summer 1979.

ROSS, RONALD G. *Data Base Systems*. New York: AMACOM, 1978.

5

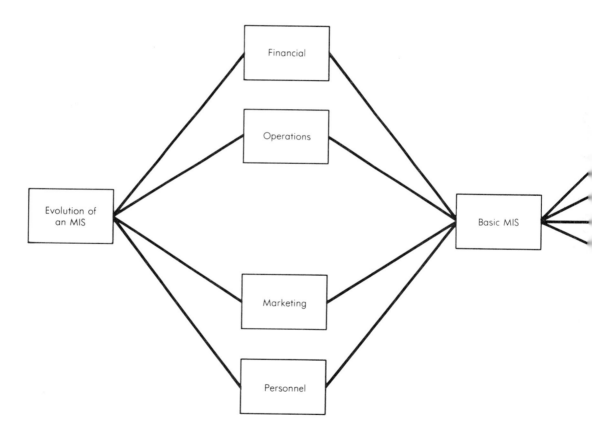

Information Systems for Decision Making

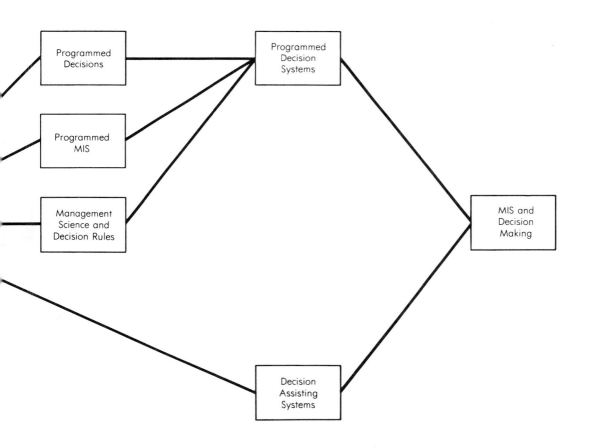

Although the great need for information systems should appear obvious to most managers, it is necessary to underscore their importance. Without information, a business simply cannot survive. Information flows are to the life and health of a business what the flow of blood is to the life and health of an individual. This applies to small organizations as well as to large ones. Indeed, superior information systems have enabled many small companies to more than offset the economies of scale enjoyed by their bigger competitors.

It has been said that the recipe for a good decision is "90 percent information and 10 percent inspiration." Information is the catalyst of management and the ingredient that coalesces the managerial functions of planning, operating, and controlling. Managers depend on one specific tool, *information*, and although they "get things done through people," their tool for achieving this is the spoken or written word or the language of numbers. As Norbert Wiener remarked, "any organism is held together by the possession of means for the acquisition, use, retention, and transmission of information."[1]

In Chapter 2 we examined the managerial processes of planning, organizing, and controlling and how these were facilitated by information. In this chapter we want to get more specific with regard to how particular information systems aid in the decision-making process. The task of this chapter is to integrate the topics of management, decision making, and computer-based MIS to set the stage for MIS planning and design considerations to follow. Hence, we must demonstrate the relationship between the computer and its use for decision-making applications. We will be concerned with (1) how the computer "makes" programmed decisions, provided that it is programmed with appropriate decision rules, and (2) how the computer can provide decision-assisting information for complex decisions that do not lend themselves to automation. These considerations are of primary importance for managers if they are to utilize the computer and management information systems in improving their decisions and their operations. We will also examine some typical computer-based information systems.

---

[1] Norbert Wiener, *Cybernetics* (New York: John Wiley, 1948), p. 187.

EVOLUTION OF AN INFORMATION SYSTEM

By examining the basic information needs of a company (large or small) and what constitutes a satisfactory management information system, we can gain a better understanding of how information needs become more complex as organization operations expand. We learn also how information systems may be improved through modification of a manual system or design of a computer-based system.

Figure 5-1 portrays a small company (Owner & Sons) not so many years ago. Mr. Owner is president, proprietor, chief executive, and chairman of the board. Mr. Owner, Jr., is vice president of sales, director of market research, controller, treasurer, and director of research and development. Their entire work force consists of two helpers.

Figure 5-1 also demonstrates Mr. Owner's complete information processing system. His transaction tickets are skewered on the spindle as the transactions occur. Historical information is contained in storage books on top of Mr. Owner's

FIGURE 5-1   Owner & Sons Information System

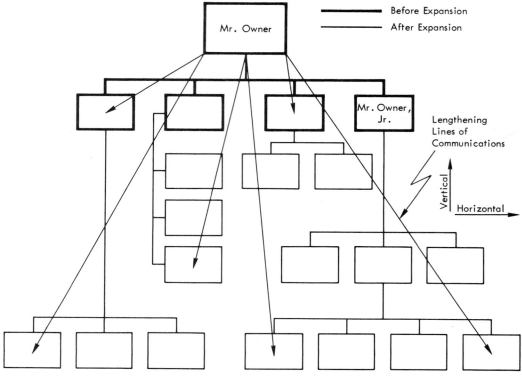

FIGURE 5-2 Complexities of Growth (Communication, Delegation, Information)

desk. With this system, upper management has on-line entry into the basic resource records of the company and immediate access to its entire data bank. Cash flow and balance information are within sight in the safe in the corner of the office. There is even an advanced system of exception reporting on the blackboard on the washroom door. What Mr. Owner has developed is a *real-time* information system—all information required to run the business is within reaching distance of the president and is available within seconds.[2]

Times change, however, and Mr. Owner's business has grown into the larger company depicted in Figure 5-2. The functions have remained basically the same, but the volume and complexity of information needs have increased enormously. As with all growing companies, new products are developed, sales volume grows, number of employees increases, factors outside the company become increasingly important, and generally the complexities of the operation expand more rapidly than company size.

[2]As opposed to batch processing, a real-time information system provides response to information inquiries in a time frame short enough to permit the user to shape an ongoing situation or make an immediate decision. The best known illustrations are telephone systems (communications), aerospace systems (command and control), and airline reservation systems (logistics).

This increase in company size results in an increase in information collecting, processing, and distribution. It now becomes necessary to handle many customer accounts and many production records with many more interrelationships. In addition to the increased records, information needs, and associated difficulties, there are now the problems connected with delegation of authority and responsibility. It is now necessary to assign people to supervise other people, and this development expands communication lines and compounds these problems.

As the need for information grows, additional people and equipment must be added to handle the information. Typewriters and calculators are purchased and additional clerks are hired. The next step is to procure tabulating and punched-card equipment. Finally, each generation of electronic computers is acquired as it becomes available to take advantage of the latest information processing technology.

Meanwhile, what has happened to management? As have the other basic functions of the company (production, sales, finance, etc.), management functions have not changed and will not. Management still plans, organizes, staffs, directs, and controls. However, the communication network for information has increased fantastically.[3] A succession of delegations of duties and authority has lengthened the lines of communications and has increased the complexity of the communication network of Mr. Owner's business a thousandfold. The functions of the company and of its management are essentially the same regardless of size, but the complexities associated with size have vastly increased the need for information in order to manage the organization.

Despite these complexities, the management of the now larger company would like to be able to operate in the same fashion and with the same information requirements that old Mr. Owner enjoyed. The objective of developing or improving a management information system can be explained largely in terms of the new Mr. Owner's problems: (1) to provide the type of information environment that will integrate the basic operating functions and (2) to provide management with access to information relative to complex activities in decentralized organizations. Both (1) and (2) need to be done with approximately the same ease that Mr. Owner enjoyed in his small operation with four persons and the information system contained in his rolltop desk.

Notice also that as the small company grows and becomes more complex, the basic functions and much of the basic information needs remain the same. This is portrayed in Figure 5-3. In other words, although complexity may be a geometric function of size, this is not necessarily true of the volume of data or the categories of information needs.

It is apparent that change will continue to take place in management and in the operation of organizations. To handle the changes properly, the manager of

---

[3]V. A. Graicunas, "Relationship in Organization," *Bulletin of the International Management Institute* (Geneva: International Labour Office, 1933), in L. Gulick and L. Urwick, eds., *Papers on the Science of Administration* (New York: Institute of Public Administration, 1937), pp. 181–187.

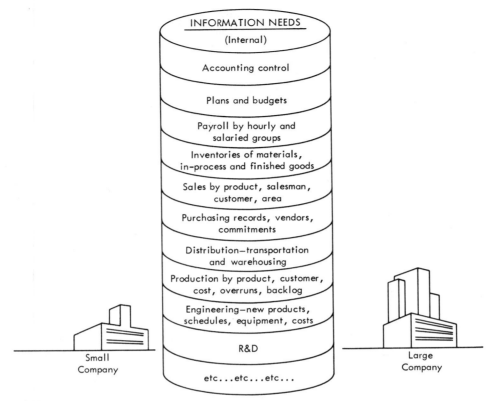

FIGURE 5-3 Internal Information Needs — Large or Small Company

the 1980s must learn what to do with information to deal with the resultant increased complexity. In other words, the manager must be prepared to take an active part in the design and installation of management information systems. This is worth repeating: *the manager must be prepared to take an active part in the design and installation of management information systems.*

BASIC INFORMATION SYSTEMS

Although many companies and organizations are making valiant efforts to extend computer applications from areas now considered proven and routine, nevertheless the bulk of information systems (manual or computer based) remain in the categories discussed in this chapter. The gathering and dissemination of information is usually the company's most difficult problem. Information is voluminous, scattered, and often difficult to obtain. If managers become embroiled in paperwork, they have no time for evaluation, planning, or decision making. Their workday is fraught with searches for information to handle the various crises that arise in addition to the normal work flow.

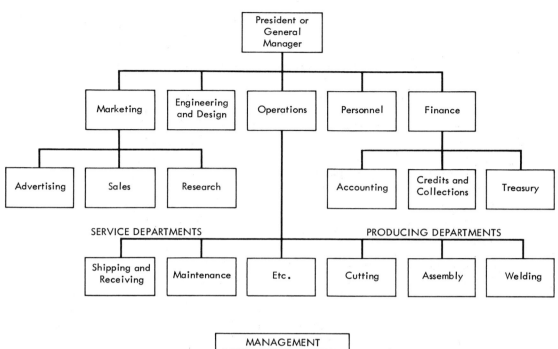

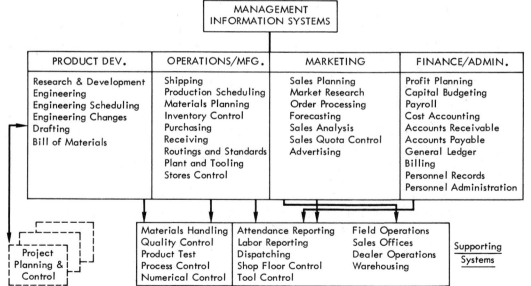

FIGURE 5-4 Basic Information Systems

Over time, the typical manufacturing company has developed the major information systems shown in Figure 5-4 to provide planning, operating, and control information to decision makers throughout the organization. These major systems are (1) engineering/design, (2) manufacturing/operations, (3) marketing, (4) finance/administration, (5) project planning/control, and (6) support systems. As we will show, these systems are not separate and distinct; they connect, interact, and otherwise tie the subsystems of the organization together through the medium of information. Note also in Figure 5-4 that although these major systems serve to integrate the basic functions of planning, operating, and controlling, most are designed and utilized primarily for one or two of these functions. Although virtually all planning information can be used for subsequent control, we are concerned here with major uses.

Financial Information Systems

All companies have some kind of financial information system; this category of information is the most common in use today. The basis of the system is the flow of dollars throughout the organization, and if they are designed correctly, the profitability and responsibility accounting systems follow the organization structure. These systems involve large amounts of data concerned primarily with historical and internal information, although in some areas of financial planning, the system provides the futuristic look associated with planning. Budgeting is wholly futuristic.

By and large, the conversion of a *manual* financial system to a *computer-based* system is subject to less improvement as a managerial device than are other types of information systems. From a data handling and cost point of view, financial systems are usually the first candidates for conversion, but there is less opportunity to improve the quality of the information system because of the nature of its operations, which are usually concerned primarily with budgetary control. Improvement is obtained in promptness and accuracy of reporting.

Periodically, management approves some type of financial plan (the master budget) that assigns responsibility for maintaining incomes, investments, and costs within standard limits. This plan then becomes the basis for periodic reports on performance against plan, and these reports become the device by which control is exercised. Major problems in such a system involve (1) determining equitable standards for control, (2) determining when action is required, and (3) obtaining rapid, up-to-date information on variances. It is unlikely that the automation of financial records will decrease the problems associated with the first two attributes. It will, however, materially assist in speeding up reporting.

The financial system is probably the most important single management information system in the company, and in most companies it is the oldest and best developed. The major concern associated with this system is the necessary design actions to make it a vital tool for operating and planning. Moreover, the

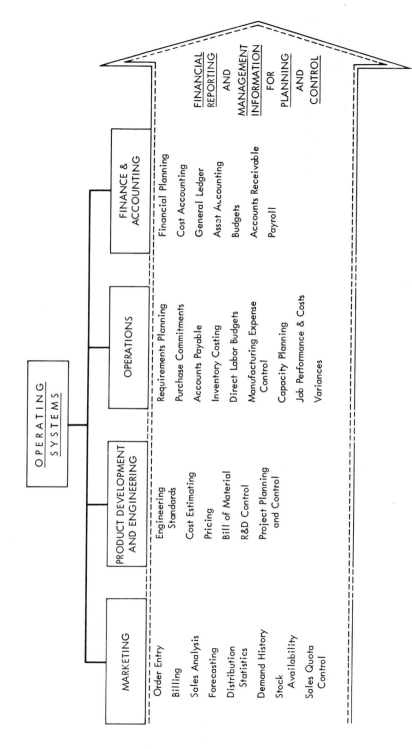

FIGURE 5-5 Integration of Operating Systems with Accounting and Financial Information Systems

173

financial system has a very significant impact on other information systems when one considers that the ultimate common denominator of many operating decisions is the dollar. The interface between these subsystems and the interdependence between them are highlighted in Figure 5-5.

Example—Billing

Billing is perhaps the most widely used data processing application. Despite the fact that the preparation of invoices is often viewed as a somewhat casual clerical function, the speed and accuracy of the operation can have a significant impact upon cash flow as well as customer goodwill. Additional advantages include clerical savings, more timely processing, the release of high-salaried employees for other functions, and the flexibility to absorb additional work load during times of increased growth.

A customer's invoice, the output of the typical billing system, is illustrated in Figure 5-6. Notice that in addition to the managerial objectives indicated, the customer's invoice also can provide the input for additional vital subsystems. Here we see an excellent example of how an otherwise routine clerical operation can be upgraded for managerial decision making.

BILLING

Objectives: Provide Input to Other Subsystems
Improve Cash Flow
Maintain Customer Good Will
Timely Invoice Processing
Keep Salesmen Informed

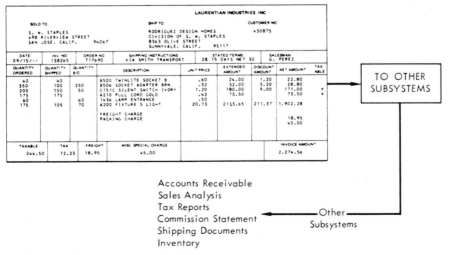

Accounts Receivable
Sales Analysis
Tax Reports
Commission Statement
Shipping Documents
Inventory

FIGURE 5-6 Customer's Invoice

Source: Courtesy of IBM Corporation.

Production / Operations Systems

The production/operations system is concerned with information about the physical flow of goods or the production of goods and services. It covers such activities as production planning and control, inventory control and management, purchasing, distribution, and transportation. (It is also worth noting that the principles involved in the traditional manufacturing production planning, scheduling, and control system are frequently transferable to many service, white-collar, or "paperwork" applications. After all, these applications are involved with the production of "paperwork.")

Because the quantities of data are so large and the timing of information so essential, the production/operations system is the most adaptable to automation and yields the largest benefits in terms of immediate solution of critical and costly problems. Although other applications (e.g., decision making, total system stimulation) may offer greater potential, this functional area usually offers immediate payoffs.

There are six characteristics of the type of information that lends itself best to computer use:

1. *Speed.* Computers are extremely valuable if speed is required in processing data.
2. *Quantity.* Large amounts of data can be processed very quickly.
3. *Repetitiveness.* The more repetitive the task, the more profitable it is to automate this task.
4. *Complexity.* Problems with several interacting variables can be solved quickly and accurately.
5. *Exact input.* Computers require inputs that are exact. Intuition and judgment are not attributes of machines.
6. *Accurate output.* Great accuracy can be obtained as needed; also, accuracy is not affected by boredom and fatigue.

These six characteristics are clearly present in production-related information.

Because the information needed for effective management of production/operations has all these characteristics, these systems are probably the most adaptable to automation of any in the company. Moreover, because of the requirement for timeliness in handling large quantities of data, the greatest advances in improvements and economy are likely to be made in the production/operations area.

The production/operations system, particularly in a manufacturing company, is unquestionably the most important from an operating standpoint. It crosses all subsystem boundaries and has an effect throughout the company. Yet despite this importance, the production/operations system has had less management involvement and consequently less development than the financial system. This is unfortunate, because in most companies this area offers more opportunity for development, cost saving, and management improvement than any other. Indeed, much of the "total systems" activity in recent years has begun because of

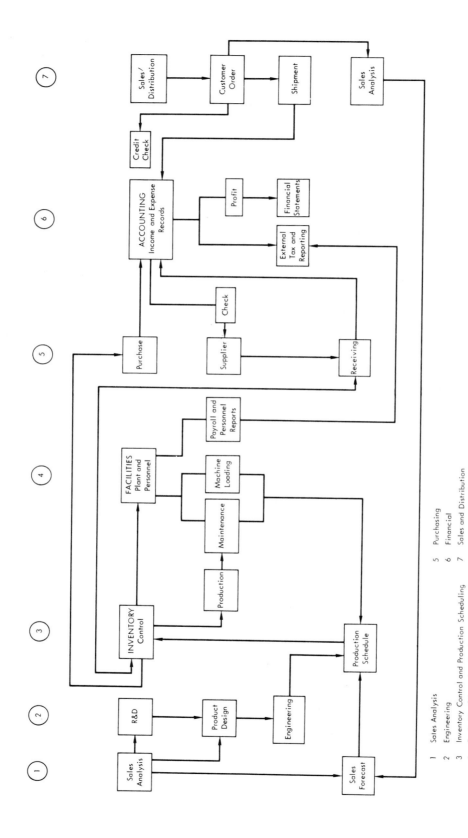

FIGURE 5-7 Integration of Subsystems Through the Information Flow in the Production / Operations System

1 Sales Analysis
2 Engineering
3 Inventory Control and Production Scheduling
4 Production/Operations Facilities
5 Purchasing
6 Financial
7 Sales and Distribution

problems in the production/operations area and because once begun, an examination of this area leads to the design of related and integrated subsystems throughout the company. This attribute and the importance of the production/operations system and its impact on systems elsewhere in the organization can be seen in Figure 5-7, which demonstrates how the production subsystem interacts with all major functions of a manufacturing company. Note that the critical input to this system is the customer order.

Examples—Purchasing, Materials Planning, Operations Scheduling

Some of the operations involved in this major system can be understood by examining three of the most widespread information subsystems. Critical objectives and information needs are

Purchasing Objectives

Determine economic order quantity to buy.
Reduce clerical costs.
Monitor buyer performance.
Identify high-volume vendors to negotiate higher discounts.
Determine supplier performance by identifying late deliveries and poor quality.
(See Figure 5-8.)

Materials Planning Objectives

Plan and control parts from a predetermined production schedule.
Reduce the time and costs of determining and ordering material requirements.
Allow nondisruptive changes to production schedule.
Forecast future needs for ordering material.
Forecast changes in material requirements resulting from production schedule change.
(See Figure 5-9.)

Capacity Planning and Operation Scheduling Objectives

Identify work center loads for future time periods and those that are over- or underloaded.
Evaluate alternatives of subcontracting or overtime to meet delivery dates.
Identify orders to be rescheduled to level the load.
Forecast time and location of equipment and tooling needs.
Compute start dates for shop orders to meet delivery dates.
Forecast skills and trades required.
Forecast order release dates.
(See Figure 5-10.)

Buyer Price Analysis Report									Date of report OCT 5 Buyer's name D Chambers For qtr. ending 9/30
Material code	Product code	Part no.	Supplier name	Unit cost base period	Unit cost current period	Total costs base period	Total costs current period	Variance	
877	36	2919067	MACILVAINE BROS.	1.27	1.27	4,216	4,216		
877	40	4319108	DUNSMUIRE	8.10	7.60	13,110	12,660	450	
877	45	1437001	CARLSON	4.23	4.47	460	378	82-	

Determine buyer performance by comparing actual purchase amounts with amount figured at base or standard prices.

Vendor Delivery Performance Report							10/06		
Buyer	Vendor name	Vendor no.	Total value open orders	Open orders	Orders behind	Percent behind	YTD purchase percent behind	YTD orders behind	
CA	GENERAL MFG. CO.	19080	792.00	16	4	25	15	27	
CA	POWER DESIGN CO.	40001	2,103.75	2	1	50	25	8	
CA	CENTRAL TOOL CO.	56012	301.20	10	1	10	2	50	
	BUYER TOTAL		3,196.95	28	6	21	7	85	
TK	ORIN FORGE CO.	49045	3,115.00	30	6	20	20	50	
TK	LAKE MILLING	73111	603.00	23	0	0	4	30	
	BUYER TOTAL		3,718.00	53	6	11	12	80	
	DEPT. TOTAL		6,914.95	81	12	15	9	165	

Highlights trend of vendor delivery performance by comparison of current and year-to-date (YTD) figures.

Open Purchase Order Status					Date 02/03		By P/O ☐ By Supplier ☒ By Part ☐			
Purchase order no.	Part no.	Mat. code	Supplier no.	Supplier name	Qty. on order	Qty. rec'd	Balance date	Delivery date	Value outstanding $	Action
140562	201610	924	0021	BAILY & CO.	220	110	110	03/06	200	
144250	222521	924	0021	BAILY & CO.	25		25	04/05	47	
146402	368065	924	0021	BAILY & CO.	200		200	04/03	634	
									881	
136781	179923	801	0027	ACTION INC.	4,000	3,500	500	01/03	774	EXP.
144548	474149	801	0027	ACTION INC.	800		800	03/06	175	

All orders placed with suppliers can be listed in a variety of categories (e.g., supplier, part number, order number).

FIGURE 5-8 Output Reports from Purchasing Subsystem

Source: Courtesy of IBM Corporation.

End product requirements

Stock no.	Description	Six month projection					
		1	2	3	4	5	6
1016H	ENGINE	100	0	100	50	100	100
6094HD	ENGINE	50	0	50	50	0	75
4377L	POWER UNIT	60	60	0	120	60	0
3355LD	ENGINE	0	50	0	25	0	25
3355B	ENGINE	0	25	25	25	25	25
9774AB	POWER UNIT	125	75	125	0	50	100

Summary of demand for end items and/or service assemblies that can be exploded to determine parts requirements.

Requirements planning report

Item no.	Description	Stock	10/08	10/22	11/05	11/19	12/03	12/17
A300-9965	FILTER	50						
	GROSS REQ.		337	196	231	175	372	563
	NET REQ.		287	196	231	175	372	563
	PLANNED ORDERS				700			700
	LEADTIME OFFSET			700			700	
A403-4773	GAUGE	150						
	GROSS REQ.			600		300	265	
	NET REQ.			450		300	265	
	PLANNED ORDERS			500		250	250	
	LEADTIME OFFSET		500		250	250		500

Consolidated gross requirements by time period, and orders necessary to meet requirements.

Requirements planning exception report

Item no.	Item description	Exception code	Req. date	Req. qty.	Comments
A320-4447	FILTER	01	10/08	254	ORDER SIZE EXCEEDS MAX. ALLOWABLE
A340-6674	BRACE UNIT	05	9/08	20	OPEN ORDER DOES NOT COVER REQ.
A449-3754	REGULATOR	10	12/08	187	NOT PROCESSED-OUTSIDE OF HORIZON
C203-8883	CONNECTOR	01	10/08	144	ORDER SIZE EXCEEDS MAX. ALLOWABLE
C493-7655	ASSEMBLY UNIT	05	9/08	20	OPEN ORDER DOES NOT COVER REQ.
E212-3993	VALVE SWITCH	10	12/08	163	NOT PROCESSED-OUTSIDE OF HORIZON
E222-7063	PUMP METER B	18	10/08	15	OPEN ORDER DUE-NO REQ.

Exception report that highlights areas that require special handling.

FIGURE 5-9 Materials Planning Reports

Source: Courtesy of IBM Corporation.

Dept. no.	GRP no.	Description	No. of mach.	Wk.	Capacity	Load	Available capacity	Overload
1	01	BENCH MILLS	5	1	136.0	130.0	6.0	
				2	170.0	150.0	20.0	
				3	170.0	165.5	4.5	
				4	170.0	179.0		9.0
				5	170.0	162.3	7.7	
				6	170.0	185.1		15.1

Work center load summary — 07/15 — Machine shop A

Summary of labor operations required for shop orders by time period and machine group.

Mach./GRP	Hrs./day	Scheduled Day	Scheduled Hr.	Part no.	Job	Oper.	Priority code	Order qty.	Claimed qty.
1609-01	7.50	622	.0	461235	3422	020	1	2,100	210
		622	4.50	461747	6343	035	5	1,988	
		623	5.50	461396	4211	020	5	113	
1207-01	15.00	622	.0	537141	3762	055	2	2,759	500
		622	6.25	537593	4727	030	3	457	
		623	13.40	537547	3249	040	5	637	

Shop load schedule — 07/15

Utilized for scheduling jobs and improving use of men and machines.

Part no.	Job	Oper.	Dept.	Mach./GRP	Scheduled Day	Scheduled Hr.	Tool no.	Tool code	Description
131634	1700	0040	018	1610-01	624	11.1	31665	B	FIXTURE
							1021545	B	CUTTER
133195	1800	0045	005	1609-02	622	.0	1000555	B	VISE JAWS
133694	6601	0090	011	1400-01	622	8.7	153310	D	INDEX GAUGE
							151347	D	COMP. CHART
							95601	B	COMP. FIXT.

Tooling list — Date 07/15

Allows prepacking of tools by listing those required by each operation.

FIGURE 5-10 Operations Scheduling Reports

Source: Courtesy of IBM Corporation.

Marketing Information Systems

The basic areas of the marketing function that lend themselves to improvement through information systems include (1) forecasting/sales planning, (2) market research, (3) advertising, and (4) operating and control information required to manage the marketing function. Examples of the last include such information as sales reports and distribution cost reports.

Marketing information is one of the most important information systems to most businesses, yet it is most often the one overlooked. Few marketing executives use information effectively on their jobs; many of them rely on intuition as a basis for decisions. The vast majority of firms tend to maintain information only about sales records or orders and shipments. What is needed is a system that will give marketing managers information to help them make better decisions about pricing, advertising, product promotion policy, sales force effort, and other vital marketing matters. Such a system should also take account of the necessity elsewhere in the organization for information concerning marketing sales, and other internal information that affects decisions in other subsystems of the company.

The effectiveness of marketing information systems depends to a large extent on feedback from the marketplace to the firm, so that the firm can judge the adequacy of its past performance as well as appraise the opportunities for new activity. Despite this feedback need, many firms consider their marketing information system to be some type of "sales analysis" activity that has been superimposed onto an accounting system. Yet there is no reason why this vital area of management activity should not take an approach similar to that of other areas of the firm whose information needs are designed around the managerial functions of planning, operating, and controlling.

Table 5-1 summarizes some of the more important types of information systems applications in the marketing area and indicates selected outputs that are useful for market planning, market research, and marketing control. These

TABLE 5-1 Selected Applications and Outputs of a Marketing Information System

Application	Output
Marketing planning	
Forecasting	Parts requirements and production schedule based on demand for industrial goods
Purchasing	Automatic optimization of purchasing function and inventory control based on decision rules
Credit management	Automatic computer processing of credit decisions
Market research	
Pricing policy	Policy based on historical analysis of past
Advertising strategy	Strategy based on sales analysis of a variety of market segment breakdowns
Advertising expenditure	Correlation by numerous market segments of sales and advertising expenditures
Marketing control	
Marketing costs	Current reports of deviation from standard and undesirable trends
Sales performance	A variety of data to help discover reasons for sales performance and correct deviations
Territorial control of sales, distribution, costs, etc.	Timely reports of performance on territorial basis to permit reallocation of resources to substandard areas

three types of marketing systems are summarized:

1. *Control systems*. Provide monitoring and review of performance against plan. Also provide information concerning trends, problems, and possible marketing opportunities.
2. *Planning systems*. Provide information needed for planning the marketing and sales program. A good system furnishes information to permit the marketing manager to weigh the effects of alternate plans in trade promotion, pricing, and other variables in the forecasting equation.
3. *Market research systems*. Used to develop, test, and predict the effects of actions taken or planned in the basic subsystems of marketing (pricing, advertising, design, etc.).

The sales/marketing function has historically been serviced with information contained in month-end sales reports. Generally, these reports have suffered from two shortcomings; they were clerical in nature and therefore did not contain decision-making information, and they arrived too late for remedial action.

These shortcomings can be overcome with a general marketing system somewhat along the lines depicted in Figure 5-11. Characteristic of this type of system is an inquiry capability located in field, branch, district, and headquarters offices. These terminals are connected via teleprocessing facilities to a computer, and the system can provide a broad inquiry coverage relating to sales activity updated on a daily basis.

The systems designer and marketing manager who uses the system can design inquiry formats to fit his or her particular needs. The four formats depicted in Figure 5-11 can be described as follows:

1. *Sales Recap*. An overall performance summary to date, compared with previous periods, budgets, or other standards. This recap can be programmed to trigger successive levels of detailed reports when the analysis indicates substandard performance. Major areas of performance analysis might include total sales by product, sales expense, new accounts, replacement sales, cancellation rates, and a variety of profitability analyses.
2. *Record Summaries*. Optional levels of detail that permit in-depth analysis of deviations spotted by the sales recap. Ideally, this format should be programmed so that the user can structure his or her own reporting needs. These might include such items as sales by model, by sales plan, by industry, by customer type, and sales to major and national accounts. Additionally, a variety of ratios, such as sales units to travel expenses, should be available if desired.
3. *Transaction Analysis*. This format might be called the *significant* transaction analysis because its purpose is to provide a "management by exception" approach to transactions that are so out of the ordinary that they require special treatment. Such transactions might be defined in terms of dollar volume, number of sales, or other significant measures that exceed control limits.
4. *Exception Inquiries*. This is the highest level of systems sophistication in that it gives a true inquiry capability to the user. This can be understood by such questions as, "Which sales offices have achieved a level of 50 percent of their sales in the manufacturing industry but are less than 80 percent sales quota in the retail industry?" It is easy to see how this inquiry capability is a vital tool to any marketing/sales manager.

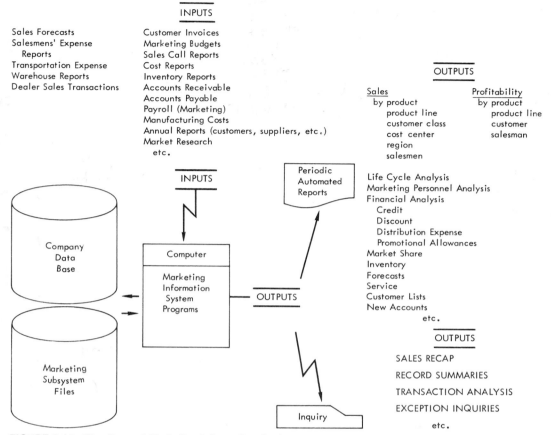

FIGURE 5-11 The General Marketing Information System

Example—Inventory Management

A marketing-related system of immense importance is inventory management, a process of vital importance to profitability. Too little inventory means lost sales and costly rush orders. Too much inventory means carrying costs, interest costs, warehousing costs, and the chance of obsolescence. Two typical inventory management reports are shown in Figure 5-12. They are

1. *Distribution-by-Value Report.* Items are shown in sequence by sales dollars, so that the item with the largest annual sales comes first and the item with the smallest annual sales comes last. Percentages are also shown. From Figure 5-12 it can be seen that the top 1 percent of items accounts for almost 18 percent of sales—six items accounting for nearly one-fifth of sales. The top 20 percent of items accounts for 70 percent of sales.

Distribution-by-Value Report

Item No	Cumulative Count		Annual Units	Unit Cost	Annual $ Sales	Cumulative Sales	
	Rank by $ Sales	%				$	%
411045	1	.2	104,578	.966	101,023	101,023	3.8
411118	2	.4	375,959	.246	92,486	193,509	7.3
411063	3	.5	40,602	2.012	81,693	275,202	10.4
411075	4	.7	69,570	1.123	78,128	353,330	13.3
411176	5	.9	133,534	.490	65,432	418,762	15.8
411381	6	1.1	106,651	.510	54,392	473,154	17.8
411368	110	20.0	90,191	.073	6,584	1,886,385	71.0
411425	111	20.2	7,513	.800	6,011	1,892,396	71.2
411263	112	20.4	1,820	3.286	5,983	1,898,379	71.4
411503	113	20.5	10,611	.553	5,868	1,904,247	71.6
411444	545	99.2	813	.145	118	2,657,997	100.0
411465	546	99.4	4,227	.022	93	2,658,090	100.0
411243	547	99.6	90	.715	65	2,658,155	100.0
411516	548	99.8	4	2.916	12	2,659,167	100.0
411541	549	100.0	0	0	0	2,658,167	100.0

Distribution-by-Value with Item Movement Activity

LAURENTIAN INDUSTRIES, INC.
ANALYSIS OF INVENTORY ACTIVITY

12 MONTH PERIOD ENDING 7/1/--

STOCK LOCATION	STOCK NUMBER	DESCRIPTION	UNIT	DATE OF LAST ACTIVITY	NET ISSUES FOR PERIOD			BALANCE ON HAND		
					NUMBER OF TRANS	QUANTITY	AVERAGE PER MONTH	QUANTITY	MONTHS SUPPLY	VALUE
2715-237	127205	LIGHT RECEPTACLE	EA	7/--	2	4	.3	16	53.3	$ 4.32
2715-420	247389	SOLENOID. HEATER	EA	7/--	1	1	.1	7	70.0	4.48
2715-267	111462	SWITCH, STARTER	EA	8/--	1	4	.3	4	13.3	8.64
2715-601	896124	PINION STUD	EA	9/--	4	16	1.3	84	64.6	9.24
2716-234	59827	GASKET. MANIFOLD	EA	11/--	2	12	1.0	16	16.0	7.52
2716-320	614	WASHER, RUBBER	DZ	12/--	1	3	.2	14	70.0	2.52
2717-086	6213	BOLT, CARRIAGE	DZ	12/--	1	2	.2	27	135.0	32.40
2717-742	1032	BEARING, CLUTCH	EA	1/--	1	1	.1	9	90.0	34.83
2717-748	148722	AXLE	EA	3/--	1	1	.1	3	30.0	24.60
2719-147	2642	BRUSH, GENERATOR	EA	3/--	3	9	.7	42	60.0	7.14
2719-382	222649	REGULATOR	EA	3/--	4	4	.3	3	10.0	3.78

FIGURE 5-12 Inventory Management Reports

Source: Courtesy of IBM Corporation.

2. *Distribution-by-Value with Item Movement.* This report permits (a) life-cycle analysis, (b) segmentation of inventory to allow concentration on high investment items, (c) establishment of order quantities and order points, and (d) cycle review of vendor lines.

Personnel Information Systems

The personnel information system deals with the flow of information about people working in the organization as well as future personnel needs. In most organizations, the system is concerned primarily with the five basic subsystems of the personnel function: recruiting, placement, training, compensation, and maintenance.

It is probably not unfair to say that many personnel managers are proving to be myopic in their conventional specialization and concern with personnel records for their own sake. Human resource management, as opposed to the traditional view of the personnel function, should be considered a total system that interacts with the other major systems of the organization—marketing, production, finance, and the external environment. Indeed, the primary purpose of the human resource management program is to service these major systems. Forecasting and planning the personnel needs of the organization, maintaining an adequate and satisfactory work force, and controlling the personnel policies and programs of the company are the major responsibilities of human resource management.

To achieve the foregoing, a *human resource management system* is necessary. Like any system, it consists of a number of inputs and outputs and a number of related subsystems, processes, and activities, all operating through the medium of information. Such a system is shown in Figure 5-13. Note that the output from the subsystems goes to personnel staff specialists as well as to line operating managers. Many personnel managers mistakenly conceive of their information systems as a tool of the personnel function alone rather than as the real reason for a human resource management system—organizational effectiveness. A systems-oriented approach to human resource management interrelates and integrates the functions of the personnel manager with the duties of the operating personnel, who benefit most from an information system.

Briefly, the five classical subsystems of the personnel information system, designed to accomplish these objectives, are

1. *Recruitment.* Properly managed, the recruitment system forecasts personnel needs and skills and recruits the personnel at the proper time to meet organizational needs. A properly designed information system will furnish information concerning (a) skills required for company programs and processes and (b) inventory of skills available in the organization. Work force tables, job specifications, and other personnel data are also useful in this subsystem.

2. *Placement.* This system is perhaps the most vital of all personnel functions because it matches available personnel with requirements, and hence the effective use of labor as a resource takes place within this system. A properly designed placement information system takes account of the latest behavioral tools and techniques to ensure that the capabilities of people are identified and placed with properly organized work requirements.

3. *Training and development.* As technological changes and demands for new skills accelerate, many companies find that they must necessarily develop much of their talent requirements from internal sources. In addition, a large part of the work force must constantly be updated in new techniques and developments. This task is the function of the training and development system. Basic information requirements include a continuing skills inventory of company personnel matched against a forecast of current and estimated needs for improved skills.

4. *Compensation.* The pay and other values (fringe benefits, for example) for the satisfaction of individual wants and needs and for compliance with government,

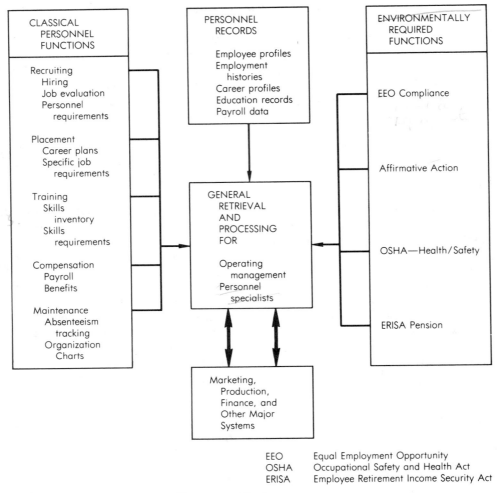

| CLASSICAL PERSONNEL FUNCTIONS | PERSONNEL RECORDS | ENVIRONMENTALLY REQUIRED FUNCTIONS |

Recruiting
  Hiring
  Job evaluation
  Personnel
    requirements

Placement
  Career plans
  Specific job
    requirements

Training
  Skills
    inventory
  Skills
    requirements

Compensation
  Payroll
  Benefits

Maintenance
  Absenteeism
    tracking
  Organization
  Charts

PERSONNEL RECORDS

Employee profiles
Employment
  histories
Career profiles
Education records
Payroll data

GENERAL
RETRIEVAL
AND
PROCESSING
FOR

Operating
  management
Personnel
  specialists

ENVIRONMENTALLY REQUIRED FUNCTIONS

EEO Compliance

Affirmative Action

OSHA—Health/Safety

ERISA Pension

Marketing,
Production,
Finance, and
Other Major
Systems

EEO   Equal Employment Opportunity
OSHA   Occupational Safety and Health Act
ERISA   Employee Retirement Income Security Act

FIGURE 5-13 Human Resource Management System

union, and other requirements is the basic function of the compensation system. Information included in or required by this system is largely that associated with the traditional payroll and other financial records.

5. *Maintenance.* This system, largely for the benefit of operating managers, should be designed to ensure that personnel policies and procedures are achieved. It may extend to the operation of systems to control work standards, those required to measure performance against financial plans or other programs, and the many subsidiary records normally associated with the collection, maintenance, and dissemination of personnel data.

In recent years, government and other influences from the company's external environment have placed requirements on the human resource management system. Four of these requirements are discussed next:

1. *Equal employment opportunity.* The law requires equal employment opportunity for all applicants regardless of race, sex, and so on. Companies must keep statistical information of various types to show compliance with these laws.
2. *Affirmative action.* Once employed, the law requires fair treatment of minorities and women in placement, compensation, promotion, and so on. Again, statistics must be kept available to show compliance with the law.
3. *Occupational Safety and Health Act.* Employers are required to provide a (provably) safe and healthy work environment. Records must be maintained of all injuries and illnesses.
4. *Employee Retirement Income Security Act.* Firms are required to show that pension plans and other benefit plans are being properly administered.

Recently, a good deal of attention has been focused on the design and utilization of skills inventory programs. These are sometimes called "skills banks" or "manpower assessment programs." The objective of such programs is to identify and locate the talent resources of the organization to maximize their use. It is easy to see how such an objective could be essential in the engineering, research, or other firms where talent is the most costly and valuable resource.

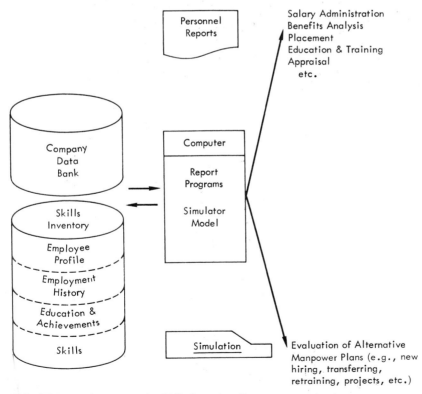

FIGURE 5-14   Operation of a Skills Inventory Program

Figure 5-14 depicts the conceptual operation of a skills inventory program. Notice that in addition to the regular reports generated by the program, it may also include a computer simulation model. We can call this the "personnel simulator" or the "work force simulator" or another appropriate title. It is a valuable tool for gaining information about different manpower approaches under varying conditions.

Other Information Systems

In addition to the major systems described, many organizations have a variety of less important information requirements for which the design of an information system is desirable. Some are manual, some computer based, and some may be combinations of manual and computer. Among the most common are

1. *Purchasing.* In this rapidly growing area of application, some purchasing uses are automatic preparation of quote requests, updating order records, handling routine follow-ups, processing requisitions, and checking history files as a means of vendor selection. More advanced applications include order writing, vendor rating, computation of economic order quantity, and preparation of accounts payable checks.

2. *PERT.* Program evaluation and review technique, PERT, has become a widely used information device for controlling the time, cost, and work in a project or program. Modifications of the basic technique include PERT/TIME, PERT/COST, PERT/CPM (critical path method) and PERT/LOB (line of balance).

3. *Research and development.* This is a vital area for industrial companies but of less importance for financial and service organizations. This information system may include some method for exchanging information on the results of research findings, or in a more sophisticated system, provision can be made for the examination, storage, and retrieval of research information.

4. *Simulation.* Although, strictly speaking, simulation is not an information system, it may be classified as such because it is computer based and it depends upon access to the company's data bank. It is a method for simulating decisions and hence is a vital tool of planning.

5. *Strategic planning.* This system deals with projections of the future and for the most part uses information developed for other purposes. It is one of the few information systems that utilizes the entire range of information developed in the company, both external and internal.

DECISION MAKING AND MIS

Despite the fact that decision making can be treated as a central aspect of managing, the literature and teaching surrounding decision making have generally focused on the *moment* of decision rather than on the whole lengthy, complex process of defining and exploring the many alternatives in a decision that precedes the final act of deciding. For the systems analyst and for the manager who participates in or utilizes the management information system to assist in the decision-making *process*, the steps in problem solving and systems design are extremely important. Peter Drucker's comment that "over the next 20 years the emphasis in management will be on the understanding of decision making" reflects a growing need to formalize the process as a fundamental and necessary part of management and of information systems design. And because information is the essential ingredient of management and decision making, the aspect of the organization described by the information flow process is a growing concern. The ultimate purpose of the MIS is to make decisions at all levels of operations based upon the information flow. If decisions cannot be automated through MIS design, the objective becomes one of providing information to improve the decision-making ability of the manager.

Programmed and Nonprogrammed Decisions

It is very important to distinguish between two types of decisions representing the extremities of the range of decisions: *programmed* and *nonprogrammed decisions*. These labels are derived from the jargon of the computer field, where a program is defined as a plan for the automatic solution of a problem. Programs are simply a string of instructions to accomplish an assignment. Because few problems lend themselves totally to automatic solutions, we have few totally programmed decisions. We do have many cases of problem solving that combine varying mixtures of programmed and nonprogrammed problem solving. The concept of programmed decisions is important because *the ultimate* (and unachievable) *goal of information systems is to provide purely programmed decisions*. Because this is not possible, we seek to provide the optimum type of information to the human decision maker, who then makes nonprogrammable decisions.

Decisions lend themselves to programming techniques if they are repetitive and routine and if a procedure can be worked out for handling them so that each is neither an ad hoc decision nor one to be treated as a new situation each time it arises. Numerous examples of programmed decisions are available in almost any organization, the most familiar being the computation of pay in accordance with a union agreement, contract, company policy, or regulation. Hence the *program* or *decision rule* is contained in the agreement, contract, policy, or regulation. Other examples are pricing orders, credit checks, payment of accounts receivable, and the dozens of decisions made daily in accordance with company policy (decision rule).

Decisions are nonprogrammed to the extent that they are unstructured, new, of high consequence, elusive, or complex, or involve major commitments. Advertising budgets, new product decisions, acquisition and merger considerations, board member selection, and similar problems illustrate the nonprogrammed type of decision that cannot be automated.

Can we not say that the hypothetically ideal situation in an organization would be to have all decisions programmed? Without a decision rule to cover a

TYPE OF DECISION	METHODS OF DECISION MAKING	
	OLD	NEW
PROGRAMMED Repetitive and Routine	Habit Standard Operating Procedure Organization Structure Policy etc...	Management Information Systems (Includes Management Science Techniques and the Computer)
NONPROGRAMMED One-shot, Ill-structured	Judgment, Intuition, Insight Experience Training and Learning	Systematic Approach to Problem Solving & Decision Making (See Case 3)

FIGURE 5-15   Methods of Decision Making

situation, the manager must fall back upon the general problem-solving methodology, which depends so much on human judgment. The cost of solving the organization's problems in this manner is usually high, and solutions may sometimes be unsatisfactory. One of the goals then of MIS design is to devise decision rules for the problems that lend themselves to solution by decision rule and the programmed approach.

The major reason for distinguishing between these two types of decisions is to arrive at some classification of decision-making methods in order to improve decision making. This is done in Figure 5-15, which classifies two types of decisions, programmed and nonprogrammed, and two general approaches, old and new, to the techniques involved.

Making Nonprogrammed Decisions

It is apparent that we do not have a complete theory of decision making. Equally clear is the lack of understanding among practicing executives and academicians on just how decisions are made in organizations. When asked to explain the decision-making process in business organizations, we usually say that executives exercise "judgment" and that this judgment is largely a function of experience, intuition, and insight.

Managers seem to make better decisions when exposed to training in an orderly thinking process. For example, military officers attend war colleges to learn the military problem-solving and planning steps: (1) determination of the mission, (2) description of the situation and courses of action, (3) analysis of opposing courses of action, (4) comparison of own courses of action, and (5) the decision. The Harvard Graduate School of Business exposes the would-be executive to hundreds of case situations, presumably with the expectation that by solving many problems, the student will become proficient at the process. Over the years, the manager has been urged to learn, practice, and acquire the habit of making decisions based on the problem-solving process: (1) define the problem, (2) identify the alternatives, and (3) choose the best alternative. This process, defined by Dewey decades ago, is largely intact today and is still good advice for solving the unstructured, nonprogrammed problem.

There is some evidence that problem solving can be learned. At least we recognize and reward those who have had some success at it. Selection processes for managerial advancement are largely devoted to identifying past success at decision making and attempting to predict future success. We also tacitly admit that experience improves problem solving by our practice of exposing managers to increasingly varied and difficult decision-making situations as they advance in a career.

Despite the abundance of research and literature on the topic, we still do not have an exact science of nonprogrammed decision making. In Case 3, we review a systematic approach to both problem solving and decision making. For purposes of MIS design, we want to program more of our decisions through the use of management science techniques. A brief discussion of these is contained in the paragraphs that follow, and an in-depth analysis appears in Chapter 12.

Making Programmed Decisions

By far the greatest number of business decisions are repetitive and routine. One survey found that about 90 percent of management decisions are routine ones. If this is true, then there is an overriding need to automate or *program* these decisions so that the executive can get on about his or her true task, the design and plans for improved organizations and operations. If the manager's job is primarily that of decision making, he or she should get away from short-term tactics and routine, place these types of decisions in the programmed category, and have them made by one or more techniques of programmed decisions. To draw an analogy, there is no reason why we should not standardize information for mass production of programmed decisions in much the same way we standardize materials for production of products.

Some of the traditional ways of making programmed decisions are shown in Figure 5-15. The most general and most pervasive is by force of habit. We go to the office, make decisions regarding the disposition of the inbasket correspondence, and take dozens of actions daily that are "programmed" through force of habit. These habits and skills are valuable to the organization; one of the major costs in personnel turnover is involved in having new people acquire the habits of the organization and the job.

Following habit, the most prevalent technique for programming decisions is with the company procedure—written, oral, or understood. Standard operating procedures provide a means for indoctrinating and training new personnel and for guiding experienced personnel in the performance of specific tasks. The procedure has the additional advantage of forcing a certain amount of detailed planning, because it cannot be adequately designed, reviewed, or implemented without careful thought. In a strict sense, policy cannot be classified as a programming technique; by definition it provides only a general guide to action. However, the decision-making process in the organization is vastly improved by the establishment and communication of clearly understood policies.

MIS AS A TECHNIQUE FOR MAKING PROGRAMMED DECISIONS

Future prospects for programming the decisions of the organization through the proper design of an MIS are enormous. If we include the *computer* and *management science* as integral parts or tools of computer-based information systems, the prospects for a revolution in programmed decision making are very real. Just as the manufacturing process is becoming more and more automated, so is the automation of programmed decisions increasing to support this production and other information needs throughout the organization.

How will this revolution come about? What is there about management information systems that will program so many of our routine decisions? The answer lies in three basic considerations surrounding the design of an MIS:

1. The problem to be solved, the decision process to be programmed, or the process for which information is desired. The essential element in programming a decision is the *decision rule* (e.g., reorder if inventory declines below x level).
2. Management science. We define this broadly to include operations research, associated mathematical tools, and the scientific approach to problem solving. Management science, thus defined, gives us the methods and techniques to design the *decision rules.*
3. The computer. This is a powerful device for processing information and "making" programmed decisions in accordance with predetermined decision rules.

The Decision Rule and the Computer

The programmed information system is theoretically the ultimate in design and application because discretion is removed from the human decision maker and turned over to the information decision system. In the "never-never land" of total systems, the complete automation of decisions will have been accomplished and the organization will remain in dynamic equilibrium by means of self-correction obtained by cybernetic feedback.[4]

[4] In cybernetic terms we might call the organization "a homeostatic machine for regulating itself through feedback." Despite the fact that thousands of examples of this kind of control exist for mechanical systems (machines), economic systems (Keynesian theory), biological systems (human brain), and so on, it is difficult to think of the company or the organization in these terms; yet the fundamental design idea is the same.

Figure 5-16 illustrates schematically the notion of programmed information systems. The objective is to design the information production process in such a way that the computer automatically "makes" the decisions. This is accomplished in three steps:

1. Analyze the problem by means of the *management science* approach and design a *decision rule* that solves all applications.
2. Program the *decision rule* for the computer.
3. Design the input and output of the computer information system to provide for automatic decisions by the computer.

Note that under the decision rule concept of programmed decision systems (Figure 5-16), the control component of the information system now becomes a part of the processor (the computer), and the human judgment in control and decision making formerly required is now accomplished automatically by computations performed in the computer.

This concept is essential for an understanding of how programmed decision systems are designed for computer-based information systems. A word of caution, however: in actual practice the complete removal of human intervention for management applications is unlikely, owing to the need to *periodically review the*

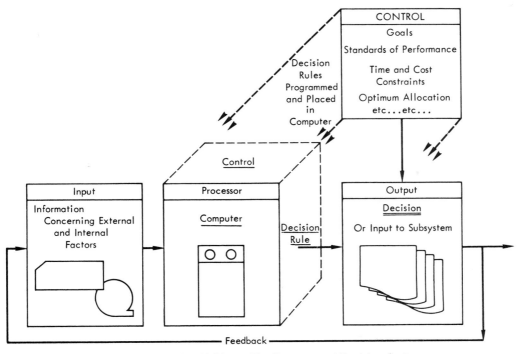

FIGURE 5-16 Automation of Decision Making — The Programmed Decision System

decision rule. So in the sense that the decision rule is subject to change, for whatever reason, the system is not 100 percent programmed.

Figure 5-17 illustrates some programmed decision systems in manufacturing, planning, and control. From this illustration it can be seen that the systems that are totally programmed are, for the most part, somewhat primitive, consisting primarily of applications that automate the paperwork involved in clerical operations and output decisions formerly supervisory in nature and made by humans. Routine decisions such as accounts receivable, payroll, inventory quantity determination, order placement, customer billing, shipping schedules, and a host of others formerly covered by standard operating procedure for manual processing lend themselves admirably to absorption in a programmed decision system.

Figure 5-18 provides a much more sophisticated distribution logistics model (sometimes called distribution management, physical distribution control, or rhochrematics) that, in its more advanced stage, treats the entire logistics of a business, from sales forecast through purchase and processing of material and inventory to shipping of finished goods. The objectives of this system include the

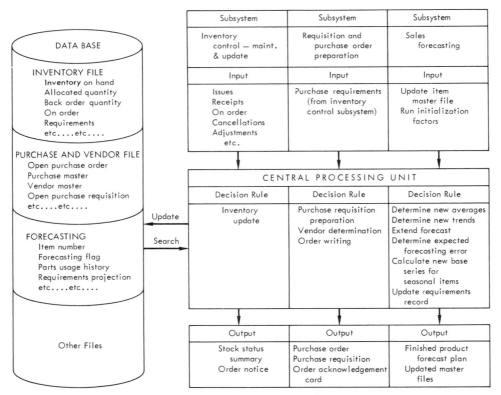

FIGURE 5-17   Examples of Programmed Decisions in Manufacturing Subsystems

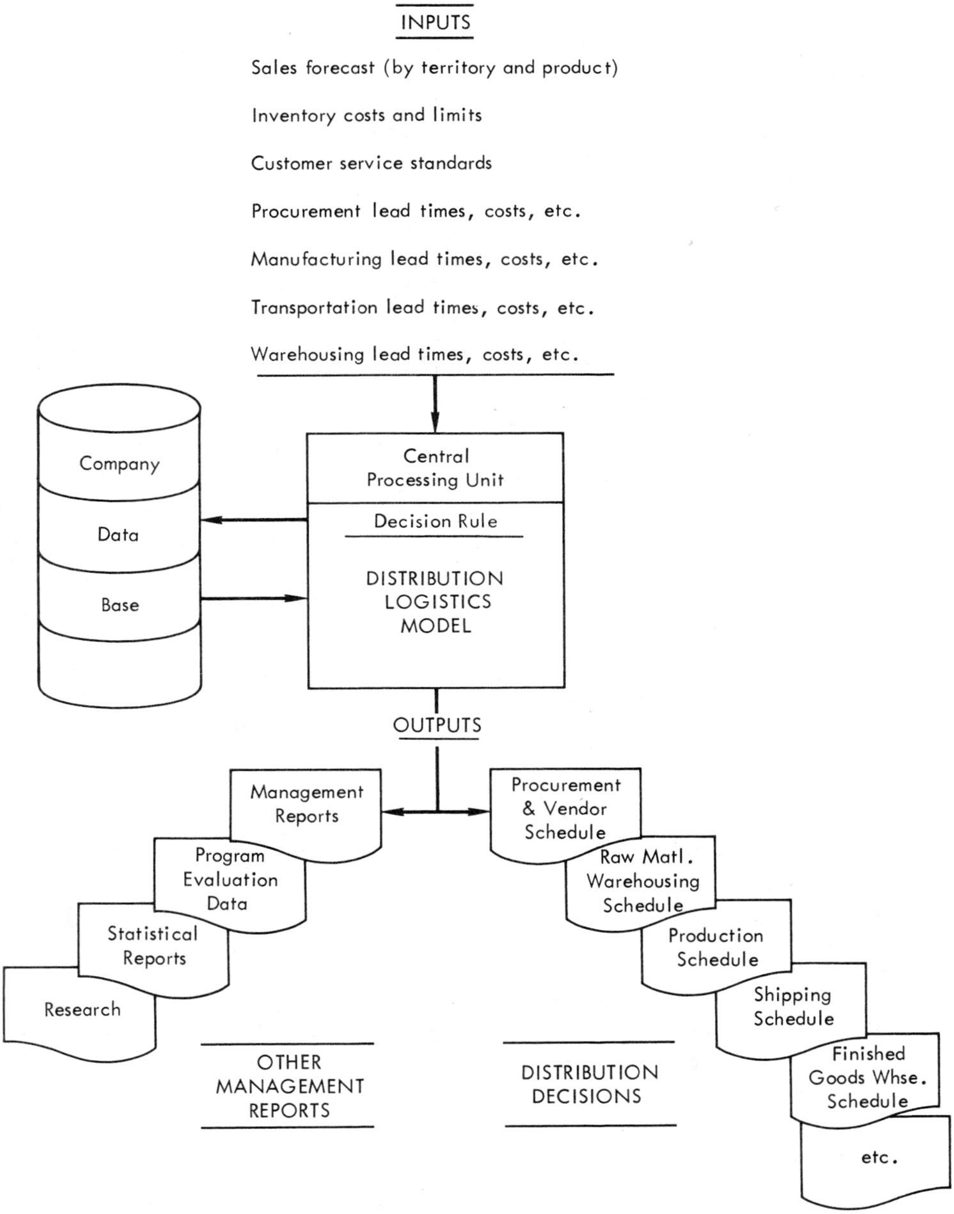

INPUTS

Sales forecast (by territory and product)

Inventory costs and limits

Customer service standards

Procurement lead times, costs, etc.

Manufacturing lead times, costs, etc.

Transportation lead times, costs, etc.

Warehousing lead times, costs, etc.

Company Data Base

Central Processing Unit

Decision Rule

DISTRIBUTION LOGISTICS MODEL

OUTPUTS

Management Reports

Program Evaluation Data

Statistical Reports

Research

OTHER MANAGEMENT REPORTS

Procurement & Vendor Schedule

Raw Matl. Warehousing Schedule

Production Schedule

Shipping Schedule

Finished Goods Whse. Schedule

etc.

DISTRIBUTION DECISIONS

FIGURE 5-18 Programmed Distribution Logistics System

optimization of total costs and at the same time the meeting of established constraints such as capital cost and customer satisfaction.

From the model illustrated in Figure 5-18, it can be seen not only that the system is exceedingly complex but also that it can be a fine instrument of planning and control. The system is shown as a group of subsystems that are integrated, interrelated, and connected in a total system of distribution. It goes without saying that such a system requires constant review of the variables involved to ensure that the inputs as well as the decision rules have been and remain correct. In this sense it is not truly a fully programmed system.

In practice, the totally programmed decision system is rare, except for the clerical operations involved in routine paperwork. Expansion of applications in the programmed area is unquestionably one of the most fruitful fields for research and also offers the greatest payoff in the future for designing better information systems. Moreover, *and this is important,* the present lack of totally programmed systems for middle- and top-management use does not invalidate the approach. On the contrary, the management science techniques involved in the design of decision rules are fundamental and necessary for improving the *decision information systems* that promise to revolutionize management in the very near future.

Management Science and the Decision Rule

How do we design the decision rule for programming or automating decisions? The answer lies in the utilization of management science techniques and a general procedure for constructing models and decision rules in complex situations. In general terms, this consists of specifying the management decision, identifying the most influential parameters and variables (controllable and noncontrollable) and the interrelations, combining relationships into a system of symbolic relationships, manipulating and solving the equations, and testing and revising the model.

Let us amplify some aspects of this procedure with the aid of the model pictured in Figure 5-19. We begin with the goals of the manager. The manager is faced with a decision problem in achieving a particular set of goals. The decision problem involves the selection of one alternative from among many possible alternatives that are available because of his or her control over certain variables of the situation. The manager seeks an alternative that will maximize some benefit, minimize some cost, or optimize some conflicting conditions.

The alternatives in the problem are depicted as A, B, C, and so on in Figure 5-19, and the problem is to choose the one that will best achieve the goal. The business may choose, for example, the number of salespeople to hire, the amount to be spent on advertising or research, the reorder inventory level, or the products in the product line. The *independent* variables in the system consist of the factors that are internal to the firm, and therefore controllable, and the factors that are

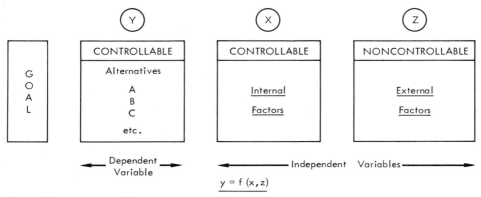

FIGURE 5-19 General Model of the Management Science Solution to Decision Problems

external to the firm, and generally *noncontrollable*. (A company may exert significant influence on external variables through a trade association, political lobbying, market position, or economic leadership.) The decision maker may control *resources* of the firm or *activities*—for example, the mix of labor and capital, pricing, maintenance policy, or product strategy. With regard to most *external* factors, such as the vagaries and intransigence of nature and society, the whims of politicians, and the activities of competitors, the decision maker can exercise little or no influence.

The decision maker must identify the factors, internal or external, that will have a bearing on the dependent variable he or she seeks to optimize. In practice, the mathematical model should be kept as simple as possible by selecting the factors that have a significant effect on the goal to be achieved and dropping those that add only small refinements. The relationships should be verbalized in complex situations as the first step in structuring relationships. A decision maker who believes that the firm's inventory costs are high might structure the problem in this fashion:

"I'm tying up a lot of money in inventory. In fact, we carry so much inventory that we're running out of warehouse space. Carrying cost is a controllable variable that I could reduce by improving efficiency in warehousing, but I think we're doing well there; I'll consider the cost of storage per unit per year as fixed at $5. What I should do is to lower the amount of inventory I carry at any one time by ordering in small quantities. (The order size is a controllable variable.)

"If I order smaller quantities I'll have less average inventory, but I'll have to place more orders, at $10 for the paperwork on each order. Also, if I can stand short periods of stockout to build up backorders, my average inventory will be lower, but there is a penalty cost in loss of goodwill, probably $5 for each unit per period of time. The length of time of stockout will depend on order size and lead time from ordering to receiving goods (both controllable and independent variables)."

The management scientist would then draw a representation of the model and introduce symbols to identify the variables in Figure 5-20 as

L = lead time = 2 periods
Q = order quantity (independent variable)
C = cost of placing a purchase order = \$10
K = carrying cost per unit of product per period = \$.25
P = shortage penalty cost per unit per period = \$.50
D = demand in units per period = 12
R = reorder level (independent variable) related to Q and S
S = maximum shortage to be allowed (independent variable) = $R - DL$

The system cost is first stated in words to express the relationship among the variables, and then in symbols:

total system cost/period = carrying cost/period + purchase cost/period
+ shortage cost/period

In symbols,

$$\text{total system cost/period} = \frac{K(Q+S)^2}{2Q} + \frac{CD}{Q} + \frac{PS^2}{2Q}$$

The model is then manipulated (by setting the derivatives of total system cost with respect to Q and S equal to zero and solving for Q and S) to yield, for

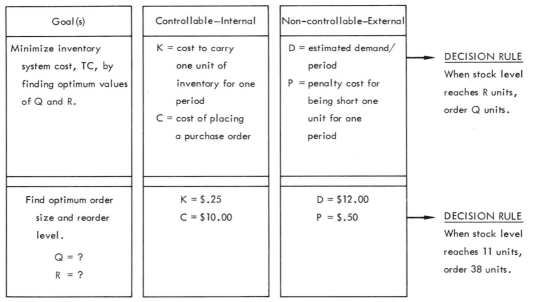

Goal(s)	Controllable—Internal	Non-controllable—External	
Minimize inventory system cost, TC, by finding optimum values of Q and R.	K = cost to carry one unit of inventory for one period C = cost of placing a purchase order	D = estimated demand/period P = penalty cost for being short one unit for one period	DECISION RULE When stock level reaches R units, order Q units.
Find optimum order size and reorder level. Q = ? R = ?	K = \$.25 C = \$10.00	D = \$12.00 P = \$.50	DECISION RULE When stock level reaches 11 units, order 38 units.

FIGURE 5-20 Inventory Model

minimum cost,

$$Q = \sqrt{2CD(1/K + 1/P)} = \text{(about) } 38 \text{ units}$$
$$R = DL - KQ/(K + P) = \text{(about) } 11 \text{ units}$$

Figure 5-20 illustrates this situation in which a *decision rule* is determined, a decision rule that can be programmed on a computer so that the computer can "make" the reorder decision. We must keep in mind two very important considerations in using the quantitative techniques related to this model. First, the external factors are not controlled by the decision maker, and hence the *values assigned to these variables must be estimated*, predicted, or forecast by him. For example, the demand per period in Figure 5-20 must be estimated. A second important consideration involves the assignment of values and relationships among the controllable (internal) factors, particularly cost, price, and volume relationships. In many cases, the conventional accounting system does not yield this kind of decision information properly, and care should be taken to determine real (not necessarily accounting) costs. In Figure 5-20, the cost of holding in inventory one unit of product for one period of time is an example. Finally, the restrictions that limit the value of internal factors must be stated for values that exceed the capacity of the warehouse.

DECISION-ASSISTING INFORMATION SYSTEMS

Unfortunately, all the manager's decisions do not lend themselves to total automation by programmed decision rule. Indeed, the most important and costly ones do not. We must therefore look to computer-based MIS as a source of information to aid the decision maker in the human process of problem solving and decision making. The general concept of the two types of output is shown in Figure 5-21.

The type of system that we have chosen to call the *decision-assisting information system* is characterized by the fact that it concentrates on the information required by the manager as decision maker. This information may be furnished independently (as in output reports) or in an interactive sense where

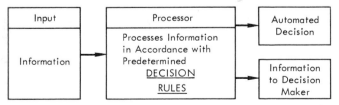

FIGURE 5-21   Making Programmed Decisions with a Management Information System

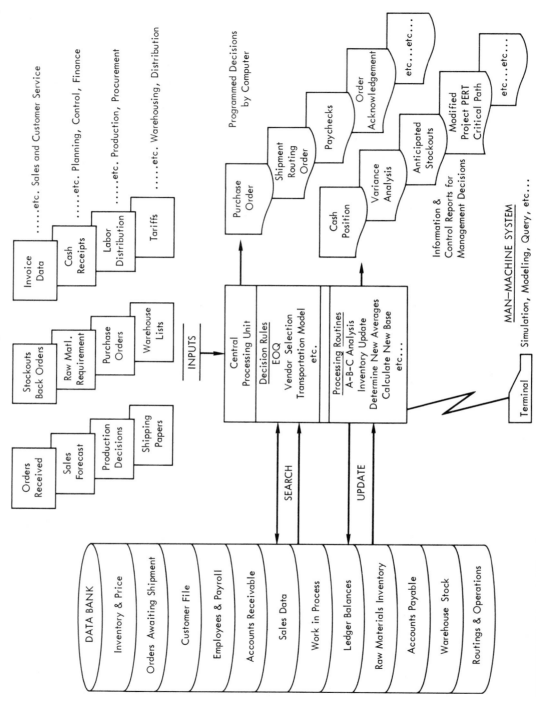

FIGURE 5-22 Integrated Manufacturing Information System

there is a person-machine relationship in a problem-solving network. This latter mode usually takes the form of modeling or simulation in which the decision maker can ask "what if" questions.

The manner in which information can be automated and programmed for use in a *decision-assisting information system* is shown in Figure 5-22. Notice that in this illustration the characteristics and outputs of this vital type of system are shown:

1. Some outputs are decisions; the computer has "made" a decision in accordance with a *programmed decision rule*. (The shipment routing order)
2. Some outputs are secondary information in the form of reports to be used by a subsequent human decision maker. (Variance analysis)
3. The methods of management science have been utilized in both types of systems for the design of decision rules.
4. There are provisions for person-machine-type interactions in the sense that the manager/decision maker can "*model*" his or her decisions prior to commitment.
5. *Optimum* solutions are provided by management science decision rules.

Another example of the distinction between automated decisions and decision assistance is warranted. In almost any business, there is a billing function. Someone goes through the accounts receivable files and bills all outstanding accounts. This can be completely automated. A computer program can go through the accounts receivable file, decide who owes how much money, and print out the bills and mailing labels. This is truly automated decision making. Most businesses also have sales representatives who market their goods and services. The computer can figure up exactly how much each salesperson sold of each item, how many new customers were contacted, and whether those figures meet the goals set by management. However, a good marketing manager will not make the salesperson's evaluation a completely automated decision. Salespeople could be ridiculously overrewarded if they are given full credit for large "blue-bird" orders (orders that come to them with little or no effort). Similarly, they could be grossly underrewarded if sales in their region dropped due to a large customer moving away (e.g., General Motors closing a plant). To avoid these inequities, the marketing manager takes the automated sales analysis output as information to assist in evaluating the sales force. The manager then adds his or her special knowledge of unique, modifying circumstances to reach the final decision.

Improve Decision Making by Upgrading Clerical Systems

Although in a strict sense the clerical and supervisory types of application are not oriented to decision making, it is worthwhile to review some of them and see how they may be improved.

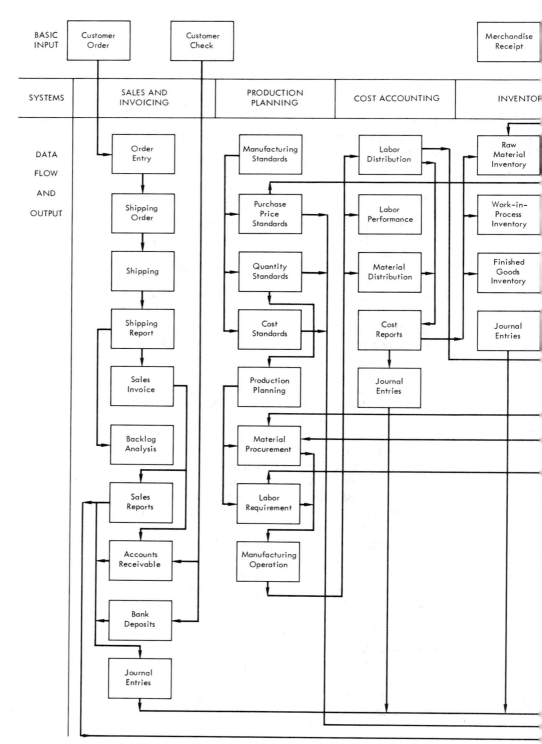

FIGURE 5-23 Total Systems Concept — A Manufacturing Company

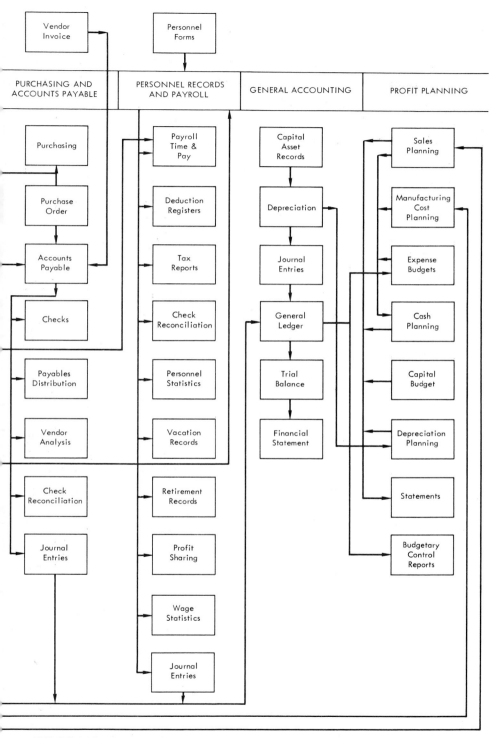

FIGURE 5-23 (continued)

Source: C. C. Wendler, *Total Systems* (Cleveland: Systems and Procedures Association, 1966), p. 33.

Despite the thousands of computer-based installations in the United States, the overwhelming share of applications are concerned with standard tasks of accounting and financial record keeping. Until now, computers have been doing largely what clerks had done before, but doing it electronically. The value of the computer, when it was measured at all, was calculated by a method that compared its cost against the cost displacement of clerical and machine resources such as clerks and tabulating equipment. Naturally, with this view of cost in mind, management turned to the automation of clerical paperwork as the first and frequently the only application.

Most of these clerical applications are not advanced or sophisticated; they are functionally similar to the punched card tabulating (unit record) equipment that the larger electronic data processing (EDP) systems replaced. The great majority of smaller firms are just beginning to consider the use of EDP. Even in the country's largest firms, the EDP applications are largely clerical. The most common uses are

Inventory control	Production planning
Payroll	Raw materials ordering
Cost studies and reports	Parts ordering

The intention here is not to downgrade the use of the computer for clerical applications. On the contrary, the clerical area offers applications with immediate payoff in cost reduction as well as improved accuracy of information. Moreover, much of the information furnished as output from clerical systems has decision-making applications at the supervisory level and elsewhere. The illustrations of Figure 5-23 give a further insight into how sophisticated clerical information systems can integrate the functions of a manufacturing company and provide outputs for decision making at supervisory and middle-management levels. Figure 5-23 also illustrates the "total systems" concept—at least as far as this concept can be adopted in a manufacturing company with the information shown. This illustration shows each subsystem segregated into the primary input of the system, the primary output of the system, and the data flow between systems.

For the purpose of *decision making* and improvement of operations, what is needed is an approach to the design of an information system and its contribution that measures these not by cost displacement of clerical expenses but by *how well the system improves the operation of the organization*. Figure 5-24 shows some of the applications and ways in which this might be done. Notice particularly the transition from clerical operations to decision applications, which demonstrates how the operations of the company are improved (e.g., customer relations, personnel stability).

In summary, it is time for the manager to advance from the already firmly established clerical base of applications to the additional use of these applications for making decisions on how operations of the organization can be improved. We should assume as given the benefits of paperwork automation and clerical cost displacement and build from there.

ADMINISTRATION AND CONTROL			DECISION MAKING AND OPERATIONAL	
Application	Objective		Application	Objective
Ledger Accounting	Clerical Displacement and Control	➤	Accounting	Cash Control Budget Control
Marketing Order Entry Billing	" "	➤	Personnel Skills Inventory	Personnel Stability
Personnel Payroll	" "	➤	Purchasing Replenishment Orders	Vendor/Buyer Relationship
Production Output Reporting	" "	➤	Production	Cost Control
		➤	Inventory	Optimize Inventory
Inventory Inventory Level	" "	➤	Marketing	Customer Relations
		➤	Distribution	Optimize Costs Customer Relations

FIGURE 5-24   Advances in Clerical and Supervisory EDP Applications

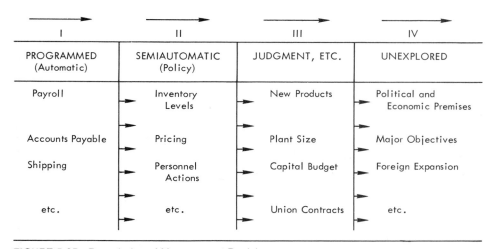

I	II	III	IV
PROGRAMMED (Automatic)	SEMIAUTOMATIC (Policy)	JUDGMENT, ETC.	UNEXPLORED
Payroll	Inventory Levels	New Products	Political and Economic Premises
Accounts Payable	Pricing	Plant Size	Major Objectives
Shipping	Personnel Actions	Capital Budget	Foreign Expansion
etc.	etc.	Union Contracts	etc.

FIGURE 5-25   Boundaries of Management Decisions

SUMMARY

Figure 5-25 demonstrates how the boundaries of management's *programmed* decisions are constantly moving to the right in order to assimilate and program increasingly complex problems. However, the progress in moving those boundaries to the right has been slow. Computers and information systems thus far have been concerned largely with clerical applications and routine reports. Our task, as manager-users and systems designers, is to move the frontiers to the right to increasingly complex and useful applications. This can be accomplished through computer-based MISs that utilize the techniques of management science for automated decisions and decision-assisting information.

PROBLEMS AND QUESTIONS

1. Work Case 4, Johnson Enterprises (C).
2. For the four systems shown in Table 5-A, page 208, mark with an (x) the system objective(s), inputs to / outputs from the system, whether the listed decision can be made from information furnished by the system, and whether the decision is programmed (made by the computer automatically) or whether is it decision assisting (made by the user with information furnished by the computer system).
3. For the four systems shown in Table 5-B, page 209, for International Medical Instruments, mark with an (x) the system objective(s), inputs to / outputs from the system, and whether the listed decision can be made from information furnished by the system. (*Note:* Give your answers as you would redesign the indicated systems, *not* as they now exist in the case study.)
4. List the objectives of the systems given for the International Medical Instruments case:

System	*Objective(s)*
Billing	
Purchasing	
Materials planning	
Production scheduling	
Inventory management	
Sales analysis	

5. What are the six characteristics of information that make successful computer applications (using this information) more probable?

   _____

   _____

   _____

   _____

   _____

   _____

6. Which of the major information systems and subsystems of Figure 5-4 would be applicable to a bank? A retail store?

7. Which of the information systems and subsystems of Figure 5-4 would you recommend for the International Medical Instruments case? Which for the Northwestern Insurance Company case?

8. For the International Medical Instruments case, list three or more clerical applications that could be upgraded into decision-making applications.

9. List five applications that lend themselves to programmed decision rules. List five that do not. For the five that do not, show how an MIS would help make the decision.

10. It is said that an *information* system will avail you nothing unless it is backed up by a *management* system. Explain.

SELECTED REFERENCES

ALTER, STEVEN L. *Decision Support Systems*. Reading, Mass.: Addison-Wesley, 1980.

CASCIO, WAYNE F., AND ELIAS M. AWAD. *Human Resources Management: An Information Systems Approach*. Reston, Va.: Reston, 1981.

EILON, SAMUEL, "What Is a Decision?" *Management Science*, December 1969.

HARRISON, E. FRANK. *The Managerial Decision Making Process*. Boston: Houghton Mifflin, 1975.

MOSCOVE, STEPHEN A., AND MARK G. SIMKIN. *Accounting Information Systems*. New York: John Wiley, 1981.

MURDICK, ROBERT G. *MIS: Concepts and Design*. Englewood Cliffs, N.J.: Prentice-Hall, 1980.

————, AND THOMAS C. FULLER. "Subsystem Cycles for MIS." *Journal of Systems Management*, June 1979.

RADFORD, K. J. *Complex Decision Problems: An Integrated Strategy for Resolution*. Reston, Va.: Reston, 1977.

SRINIVASAN, C. A., AND H. M. SCHOENFELD. "Some Problems and Prospects in Design and Development of Corporate-wide Information Systems." *Management International Review*, February 1980.

THIERAUF, ROBERT J. *Distributed Processing Systems*. Englewood Cliffs, N.J.: Prentice-Hall, 1978.

VAN GUNDY, ARTHUR B. *Techniques of Structured Problem Solving*. New York: Van Nostrand Reinhold, 1981.

TABLE 5-A

System	System Objective	Inputs From	Outputs To	Decision	Decision Programmed	Decision Assisting
Billing Output: Customer's invoice	( ) Bill customer ( ) Improve cash flow ( ) Inform sales people ( ) Prepare tax reports	( ) Order process ( ) Shipping ( ) Receiving ( ) Sales planning	( ) Sales analysis ( ) Shipping ( ) Profit planning ( ) Bill of materials	( ) Compute discount ( ) Improve pricing policy	( ) Yes ( ) Yes	( ) Yes ( ) Yes
Purchasing Output: Purchase order	( ) Determine EOQ to buy ( ) Monitor buyer performance ( ) Inventory control ( ) Requisition preparation	( ) Receiving ( ) Vendor file ( ) Sales analysis ( ) Open customer order file	( ) Cash budget ( ) Receiving ( ) Accounts payable ( ) Billing	( ) Compute percentage of orders behind schedule by vendor ( ) Determine demand for end items of components in manufacturing schedule ( ) Determine vendors to drop	( ) Yes ( ) Yes ( ) Yes	( ) Yes ( ) Yes ( ) Yes
Inventory Management (finished goods) Output: Distribution by value reports	( ) Compute shop order loads ( ) Reduce time of purchase ( ) Optimize inventory costs ( ) Reduce stockouts to absolute minimum	( ) Billing ( ) Shipping ( ) Sales analysis ( ) Receiving	( ) Sales planning ( ) Purchasing ( ) Production scheduling ( ) Bill of materials	( ) Cumulative rank of items by dollar sales ( ) Life-cycle analysis	( ) Yes ( ) Yes	( ) Yes ( ) Yes
Operations Scheduling Outputs: Work center, load summary, and shop load schedule	( ) Compute material requirements ( ) Locate customer order ( ) Forecast labor required ( ) Schedule jobs to machines	( ) Customer orders ( ) Production schedule ( ) Materials planning ( ) Shipping	( ) Tool control ( ) Labor distribution ( ) Payroll ( ) Backorder file	( ) What work centers are over / under-loaded? ( ) Should overload be accomplished by overtime or subcontracting?	( ) Yes ( ) Yes	( ) Yes ( ) Yes

TABLE 5-B

System	Product Development (Bill of Materials)	Manufacturing (Materials Planning)	Marketing (Sales Analysis)	Finance (Profit Planning)
Objective(s)	( ) Control backorders ( ) Forecast labor requirements ( ) Explosion of parts requirements ( ) Forecast material requirements	( ) Compute parts from production schedule ( ) Minimize production schedule changes ( ) Reduce clerical costs ( ) Control backorders	( ) Identify marginal customers ( ) Provide life-cycle analysis ( ) Monitor sales people's performance ( ) Schedule sales plan	( ) Provide market research ( ) Provide plan and control for reaching profitability objective ( ) Integrate organizational subsystems
Receives Inputs from	( ) Engineering changes ( ) Master file list ( ) Customer orders ( ) Sales analysis	( ) Bill of materials ( ) End item demand schedule ( ) Production schedule ( ) Purchasing	( ) Billing ( ) Sales plan ( ) Accounts payable ( ) Profit plan	( ) Sales planning ( ) Purchasing ( ) Order processing ( ) Materials planning
Provides Outputs to	( ) Material status ( ) Parts requirements list ( ) Finished goods inventory ( ) Open order file	( ) Purchasing ( ) Sales planning ( ) Labor distribution ( ) Shop loading	( ) Market research ( ) Cost accounting ( ) Sales planning ( ) Billing	( ) Cost accounting ( ) Sales quota control ( ) Bill of materials ( ) Shipping
Decisions	( ) Requirements resulting from engineering change ( ) Cost of labor for engineering change ( ) Delay in shop loading ( ) Parts shortages	( ) Material requirements by time periods ( ) Orders necessary to meet requirements ( ) End item requirements ( ) Sales plan	( ) Identify low margin-low profit customers ( ) Profit contribution by line and territory	( ) Labor standards ( ) Purchase budget ( ) Shop floor control ( ) Dealer operations

6

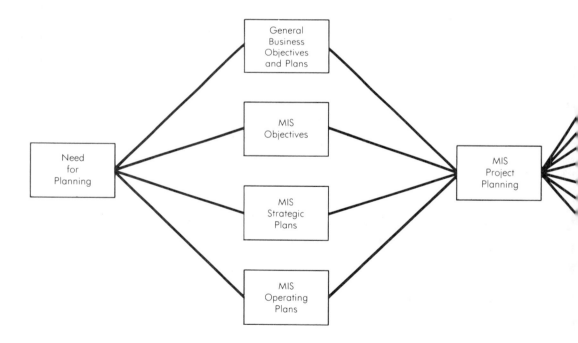

Strategic and Project Planning for MIS

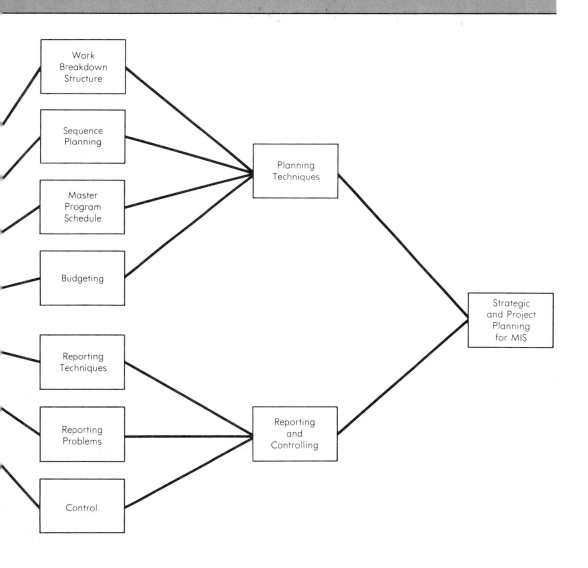

It is evident that the rapidly improving capability and capacity of modern computers are outracing the ability of the average company to utilize them properly. For example,

> *The auto parts store in a large Florida city is reasonably efficient and modern. Yet when asked for a 1982 Jeep windshield frame and gasket, the attendant drags out his books and his microfilm to translate the request to a part number. With today's technology, the attendant should enter his request for a 1982 Jeep windshield frame and gasket via the terminal. The processor decides what part number that is and determines if it is in stock; of so, it tells the clerk what aisle and shelf to find it on; if not, it prints the backorder request.*

> *The hospital in a nearby city is modern and has a competent staff and good equipment. The hospital still does nurse scheduling manually, even though scheduling of resources was one of the earliest automated management solutions.*

The applications just mentioned are not very sophisticated; in fact, they represent low-level operating decisions. Numerous other examples of this type will occur to the reader.

There has been very little done to assist top-level managers in their decision making. Imagine a chief executive turning to his MIS manager and saying, "Have the computer prepare a merger analysis for Company XYZ and have it on my desk by 8 : 00 A.M. tomorrow." Although most executives and managers would think this scenario nothing short of ludicrous, the computer is capable of extensive assistance in this and many other cases. It is fair to say that one major reason for the underutilization of computers and the failure to utilize fully the potential of information systems is lack of *managerial* involvement in the strategic planning for systems development and design activities.

In this book we have divided the MIS development work into four phases:

1. *Strategic and project planning.* This chapter addresses the problems of meeting short-term and long-term objectives with current projects that flow into a larger strategy covering the long term. Only with careful planning can these projects be successfully completed.

2. *Conceptual system design.* The feasibility study is conducted during this phase. Also, a broad-brush picture is created by the technical leaders. At the end of this phase, we know the project can be done and roughly how. Chapter 7 covers these topics.

3. *Detailed system design.* Given the critical decision on the conceptual system design, this phase provides the details of how the system will work. This is discussed in Chapter 8.

4. *Implementation, evaluation, and maintenance.* The output of detailed design is a set of specifications. Implementation is converting these specifications to a working system. When the system is running, it must be evaluated against the original objectives. Finally, it must be maintained. Chapter 9 covers these topics.

To a great extent, these phases overlap. For example, project architecture cannot be completed until some system design is done. We will treat the phases as distinct, all the while remembering that they overlap and that the process is really one of iterative refinement.

All topics will be considered from the manager's viewpoint. Although this will limit our discussion of some of the technical aspects of implementation, it will properly emphasize objectives, strategy, and planning as they apply to MIS.

GENERAL BUSINESS PLANNING

The starting point for MIS planning is general business planning. No MIS department can decide what they should do or how they should do it without the groundwork provided by objectives and plans for the company they are supporting. Chapter 2 discussed general business planning in some depth, and the reader may wish to review that section. Before turning to MIS planning, let us recall the following:

General Business Item	*Importance*
• Statement of mission or purpose	Clearly defines the business of the firm.
• Objectives	Set goals for the company in all key performance areas.
• Strategic plans	Provide general guidance on how to get to the long-range objectives.
• Operating plans	Provide detailed guidance on how to get to the short-term objectives.

Figure 6-1 summarizes general business planning.

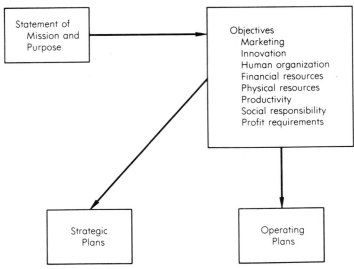

FIGURE 6-1   General Business Planning Overview

APPROPRIATE MIS RESPONSE

What does a mission statement for the business have to do with the MIS group? What do general business objectives and plans have to do with the MIS department? Everything! Recall that management information systems exist solely to support and aid line management in meeting the objectives of the business.

Let us look at each of the general business items just noted and see what the proper response from the MIS department should be.

Mission Statement

The general statement of purpose for the business has value to the MIS group in two ways. First, it serves as a constant reminder that computers and information systems are *not* the point of the business—they are tools to aid management in the real, stated business purpose. Second, the mission statement serves as the outline for the MIS department's mission statement, which in some form must say, "We will provide information support to management to enhance...".

Objectives

These general business objectives represent valuable opportunities for the MIS department to identify and understand the challenges the company faces. Each of these goals has an attendant information need that must be satisfied before the objective can be met. The information part is not the whole solution, but it is a part, and it can facilitate the total solution.

It is the responsibility of the MIS group to produce department objectives that dovetail with and support the objectives of the larger enterprise.

Strategic and Operating Plans

The various strategic and operating plans that the business has produced to meet its objectives are another source of valuable input to the MIS group. If the company plans to introduce a new short-life product next year, there is an opportunity to provide marketing, production, and financial information/analysis relative to that product. And if the management information system is correctly designed and implemented, it can be used for the next product or set of products.

REVIEW

We have seen that business defines its mission and purpose, sets its objectives, and then produces its strategic and operating plans. To be effective, the MIS department must state its mission and purpose, set its objectives, and lay out plans in support of the larger business. Only then is the whole organization pulling in the same direction, all contributing to the meeting of the same objectives. Figure 6-2 reemphasizes the required relationship of business plans and MIS plans.

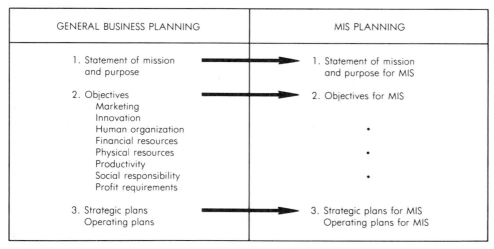

FIGURE 6-2 MIS Planning as a Derivative of Business Planning

MIS PLANNING: GENERAL

Now that the groundwork of general business objectives and planning has been laid, we can turn to these same activities narrowed to the MIS scope. Just as with the larger business, there can be no long-term success with management information systems unless those involved know where they are going and how they will get there.

The Need for a Systems View

Judging from the literature and from observations of real-life applications, little more than lip service has been paid to the widely promoted concept of a "total" single system or to the goal of a highly integrated set of subsystems. Instead, we have seen the development of "islands of mechanization" following unrelated starts in quick payoff areas such as payroll and some clerical accounting functions. This patchwork approach has resulted in the development of unrelated and sometimes incompatible subsystems.

This patchwork or piecemeal approach to systems development, which has no unifying framework and is without a master plan, has several disadvantages. One stems from the unrelated nature of the subsystems developed. Frequently autonomous departments and divisions have developed individualistic systems without regard to the interface of such systems elsewhere in the organization. The result has been an inability to communicate between systems and the incompatibility of subsystems of a like nature throughout the company.

A fairly common example of failure to relate subsystems is the way in which personnel information is structured. Several departments (sales, production, accounting, personnel) may maintain employee files that overlap with other similar files but do not provide for interface between them. In one instance, critical engineering and labor skills shortages developed in several geographically separated divisions of a multidivision company. But despite the fact that these skills were available elsewhere in the company, no identification could be made because of the lack of a common personnel skills information system.

A second and serious disadvantage is the cost involved—cost in time, resources, and money. The longer a master plan is put off, the more costly will be the inevitable need to overhaul, unify, and standardize the approach to integrated systems design. Many companies have invested in the automation of clerical records and subsequently discovered that a complete overhaul of the system is necessary when it becomes integrated with a larger effort. A popular one-for-one conversion in the past has been the materials inventory "tab" system, which frequently requires complete rework when a production planning and control system is implemented.

The questions arise, first, "Why has the piecemeal approach been allowed to develop?" and, second, "What should and can be done to improve the design situation so that an improved, integrated approach can be taken?"

There are multiple reasons why the piecemeal approach developed. First, a systems view and system plan take time, money, and upper-management involvement to create. When something is difficult to do, people try to find an easier way. Second, the financial payoffs come quickly and painlessly for isolated applications like materials inventory. Only recently have managers realized what a mess they created. Third, managers failed to understand the future of the computer and information systems. The impact of the electronic age is just now seriously reaching the average person. Using excellent hindsight, we now see the need for integrated information systems.

What of the future—will the piecemeal approach continue? There are favorable signs:

- We have past mistakes from which to learn.
- We have some positive experience with (partially) automated decision systems.
- Upper management generally recognizes the need for the information and systems components of all modern projects (and funds accordingly).
- A larger percentage of project expenditures is going to design and software as opposed to hardware.

Although there is reason for hope, overconfidence is not warranted. Consider the three reasons given for the piecemeal approach originally being taken. It still takes time, money, and management involvement to produce a good systems plan. Quick payoffs are still available from isolated applications. And although we believe we now understand the impact of computer information systems on business, the next several years will almost certainly bring some substantial and revolutionary changes we do not foresee. When the pros and cons are balanced out, we can expect the more successful companies to have extensive systems plans into which their computer information applications fit. The average company will continue to have only isolated applications that automate clerical work or assist management decision making. Within the next two decades, the quality of management information systems will widen the gulf between successful companies and "also-rans." In fact, successful companies will be successful based on a good management team taking full advantage of computer assistance with their information needs.

The answer to the second question, regarding the means to achieve an integrated approach to systems development, lies clearly in the adoption of a master plan. Working to a long-range blueprint is desirable; it is proven, and it is practical. Indeed, the same reasons that can be advanced for business planning in general can apply to the argument for systems planning.

These four special reasons for systems planning are

1. *To offset uncertainty*
2. *To improve economy of operations*
3. *To focus on objectives*
4. *To provide a device for control of operations*

Aside from the uncertainty of business operations and the resulting need for better forecasting information, the special need for a systems plan is evident because of advancing computer technology and its widespread effect on business operations. Both software and hardware have become so complex that the job of selection and utilization is much more difficult. As a result, the majority of organizations have fallen far short of their potential to use computers for processing the information necessary to manage the company effectively. A master plan may not remove the uncertainty, but it will almost surely place the firm in a better position to deal with the unknowns and to take advantage of developments as they occur.

Planning the overall approach to an integrated system is also *economical*. The prevailing pattern of design effort in most companies reflects the short-term approach of automating those clerical operations that offer an immediate payoff in terms of reduction of paperwork and staff. However, experience has shown that in the long run this approach is likely to be more costly than is proceeding under a predetermined plan. Once one job or function has been automated, the need for the design and automation of contiguous functions frequently becomes obvious. Money can be saved and performance improved by an effective linking together of these neighboring functions through a good plan for integrated systems design.

A good plan for systems development also serves to *focus on company and systems objectives*. Conversely, firms without explicit organizational objectives and explicit plans for achieving them, that make expedient responses to environmental factors rather than shape their own environment, are unlikely to have definite systems objectives and a plan for their attainment. Indeed, if we review the fundamental process of planning, we discover that planning cannot proceed in any area of endeavor until adequate objectives have first been set. It follows that development of a master systems plan forces examination and definition of objectives.

Systems development, implementation, and operations are among the most difficult of activities within the company to control. The fourth major advantage of the development of systems effort under a predetermined plan is that the plan provides a means for subsequent *control*. Plans and objectives also provide the means for measuring progress. If systems development activities and events are organized on a project basis with specific objectives (e.g., optimize cost of raw materials inventory) to be achieved within a certain time period and at a predetermined cost, then these goals can be used as yardsticks to measure subsequent accomplishments.

Finally, the existence of a systems plan does not mean that all of it has to be implemented, let alone immediately. Priorities for development of subsystems should be set on the basis of payoff and implemented as management sees fit.

MIS Objectives

It cannot be too strongly stated or too often repeated—the reason for an MIS group's existence is to support line management in whatever business they are engaged. The temptation of every support group is to take on an independent life of its own. The enormity of this error cannot be overemphasized. THE PURPOSE OF MIS IS TO SUPPORT AND ASSIST MANAGEMENT IN THE COMPANY'S BUSINESS.

As we stated, MIS objectives are derived from the company's objectives. Ideally, these business objectives are clearly stated in writing. If that is not the case, these objectives are available from the key executives in the business. Although an executive may not have written objectives, almost certainly he or she can answer the questions

1. What do you want to achieve in area XYZ?
2. What is your schedule for this achievement?
3. What are the cost and completion criteria?
4. How can the MIS group assist you?

Hence, we have the company's objectives as a starting point.

Each company objective should be reflected in at least one MIS objective. The MIS objective calls for a supporting contribution to meet the company's goals. Let us take an example. Suppose the company wants to increase its market share in market segment A from 10 percent to 14 percent next year. Numerous information needs present themselves:

- How is the market currently allocated?
- What products did each competitor offer to get and hold its share of the market?
- What are the pros and cons of these products?
- To what customer set does each of these products appeal?
- How much advertising is spent on each product?
- In what stage of the product life cycle is each product?
- And so on...

The marketing group may have the answers to some of these questions. They do not have answers to all of them. The ones that are not yet answered are the opportunities for the MIS department to make a contribution. MIS objectives can be created from these unfulfilled information needs. The MIS department will also set itself a long-range objective to create an MIS that answers as many of these types of marketing questions as possible for use with the next market share problem.

One final point should be made on setting MIS objectives. Each MIS objective must tie back to a company objective (i.e., everything done by the MIS department is in support of the company's business).

Strategic Planning, Project Planning, and MIS

As already mentioned, it is imperative to have a long-range, total MIS plan into which all shorter-range plans and projects fit. This prevents the creation of fragments (single-function systems) that are incompatible with other management information systems. The long-range, total MIS plan evolves from reflecting support for the company's overall goals.

The total MIS plan should be checked periodically to verify that it still answers to the needs of the larger business (i.e., Is it a sufficient overview and framework to accommodate and guide all the MIS activity for the company?). The total MIS plan is always consulted when a strategic or project plan for a management information system is proposed. The key question asked is, "Does this specific MIS plan fit within the framework of the total MIS plan?"

There should again be a correspondence between business plans and MIS plans, this time at the strategic level. Each business strategy should be supported by an information management strategy. Each information management strategy should tie in to some business strategy; similarly for project planning. The MIS department must produce an operating plan that meshes with the other operating plans in the company. That operating plan will contain a number of project plans, each of these in support of a project in the business mainline. Now let us look at project planning in more detail.

MIS PLANNING: DETAILS

The heart of this section deals with a concept we have already used intuitively and will now define: the *project*. Business is usually described in terms of the flow of work. This continuous process changes very gradually over time. However, sometimes there are major dislocations, caused by needs for major innovations. The introduction of a new management information system is such an innovation. A number of tasks related in a complex fashion to achieve a one-time objective, such as the creation of an MIS, is called a *project*.

Projects differ from processes in that they are discrete—they have clearly specified beginning and end dates, as opposed to company functional operations such as marketing, manufacturing, or accounting. Projects are complex because they require a wide variety of skills. Moreover, they cut across traditional organizational lines and involve a substantial number of interrelated activities. And because each project is a one-time effort, unusual problems arise that call for nontraditional solutions. In addition, projects usually require the development of new techniques and advances in the state of the art while the project is in progress.

Needs and Objectives

Many prescriptions for project planning call for starting with a search for problems needing solutions. We do not recommend that. By the time a company is ready to do project planning, it is far too late to search for problems needing solutions. In fact, we already have that list at hand—it evolved from business objectives to MIS objectives, from business strategic plans to MIS strategic plans, from business operating plans to MIS operating plans. We know what project we are working on and what the general needs and objectives are. We now need to refine these statements of need.

The statement of general needs and objectives is almost always too high level and vague to be implemented. The process of refining these vague requirements is a crucial factor in project success. These key steps should be taken:

1. The *problem statement* must be made comprehensible to those who will design and implement the MIS. For example, the management need may have been for an in-depth market analysis. The computer specialists may have no idea what all that includes; hence the importance of breaking down the idea "market analysis" to include and define "competition," "market share," "distribution channels," "sales force size," and so on. In other words, first determine the *users' needs* in specific terms.

2. *Input.* From the user's perspective, what items can the user reasonably be expected to provide? Human-to-machine interface may be important, and if it is, these requirements need to be detailed during this phase. For example, if a clerk will be the user, very clear messages prompting for input are required.

3. *How* the system will work should be specified only in very general terms at this time. In fact, the designers should concentrate on "what" the system should do and leave as many implementation details as reasonable to the specialists who will actually produce the MIS. For example, a permanent payroll record may be a valid need or objective. But the internal format in which the file is maintained is probably too much detail for this phase of design.

4. *Output.* If the user has expectations about, or requirements for, the results of the system, those need to be detailed. For example, sample user reports should be drawn up at this stage and taken to the future users for approval.

5. *Budgets* are a key part of detailing the needs of a project. The firm may need a $100,000 market analysis system very badly, but have no need for a $1,000,000 system. It may also not have the funds for the $1,000,000 system.

6. *Schedules.* Next year can be the perfect time for a system to be working while five years from now it would be another Edsel.

In summary, the management statement of the problem (general needs and objectives) must be taken and broken down into a language the computer specialists will understand. It must also be clarified by making more specific statements of requirements and then reviewing these with the managers who originally posed the problem.

We now need to understand the planning cycle. Figure 6-3 shows the general needs and objectives being transformed into specific needs and objectives. Only at this point is the project understood well enough to start serious project planning. As indicated, planning is a cyclic activity. A high-level plan is made first and will be very rough (not detailed, but approximate). As more becomes known about the project, we iterate on the plan until eventually it is both detailed and refined. The planning side of a project is not complete until the project has been implemented, tested, documented, and been working for a while. For this reason, implementation and testing data feed into successive levels of the plan to improve its detail and accuracy.

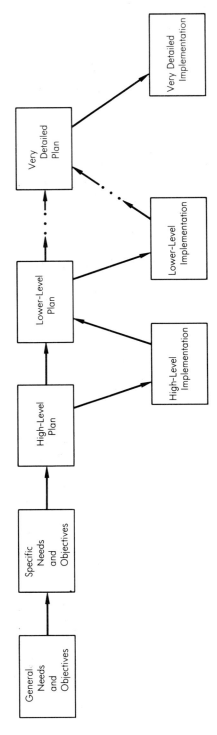

FIGURE 6-3 Planning Cycle

All of this discussion hinges on understanding what constitutes a plan. The following items should certainly be included:

1. Summary statement of the problem being solved by this project is required.
2. A breakdown of the work to be done (as detailed as practical) is required. Also, estimates of how long each piece will take are needed. Documentation, testing, and maintenance efforts should be included.
3. A list of dependencies on outside groups with target dates for "delivery" of services or equipment is required.
4. A list of outside groups that depend on this project with target dates for delivery is required.
5. A list of interdependencies of various pieces within this project with dates of need/delivery is required.
6. The skills needed to complete the project should be listed. Eventually, the people who work on the project must match this list exactly.
7. Other resources needed to complete the project must be identified (e.g., space, computer hardware, and telephones). Dates these items are needed must be specified.
8. A budget covering salaries, rent, capital expenditures, and so on must be part of the plan.
9. A statement of the reporting and tracking system to be used must be included.
10. A schedule of activities reflecting all the above work and interdependencies is required.
11. A backup plan if any piece of the plan fails must be supplied.

We have discussed the evolution of a management need for information through a detailed statement of project objectives on to the project planning cycle and project plan content. Now let us turn to some specific planning techniques that are useful if the project is large or complex.

Planning Techniques

For very small projects, commonsense techniques for planning and documenting the plans for the MIS project are sufficient. We will discuss here the more elaborate techniques for planning for larger projects. Most of these techniques and tools have been borrowed from engineering project management theory and practice, where they originated.

The planning techniques rest on some fundamental management premises. The first is that all work can be planned and controlled. The second is that the greater the difficulty in planning the work, the greater the need for such planning. Techniques exist for a rational approach to planning the design and implementation of large systems. The third premise is that the assignment of project management to a project manager with wide responsibilities is an important factor in increasing the probability of success of a project. The project manager must control all funds required for the project. However, the project manager may direct the activities of a program without having direct-line command over all persons involved in the program. He or she achieves this by means of a clearly defined work breakdown structure for the project.

Work Breakdown Structure

A fundamental concept in project management is the work breakdown structure, which starts with the total end result desired and terminates with the individual detailed tasks. The project breakdown structure is a natural *decomposition* of the project end result. It is created in a level-by-level breakdown from:

1. System to subsystem
2. Subsystem to task
3. Task to subtask
4. Subtask to work package

The manner in which the project is broken down into tasks is illustrated in Table 6-1.

TABLE 6-1   Standard Task List of the Work Breakdown Structure for Project Control

I. Study Phase
Task 1 Study organization goals and problems.
  Subtask 1.1 Interview managers and study internal documents.
  Subtask 1.2 Survey operating problems.
  Subtask 1.3 Study informational problems.
Task 2 Study company resources and opportunities.
  Subtask 2.1 Evaluate company resources.
  Subtask 2.2 Study needs of the market and environmental trends.
  Subtask 2.3 Evaluate competitive position.
Task 3 Study computer capabilities — equipment and labor skills.
Task 4 Prepare proposal for MIS design study.
II. Gross Design Phase
Task 1 Identify required subsystems.
  Subtask 1.1 Study work flow and natural boundaries of skill groupings and information needs.
  Subtask 1.2 Develop alternative lists of subsystems.
  Subtask 1.3 Develop conceptual total system alternatives based upon the lists of subsystems.
  Subtask 1.4 Develop scope of work to be undertaken based on need of the company and estimated resources to be allocated to the MIS.
  Subtask 1.5 Prepare a reference design showing key aspects of the system, organizational changes, and computer equipment and software required.
III. Detailed Design Phase
Task 1 Disseminate to the organization the nature of the prospective project.
Task 2 Identify dominant and principal trade-off criteria for the MIS.
Task 3 Redefine the subsystems in greater detail.
  Subtask 3.1 Flowchart the operating systems.
  Subtask 3.2 Interview managers and key operating personnel.
  Subtask 3.3 Flowchart the information flows.
Task 4 Determine the degree of automation possible for each activity or transaction.

TABLE 6-1 Standard Task List of the Work Breakdown Structure for Project Control (Cont.)

Task 5		Design the database or master file.
Subtask	5.1	Determine routine decisions and the nature of nonroutine decisions.
Subtask	5.2	Determine internal and external data required.
Subtask	5.3	Determine optimum data to be stored in terms of cost, time, cross-functional needs, and storage capacity.
Task 6		Model the system quantitatively.
Task 7		Develop computer support.
Subtask	7.1	Develop computer hardware requirements.
Subtask	7.2	Develop software requirements.
Task 8		Establish input and output formats.
Subtask	8.1	Develop input formats (design forms).
Subtask	8.2	Develop output formats for decision makers.
Task 9		Test the system.
Subtask	9.1	Test the system by using the model previously developed.
Subtask	9.2	Test the system by simulation, using extreme value inputs.
Task 10		Propose the formal organization structure to operate the system.
Task 11		Document the detailed design.
IV. Implementation Phase		
Task 1		Plan the implementation sequence.
Subtask	1.1	Identify implementation tasks.
Subtask	1.2	Establish interrelationships among tasks and subtasks.
Subtask	1.3	Establish the performance / cost / time program.
Task 2		Organize for implementation.
Task 3		Develop procedures for the installation process.
Task 4		Train operating personnel.
Task 5		Obtain hardware.
Task 6		Obtain or develop the software.
Task 7		Obtain forms specified in detail design or develop forms as necessary.
Task 8		Obtain data and construct the master files.
Task 9		Test the system by parts.
Task 10		Test the complete system.
Task 11		Cut over to the new MIS.
Task 12		Debug the system.
Task 13		Document the operational MIS.
Task 14		Evaluate the system in operation.

The work breakdown structure, referred to as WBS, starts with a word description of the entire project and is then decomposed by word descriptions for each element of each subdivision. The organizational structure should have no influence on the development of the WBS. The primary question to be answered is, "What is to be accomplished?" Next, an acceptable way of classifying the work must be found. The classification should be such that natural systems and components are identified and milestone tasks for accomplishing their design are related. Neither gaps nor overlaps must be allowed, yet the structure should interlock all tasks and work packages.

The smallest element in the WBS, usually appearing at the lowest level, is the work package, a paragraph description of the work that is to be done to

TABLE 6-2 Work Package Information Checklist

1. Project identification, title, and number
2. Title and number of work package
3. Responsible organization and manager
4. Interface events and dates
5. Start and end date for work package
6. Dollar and labor estimates, projections of dollars and labor on a weekly or monthly basis, and a schedule of actual application of resources maintained as current
7. Contract or funding source identification
8. Account charge number
9. Work order or shop order, to be opened when authorization is obtained to expend a specified amount of money under a particular account number

achieve an intermediate goal. Requirements of time, resources, and cost are listed, including definite dates for starting and completing the work—a short duration compared with that of the total project. The breakdown of the project into work packages, each assigned to a single responsible manager, provides the means for control of the entire project. A typical list of items of information contained in a work package form is given in Table 6-2.

Sequence Planning

The relationships among tasks must be set forth by a chronological ordering, starting with the terminal task of the project and working backward. As each task is set down, it is necessary to determine what immediately preceding tasks must first be completed. When a network of events has been established, estimates of the time required to complete each event, based upon the work package information, may be entered.

There are a number of time paths through a network that run from the starting event to the terminal event. The longest is called the *critical path*. On the basis of management decisions, resources may be added or redeployed to change the length of time of a current critical path to yield a new one, thus gaining time by a trade-off involving increased costs. The final network is sometimes called the *master project network plan*.

Master Program Schedule

The master program schedule (MPS) is a management document giving the *calendar dates* for milestones (major tasks and critical path minors tasks), thus providing the control points for management review. The MPS may be in the form of a Gantt chart for small MIS projects or in machine (computer) printout for large projects whose networks have been programmed for computer analysis and reporting. In the latter case, the MPS is derived from the network schedule by establishing a calendar data for the starting event.

Budgeting

The establishment of cost and resource targets for a planned series of periods in advance is project budgeting. Although cost constraints may be applied in a top-down fashion during planning, such constraints must be reconciled with a *bottom-up* approach through the work breakdown structure. Reconciliation is accomplished by either (1) allocating more funds or (2) narrowing and reducing the scope of the work and redefining the objectives of the project.

Cost and resource targets must be established for a work package by

1. Performing organization
2. Funding organization
3. Elements of cost: labor, materials, and facilities

Only direct costs are included in the project budget, because they are the only costs over which the project manager has control.

Cushioning should not be added to the resource costs because meaningful measures of control depend upon realistic goals. However, because experience has shown that project cost overruns are far more common than underruns, a contingency fund should be budgeted to cover unanticipated problems. The project manager's use of the contingency fund is also a measure of his performance.

Reporting and Controlling

Control of the project means control of performance/cost/time (P/C/T). These elements, P/C/T, must be reported in a way that ties them all together, otherwise the report is meaningless. Consider, for instance, a project in which performance and costs are on target. It is possible for such a project to be behind and in trouble from the time standpoint. On the other hand, a project may show an overrun of costs as of a particular date, yet if the work performance is ahead of schedule, this is good news instead of bad news.

Reporting Techniques

The reporting system for a project is its own MIS. Some methods of project reporting are

1. Integrated P/C/T charts as shown in Figure 6-4.
2. Financial schedules and variance reports.
3. Time-scaled network plans and computerized reports based on them.
4. Problem analysis and trend charts.
5. Progress reports.
6. Project control room and computerized graphic systems.

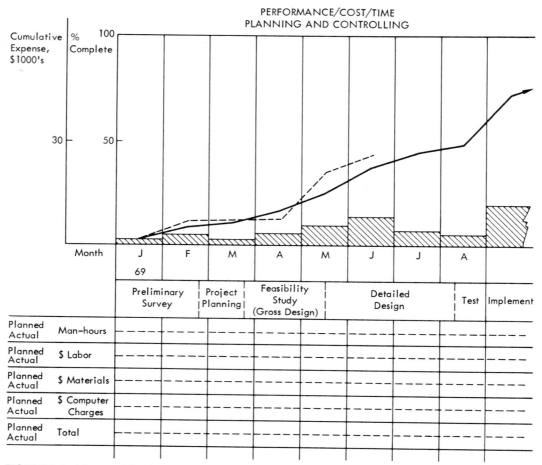

FIGURE 6-4   Integrated P / C / T Chart

7. Design review meetings and "reference designs." A common "reference design" must provide a formal description of system specifications and goals at any particular time. All designers work on the basis of assumptions about parts of the system other than theirs. If they are not working on the same assumptions, chaos results. The reference design may change with time, and the design review meeting of all key personnel is a good time to make formal changes.

Reporting Problems

Control is difficult if the only reports are written narratives requiring interpretation by management. At the other extreme, reams of computer data reports are equally poor. Managers prefer graphic displays, which reduce large amounts of complex information into easily understood pictorial form. Comparisons and trends of major variables are also effective in communicating. Graphic display must be designed to guard against too gross a level of reporting, however, or else growing problems may be obscured.

Other problems in reporting are the use of complex grammatical structure; high "fog index" of writing; excessive and unexplained abbreviations, codes, and symbols; and too much technical jargon. Projects may fail if the project manager and his or her technical specialists do not make clear to management what is happening and how the money is being spent.

Control Through "Completed Action"

Managers in a chain of command cannot divest themselves of accountability for tasks that are delegated to them. Responsibility for a work package may be delegated to the lowest level in the organizational hierarchy, but each manager up the line is evaluated on the basis of completed action on the work package. The worker who has responsibility for a work package should be supplied with adequate reports of P/C/T. As variances are reported to the responsible performer, the burden is on that person to take corrective action. His or her ultimate responsibility is "completed action," the presentation of a completed job to the manager. Only in emergencies and cases of wide variances from planned action should the managers at various levels in the organization step in to reclaim delegated responsibility. The control in a well-run project is essentially self-control, based upon a good reporting system.

SUMMARY

The design and implementation of an MIS cannot be carried out on an unplanned trial-and-error basis. The complex assemblage of tasks involved and the cost of the design and implementation are such as to constitute a major project. Project management is conducted with special management techniques of its own, techniques related to establishment of project needs and objectives and to planning, scheduling, budgeting, reporting, and controlling.

The outstanding characteristics of these techniques are the breakdown structure, the network approach to defining task relationships, and the integration of performance/cost/time for planning and control. The detailed techniques for implementing these major project management techniques have provided powerful aids to organizations. We have summarized the project planning and control cycle in Figure 6-5.

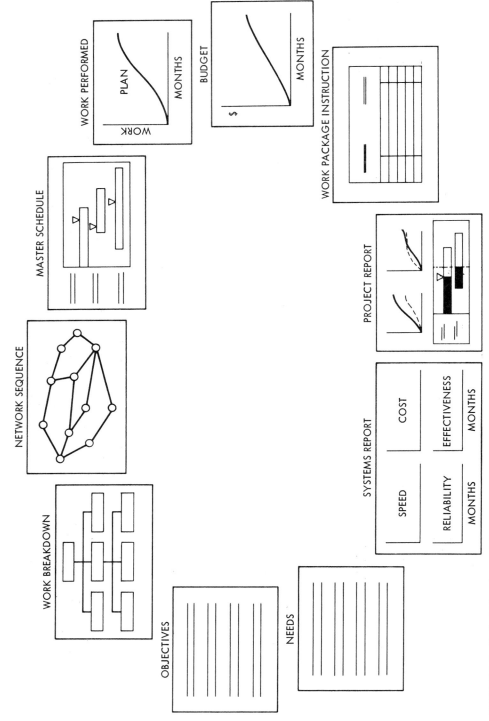

FIGURE 6-5 Project Planning and Control Cycle

PROBLEMS AND QUESTIONS

1. Case 4 discusses the need for a systems view and a good set of plans. Work Johnson Enterprises (D).

2. Propose a statement of mission and purpose for General Motors' Chevrolet division; for the Audubon Society; for the American Medical Association.

3. In the short-term, some companies seem to make good profits even though their only mission statement (if they gave it that much thought) would be "make money." Explain. Also explain why the statement of purpose "make money" will not be sufficient guidance for a company over the long run.

4. Choose a firm with which you are familiar and create realistic objectives for the eight categories suggested by Figure 6-1.

	Category	*Objective of Firm*
1.	_____	_____
2.	_____	_____
3.	_____	_____
4.	_____	_____
5.	_____	_____
6.	_____	_____
7.	_____	_____
8.	_____	_____

5. Explain the relationship between general business plans and MIS plans. Figure 6-2 may be useful.

6. List five systems problems that you have noticed in your recent dealings with stores, service firms, or manufacturing plants.

_____
_____
_____
_____
_____

7. If you were or are working for a company, what kinds of systems problems would you look for whose solutions would provide the greatest payoff?

8. Consider some major project on which you are currently working (getting through college, for example), and develop a work breakdown structure.

9. A systems project is planned for a small store. The "start" event is labeled Event 1. The subsequent activities and required times are

Activity	1-2	Determine information needs	2.6 weeks
	1-3	Analyze store operations	4.0 weeks
	2-3	Define subsystems	1.5 weeks
	2-4	Develop database	2.1 weeks
	3-4	Identify system constraints	.2 weeks
	4-5	Design the MIS	4.2 weeks

Draw the network diagram, indicate the critical path, find the time for the critical path, and find the slack time for each activity.

10. Referring to Figure 6-A, review the definitions given and answer the following questions. Definitions:

   a. The circles with numbers in them are events.
   b. The arrows between the circles (labeled with capital letters) are work activities.
   c. The numbers in parentheses associated with each arrow are the numbers of days required to complete that work activity.

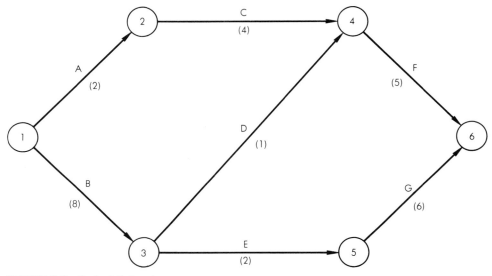

FIGURE 6-A   Project Network

Questions:

   a. List all events that must complete prior to event 4 being completed. _____
      _____ List all events that must complete prior to event 5 being completed. _____
   b. How many days minimum are required to reach event 4? _____
      To reach event 5? _____
   c. Which events are on the critical path (to reach event 6)? _____
      What is the critical path length (in days)? _____

SELECTED REFERENCES

Andrews, William C. "Business System Proposal." *Journal of Systems Management,* February 1978.

Bush, Robert L., and K. Eric Knutsen. "Integration of Corporate and MIS Planning: The Impact of Productivity." *Data Base,* Winter 1978.

Business Systems Planning (GE-20-0527-2). White Plains, N.Y.: IBM, 1978.

CHRYSLER, EARL. "Improved Management of Information Systems Development." *Journal of Systems Management*, March 1980.

GUNDERMAN, JAMES R., AND FRANK W. McMURRY. "Making Project Management Effective." *Journal of Systems Management*, February 1975.

HEAD, ROBERT V. "Strategic Planning for Information Systems." *Infosystems*, October 1978.

KANTER, JERRY. "MIS Long Range Planning: Why Don't More Companies Do It?" *Infosystems*, June 1982.

KEIN, ROBERT T., AND RALPH JANARO. "Cost/Benefit Analysis of MIS." *Journal of Systems Management*, September 1982.

KERZNER, HAROLD. "Tradeoff Analysis in a Project Environment, Part I." *Journal of Systems Management*, October 1982.

KRAMER, OTTO P. "Management of the Systems Function." *Journal of Systems Management*, August 1978.

LIENTZ, BENNET P., AND MYLES CHEN. "Long-Range Planning for Information Services." *Long-Range Planning*, February 1980.

McLEAN, EPHRAIM R., AND JOHN V. SODEN. *Strategic Planning for MIS*. New York: John Wiley, 1977.

METZGER, PHILIP W. *Managing a Programming Project*. Englewood Cliffs, N.J.: Prentice-Hall, 1973.

MURDICK, ROBERT G. *MIS: Concepts and Design*. Englewood Cliffs, N.J.: Prentice-Hall, 1980.

PAGE, JOHN R., AND H. PAUL HOOPER. "Basics of Information Systems Development." *Journal of Systems Management*, August 1975.

ROSSOTTI, CHARLES O. "The Computer Alternative." *Infosystems*, September 1982.

SCHWARTZ, H. H. "MIS Planning." *Datamation*, September 1970.

SIEGEL, PAUL. *Strategic Planning of Management Information Systems*. New York: Petrocelli, 1975.

STRASSMAN, PAUL A. "Stages of Growth." *Datamation*, October 1976.

THOMPSON, ARTHUR A., JR., AND A. J. STRICKLAND III. *Strategy Formulation and Implementation*. Dallas: Business Publications, 1980.

ZACHMAN, JOHN A. "The Information Systems Management System: A Framework for Planning." *Data Base*, Winter 1978.

7

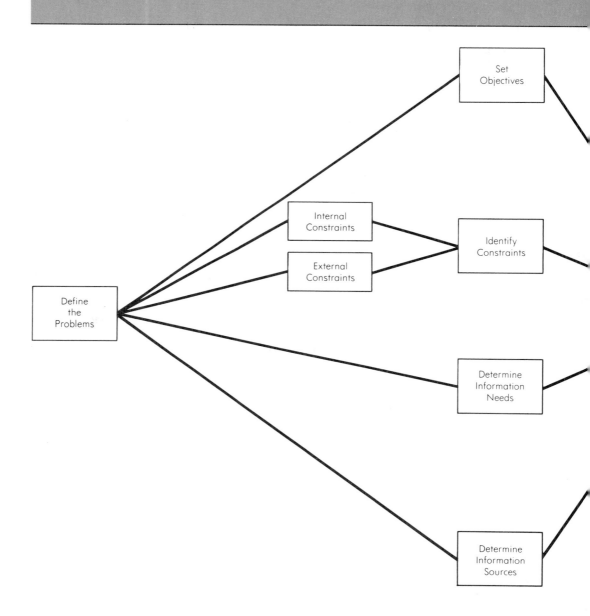

Conceptual System Design

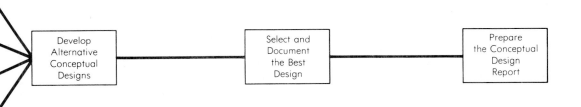

Because the conceptual design sets the direction for the MIS project, it is vital that managers participate heavily at this stage. The conceptual design should not be relinquished to technicians.

Conceptual design is sometimes called *feasibility design, gross design,* or *high-level design.* All these terms carry a portion of the complete meaning of this phase of MIS development. The conceptual design phase takes as input

1. A crisp statement of a management information requirement and
2. A set of management objectives for the MIS.

The process of doing the conceptual design involves showing the feasibility of meeting the management objectives for the MIS, painting the broad-brush picture of the system, showing *how* the system will work at a gross or high-level. The output of the conceptual design phase is a set of documents describing the MIS in sufficient detail for the technicians to begin their work on detailed design.

The key tasks performed during conceptual design are

1. Defining the problem(s) in more detail
2. Refining the management objectives to set system objectives
3. Establishing system constraints
4. Determining information needs and sources
5. Developing alternative designs and selecting one
6. Documenting the conceptual system design

Figure 7-1 shows an overview of the MIS development process. Note that conceptual design is the "centerpiece," the fulcrum, of the process. Only after the conceptual design is completed do we know for sure that the MIS can successfully be constructed.

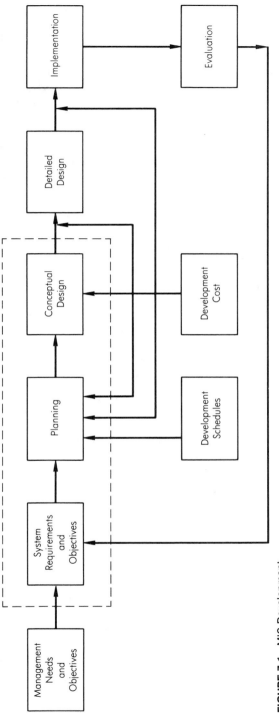

FIGURE 7-1 MIS Development

237

DEFINE THE PROBLEMS

Problems undoubtedly exist in any dynamic business. What are usually lacking are clear definitions of the problems and a priority system for their solution. Therefore, management must take the first step in MIS design by formulating problems to be solved. Let us briefly review the methods suggested in Chapter 6 for detailing problems.

The mission statement for the business as a whole leads to objectives for the general business. From the objectives we derive plans. Associated with each business objective and business plan are information needs. These information needs are the problems to be solved by the MIS function. As noted in Chapter 6, these general statements of need are seldom clear enough or sufficient for starting the design process. We must go through an iterative process of

1. Stating the information need
2. Asking questions about that need
3. Suggesting interpretations of that need
4. Detailing the original statement
5. Reviewing the more detailed statement of need with management

The steps just listed are repeated until we really understand the information need and the problem to be solved.

As mentioned in an earlier chapter, the phases of a project overlap and flow into one another. The process of problem refinement just discussed flows naturally into (and overlaps with) setting system objectives.

SET SYSTEM OBJECTIVES

Despite our understanding of the nature of objectives in the operating activities of the company, it is frequently quite difficult to state objectives for systems that cut across all functional areas.

Unlike the *technician*, who frequently turns to topics such as file structure and retrieval techniques and who views the objectives of a subsystem only in terms of its input to a larger system, the *manager* must define system objectives in terms of legitimacy of information demands and not in terms of the satisfaction of demands that are not related to an objective. Systems analysts (and computer sales representatives) tend to stress processing efficiency, and staff and functional supervisors commonly believe that their objective is "to complete the required report on time for management use." This view disregards the real objective of the systems design—*management effectiveness*. The value of systems lies in the benefits to their users, not in mere efficiency of transactions. We have witnessed the design of information systems in several government agencies where the system objective was the automation of hundreds of reports, without regard to management of the many tasks related or to functional or resource subsystems represented by the reports (e.g., training, employee relations, safety, recruitment, staffing, etc.). Such focus on the automation of records or the processing of existing data overlooks the true objectives of the operational organizational entity represented by the subsystem.

Yet it is not an easy matter to determine the real objectives of an information system any more than it is easy to determine the objectives of the operational system served by it. A common fallacy in stating objectives is to emphasize the obvious or to state objectives in vague terms: "reduce costs," "improve efficiency," "keep accurate records," "meet the production schedule." When asked for his objectives, a university president may reply, "Provide quality education," and a government bureaucrat may say, "Provide more jobs for the unemployed"; yet in neither case is the objective stated in terms specific enough to provide a measure of performance of the system or to design an information system to help achieve the objective.

Despite its difficulty, being specific is necessary. System objectives must ultimately be stated in terms of the objectives of the department, group, function, or manager to be served or in terms of the functions the information

TABLE 7-1 Objectives of Material Control System: Major Electrical Manufacturer

Subsystem	Objective
Routings	Capture routing information and time values that can be used by manufacturing for cost of completed work, labor status by contract, effect of changes by rerouting, etc.
Status	Establish a system that can be used by manufacturing to determine work load in shop, effect of accepting additional work, overload in various cost centers, status of self-manufactured work-in-process, etc.
Tools	Capture all tool information that can be used by manufacturing to determine tool status *prior* to release of work to shop, and maintain a tool inventory by contract for auditing purposes both by the company and the government on government contracts.
Cost control	Establish an overall system that can be used by manufacturing to very quickly determine labor costs, material costs, tool costs, overruns, etc., by contract.
Scheduling	Determine effect of engineering changes, lack of material, tool shortages, etc.
Make or buy	Make decisions on those items to subcontract, based on cost, load, schedule, etc.
Request for proposal information	Establish a system that can be used by manufacturing to produce immediately the necessary information needed for customer requests and requests for proposals.
Elapsed time	Analyze, improve, and prepare an orderly procedure that can be used by manufacturing to report elapsed time, if required by contractual obligation.

system is to perform. In other words, system objectives should be expressed in terms of what managers can do after their information requirements have been met. Such expression may use descriptive statements, flowcharts, or any other means that will convey to management the objectives that the systems designer must meet to develop the system. If possible, the objectives should be stated in quantitative rather than qualitative terms so that alternative system designs as well as system performance can be measured for effectiveness. That is, a statement of objectives should include exactly what it is that the system is supposed to accomplish and the means by which it will subsequently be evaluated. Table 7-1 shows an example of such a statement. This table contains a statement of objectives for the material control system of one of the nation's major electrical manufacturers. Notice how specific objectives are defined.

Listed next is an additional group of functional subsystems and a hypothetical statement of objectives for each. *These examples will be used for illustration throughout the remainder of this chapter.*

Subsystem	Objective
Inventory	Optimize inventory costs through the design of decision rules containing optimum reorder points, safety stock levels, and reorder quantities, each capable of continuous and automatic reassessment.
Accounts payable	Pay 100 percent of invoices before due date.
Purchasing	Provide performance information on buyer's price negotiations with suppliers so that purchase variance can be controlled within set limits.
Production control	Identify cost and quantity variances within one day to institute closer control over these variables.
Project control	Identify performance against plan so that events, costs, and specifications of the project can be met.

In summary, the first steps in systems design attempt to answer the questions: "What is the purpose of the system?" "Why is it needed?" "What is it expected to do?" "Who are the users and what are their objectives?" These questions relate to the *what* of systems design and the remainder of the steps relate to *how* it is to be achieved.

Finally, the establishment of management information system objectives cannot be divorced from a consideration of organizational objectives, near term and long range. Over the near term, system objectives can usually be framed in terms of management planning and control and decision making: lowering costs, strengthening operating controls, improving data flow, and meeting customer and external requirements. These short-range system objectives must, however, take into account the environment in which a business will be operating 5 to 10 years hence. *Today's* system design must take account of *tomorrow's* environment.

ESTABLISH SYSTEM CONSTRAINTS

The iterative nature of the systems design process is easily understood when we consider the third step in the process—establishing constraints. Sometimes called *problem boundaries* or *restrictions*, constraints enable the designer to stipulate the conditions under which objectives may be attained and to consider the limitations that restrict the design. To state it another way, constraints, which are provided by the manager-user or the designer himself, limit freedom of action in designing a system to achieve the objective. It is clear then that a constant review of objectives is necessary when considering system constraints. Indeed, the two steps of setting objectives and establishing constraints may be considered together as one.

Although constraints may be viewed as a negative limitation on systems design, there is a positive benefit as well. We should not let our desire to design sophisticated systems run away with reality, or make promises that cannot be kept. Identification of the problem or setting the objective may be evident, but the solution is not always easy. Moreover, the designer who thinks that his system can run the organization is as mistaken as the manager who believes that he can run his organization without a system. Establishing constraints will help to ensure that the design is realistic.

Constraints may be classified as internal or external to the organization. This concept is shown in Figure 7-2, which forms the basis of the following discussion.

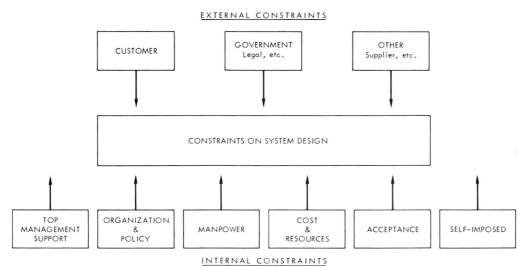

FIGURE 7-2 Constraints on Management Information Systems Design

Internal Constraints

If *top management support* is not obtained for the systems concept and for the notion that computer-based information systems are vital for management planning and control, the type of design effort discussed in these chapters cannot be implemented. A good environment for information systems must be set, and one essential ingredient is the approval and support of top management. This constraint definitely influences the kind of system the manager-user may design.

Organizational and policy considerations frequently set limits on objectives and modify an intended approach to design of a system. The structure of the organization and the managers occupying various positions influence information flow and use of system outputs. In a decentralized multiplant organization with a wide product line, the design of common systems in cost accounting or production control is obviously less acceptable than in a more centralized organization with fewer products. An additional organizational difficulty is related to the turnover of managers. More than one head of computer operations has stated that his major difficulty is the abandonment or redesign of systems due to the turnover among manager-users. Also, company policies frequently define or limit the approach to systems design. Among these policies are those concerned with product and service, research and development, production, marketing, finance, and personnel. For example, a "promote from within" personnel policy would have an impact on the type of systems design to build a skills inventory. Other important considerations in design are those concerning audits.

Personnel needs and personnel availability are a major limiting factor in both the design and utilization of information systems. Computer and systems skills are among the most critical in the nation; rare indeed is the manager who admits to having sufficient personnel to design, implement, and operate the systems desired. Additional considerations concern the nature of the work force and the skill mix of users. Elaborate and sophisticated systems are of little value if they cannot be put to use.

Perhaps the most significant constraint of all is the one concerning *people*. "People problems" is probably the fact most often mentioned where failure to achieve expected results is concerned. Here we have the difficulties associated with the natural human reaction to change, the antagonism, and the lack of interest and support frequently met in systems design and operation. Automation, computer systems, and systems design often call for the realignment of people and facilities, organizational changes, and individual job changes. Therefore, these reactions are to be expected and should be anticipated in designing systems to achieve the objective.

Cost is a major *resource* limitation. The cost to achieve the objective should be compared with the benefits to be derived. You do not want to spend $20,000 to save $10,000. Although a cost-benefit analysis is frequently difficult, some approach to priority setting must be undertaken. Considerations similar to those surrounding cost apply also to the use of other resources. *Computer capacity* and other facilities relating to operation of data processing systems should be utilized in an optimum way.

Self-imposed restrictions are those placed on the design by the manager or the designer. In designing the system to achieve the objective, the manager may have to scale down several requirements to make the system fit with other outputs, equipment, or constraints. Usually, the manager will also restrict the amount of time and effort devoted to investigation. For example, the designer may want to design a pilot or test system around one product, one plant, or one portion of an operation before making it generally applicable elsewhere. Functional requirements also define constraints placed on the system by its users. The data requirements, the data volumes, and the rate of processing are constraints imposed by the immediate users. More remote users impose constraints by the need to integrate with related systems.

External Constraints

Foremost among the considerations surrounding the external environment are those concerning the *customer*. Order entry, billing, and other systems that interface with systems of the customer must be designed with the customer's needs in mind. If certain outputs from the system are not acceptable to the customer, a definite limitation must be faced up to. The customer may require that bills be submitted in a form that provides input to his or her system of accounts payable. For example, standard progress reporting and billing procedures are among the requirements imposed for processing data under many military procurement programs.

A variety of additional external constraints should be considered in addition to the customer. The *government* (federal, state, local) imposes certain restrictions on the processing of data. Among these are the need to maintain the security of certain classes of information (e.g., personnel) to comply with law and regulation in the conduct of business (e.g., taxes, reporting) and to meet certain procedures regarding record keeping and reporting to stockholders (e.g., outside audit). *Unions* can and do affect the operation of systems involving members in matters such as compensation, grievances, and working conditions. *Suppliers* are also an important group to be considered when designing information systems because these systems frequently interface with that group.

In summary, it is important to recognize the constraints that have an impact on systems design. Having recognized them and made appropriate allowance in the design function, the manager will then be in a position to complete the remaining steps toward the design of an operating system that will achieve the objective he has previously determined.

The nature of constraints is illustrated here by stating a hypothetical constraint for each of our selected functional subsystems.

Subsystem	Statement of Constraint
Inventory	Regardless of reorder points and reorder quantities, the supplier will not accept orders for less than carload lots for raw materials 7 and 12.
Accounts payable	The individual who prepares the check for payment of invoices must not be the same individual who approves payment.
Purchasing	It is not necessary to negotiate purchases in amounts under $500.
Production control	System output for shop control will be identified by department only and not by the individual worker or supervisor.
Project control	We are required to report weekly to the U.S. Department of Defense any slippages in time or cost exceeding 10 percent of any event in the project control critical path.

DETERMINE INFORMATION NEEDS

A clear statement of information needs is fundamental and necessary to good systems design. Too many companies spend lavish sums on hardware and software to perpetuate existing systems or build sophisticated data banks, without first determining the real information needs of management: information that can increase the perception of managers in critical areas such as problems, alternatives, opportunities, and plans.

Unless managers can provide the specifications for what they want out of an information system, the design effort will produce less than optimum results. If, on the other hand, the manager-user can define the objectives and spell out the items of information that are needed to reach the objective, he or she is then at least halfway home in systems design. Failure to be specific on these two steps probably accounts for the downfall of more design efforts than any other factor. If systems design begins without such clear-cut statements by the manager, systems analysts or technicians will provide *their* objectives and *their* information needs.

Yet it is not easy for a manager to spell out the specific information requirements of his or her job, and therein lies a basic frustration in the improvement of systems. In an attempt to get a clear statement of information needs, the analyst frequently meets with an interviewing situation along the following lines:

Analyst: Could you tell me what the objectives of this cost accounting system are, as you see them?

Financial
Manager: Sure... to get the reports out faster... to do something about keeping the costs in line... to keep management informed....

Analyst: Yes, I understand... let me put it another way. What are your responsibilities as you see them?

Financial
Manager: Whatta you mean? I'm in charge of the accounting department.

Analyst: Yes, I know, but we need to get a better statement of your department's objectives, how the cost accounting system can further these objectives, and what information is needed to do this.

Financial
Manager: Well, we need the information we've been getting, but we need it faster and with a lot more accurate input from those fellows in operations.

This hypothetical conversation reflects the difficulty of getting managers to be specific about information needs. One approach, sometimes used by consultants, is to get top management to require in writing from subordinate managers a statement containing (1) a list of four or five major responsibilities for which the manager believes himself or herself to be accountable and (2) the four or five specific items of information that are required to carry out the responsibilities. These requirements could be framed in terms of duties performed or decisions made; the idea is to get the manager to think of information needs. If this can be done, the information system is well on the way to being designed.

Another approach is avoidance of the direct question, "What information do you need?" Instead, the designer requests that the user describe what occurs in the decision-making process; then the designer concerns himself or herself with the identification of the questions that are to be resolved in the activity for which the system is being designed. This approach is also a good one for the manager-user, because the manager-user is intimately familiar with the operation and presumably with the difficult decision operations in it.

One way of determining what managers do *not* need in the way of information is to cease issuing selected periodic reports or reduce their circulation list. If managers really use a report, they will complain, and their names may be restored to the circulation list.

A manager needs information for a variety of reasons concerned with the management process. The type of need that he or she will have at various times and for various purposes depends largely upon two factors that we shall examine briefly: the personal managerial attributes of the individual manager and the organizational environment in which decisions are made.

Personal Attributes

Knowledge of Information Systems

If managers are aware of what computer-based systems can do, their information requests will probably be more sophisticated and more specific. Their knowledge of capabilities and costs places them in a much better position to aid in the design of a good system.

Managerial Style

A manager's technical background, leadership style, and decision-making ability all affect the kind and amount of information required. Some prefer a great amount of detail; others like to decide with a minimum of detail and prefer personal consultation with subordinates.

Manager's Perception of Information Needs

"You tell me what I need to know" and "Get me all the facts" represent two opposite perceptions of information needs. This dichotomy is due partly to the fact that many managers are ignorant of what information they need. Another dimension of the problem is the widely differing views of managers regarding their obligation to disseminate information to subordinates and to groups outside the firm. The manager who cannot or will not delegate authority is likely to keep information closely held.

Organizational Environment

Nature of the Company

Problems in communication and in controlling operations seem to be a function of the company's size and the complexity of its organization. The larger, more complex firms require more formal information systems, and the information needs of these systems become more critical to operations.

Level of Management

There are three levels of management (i.e., strategic planning, management control, operational control) and the varying needs for information at each. Each level needs different types of information, generally in different form. Top levels need the one-time report, the summary, the single inquiry. The management control level needs the exception report, the summary, and a variety of regular reports for periodic evaluation. The operational control level requires the formal report with fixed procedures, the day-to-day report of transactions, to maintain operational control of actions as they occur. Managers at *all* levels have changing information needs, depending on the nature and importance of the particular decision.

Structure of the Organization

The more highly structured the organization, the easier it is to determine the information needs. Where authority and responsibility are clearly spelled out, relationships understood, and decision-making areas defined, the information needs of managers can be determined more easily.

Returning to our illustrative subsystems, some information needs might be stated as follows:

Subsystem	Information Needs
Inventory	Daily report on items that have fallen below minimum inventory level so that expediting action can be taken.
Accounts payable	Incoming invoices coded according to "days to due date," because invoices should be paid no sooner than two days prior to due date to conserve cash.
Purchasing	The performance of each individual buyer, indicated by comparing actual purchases with hypothetical purchases at base or standard prices.
Production control	Exception report to identify by shop order and lot number the variances in cost and quantity that are over or under by 5 percent.
Project control	Weekly report on progress against plan for the events in critical path. Also need to know where float exists in other events so that resources may be shifted.

DETERMINE INFORMATION SOURCES

The step of determining information needs is hardly completed before it is necessary to consider the information sources. Indeed, these two steps are overlapping and, as we stated before, iterative.

Although some systems require considerable external information, for the most part the natural place to turn for information is inside the firm: books, records, files, statistical and accounting documents, and so on. Thus, most analysis refers to the step of determining information requirements as analyzing the present system.

The extent to which the existing system should be studied in a redesign effort of a new system has long been the subject of debate. One school of thought maintains that detailed analysis of the existing system should be a preliminary step to determining information requirements and that as much information as possible should be gathered and analyzed concerning the in-place system. This approach is justified on four grounds:

1. A minor modification in the existing system may satisfy the information requirements without a major redesign effort.
2. A look at the existing system is required to determine the specific areas that need improvement.
3. Because most systems utilize some common sources of input, a study of existing systems is necessary to determine these.
4. A study of existing systems is necessary to determine the data volume and costs associated with new designs.

The second theory of systems design, sometimes called the "fresh approach" or the "logical approach," holds that detail analysis of the existing system is not necessary because the new system will be substantially changed and should not be predicated on the restraints of the existing one. Moreover, too close an identification with existing systems may compromise objectivity in the construction of logical methods to satisfy the information needs required to meet the systems objectives.

The choice of one or a combination of these approaches by the manager or designer is probably a matter of the state-of-the-art of information systems in the company under study, the objectives and existing information sources of the subsystem being designed, and the preferences of the actual manager. Sooner or later during design, some examination of existing company files as well as of external sources will become necessary, if only to determine the source to satisfy a portion of the new information needs or to integrate the subsystem under study with the total system for the organization.

Analysis and Integration

During this step in systems design, the determination of information sources, the form of the new system begins to take shape. We must not only uncover information sources for the particular subsystem under consideration but also take into account how they fit into the overall integrative sources of information and techniques of analysis.

Sources of information may be categorized as follows:

1. *Internal and external records.* Internal records most often take the form of written materials and could include examples of inputs or outputs, file records, memoranda and letters, reports containing information about the existing system, and documentation of existing or planned systems. External data may come from a variety of sources such as trade publications, government statistics, and the like.
2. *Interviewing* managers and operating personnel is a valuable method of identifying possible sources of information and of analyzing the existing system. This form of data gathering can be the most fruitful method of securing information, provided that it is conducted properly. Unlike the reading of written records, the gathering of

BEFORE ANALYSIS — Input / Output Chart

Input \ Output	Paychecks	Payroll file	Payroll summary	FICA report	FICA tax	Fed. report	Fed. tax	Union relations	Gov't audit	Legal	Overtime management	Credit Union	Absentee management
Time card													
Name	•	•		•		•			•	•	•	•	•
Start time	•							•	•	•	•		•
Stop time	•							•	•	•	•		•
Hours worked	•		•					•	•	•			
Overtime	•		•					•	•	•	•		•
Payroll file													
Name	•			•		•							
Exemptions	•												
Wage rate	•							•					
Wages paid	•	•	•	•	•	•	•		•	•		•	
FICA paid	•	•	•	•	•				•	•			
Fed. tax	•	•	•			•	•		•	•			
Badge door control													
Name	•							•			•		•
Time in	•							•			•		•
Time out	•							•			•		•
Fed. tax tables	•												
Mgr. report													
Name	•							•			•		•
Vacation								•					•
Illness								•					•
Overtime	•							•			•		•

AFTER ANALYSIS — Input / Output Chart

Input \ Output	Paychecks	Payroll file	Payroll summary	FICA report	FICA tax	Fed. report	Fed. tax	Union relations	Gov't audit	Legal	Overtime management	Credit Union	Absentee management
Name	•	•		•		•		•	•	•	•	•	•
Start time	•		•					•	•	•	•		•
Stop time	•		•					•	•	•	•		•
Exemptions	•												
Wage rate	•							•					
Wages paid	•	•	•	•	•	•	•		•	•		•	
FICA paid	•	•	•	•	•				•	•			
Fed. tax	•	•	•			•	•		•	•			
Fed. tax tables	•												
Vacation								•					•
Illness								•					•

FIGURE 7-3 Input / Output Chart (Payroll System)

facts from an interview involves human communication problems; these can be largely overcome by proper planning and by gaining the confidence of persons interviewed.

3. *Sampling and estimating* methods may become necessary when the accumulation of data is so large that only a portion of it can be examined. The major advantages of sampling techniques lie in the saving of time and cost, particularly on nonrecurring events where data are not available. One frequently used form of sampling is *work sampling*, which can be used to analyze the actions of people, machines, or events in terms of time. Estimating is an acceptable method of analysis and is a timesaver; however, estimates should be checked to control totals or be verified by interview where possible.

A number of *techniques of analysis* and synthesis have been published and are in widespread use. For our purposes in discovering information sources, two of these are of particular interest: input/output analysis and multidimensional flows. These two techniques permit us to summarize the available sources of information input so that we can avoid duplication by integrating them.

Input/output analysis is demonstrated in Figure 7-3 with the input/output chart, a visual portrayal of information inputs to a system and the information output that results. With a listing of inputs along the left side and outputs across the top, the relationship can be established by the dot at the point of intersection.

Figure 7-3 also demonstrates how data can be reduced and subsystems integrated through proper design. The top half, or "before analysis" portion, reveals that several items of output appear also as input, indicating rehandling and reprocessing of the same information to produce an output. The bottom half of the figure illustrates how consolidation and integration can reduce the number

Activity	Customer file	Vendor file	Personnel information	Accounts receivable	Accounts payable
Define customer need	X				
Design and document product		X	X		X
Manufacturing		X	X		X
Marketing	X		X	X	
Distribute products	X				

FIGURE 7-4 Multiple Uses of Information

of information sources (i.e., input items). Figure 7-4 demonstrates the multiple uses of information sources and how information requirements may be identified and combined in a systems design that can serve more than one user. Files of input can be utilized by various organizational elements and various information subsystems.

Multidimensional flow is an additional technique of organizing information sources or depicting the existing design of a subsystem. A flowchart can be constructed to trace the routing or flow of information from origin to destination and to arrange this flow in a chronological sequence that shows the progression of information through the organization. Although they are not specifically required for identification of information sources, the factors of frequency, volume, time, cost, and physical distance can also be shown on such a chart.

Information Sources — Summary

Now that information sources have been identified with information needs, the next design step is to prepare a list that matches needs and sources. Such a list is evaluated and reevaluated until a final valid list of information sources is generated to match against previously determined information needs. This matching can take the form of a matrix diagram, a valuable device for the integration of subsystems as well as for use in the remainder of the systems design process. Figure 7-5 illustrates how such a matching process might be useful for the economic order quantity subsystem of the inventory management system.

	Accounting	Production	Purchasing	etc.
Ordering Costs	X			
Carrying Costs	X			
Requirements		X		
Consumption Time		X		
Usage Rate		X		
Lead Time			X	
etc.				

FIGURE 7-5 Information Needs / Information Sources Matrix

Information sources can be further illustrated by giving examples of our selected subsystems:

Subsystem		Information Sources
Inventory	need	Items falling below minimum inventory level
	source	Stock-level determination subsystem compares current balance against minimum inventory level
Accounts payable	need	Code invoices "days to due date"
	source	Coded upon entry into accounts payable subsystem
Purchasing	need	Performance of individual buyers
	source	Purchasing system compares outgoing purchase prices with predetermined standards
Production control	need	Cost variances over or under 5 percent
	source	Integration of costing with manufacturing applications: shop control, stores requisitioning, labor distribution, etc.
Project control	need	Progress against plan for events in critical path
	source	Project control subsystem

DEVELOP ALTERNATIVE CONCEPTUAL DESIGNS AND SELECT ONE

The development of a *concept* of a system is a creative process that involves synthesizing knowledge into some particular pattern. In our case, the concept of an MIS would consist of the major decision points, patterns of information flow, channels of information, and roles of managers and competitors. The concept must also include the relationship of the MIS to all functional operating systems, both existing and planned. The concept is a sketch of the structure or skeleton of the MIS, guiding and restricting the form of the detailed design. If conceptual design is the skeleton, then detailed design is the flesh.

Let us present two very simplified examples of alternative conceptual designs. For the first example, consider a company that wishes to introduce a new compact car. Two teams of engineers are put to work to conceive a design. One concept produced is a sketch showing a three-wheeled vehicle of a specified maximum length, weight, and horsepower, with the engine in the rear. The other team produces a sketch and description of a four-wheeled vehicle with front-engine drive and a specified minimum length, maximum weight, and horsepower limits.

In the second example, a company has 20 warehouses scattered about the United States to provide rapid shipment to customers. Headquarters and production facilities are at a single location. An MIS is needed to regulate production and inventories because of constant crises that have arisen with respect to deliveries. Two teams are asked to develop an MIS. The first team proposes that all orders from customers be sent directly to marketing at company headquarters. Marketing management will then provide demand forecasts to the factory and shipping instructions to the warehouses. A computer at company headquarters will maintain a perpetual inventory of all products in all warehouses. The second team proposes an MIS whereby orders are transmitted by the customers directly to the nearest warehouse. Each warehouse maintains its own inventory records; each forecasts its demand for the month ahead and transmits it to the factory.

It is obvious that each alternative concept of a system has advantages and disadvantages. Sometimes one concept will dominate all others by every major criterion. More often, a cursory evaluation will indicate that several concepts are not feasible or have little to recommend them. When there are several good contenders, careful evaluation of each is required. The bases for evaluation that appear to be most practical are

1. Compare anticipated performance of the conceptual design with the objectives of the system as previously developed.
2. Prepare a rough or preliminary cost-effectiveness analysis of the system. This forces some *quantified* comparisons among systems.
3. Examine the flowcharts and identify strong and weak points of each conceptual design. Examine the quality of the databases and information to be made available. Study the number of operations, dispersion and duplication of files, and potential breakdown points.
4. Expand the conceptual designs in more detail if none of these provides a preferred design.

DOCUMENT THE SYSTEM CONCEPT

At this point, sufficient information has been accumulated to begin a more detailed description of the system concept. This description includes essentially a flowchart or other documentation of the flow of information through the system, the inputs and outputs, and a narrative description of the operations.

Here we are describing the *manager's* participation in the system design and not the detailed specifications and documentation included in subsequent expansion by the designer. The manager's involvement in the design process is analogous to the homeowner's participation in the architect's planning, where the basic design and many of the details are shaped by the wishes and needs of the person buying the house. So it is with a computer-based information system. The manager should be involved to the extent that the system provides the information required; the designer is concerned with the nature of the materials and equipment as well as with technical processing considerations. Details to be worked out later by the designer will include explicit instructions as to *what data* are to be captured and *when*, the *files* that are to be used, the details of how *processing* is to be done, what *outputs* will be generated by the system, and how the outputs and files are to be *distributed*.

The scope of management design effort in documenting the system concept can be appreciated by recalling the previous discussion of a "black box" concept of a system. The system elements include inputs, outputs, master files, and rules for processing the data through the "black box." The processor element remains essentially "black" to the manager-user except for the decision rules that have been designed. The rules (programs) for processing the data include (1) processing of input data against the file data and producing an output, (2) processing input data for file update, (3) processing input data into outputs without reference to the file, and (4) producing an output from the file without having processed an input. Generally speaking, the system concept is not too concerned with the interior of the "black box" or the file construction. It is concerned very much with a definition of the job to be done, without specifying the detailed methods of implementation. To say it another way, the concept defines the problem without much regard to the solution of processing the information through the "black box." These processing details and some input/output specifications may be left for the implementation stage.

Major topics for managerial concern are discussed next. Once again, the design process is iterative.

General System Flow

The general system flowchart is a common method of indicating the general structure of a computer-based information system. Shown in such a chart is the description of the data processing logic in general terms. The system flow also reflects the design efforts that have gone on before this step: setting objectives, establishing constraints, and determining information needs and sources.

The system flow, as illustrated by a flowchart, is quite general in nature and indicates only the main components of the system. At this stage in the design, the chart does not indicate what processing occurs at particular steps in the flow or what specific data, equipment, or people are involved. However, the chart is extremely important because it provides the foundation upon which a great many detailed specifications will follow.

Notice some important characteristics of the conceptual design flowchart:

1. System *objectives* are achieved and are reflected in the flow diagram (e.g., optimize inventory costs through the design of decision rules containing optimum reorder points, safety stock levels, and reorder quantities).
2. Information needs and information sources are designed into the system.
3. Decision rules and decision points are shown.
4. Inputs and outputs are designated.
5. Most important—*subsystems are integrated*.

System Inputs

From the user's point of view, the inputs were structured when information sources were determined. However, there remains the task of design of input format. Because inputs frequently have to be accepted in the form in which they are received from outside the firm (e.g., sales orders, shipping documents, receiving papers, personnel information), input design becomes a matter of converting these to machine-usable form. Where inputs are from other subsystems within the firm, the problem becomes one of integrating these systems through common data elements and other means.

More detailed input data specification includes the sources of data—that is, where they come from, what form they are in, and who is responsible for their production. Some inputs may be machine readable and some may have to be converted. Because *forms* are so often used in collecting inputs and for other aids in operating a system, they are indispensable in modern business, and forms design is a primary concern of the systems designer.

Although managers are not concerned in detail with these input specifications, they should be aware that the designer must specify the source of each input, its frequency, volume, and timing plus its disposition after processing is completed. Because input must be checked for validity and volume, the editing procedures for accomplishing this are also required. Another important consideration is the specification of how inputs are to be converted into machine-readable form. These and other details of input design are usually contained on forms designed for that purpose.

System Outputs

From the technical standpoint, the output data definition includes the specification of destination (i.e., where they go, what form they take, and who is responsible for receiving them). Included in the specifications are the distribution of output (who gets what, how many copies, and by what means), the frequency with which output will be called for and its timing, and the form the output will take (tape, hard copy, data terminal, etc.). Questions that the designer will ask in the process of developing output specifications include

1. What form are the output reports to take? Can it be off line?
2. Should the information be detailed or summarized?
3. What can I do with the output data that will be reused?
4. What kind of output form will be required? How many copies?
5. Are reports generated on demand? By exception? On schedule?

Despite the need to answer these details of output specification, the manager is concerned primarily with getting his or her information needs as previously determined in some type of output format. In other words, the consideration is how to *present the information to the eye or the ear of the manager*, and the answer lies in the content and form design of the output document. The form design is a direct function of information needs and should be constructed to fill those needs in a timely fashion. Care should be taken not to ask for *too much* information *too frequently*. "Management by exception" and "information by summary" should be the guiding principles.

DAILY RAW MATERIALS EXPEDITE REPORT

Item Number	Description	Unit	EOQ	ROP	Bal	On Order	Del.	Received	Action
zz	Gasket Material	yd	900	400	327	900	6/6		Expedite with vendor
f73	Spring	doz	60	10	12	60	7/3	42	Check receipt

SHOP VARIANCE REPORT

No.	Lot	Description	Unit	Run	Start	Due Compl.	Shop		Variance $\pm$ 5%
3B2	R44	Alum. Tube	each	2	6/13	6/19	Weld		Cost variance + 7.2%
zzx4	R44	Alum. Tube	each	3	6/13	6/26	Bend		Time over 7 days

BUYER NEGOTIATIONS VARIANCE REPORT

Material	Unit	Part No.	Vendor	Standard Cost	Actual Cost	Variance	
Steel Pl.	Lb.	274345X	Bay Metals	.32	.35	.03	9.4% +
Dr. Shaft	ea.	B33–165	Zimmer	9.55	8.72	.83	8.7% **

FIGURE 7-6 Selected Outputs for Three Subsystems: Inventory Management, Production Control, Purchasing

Three illustrative subsystems that we have been using for design in this chapter are inventory management, production control, and purchasing. Figure 7-6 shows examples of outputs that might be designed to provide managerial information needs determined earlier in the design process for these subsystems.

Other Documentation

Other frequently used means of describing or documenting the system concept are the activity sheet and the system narrative. Figure 7-7 is a system description for our illustrative inventory management system and is designed to provide information on volumes, time relationships, and specific functions or requirements.

The system narrative is another way to document and describe a system. The justification for such an approach is based on the caution of the systems designer: "If you haven't written it out, you haven't thought it out." The following excerpt from our inventory management system narrative indicates the

---

ACTIVITY: Inventory Control

	Key	Name	Volume
Stock Level Subsystem		Inputs	
Freq: As received	1600	Receipts	100/day
Inputs: 1600, 1610, 1620	1610	Issues	1000/day
	1620	Misc. Transact.	100/day
Reorder Point Subsystem		Outputs	
Freq: Daily	2600	Stock Status	400/day
Inputs: 3610, 3640	2610	Purchase Orders	25/day
	2620	Expedite Report	1000 lines/day
Reporting	2630	Exceptions	200 items/day
	2640	Stock Status	5000 lines/week
Daily		Files	
Inputs: 3610	3600	EOQ & ROP File	5000 records
	3610	Master Stock	5000 records
	3620	Receiving File	5000 records
	3630	Vendor File	100 records

Note: Purchase orders for commodity class 7Q4 must be in carload lots.

FIGURE 7-7   System Description — Activity Sheet for Inventory Control Subsystem (Materials Control)

kind and level of system description that should be available at the end of detailing the system concept.

Inventory Management of Raw Materials

This system is concerned with inventory control of raw materials for manufacturing. There are four plants, each with its own computer and each utilizing the same inventory control system. Raw materials move from receiving to storekeeping and thence to manufacturing as required by the production planning and control system. There are three major groups of operations within the system: *stock level subsystem*, based on transactions; *reorder point subsystem*, including purchase order preparation; and *economic order quantity subsystem*.

Stock Level

1. As material arrives at receiving, the receiving report is marked to show quantity and quality acceptance. The receiving report is then matched against the receiving order file (prepunched card) and actual quantity received, date received, and quantity acceptance are keypunched. The receiving order card is then transmitted to the computer center for updating the inventory file.
2. As the storekeeper issues items from stores, a prepunched card is...

Once the conceptual design has been documented, the responsible manager or task force leader should prepare a report for the top managers who must authorize further development of the system.

PREPARE THE CONCEPTUAL DESIGN REPORT

The conceptual design report is, in a sense, a proposal for the expenditure of funds and for organizational changes. Because it is directed to management, it should have a concise summary of the problems that necessitate the system, the objectives, the general nature of the system, reasons why the concept was selected over others, and the time and resources required to design and implement the system. Along with this summary, possibly in a separate volume or volumes, the documentation should be provided. In essence, the proposal shows performance specifications of the system. Performance specifications describe the functions that must be performed by the system and the means by which each function is measured.

SUMMARY

The conceptual design represents the structure of the MIS. It specifies the performance requirements for those who will develop the detailed design. Because it sets the broad outlines of the MIS, the managers who will make use of the MIS must have a large role in the development and evaluation of alternative concepts.

Management must identify basic business problems and objectives of the MIS. System constraints may be of an environmental, basic business, or technical nature. Management is responsible primarily for specifying the first two. The needs of management for information are a function of the problems to be solved and of individual managerial style. Thus, only the managers can factor these into the conceptual design. Sources of information, on the other hand, are often best determined by the technical specialists.

The conceptual design is ultimately described by formal documents such as flowcharts, input/output matrices, data bank requirements, hardware and software requirements, organizational changes, and time and cost refinements of the project program proposed.

PROBLEMS AND QUESTIONS

1. Work Case 4, Johnson Enterprises (E).
2. Referring to Table 7-A, page 260, indicate by marking (x) in the appropriate answer, the gross design consideration for the indicated MIS. Assume that you are redesigning all systems for the Northwestern Insurance Company (Case 2).
3. Why is the term *feasibility design* often used to designate conceptual design? Which term do you think is more appropriate? Why?
4. Should detailed design work ever overlap the development of the conceptual design? What problems might arise? What advantages might there be?
5. Develop in detail a possible "scenario" between the systems designer and a manager of marketing at the stage of development of alternative concepts for a marketing management information system.
6. Develop a list of criteria for comparing alternative conceptual designs.
7. When the engineering department in a certain large company wishes to order materials or components for the development of a prototype model, it sends a materials request form to the purchasing department. The purchasing department selects one of several vendors that most closely meet the specs and prepares a purchase order. The purchase order must be signed by engineering management and, depending upon the amount, by the finance department or even the general manager.

    The vendor encloses a packing slip with delivery of the items, and the company's receiving department sends a receiving report to both engineering and accounting. The vendor also sends a separate invoice to the accounting department to bill the company. The company checks the invoice, the packing slip, the receiving report, and the purchase order. If they all agree, the bill is paid; otherwise an investigation is initiated. Problems arise when partial shipments are made.

    The new senior systems designer is appalled at such a cumbersome system and has told management that he can devise at least three superior conceptual designs.
8. Cooper Textile Mills has its home plant in Wycombe, Pa.; a second manufacturing plant in Puerto Rico; a dyeing plant in New Jersey; a manufacturing plant in France; and its primary sales office in New York. Cooper Mills' major product is power nets, the basic material in women's foundation garments. It is one of the most difficult

TABLE 7-A Conceptual Design Consideration

	Basic MIS		
	Policyholder	*Service*	*Personnel*
System Objective	( ) Improve accuracy of records ( ) Provide inquiry turn-around time of 24 hours	( ) Provide simulation model that can forecast service requirements ( ) Reduce reporting time of service report	( ) Identify turnover variance within 7 days ( ) Reduce personnel turnover
Constraint	( ) File storage capacity ( ) Comply with state insurance requirement	( ) End-of-month report due by fifth of next month ( ) Improve the accuracy of the report	( ) Quality of work ( ) Hourly employees must be separate from supervisory employees
Information Need	( ) Policyholder social security number for data file entry ( ) Information for reporting purposes	( ) Objective / standard for work quantity ( ) Number of policyholders by area	( ) Pay rates ( ) Available hours for each service unit per period
Information Source	( ) Accounting records ( ) Policy application	( ) Weekly service report ( ) Policy file	( ) Personnel system labor budget ( ) Design new form
Input	( ) Keypunch of manual application ( ) Special form	( ) Mark sense or MICR ( ) Simulation model	( ) Termination notices ( ) Monthly personnel report
Output	( ) Policy printout ( ) Data bank inquiry capability	( ) Report of performance against standard ( ) Forecast of service requirements	( ) Actual turnover rate compared with standard by office, service unit, salary grade, position code ( ) Monthly personnel report
Other Characteristics	( ) Real-time inquiry ( ) Microfilm storage ( ) Hardcopy printout	( ) Provide "what if" capability in inquiry ( ) Tape storage ( ) Monthly report of variance	( ) Real-time inquiry ( ) Direct access storage ( ) Hardcopy printout

materials to produce on a continuously high-quality basis. According to President Gilbert Cooper (in *Textile World*), "We need the raw materials on hand to be able to react to a sudden switch-over in customer style preference — from nylon to rayon, for example. At the same time, some of our raw materials are so expensive — up to $6 a pound — that tying up capital in a glut of stock could ruin us financially." Without knowledge of market trends, panic pricing may result in heavy losses. Trends in style could be noted early, if prompt reports of sales could be obtained and analyzed.

Could several good conceptual designs for a management information system be developed?

9. According to Walter E. Trabbold, controller of the Bank of Delaware, "We have defined it [development of management information systems] in terms of six subsystems." These are

    a. Development of a central (customer information) file
    b. Computerization of all operations: demand deposits, savings, commercial loans, mortgage loans, investments, and clubs
    c. Integrated accounting subsystem to meet reporting requirements of management, stockholders, and regulatory agencies; this includes general ledger, cost, budgeting, and statistical information
    d. A reporting subsystem in two parts: standard reports and exception reports
    e. An on-line inquiry subsystem to provide management with current operating and marketing information
    f. A sophisticated model of the entire business system

For a bank considering installation of a total management information system, draw a block diagram of the conceptual design to represent the subsystems listed and their relationships.

10. Discuss the following interview; reconstruct it in the form in which you feel it should have gone. Then assign two students to play the roles first as given and then as they would in real life if the systems designer were properly trained.

The Interview

S: *Systems designer or analyst*

M: *Accounting manager being interviewed*

S: Good morning, Ms. Millsop. I'm from the MIS section. My manager notified you that I was coming some time this week, and I found some free time this morning.

M: Yes, I agreed with Mr. Lusk, the corporate systems manager, and your manager, that I would meet with one of the systems people.

S: Right! Well, I'm the one. We've noticed that you have an awful lot of staff and clerical people in your department and we want to replace a lot of them with the computer.

M: What's that? Take away some of my highly trained people? My people are already overworked and forced to go on overtime every quarterly report period. We have about 11 supervisors with only 1 or 2 people reporting to them to handle a tremendous volume of paperwork in distinctly different accounting functional areas. If we don't get the financial reports out on time, the roof falls in.

S: You don't understand! Let me explain it to you. Let's look at this flowchart. (He unrolls a $5' \times 2'$ chart showing in great detail all aspects of a computerized MIS.) We're going to set up a master file of all customer accounts, all employee wage and salary accounts, all shipments, and all inventory on these five tapes. We'll do an updating of each file based on new data you and other departments supply before we use each of these files to accumulate costs and prepare invoices. We will sort and merge these accounts; then we'll use this canned program to (pulls out a 20-page computer program)...

M: (Fidgeting and looking at her watch) I can see that you have put a lot of thought into this, but you know that our department's output is the most important within the company. We must prepare all financial reports very carefully and provide accurate control data for customer accounts and internal expenses.

S: Not to worry! Our computer is much more accurate and faster than your people can ever be. The only unfortunate thing is that we will still have to depend on some of your staff people for input to the computer. They'll have to improve a lot, though, to keep up with the accuracy and speed of this new MIS.

M: Wait a minute! My section was cited last year by our president as the most efficient and courteous service group in the company. Do you see that plaque on the wall behind me?

S: (Lighting a cigar, puffing furiously, and leaning forward to point to his chart) Well, let's get back to the computer. I've already put in my recommendations and a cost reduction award application...

M: You've already made your recommendations before discussing them with me? (Turns red) Why are we bothering to meet? If you'll excuse me, I must leave now to meet with Mr. Lusk. I'll take this up...

S: (Interrupting) Just a minute—I have some more questions to ask. We need more data about your account classifications, transactions, update methods, and frequency and type of reports...

M: (Presses hidden button under top of desk. Secretary rushes in and tells her she's late for a meeting.) I'm sorry, Mr.—what's your name? My secretary will help you in any way he can. (To secretary) Will you show Mr.—ah, er, out?

SELECTED REFERENCES

BARIFF, M. L., AND E. J. LUSK. "Cognitive and Personality Tests for the Design of Management Information Systems." *Management Science*, April 1977.

Business Systems Planning (GE-20-0527-2). White Plains, N.Y.: IBM, 1978.

CHASE, WILTON P. *Management of Systems Engineering.* New York: John Wiley, 1974.

Communications Oriented Production Information and Control System, Vols. I–VIII. White Plains, N.Y.: IBM, 1972.

DEBRABANDER, BERT, AND ANDERS EDSTROM. "Successful Information Systems Development." *Management Science*, October 1977.

GILMORE, ROBERT W. *Business Systems Handbook.* Englewood Cliffs, N.J.: Prentice-Hall, 1979.

ISAACS, P. BRIAN. "Warnier-Orr Diagrams in Applying Structured Concepts." *Journal of Systems Management*, October 1982.

MEISTER, DAVID. *Behavioral Foundations of System Development.* New York: John Wiley, 1976.

MUNRO, MALCOLM C. "Determining the Manager's Information Needs." *Journal of Systems Management*, June 1978.

MURDICK, ROBERT G. "MIS Development Procedures." *Journal of Systems Management*, December 1970.

————. *MIS: Concepts and Design.* Englewood Cliffs, N.J.: Prentice-Hall, 1980.

ORR, KENNETH T. "System Methodologies for the 80's." *Infosystems*, June 1981.

SRINIVASSAN, C. A., AND H. M. SCHOENFELD. "Some Problems and Prospects in Design and Development of Corporate-Wide Information Systems." *Management International Review*, February 1978.

WILKINSON, JOSEPH W. "Specifying Management's Information Needs." *Cost and Management*, September–October 1974.

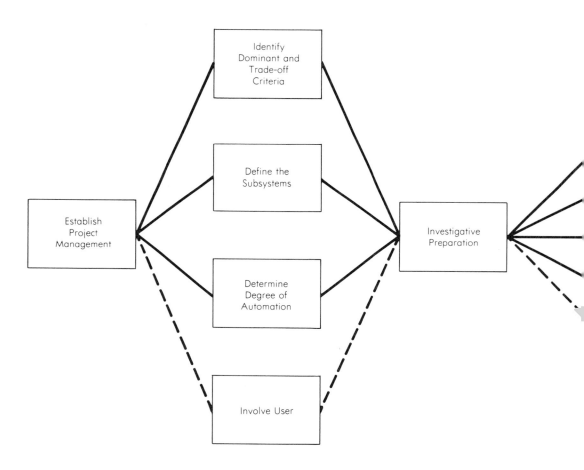

Detailed System Design

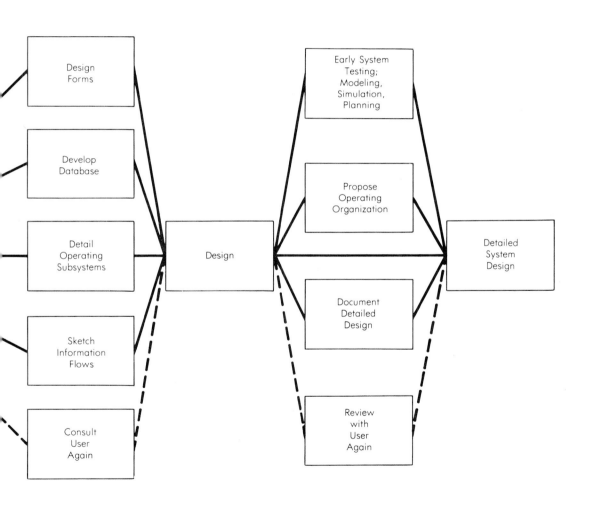

Design Forms

Develop Database

Detail Operating Subsystems

Sketch Information Flows

Consult User Again

Design

Early System Testing; Modeling, Simulation, Planning

Propose Operating Organization

Document Detailed Design

Review with User Again

Detailed System Design

Once the scope and general configuration of the MIS have been established, the detailed design of the system may be started. A step-by-step explanation of a how-to-do-it procedure for detailed system design applicable to all systems is impractical, for the following reasons:

1. There is a wide variety of approaches to system design in terms of organizing for it, conducting it, and defining its output.
2. A basic question rarely treated by writers deals with the state of the art and to what extent it should be incorporated into systems design. In other words, should we describe management information systems design as it *is* today, as it *could be* if the latest state of the art knowledge were utilized, or as it probably *will be* in five years?
3. Systems design is a complex of concurrent activities, whereas the nature of our description can proceed along only one line at a time.
4. It is difficult to describe a process of rational design that must be tested in an organization from time to time to determine the likelihood of its being accepted by the members of the organization. That is, the design of a management information system is both a rational and a social process.
5. If it is to represent the design of information systems in general, the explanation may be at such a level of generality that it gives no clues to the multitude of detailed steps involved. On the other hand, the explanation of a detailed procedure can describe only one among thousands and gives no clue to the general nature of design. Attempting to find a middle course sacrifices the advantage of one extreme without gaining much from the other.
6. An explanation of detailed system design procedure must be interrupted frequently by descriptive essays on some aspect with which the designer deals.

Within the limitations on clarity and objectives imposed by these considerations, we will attempt to present the nature of systems design at the "edge of the art." The edge of the art is broad, with part in the present and part in the near future. A general approach will provide the framework, but frequent resort to detailed procedures and descriptions will bring substance to the framework.

266

INFORM AND INVOLVE
THE ORGANIZATION

The first step in systems design is not a technical one. It is concerned with gaining support for the work that follows. Systems designers must have the support of most members of the organization to obtain information for the design of the system and to obtain acceptance of the final system. At a minimum, members of the organization should be informed of the objectives and nature of the study. It is preferable, if possible, to draw many members into the study, at least in some small way. Furthermore, it is desirable to reassure the employees, if possible, that changes will benefit them or that they will not suffer financially from the implementation of the system. Even so, the natural human resistance to change requires that sufficient information on general progress be disseminated to gradually accustom the employees to their future roles.

The contrary approach—that employees should not be disturbed during the system design—can be quite hazardous. When people are not informed, they seize upon bits of information, construct concepts that may be completely erroneous, and as a consequence often take up detrimental activities. The final system, when announced, may be met with shock, resentment, and both open and covert resistance.

AIM OF DETAILED DESIGN

The detailed design of an MIS is closely related to the design of operating systems. Sometimes, it is true, the operating system must be accepted without change and a new MIS appended to it. However, it is preferable to design both systems together, and as we discuss the detailed design of the MIS, this parallel effort will be apparent, even though our principal focus is on the MIS.

By drawing upon the analogy of engineering design, we can clarify the meaning of detailed design. The direct goal of engineering design is to furnish the engineering description of a tested and producible product. Engineering design consists of specifications in the form of drawings and specification reports for systems as a whole and for all components in the system. Further, justification documents in the form of reports of mathematical analysis and test results are part of the detailed design. Enough detail must be given so that engineering design documents and manufacturing drawings are sufficient for the shop to construct the product. The production of operating and maintenance instructions is also considered part of the design output.

The analogy of detailed design of MIS readily follows. The aim of the detailed design is to furnish a description of a system that achieves the goals of the conceptual system design requirements. This description consists of drawings, flowcharts, equipment and personnel specifications, procedures, support tasks, specification of information files, and organization and operating manuals required to run the system. Also part of the design is the documentation of analysis and testing, which justifies the design. The design must be sufficiently detailed that operating management and personnel can implement the system. Whereas conceptual design gives the overall *performance* specifications for the MIS, the detailed design yields the *construction* and *operating* specifications.

PROJECT MANAGEMENT OF MIS DETAILED DESIGN

Any effort that qualifies as a system design has the dimensions of a project. The first step in the detailed design is therefore a planning and organizing step. For small projects, all phases may be planned for, as described in Chapter 6, *before* the conceptual (feasibility) design is undertaken. Often, in large projects, not enough is known about the prospective system in advance of the conceptual design to plan for the detailed design project. Further, if the conceptual design indicated that a new system design is not appropriate at this time, any project planning for the detailed design in advance would be wasted.

Once the project manager and key project personnel have been designated, the steps in project management fall into two classes: *planning* and *control*. The amount of effort expended in each step is obviously a function of the size of the MIS project and the cost of developing the detailed design of the project. The key steps in planning and control of detailed design, based upon Chapter 6, are recapitulated here.

Project Planning

1. Establish the project objectives. This involves a review, subdivision, and refinement of the performance objectives established by the conceptual design.
2. Define the project tasks. This identifies a hierarchical structure of tasks to be performed in the design of the MIS and may be documented by work package instructions for large projects.
3. Plan the logical development of sequential and concurrent tasks and task activities. This usually requires a network diagram of events and activities.
4. Schedule the work as required by management—established end date and activity network constraints. Essentially, the work and schedule are tied together by completion of the PERT diagram.
5. Estimate labor, equipment, and other costs for the project.
6. Establish a budget for the project by allocating funds to each task and expenditures month by month over the life of the project.
7. Plan the staffing of the project organization over its life.

Project Control

1. Determine whether project objectives are being met as the project progresses.
2. Maintain control over the schedule by changing work loads and emphasis as required by delays in critical activities.

3. Evaluate expenditure of funds in terms of both work accomplished and time. Revise the budget as required to reflect changes in work definition.
4. Evaluate work force utilization and individual work progress, and make adjustments as required.
5. Evaluate time, cost, and work performance in terms of schedules, budgets, and technical plans to identify interaction problems.

IDENTIFY DOMINANT AND TRADE-OFF CRITERIA

Dominant criteria for a system are those that make an activity so important that it overrides all other activities. For example, a dominant criterion might be that the system operate so that there is never a stockout. This overrides the criterion of minimizing inventory cost. Such a criterion might hold for a company selling human blood, life-preserving drugs, or electric power. It might even hold for a company selling a consumer product where loss of a customer is permanent and all competitors have a no-stockout policy.

Examples of other dominant criteria might be one-day customer service, zero-defect product, specified price range for products, maintenance of multiple sources of supply for all materials and components purchased, or conformity of all research and engineering to long-range corporate plans. It is obvious that identification of the dominant criteria is necessary before subsequent design steps can proceed.

Trade-off criteria are those in which the criterion for performance of an activity may be reduced to increase performance of another activity. For example, the criterion of low manufacturing costs might be balanced against that of long-range public image of the firm achieved by reduction in environmental pollution. Again, the criterion of producing styles or models for many segments of the market might be balanced against that of maintaining low manufacturing and service costs.

The reason for identifying dominant and trade-off criteria is that as the detailed design is developed, decision centers (managers or computers) must be identified to achieve such criteria or make trade-offs. The MIS must be designed to provide the information for the decisions, or at lower and programmed levels, to make the trade-offs.

DEFINE THE SUBSYSTEMS

We start the process of defining the subsystems with two principal blocks of information: (1) the conceptual design and (2) the dominant and trade-off performance criteria. Although the conceptual design requires some assumptions concerning the subsystems, it is necessary now to review these subsystems and to

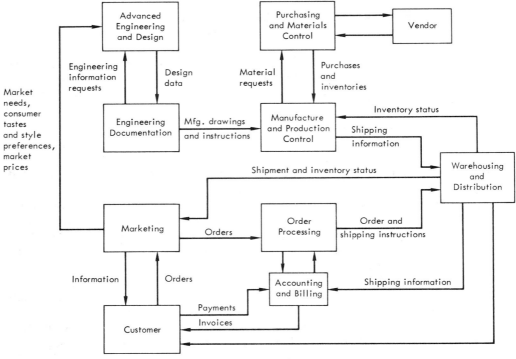

FIGURE 8-1 Conceptual System Design for a Business System

redefine them if it seems appropriate. Based upon the conceptual design, investigation of the detailed activities of each major activity block must be undertaken. Consider, for example, the conceptual design representation of a business system given in Figure 8-1. (It should be emphasized that this is a greatly simplified representation of the conceptual design. A conceptual design should be fully defined, as described in Chapter 7.) Each large block (or system) must be broken down to determine all activities required and the necessary information inputs and outputs of each activity. Careful analyses of such activities is critical in detailed design. Figure 8-2 shows a typical form, which helps to develop descriptions of each activity.

The quality control activity, one of many in the manufacturing subsystem, might be analyzed as shown in Figure 8-3. The activity processor is made up of equipment and personnel assigned. One form of information output is the revised figure for resources available after commitment to the activity. The operating input is a batch or "lot" of parts, and the output consists of reduced-size batches of a statistically specified quality plus defectives that have been separated out. The information results give the average quality of batches, the number of rejects, and the number of batches inspected per unit of time. The kind of information output captured must be based upon decisions to be made for

ACTIVITY (TRANSACTION)		NETWORK DIAGRAM ACTIVITY NUMBER
PURPOSE AND DESCRIPTION		
INPUTS	MEDIA	
OUTPUTS	MEDIA	
SEQUENCE OF ELEMENTS OF ACTIVITY	PERFORMER	DECISION RULE

FIGURE 8-2 Activity Design Form

planning and control. At this stage, only speculations on needed information for an activity may be made.

The information system must be based upon the operating system. Once this operating system is outlined by the selection of the general concept, certain basic relationships among major activities become more or less fixed. However, there is still considerable freedom in establishing the detailed activities and their

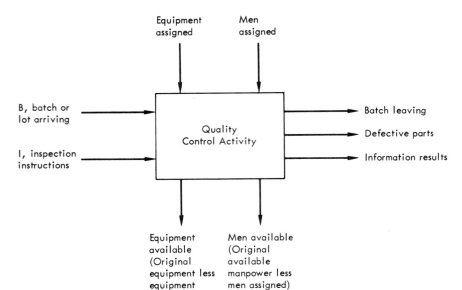

FIGURE 8-3 Model of Activity Operation and Information

relationships. The detailed activities, once defined, may be related in network form, as shown in Figure 8-4.

The degree of breakdown of the major activities, of course, determines the size and complexity of the network. If the activities are broken down too finely, the design will never be completed. If a major activity is broken down too coarsely, vital material, information, and decision needs will not be factored into

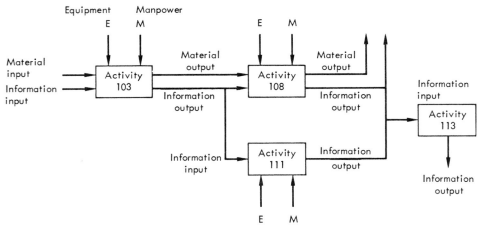

FIGURE 8-4 Interrelating Activities

the design. Furthermore, optional rearrangement or regrouping of activities will not be examined. If we could conceive of a hierarchy of activities such as

System
  Subsystem
    Functional component
      Task
        Subtask
          Operation element

then we would probably want to develop our *activity network* at the "functional component" level. Once activity networks have been developed to include each major activity of the conceptual design, the subsystems are then redefined. A subsystem may consist simply of the activities corresponding to a major block activity of the conceptual design, or some detailed activity blocks may be transferred from one group to another to make up the network of the subsystem. Any changes such as this will require a redefining of the major activity block in terms of its performance requirements. Quite often, however, a major block activity must be considered as comprising several subsystems. Grouping of activities into a subsystem may be based upon various considerations, such as (1) common functions, (2) common techniques or procedures, (3) logical flow relationships, or (4) common inputs or outputs.

The revised subsystems can be identified on the network diagrams by drawing a loop around the aggregate of activities to be included in a particular subsystem. At this point, all connecting lines for activities that cross over the loop represent either inputs or outputs to the subsystems. The loop itself is a boundary of the subsystem and an interface between two or more subsystems. Because organizational authority and responsibility structures are often divided by subsystem boundaries, problems of interfacing subsystems require careful attention; that is, inputs and outputs between interfacing systems must be matched.

The approach that we have given here for identifying subsystems is analogous to one method of development of a new company's organization structure by analysis followed by synthesis. This consists of identifying activities and tasks, grouping tasks into positions, and then grouping positions into components on some rational basis. An alternative approach that is quicker but not so thorough is simply to divide the major activities of the conceptual design into the subsystems apparently required to fulfill the major activities. Such a procedure may lead to incompletely defined subsystems, mismatches between subsystems, and missing activities.

Information for Defining Subsystems

The objective of the design search is to find a set of subsystems that satisfies the performance requirements specified by the conceptual design. To do this, we must search for information that helps us select and define the subsystems. Such information consists of

1. *Dominant and trade-off criteria for the operating and the MIS systems as a whole.* Dominant criteria—such as the decision to utilize only current manufacturing area available, to use company salespersons rather than manufacturer's representatives, to utilize current computing facilities, or to install time-sharing terminals for executive use—impose some clear limitations on alternatives for the designer. Where dominant criteria are absent, trade-offs that permit different emphasis on different functional activities must be identified, so that subsystems can be defined realistically. Analysis may indicate, for instance, that the logistics activities should be separated from both manufacturing and marketing management for greatest effectiveness and efficiency. This will require the study and development of a logistics system closely coupled to the other two systems.

2. *Available resources the company will commit.* Systems must be designed, obviously, in terms of what is available to implement them.

3. *Required activities for achievement of systems operations and performance specifications.* Each activity and its relationship to other activities must be identified.

4. *Necessary control positions in the system.* Every system has a hierarchical structure of control points, usually corresponding to the organizational responsibility structure. However, organizational responsibility for control of variances is often not well defined. The MIS designer must get control positions clarified to develop information flows.

5. *Management decision points for system planning and control.* At the upper levels of the organization, important decisions must be made regarding system operation and variances from major company goals. These top-management positions and their information requirements must be identified.

6. *Information required for programmed decision making.* Complete information requirements for decisions capable of being processed by decision tables and models with the aid of the computer must be uncovered.

7. *Specific output requirements of all systems.* This includes a detailed list of purposes to be served by the information output. The specific content of each report or communication and the method of utilization should be determined. The frequency of reports, their formats (written, visual, audio, etc.), distribution, and filing must be established. This information assists with the development of activity descriptions just discussed. Such information may be recorded on the activity form shown in Figure 8-2.

Obtaining Information

The designer utilizes four principal sources for the design of the MIS. These are

1. Task force meetings
2. Personal interviews
3. Internal and external source documents
4. Personal observation of operations and communications, when feasible

Task Force Meetings

For the design of large systems, the use of task forces for the development of information and ideas is usually advantageous. The task force for a single major activity block should consist of both managers and key specialists. The designer should chair the task force meetings. The designer's function is to draw out ideas and information, synthesize ideas, including his or her own, and present in diagrams and documents the synthesis for evaluation and modification. The task force meetings serve to bring out information gaps, operating needs, and controversial points. In repeated meetings, the design of a subsystem is hammered out.

Interviews

Instead of, or supplemental to, task force meetings, the designer should conduct interviews with key managers at top and intermediate levels, with key specialists, and with a sampling of operating employees. Although it appears obvious, it cannot be emphasized enough that the designer *must use tact in interviews.* Whether interviewing the top manager or the lowest-level employee, the designer's role is that of *a searcher* for knowledge, *not a lecturer* on systems.

In interviews with managers, the designer should seek information on

1. Objectives of the firm or organizational component
2. Major policies in force or needed to accomplish these objectives
3. The categories of information the managers desire
4. Speed of access to the various categories of information desired by managers
5. Intervals of time desired between receipt of various types of information
6. Format desired for information presented
7. Style of decision making of the managers
8. Resources that will be committed for the implementation and operation of the system
9. Degree of manager involvement in classes of decisions: individual decision making, participative decision making, or partially routine (programmed) decision making
10. Organizational relationships that would facilitate system operation and management decision making

Systems designers should not expect too much from managers in the way of defining information needs. Rather, they should work with managers to identify objectives and develop plans. The identification of necessary information will follow from this.

Internal and External Source Documents

The use of internal source documents primarily provides the systems designer with a point of departure. From a practical viewpoint, it is likely that many traditional operations and reports must be retained simply to provide some continuity of operations; and this is appropriate, because the current methods are usually the result of continued minor improvements. Modification or regrouping of activities or data batches is still feasible for the systems designer, however. The number of internal source documents may be great, depending upon the company, so that no complete listing is given here. Organization and policy guides, procedures manuals, master budgets and account structure, and the many functional reports of engineering, manufacturing, marketing, purchasing, and employee and public relations should be examined according to their relevancy to the system being designed. Sometimes, reports such as records of customers' complaints or of service calls may provide the key to system design needs.

External source documents provide economic, marketing, industry, and financial information related to the firm that may be of assistance. A review of the company by a securities analyst in a financial journal may provide very valuable insights.

Direct Observation

Designers should not isolate themselves in their offices to sketch out designs; they should make on-the-spot surveys of operations in action. It would be foolish, for example, to develop a systems design in which supervisors in the factory provide hourly personal reports to a planning/control center if the factory were a half-mile in length or if the planning/control group were in a building some distance away. Similar absurd situations could be conjectured for sales reports or physical distribution reports. On-site inspection will reveal the physical and environmental restraints that may have to be accepted in a new system. Conversely, such inspection may also lead to a major revision of the physical facilities to suit the system design.

Designers should record, as they go along, the relevant (and probably much irrelevant) data they are gathering. In the case of large documents, they would, of course, merely make notes of points vital to their investigation. At the end of certain phases, they should try to organize the data so that future information may be related to that already gathered. Finally, at some point, they sketch alternative designs for the operating subsystems.

SKETCH THE DETAILED
OPERATING SUBSYSTEMS
AND INFORMATION FLOWS

The development of the detailed design is first carried out for the subsystem, functional, and task levels of detail. It is very similar to detailed engineering design, which requires trial and error, shifting operations to find good arrangements, and performing calculations to check out the system. The equivalents of engineering sketches in MIS design are the flowcharts. Chapter 3 shows the graphic symbols and their meanings as used by designers. There are three types of systems flowcharts:

1. *Task-oriented charts*. These are block diagrams showing the relationships among the various tasks or activities. (See Figure 8-5.) Subsequently, the detailed elemental steps required to complete an activity are analyzed and described step by step on an operation analysis form (sometimes called a flow-process chart).

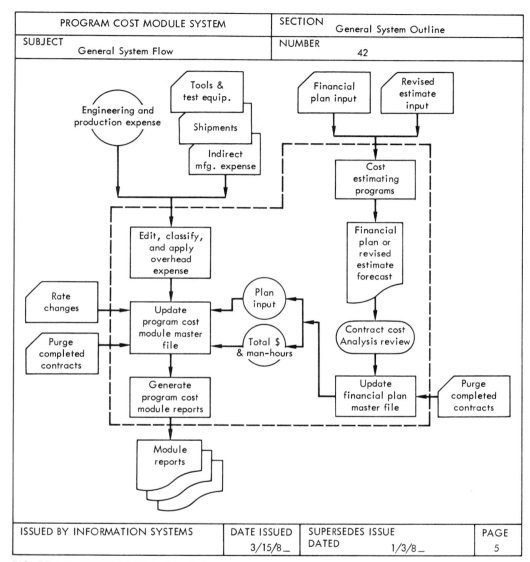

PROGRAM COST MODULE SYSTEM	SECTION General System Outline
SUBJECT General System Flow	NUMBER 42

FIGURE 8-5 Flowchart: Task Oriented

2. *Forms-oriented charts.* These charts identify the forms used in communicating or reporting and trace the flow of all copies through the organization. In some cases, the chronological movement may receive emphasis.

3. *Program flowcharts* (block diagrams). Prepared by the people who give instructions to the computer, the program flowchart is a fundamental tool of programming, designed to show the logical sequence of steps to be carried out by the computer. It structures the logic that the coding of the programs will follow. Program flowcharts will be of interest at a later stage in the design, but we include them here for completeness.

The flowcharts are *not* the complete detailed design. They show primarily flows and relationships. Inputs and outputs are shown only in gross form. The quantitative relations among elements in the systems must be expressed in terms of mathematical models. Where this is not possible, detailed verbal descriptions must be used to actually develop the detailed operating design. The flowcharts are important, however, in developing the information necessary for managerial decisions with respect to the design for model constructions, and for programmed decision making in system operation.

DETERMINE THE DEGREE OF AUTOMATION OF EACH OPERATION

Each operation in the flowchart should next be examined to establish the level of automation possible and the level desired. We can automate most processes to different degrees, depending on management desires:

1. *No automation.* People continue to do the work with at most manual aids. (A mechanic uses a wrench to put a nut on a bolt.)
2. *Work automated, control manual.* Electromechanical devices now *do* the work, but they must be *caused* to do the work by some human intervention. (A tool and die maker sets up a lathe to shave off a thousandth of an inch, then starts the process, and leaves.)
3. *Work automated, feedback automated, control manual.* We have added a feedback loop that gives the operator information but still relies on manual intervention to modify the process. (A badge reader that controls door access opens the door for valid badges and sounds an alarm in the security office for invalid badges.)
4. *Work automated, feedback automated, control automated.* This system requires little or no human intervention after it is installed and started. (Many power management systems—air conditioning, heating, lights, humidity control—are fully automated and "correct" themselves as they operate.)

It is important to remember here that the highest possible degree of automation may not be the best for the firm and task in question. Each aspect of the MIS should be in support of the company's objectives and should mesh with management's desires for the function being automated.

Widely contrasting levels of automation in a system may be suspect and should be examined. It is not at all incorrect, however, to choose an "all manual" (low-level automation) system. Low-level automation may be preferred when

1. Problems are not well structured
2. The decision criteria cannot be well defined
3. The rules for making decisions must be constantly modified or changed
4. There are gaps in the data entering the system
5. The data entering the system are ambiguous, inconsistent, or somewhat unreliable

6. The processing steps are simple and few in number
7. The cost of human labor is low relative to the cost of the equipment
8. Storage of data is negligible

INFORM AND INVOLVE
THE ORGANIZATION AGAIN

Although it is important not to disrupt the company's main business as we build the MIS, this is an ideal time to do some work that increases the acceptance of the MIS being designed. Upper management should be given a brief overview of the design and a status of the design effort as a project. Lower-level management should be shown the system and subsystem flowcharts, requested to comment on their accuracy, and solicited for guidance on the degree of automation desired in each case. Although this may generate lots of argument and conflicting comments and guidance, it is a valuable tool for determining which managers are supportive and which ones are resisting change; it also starts to generate feelings of acceptance and ownership by the mere facts of participation and involvement. And, finally, good ideas and suggestions almost always emerge.

Last, but by no means least important, explain the system in detail to the final users of the system/subsystem. Although this may be a tedious process, acceptance at this level is critical. If this is approached from an "I need your help and guidance" point of view, a flood of detailed suggestions will come out, pitfalls to avoid will be pointed out, and the acceptance and involvement process will have been started.

The activities just discussed will help to avoid the fate of many management information systems: "It's *their* system, *they* designed it; let *them* make it work!"

INPUTS, OUTPUTS,
AND PROCESSING

Armed with the flow diagrams for each subsystem and a substantial amount of constructive criticism from the future users of the MIS, we are now prepared to put more flesh on the design. We turn to defining the subsystem inputs and outputs in more detail and to providing a better description of how each subsystem will perform its task.

Inputs and Outputs: Forms

Each subsystem has requirements for information coming in and produces outgoing information to be used by another subsystem or an end user. These inputs and outputs are often forms, especially when forms are considered in the light of their modern definition: *any standardized communication that is an essential link in an operating procedure is the equivalent of a form*. This covers paper forms such as the IRS 1040 tax form, punched cards such as those used by many large companies for billing, envelopes, mailing labels, microfilm, and computer printouts of sales analysis reports.

Two tasks face us here:

1. Specify the inputs and outputs exactly. Also show where the information can be obtained or to whom it will go.
2. Design forms that fulfill their function *and* are easy to use.

The first of these tasks is fairly straightforward but not so easy to accomplish. Existing systems must be studied in detail, and many people must be interviewed to do a thorough job. Anything less than a thorough analysis of inputs and outputs exposes the system to not being able to get the input or not being able to provide the required output.

The second task, designing useful forms, is difficult. We must first identify

- The function of the form
- When the form is used
- How many copies are used in a single cycle for the transaction, transmission, and storage
- Who fills out the forms and who uses the form
- How many units of the form are required per year

A number of specific factors should be considered in forms design:

1. After all the following factors have been considered, the form should be attractive and easy to read.
2. Most forms should have a title. Examples of those that do not may be checks, labels, tags, and video displays. The title should be specific enough so that the function of the form may be determined, in most cases, without seeing the form.
3. Forms should have an identification number with the date of issuance.
4. Group information into related areas on the form. Use a box design with captions printed in small, distinct type in the upper left-hand corner of the boxes.
5. Arrange the items in that there is a logical flow from left to right and from top to bottom in filling out the form. Reporting forms usually have summaries in the right columns and bottom rows. Shading may also be used to make report forms more readable.
6. The use of box items to be checked or coded improves the readability of the design. When extreme emphasis is on accuracy, large boxes, heavily blocked sections, and lots of open space help.
7. Provide sufficient space for entering data and do not bleed lines off the sides of the forms. If horizontal lines stop short of the edge of the sheets, it is less likely that variable data will run off the edge.

8. Consider colored ink for captions to make variable data stand out. Colored ink may also be used for serial identification numbers.

9. "Boiler plate" or standard contract information is often on the back of forms such as purchase orders. Alternatively, detailed instructions on how to fill out the form may be printed on the back.

10. Routing instructions for each copy may be indicated by using a different color paper for each copy and printing routing instructions on the margin.

11. Type faces, the use of heavy and light lines, shaded areas, and color should be combined to provide an aesthetic form that makes the variable data stand out.

12. Standard form sizes should be used. These range from label sizes and shapes to the usual $8\frac{1}{2}'' \times 11''$ forms to $11'' \times 17''$ foldouts. If forms are kept small, they may be cramped in appearance, difficult to handle, and awkward to file. On the other hand, cost savings may be realized, since less paper or cardboard is required. Size is also related to the standard equipment available to process the forms—for example, sorters for checks at banks.

13. If the form is to be placed in a binder, leave adequate blank space at the top or sides.

14. If forms and envelopes are designed to match, the location of the address shown on the form must show through the envelope window with normal folding.

15. When multiple copies of a form are desired, they may be obtained in several ways. Multiple sheets may have carbon interleaves, or special no-carbon-required paper may be used. The form may be a ditto master from which, after the variable data have been added, copies may be run off. (This is appropriate for five or more copies.) Finally, a single copy of the form may be completed and then copies run off on an office copier.

16. Formats to be shown on video terminals should separate blocks of information adequately. If too many data are attempted in one display, they will be difficult to read. It is no problem to show a series of formats for clear presentation.

Even with all the care taken in designing the forms to be used in input and output, we must be sure to test the forms thoroughly by discussing them with the users and letting them actually try using the forms.

Inputs and Outputs: Database

The database is the data that must be obtained (sometimes called "captured") and usually stored for later retrieval for managerial decision making. It also consists of data that will be utilized in programmed decision making and real-time control. As discussed in Chapter 4, the database is derived from the needs of management for information to guide the total business system. We start with the study of management's problems and information needs, develop flowcharts of systems that meet management's requirements, and then detail the data requirements of the systems.

A systematic approach to the development of the database is as follows:

1. Identify all points on the flowcharts that require data inputs. Generally these are inputs to activities or transactions as well as decision tables or modeling operations.

2. Prepare a data or file worksheet for each data element, giving
   a. Source of data
   b. Length and format
   c. Current and potential frequency of updating
   d. Retention schedule for the data
   e. End use of the data
3. Group all data worksheets by system and check for omissions.
4. Group all data worksheets by activity and by organizational component and note duplications.
5. Eliminate duplicated data requirements to develop an integrated database for which cross-functional use of the master file is employed.
6. Evaluate the items in the master file for frequency of need and value of the data to the system versus cost of obtaining the data. Judgment must now be used to prune the file for possible revision of the system design if the cost of file construction and file maintenance exceeds the estimated value of the system or the available resources.

The database deserves careful attention because of its cost and operational impacts on the MIS and the larger organization. Chapter 4 discussed database management in some detail. The reader may wish to review that chapter.

Processing

A great deal of information has been gathered since the flowcharts for the subsystems were sketched. Inputs and outputs have been detailed. Numerous users have reviewed those flowcharts. At this point, corrections should be made to the subsystem flowcharts. In addition, each task specified inside the subsystem should be broken down further in either mathematical or narrative format. This process ties all the pieces of information we have gathered back to the original MIS goal. It also serves to reverify the detailed design and add flesh to the outline.

EARLY SYSTEM TESTING

There are three ways to get early feedback on the viability of the MIS just designed:

- Modeling
- Simulation
- Test planning

We will consider each in turn. Their importance lies in the impact that early problem discovery has on project cost. A problem discovered at design time is *much* cheaper to fix than is one found after the system has been put into operation.

Modeling the System Quantitatively

During our design efforts, we have quantified as much of the system as possible. We now attempt to determine quantitative ranges for inputs and outputs, quantitative relationships for the transfer functions, and time and reliability responses for operations in the system. Decision models are developed in both mathematical equation form and decision table form. The purpose of modeling at this stage is to define the system more precisely and to improve it.

Besides the mathematical modeling of systems discussed in Chapter 12, logic tables may be developed for decision models. Such "decision tables" may include both quantitative and qualitative bases for decision making. Decision tables are valuable for both design and documentation of systems. Decision structure tables are in the form of

if these conditions exist ...
then perform these actions....

The "if" listings form the *condition stub*. The "then" listings make up the *action stub*. Figure 8-6 shows a simplified decision table for purposes of explanation. The first column, under "Decision Rules," is read as follows:

if the car is driven less than 10,000 miles a year and
if the age of the youngest driver is over age 25 and
if no drivers have major physical defects and
if no driver has had more than one accident in the past 3 years and
if no driver has had a speeding conviction and
if the major use for the car is pleasure driving,

then the policy limit is $100,000 / $300,000
and the policy rate is $1.12 / $1000
and our policy identification type is A.

Auto Insurance Policy Coverage	Decision Rules			
Miles driven per year	< 10,000	< 10,000	< 15,000	< 15,000
Age of youngest driver	> 25	> 25	< 25	< 25
Physical defects of driver (one eye, one arm)	None	None	None	None
Accidents in last 3 years	≦ 1	≦ 1	≦ 2	≦ 2
Speeding convictions	None	None	None	None
Major use	pleasure	business	pleasure	business
Policy limit, $1,000's	100/300	100/200	50/100	25/50
Policy rate per $1,000	1.12	1.50	1.74	2.50
Type of policy	A	D	F	H

FIGURE 8-6 Decision Table for Insurance Decisions

Testing the System by Simulation

For very small systems, the best test may be conversion to on-line operations. In very large systems, simulation of the entire system may be too complex and costly. However, for many systems and for subsystems and functional components of large systems, testing by simulation should be carried out. The alternative, conversion to the new system and debugging and redesigning during changeover, should be held to a minimum. It is costly and damaging to the morale of the people responsible for implementing the system. Simulation has a further advantage in permitting evaluation of the system against the criteria of the conceptual design performance specifications.

The procedure for a simulation test of the whole system is as follows:

1. By random methods, select values of exogenous data from within the anticipated ranges of each variable. Let us illustrate with the input to our business of the variable we identify as share of market held by our principal competitor. The range for this is 20 to 35 percent. By the Monte Carlo technique, described in Chapter 12, we choose a random number and find the corresponding value of our competitor's market share is 23 percent. We do the same for other exogenous inputs, such as economic indexes, interest rates, cost of raw materials, size of new markets, and labor costs. Nonquantitative inputs may be handled just as easily by listing alternatives and selecting one by random number means.

2. Trace the effect of the exogenous inputs through the system. Where the activity processors are automatic, as in the case for computerized systems or decision tables, the process is straightforward. Where humans are involved, errors and time lags of a random nature may be introduced, or as a first approximation, the humans may be considered to perform routine operations with machinelike efficiency.

   There will be numerous points in the system at which human decisions, and more important, managerial decisions, will be required. If the system is to be properly tested, it is necessary to have an appropriate manager make the decision based on the information available from the system at that stage of the simulation. Inadequate information, lack of understanding of the situation by the manager, and inability of the system to control errors in judgment may be uncovered by this realistic type of simulation.

3. Examine outputs of various subsystems. Have cost variables been kept under control? Have outputs been restricted to specified ranges? Will the subsystems be able to respond rapidly enough to inputs so that the entire system will respond in time to maintain itself in its environment? Are all operations being performed according to specifications, or are crisis decisions being made constantly to keep them in line?

4. Repeat steps 1 through 3 several times. It is not feasible to test the whole system in the way that some operations are checked out. That is, a Monte Carlo simulation of a stochastic inventory system may require several thousand simulation cycles, but the process is mechanistic enough so that they can be carried out on a computer.

Planning to Test the MIS

When an individual or set of people lay out detailed plans for verifying the final version of the MIS, errors and omissions often show up. A detailed plan for testing the MIS requires that the following types of questions be asked (and answered in detail):

- Exactly which subsystems are available on various dates?
- What are all of the external (user) interfaces?
- What are some typical scenarios that can be tried out against the MIS?
- Who are some likely test subjects (users and managers)?
- And so on . . .

The process of asking and answering these questions makes the design more thorough and accurate.

SOFTWARE, HARDWARE, AND TOOLS

The software design should be done during this phase so that it will be available to merge with the larger system at the appropriate time. In fact, the coordination of the systems design group and the computer organization should start at the time of the conceptual design. Trained programmers should be on hand at the start of the detailed design work and at least nine months prior to installation. There are some principal steps in software development for systems over which management, through the systems designers, should maintain surveillance. These steps, carried out by the computer organization, are

1. Develop standards and procedures for programming. Standardized charting symbols, techniques, and records should be maintained.
2. Study the conceptual design specifications and work with the system designers in the development of the detailed design. The computer programmers should be a part of the design team by contributing their expertise as needed.
3. Develop the data processing logic and prepare the programming flowcharts. When the programming charts are completed, they should be reviewed by the systems design group.

Similarly, by now the system designers should be considering possible hardware configurations seriously. Without going into detail on how to choose computer hardware, the following items should guide the designers in their deliberations:

1. Buy enough computing power to do the whole job. Buy a little extra computing power, but remember that the MIS department is a support function.
2. Buy enough external storage to hold the required database and any application code planned. Leave some room for growth here also.
3. Buy other peripheral devices only as needed to support the problems the MIS is solving (printers to print the reports, displays to allow data entry, etc.).
4. Buy computer supplies as needed (paper, ribbons, tapes, etc.).
5. Buy enough computer power to provide the required user response.
6. Buy the best documentation.
7. Buy a sufficient maintenance/support package.

Finally, the system designers need to look ahead to the implementation phase and decide if any tools, methodologies, or procedures are needed. For example, if today's records are kept on punched cards and the new MIS has a disk database, a software tool is needed to transfer those records. The tools should be planned for so they will be available when needed.

PROPOSE AN ORGANIZATION TO OPERATE THE SYSTEM

The development of a new organization structure when the company executives and organization are in place is fraught with practical obstacles. Managers would consider it an imposition if the MIS group were to suggest regroupings, particularly if an individual manager's position may be abolished. The MIS group should work with incumbent and top managers to *suggest* organizational changes that will correspond to requirements of the new system. The group should not attempt to press or sell a reorganization. Major changes in organization are the prerogatives of top management.

Organization for systems management requires an outlook different from that of organization for functional component management. Subsystem managers should recognize that their main objective is that the subsystem should function in a way that is best for the whole system. Subsystem management requires a knowledge of the dynamics of systems and of the need for trade-offs to optimize system performance. The manager must be able to interface his or her subsystem operations effectively with coupled subsystems.

The hierarchy of management should follow the hierarchy of systems and subsystems rather than of technical disciplines. Assignment to activities by technical discipline should be primarily at the lower level, except for some overlay service systems such as financial planning and control.

DOCUMENT THE DETAILED DESIGN

The end of the detailed design project is production of the documents that specify the system, its operation, and its design justification. Documentation consists of

1. A summary flowchart.
2. Detailed flowcharts.
3. Operations activity sheets showing inputs, outputs, and transfer functions.
4. Specification of the database or master file.
5. Computer hardware requirements.
6. Software (programs).

7. Personnel requirements by type of skill or discipline.
8. Final (updated) performance specifications.
9. Cost of installation and implementation of the system.
10. Cost of operating the system per unit of time.
11. Program for modification or termination of the system.
12. An executive digest of the MIS design. This is a report that top management can read rapidly to get the essence of the system, its potential for the company, its cost, and its general configuration. We point out that a high-level MIS official at General Electric remarked, "If the MIS can be justified on the basis of cost savings, it isn't an MIS." The executive digest should be directed toward showing how the system will aid managers' decision making by gains in information or in time.

Some documentation should be on standardized forms. Input-output-activity diagrams or listings are an example. Obviously, standard symbols should be used on flowcharts and guidelines should be established for flowchart format. Some documentation is unique to a project, such as the database, and the format and classification of items should be determined by the needs of the particular user. Other documentation should simply follow good reporting style.

REVISIT THE MANAGER-USER

The system design is much firmer now and it is time to repeat the procedures of

- Reporting the status to upper management
- Feedback to and request for support from lower-level management
- Education and gentle selling to nonmanagement users

SUMMARY

Detailed design of the MIS commences after the conceptual framework has been formulated. Detailed design begins with the performance specifications given by the conceptual design and ends with a set of specifications for the construction of the MIS. Unless the operating system is to remain unchanged, the design of the MIS must be developed in conjunction with the design of the operating system.

A unique recipe for detailed design cannot be given, because design work is a creative, problem-solving activity. Blind alleys, iterative cycling processes, and new techniques are developed during the design process itself. We have tried here to describe major phases and activities of the design process. These design activities utilize all the concepts and tools developed so far in this book. This chapter can supply only an indication of their application. Prospective MIS professionals must develop in-depth skill in the problem-solving, decision-making, and management science areas by further study. They must develop their skill in systems design through actual experience. A textbook can only point the direction.

PROBLEMS AND QUESTIONS

1. Help Johnson Enterprises with its detailed design problems — Case 4(F).

2. Match the items in column A (hierarchy of parts of an MIS) with those in column B (example of each item in column A).

A	B
1. System	_____ Accounts receivable
2. Subsystem	_____ Type customer name
3. Functional component	_____ Update customer file
4. Task	_____ Find customer record
5. Subtask	_____ Accounting package
6. Operational element	_____ Customer file processing

3. List the four major sources of design information:

_____

_____

_____

_____

4. Give examples (other than those in the text) of these levels of automation in an MIS:

   a. No automation:_____
   b. Work automated, control manual:_____

   c. Work automated, feedback automated,
      control manual:_____

   d. Work, feedback, and control all automated:_____

5. Identify 10 specific factors that should be considered in forms design.

_____

_____

_____

_____

_____

_____

_____

_____

_____

_____

6. Obtain a copy of your school's enrollment form and critique it relative to good forms design criteria.

7. Figure 8-1 provides a general system concept for a business system. Assume that this is the conceptual design for a typical manufacturing firm.

   Three of the subsystems (order processing, warehousing, purchasing) are given along with a list of activities, inputs, and outputs relating to the subsystems. Match the activities, inputs and outputs by placing an (x) under the appropriate subsystem. Only one subsystem should be marked (x) per item.

	Order Processing	Warehousing	Purchasing
Activities			
Correct inventory record balance	( )	( )	( )
Order delivered by sales representative	( )	( )	( )
Prepare sales order form	( )	( )	( )
Stamp receipt time	( )	( )	( )
Pick item and deliver to shipping	( )	( )	( )
Mark "BO"	( )	( )	( )
Edit for customer account number	( )	( )	( )
Stamp shipping copy	( )	( )	( )
Edit requisition	( )	( )	( )
File requisition in open order file	( )	( )	( )
Arrange requisition by buyer specialization	( )	( )	( )
Credit check	( )	( )	( )
Compare against company catalog	( )	( )	( )
File in sales order file	( )	( )	( )
Compare to vendor historical file	( )	( )	( )
Inputs			
Customer list	( )	( )	( )
Receiving report	( )	( )	( )
Sales order log	( )	( )	( )
Inventory records	( )	( )	( )
Requisition	( )	( )	( )
Master customer file	( )	( )	( )
Customer's invoice (copies 3, 4, 5)	( )	( )	( )
Warehouse sales order file	( )	( )	( )
Customer order	( )	( )	( )
Vendor historical file	( )	( )	( )
Catalog	( )	( )	( )
Customer credit file	( )	( )	( )
Price list	( )	( )	( )
Sales order	( )	( )	( )
Purchase order	( )	( )	( )
Backorder production request for items to be manufactured (copy)	( )	( )	( )
Backorder purchase request for items to be purchased (original)	( )	( )	( )
Outputs			
Requisition for stock items	( )	( )	( )
Purchase order	( )	( )	( )
Bill of lading	( )	( )	( )
Sales order	( )	( )	( )
Customer's invoice (with items)	( )	( )	( )
Updated vendor performance history file	( )	( )	( )
Manual sales order marked with inventory check (to data processing)	( )	( )	( )
Updated customer credit file	( )	( )	( )
Updated master customer file	( )	( )	( )
Shipping order	( )	( )	( )

8. How are dominant criteria for systems design related to policies of the company?

9. Develop a decision table for an automobile rental firm for accepting or rejecting applicants.

10. In the R & D project type of organization, the performance specifications for a financial reporting system are

    a. Summary report of expenditures by task and by direct labor and materials for each task is to go to the project manager.

    b. Report of expenditures for each section's own task and subtasks, broken down by direct labor, materials, and organizational unit within the section, is to go to the section manager.

    c. Report of charges for work performed for other sections is to go to each section manager.

    d. Report of direct labor and materials, broken down for task and subtask and for all "shop orders" making up each subtask, is to go to all "fund owners" (i.e., engineers and managers responsible for a shop-order job, subtask, or task).

    e. All the reports listed are to be distributed within five working days after the close of each month.

    f. Cumulative year-to-date expenditures are to be included. [*Note:* One of the problems is gathering materials expenditures and determining assignment of personnel (labor) to different shop orders. Also, travel expense and training programs are considered direct labor charges to keep the overhead rate low.]

Develop a detailed design for the system, except for the computer programming. Make assumptions or estimates for missing data.

SELECTED REFERENCES

Blake, George B. "Graphic Shorthand as an Aid for Managers." *Harvard Business Review*, March–April 1978.

Burch, John G., Jr., Felix R. Strater, Jr., and Gary Grudnitski. *Information Systems: Theory and Practice*, 2nd ed. New York: John Wiley, 1979.

Cushing, Barry E. *Accounting Information Systems and Business Organizations*, 2nd ed. Reading, Mass.: Addison-Wesley, 1978.

Friend, David. "Graphics for Managers: The Distributed Approach." *Datamation*, July 1982.

Gilmour, Robert W. *Business Systems Handbook*. Englewood Cliffs, N.J.: Prentice-Hall, 1979.

Hartman, W., H. Mathes, and A. Proeme. *Management Information Systems Handbook*. New York: McGraw-Hill, 1968.

Hicks, James O., Jr., and Wayne E. Leininger. *Accounting Information Systems*. St. Paul: West, 1981.

Martin, Merle P. "Management Reports." *Journal of Systems Management*, June 1982.

McEwan, Charles E. "Computer Graphics: Getting More from a Management Information System." *Data Management*, July 1981.

Mitchell, William E. "Records Retention Schedules." *Journal of Systems Management*, August 1977.

MORAN, ALFRED J., JR. "Fighting the Paper War—and Winning." *Financial Executive*, September 1982.

MURDICK, ROBERT G. *MIS: Concepts and Design*. Englewood Cliffs, N.J.: Prentice-Hall, 1980.

Records Retention Timetable. Electric Wastebasket Corp., 145 West 45th Street, New York, N.Y. 10036.

SEBENIUS, W. G. "Cost Reporting by Exception." *Journal of Systems Management*, May 1975.

9

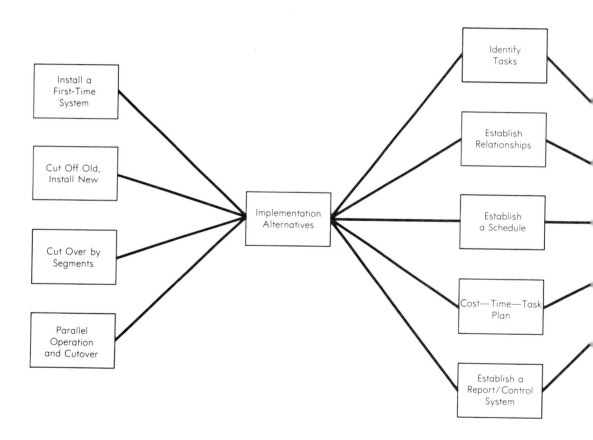

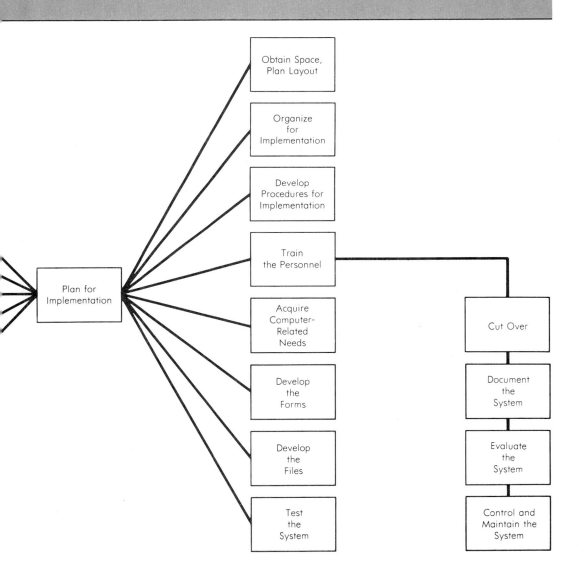

Although the design of a management information system may seem to management to be an expensive project, the cost of getting the MIS on line satisfactorily may often be comparable to that of its design. The cumulative expenditures for the design and installation of an MIS follow the pattern sketched in Figure 9-1. The implementation has been accomplished when the outputs of the MIS are continuously utilized by decision makers.

There are four basic methods for implementing the MIS once the design has been completed. These are

1. Install a system in a new operation or organization, one just being formed.
2. Cut off the old system and install the new. This produces a time gap during which no system is in operation. It is practical only for small companies or small systems where installation requires one or two days. An exception to this would be the installation of a larger system during a plant's vacation shutdown or some other period of inactivity.
3. Cut over by segments. This method is also referred to as "phasing in" the new system. Small parts or subsystems are substituted for the old. If this method is possible, some careful questions should be asked about the design of the new system. Is it really just an automation of isolated groups of clerical activities? Generally, new *systems* are not substitutable piece by piece for previous *nonsystems*. However, in the case of upgrading old systems, this may be a very desirable method.
4. Operate in parallel and cut over. The new system is installed and operated in parallel with the current system until it has been checked out; then the current system is cut out. This method is expensive because of personnel and related costs. However, it is required in certain essential systems, such as payroll or customer billing. Its big advantage is that the system is fairly well debugged when it becomes the essential information system of the company.

Except for the timing and for obvious variations, the implementation steps for all four methods may be covered together. We now proceed to give step-by-step procedures for implementation, support, test, and control of the specified MIS. We assume that the specification provides the system description both in general and in detail, procedures for operation, forms and database required, the new

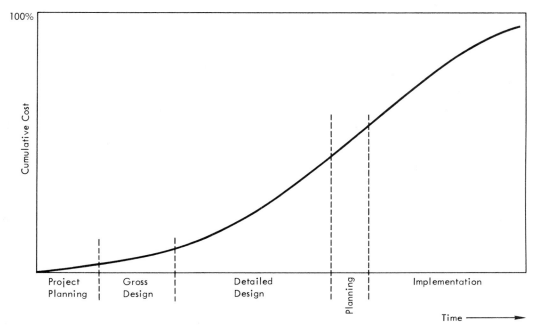

FIGURE 9-1　Growth of MIS Project Costs

organization structure including position descriptions, and facilities and equipment required. The step-by-step procedures are given for major phases of the implementation that are usually conducted in a parallel or network time format.

It should be pointed out that occasionally design and implementation are carried on simultaneously. Such a process provides operational testing of the design on a continuous basis, but it limits consideration of major design alternatives. It is a trial-and-error process. Completion of conceptual and analytical design in advance of equipment installation offers many advantages besides cost.

PLAN THE IMPLEMENTATION

The three main phases in implementation take place in series; these are the initial installation; the test of the system as a whole; and the evaluation, maintenance, and control of the system. On the other hand, many implementation activities should be undertaken in parallel to reduce implementation time. For example, acquisition of data for the database and forms design for collection and dissemination of information may be carried out in parallel. Training of personnel and preparation of software may be in parallel with each other and with other implementation activities.

It is apparent, then, that the first step in the implementation procedure is to *plan the implementation*. Although some analysts include the planning of the implementation with the design of the system, we believe that it is operationally significant to include it in the implementation stage, for several reasons. First, the planning and the action to implement the plan should be bound closely together. Planning is the first step of management, not the last. Further, the MIS design and the urgent need for the system at the time the design is completed will weigh heavily on the plan for implementation. And, finally, the planning process is a function of line management, at least as far as key decisions or alternative plans are concerned. The systems analyst may prepare plans to assist managers, but *managers must have the last say.* At the same time, managers require the services of the systems analyst to detail plans. The managers prefer to make decisions based upon the most recent information: the MIS specifications, the proposed plans of the systems analyst, and the current operating situation.

The planning for the project of implementation should follow the procedures for project planning described in Chapter 6. Once the conversion method has been described, the specific steps are as we shall delineate here.

Identify the Implementation Tasks

The major implementation tasks, or milestones, usually consist of

1. Planning the implementation activities
2. Acquiring and laying out facilities and offices
3. Organizing the personnel for implementation
4. Developing procedures for installation and testing
5. Developing the training program for operating personnel
6. Completing the system's software
7. Acquiring required hardware
8. Generating files
9. Designing forms
10. Testing of the entire system
11. Completing cutover to the new system
12. Documenting the system
13. Evaluating the MIS
14. Providing system maintenance (debugging and improving)

The plans should list all subtasks for each of these major tasks so that individuals in the organization may be assigned specific responsibilities.

Establish Relationships Among Tasks

For small projects, the order of performance may simply be described in text form. However, even in small projects, a Gantt chart or network diagram makes visualization of the plan and schedule much clearer. In large projects, many

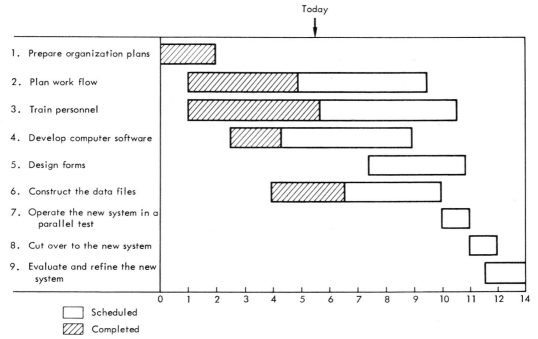

FIGURE 9-2   Gantt Chart for MIS Implementation

concurrent and sequential activities are interrelated, so that a network diagram must be employed in any good plan. Figure 9-2 shows a Gantt chart and Figure 9-3 shows a network diagram (condensed) for illustrating task relationships.

Establish a Schedule

A first estimate of the schedule is prepared by having the system designers estimate the times between the events in the program network. The critical path (longest time through the network) can then be calculated. The end date is thus established once the starting date is specified. Figures 9-2 and 9-3 indicate how times are shown for the implementation activities.

The actual desired end date is then usually specified by management on the basis of this information. Obviously, management may apply pressure or provide additional personnel to shorten the network times.

Prepare a Cost Schedule Tied to Tasks and Time

The cost for completing each milestone, and possibly each task required to complete a milestone, should be established as part of the plan; then the rate of expenditures should be budgeted. The techniques for this phase of planning were covered in Chapter 6.

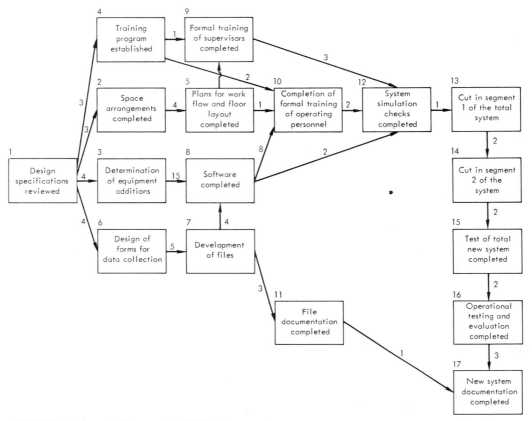

FIGURE 9-3 Network Diagram for MIS Implementation

Establish a Reporting and Control System

Reporting and control of the work in progress may be obtained by weekly meetings of the key people involved or by brief written progress reports. The financial personnel must make certain that report formats allow them to show cost and technical progress relationships as well as cost and time relationships. When large numbers of people are both conducting regular operations and introducing new equipment, arrangements, and operations, some confusion is inevitable. The object of the control system is to minimize this confusion and the associated delays and costs.

ACQUIRE FLOOR SPACE AND PLAN SPACE LAYOUTS

The installation of a new system to replace a current one may require a major revision of facilities as well as completely new office, computer room, and production layouts. The MIS project manager must prepare rough layouts and estimates of particular floor areas he or she feels will be needed. The manager should then prepare cost estimates and submit a proposal for management's approval.

Facilities and space planning should begin as soon as approval of gross space allocations has been obtained. The urgency for such planning is twofold. First, there may be a long lead time if new partitions, electrical work, air conditioning, or even new buildings are required. Second, the detailed work flow depends upon the physical arrangements of the buildings. The training of operations personnel will be more successful if it is based on exact physical relationships among the people and the equipment.

Space planning must take into account the space occupied by people, the space occupied by equipment, and the movement of people and equipment in the work process. Related to these are the number and kinds of exits; storage areas; location of utilities, outlets, and controls; environmental requirements for the equipment; safety factors; and working conditions for the personnel. A large investment in good working conditions will repay its cost many times. It is a shortsighted and costly policy to scrimp on facilities and human environment when a major renovation is required to install a new system.

ORGANIZE FOR IMPLEMENTATION

Once the implementation tasks have been defined in the planning phase, management usually assigns a project manager to guide the implementation. A manager of management information systems may assume this responsibility by virtue of a permanent assignment. In smaller companies, someone from the finance/ accounting department, or even the computer center manager, may be placed in charge. A project manager, who is responsible for the entire MIS development and implementation, usually works best.

The role of line managers must be made clear. Because the purpose of the MIS is to increase the amount and quality of their contributions, the system is really *their* system. Top management must take explicit steps to make the middle managers aware of this and of the necessity for their involvement in implementation. Essentially, the systems specialists are there to *assist* management with the implementation; they are assigned to the project as needed for this purpose.

Besides assigning responsibilities to line managers, systems specialists, and computer programmers, top management should make sure that line functional personnel have active parts in the implementation. These are the people who will operate the system, and they also must feel that it is *their* system.

Proper organization by assignment of specific leadership and task responsibility diffused widely throughout the whole organization can prevent the moans and wails so often heard after a new MIS is installed and fails. Mature people respond to work assignments that call forth their full talents. They resist the control that is implied when they are simply handed a system installed by specialists and told exactly how to operate it. But when they have a hand in shaping and constructing the system they must operate, employees react favorably. Without such acceptance, management finds that new systems fail because of inertia, apathy, resistance to change, and employee feelings of insecurity.

DEVELOP PROCEDURES
FOR IMPLEMENTATION

The project leader has available the network plan for proceeding with the implementation. The leader must now call upon key people in the project to prepare more detailed procedures for system installation. For example, suppose the detailed design specification calls for the manufacturing manager to receive a report on raw materials stored on the factory floor at the end of each day. The source of data is the supervisor, who will fill out forms and send them to a production planner for compilation. The systems analyst must develop the procedure for delivering instructions and forms to supervisors, for coordinating and integrating this very small portion of the MIS with other parts of the manufacturing system, and for working out problems with the people involved.

As another example, suppose some files must be converted from filing cabinets to magnetic tape or to some kind of random access storage. The systems analyst must develop the procedures for making this conversion without upsetting current use of the files.

Procedures for evaluating and selecting hardware must be spelled out. Procedures for buying or constructing software should be established. Procedures for phasing in parts of the MIS or for operating the MIS in parallel must be developed. Obviously there are *many* procedures that must be delineated in advance if the entire implementation is to be saved from chaos.

A major part of implementing the MIS is the testing of each segment of the total system as it is installed. So far, the only testing that has been done is a simulation of the system during the detailed design stage. The testing of segments of the MIS during installation requires application of line personnel to actual files, software, and hardware for either current operations or specially designed test problems. This is equivalent to the physical laboratory testing of parts of an engineered product after the theoretical evaluation (testing) and before construction of the parts.

It is necessary to develop the testing procedures on the basis of the design and test specifications. The procedures should prescribe

1. Which segments of the system will be tested
2. When such tests are to be performed
3. Test problems to be run
4. Who will perform the tests
5. How the tests will be run
6. Who will evaluate test results and approve the system segment or recommend modification

We might review at this time the sequence of test development and conduct up to the point before system acceptance. The steps are listed under the appropriate steps of system development.

1. *Detailed design stage.* Prepare a test description for each test. The test description is a concise statement of the ultimate objective of the test and the systems, components, and facilities involved in its accomplishment.
2. *Detailed design stage or implementation stage.* Prepare a test specification for each test. The test specification is derived from the test description. It is a completely detailed statement giving information on conditions under which the test is to be run, duration of the test, method and procedure to be followed, data to be taken and frequency, and analysis to be performed on the data.
3. *Implementation stage.* Prepare a test operating procedure for each test. A completely detailed procedure for the accomplishment of the test specification includes organization of personnel for conduct of the test; provision of necessary test forms and data sheets; statement of conditions to exist at the start of the test; a list of all equipment, software, and file data required for the test; and step-by-step procedure for all the people participating in the test.
4. *Implementation stage.* Prepare an acceptance test program. This requires a test description, test specification, and test operating procedure for the entire MIS, to check out the system before it is accepted by operating personnel for sole continuous use.

TRAIN THE OPERATING PERSONNEL

A program should be developed to impress upon management and support personnel the nature and goals of the MIS and to train operating personnel in their new duties. In the case of management, many of whom participate in the development of the system, two short seminars are usually adequate. If the first meeting is held at a time when the detailed design is well along, some valuable proposals may be offered that can then be incorporated in the design. Another meeting near the end of the implementation stage may review the benefits of the system and the roles of the executives.

Particular attention should be paid to the training of first-line supervisors. They must have a thorough understanding of what the new MIS is like and what it is supposed to do. Because, in essence, they oversee the operation of the system, they must learn how it will operate. They are faced with many changes in their work and they must obtain acceptance of changes by their subordinates. Supervisors will therefore have an intense interest in the answers to

1. What new skills must we and our people learn?
2. How many people do we gain or lose?
3. What changes in procedures do we make?
4. What are the new forms? Are there more or fewer?
5. What jobs will be upgraded or downgraded?
6. How will our performance be measured?

Certain professional support personnel—such as computer center personnel, marketing researchers, production planners, and accounting personnel who provide input to the MIS or are concerned with processing data and information—should also attend one or several orientation meetings. Because these people will be working with only a small part of the MIS, the seminars should be designed to provide them with an understanding of the complete system. This will furnish direction for their own jobs and give them a perspective that may reduce the likelihood of blunders.

Finally, longer and more formal training programs should be established for people who perform the daily operational tasks of the MIS. These are the clerks, the computer operators, the input and output machine operators, file maintenance personnel, and possibly printing production and graphic arts personnel.

In most medium and large companies, a training specialist arranges such programs. The specialist schedules classes, arranges for facilities, and assists the technical people (in this case, the systems analysts) in developing course content and notes for distribution. In small companies, the MIS manager will probably have to develop the training program.

COMPUTER-RELATED ACQUISITIONS

A comprehensive discussion of the preparation of computer programs and the evaluation and acquisition of computer and peripheral equipment does not fall within the objective of this text. We are concerned rather with identifying the managerial considerations of MIS design. The *management* of automation of logic, communication, and display is important as a *basis for systems design* and as a *factor in systems implementation.* To a great extent, the detailed design of the MIS has provided some criteria for the hardware and software, if it has not in fact specified it. One complicating factor in systems installation is that a new computer is often required along with the new MIS.

Acquisition consists of bringing on site

1. Hardware
2. Software
3. Personnel
4. Materials

These acquisitions are usually the limiting items in getting an MIS implemented. When possible, these tasks should be started during the design stage. There is, of course, some risk of loss in starting early, but it must be balanced against the considerable delay involved in the sequential approach to design and implementation of the MIS.

Hardware

The acquisition of computer system equipment is a complex subject more suitable for a specialized book. Basically, the design of the computer system and the architecture available from vendors are closely tied together. Once a choice of CPU and peripheral equipment has been made, a major decision is whether to buy or lease. Capital expenditure analysis is only one of many factors involved in this decision. Others are prestige, usage, anticipated replacement schedule, and vendor's options.

An alternative used by smaller companies is simply to lease computer time from a service bureau.

Software

Today many software packages are commercially available. Therefore, for small companies all software might be purchased. In large companies with specialized forecasting, planning, operating, and control models, most software must be developed internally or under contract. In either case, the software development must take into account the nature of the hardware.

Purchase of software packages has a pitfall. Often, so much modification of the software is required to fit the company that it would have been cheaper to have developed the entire software internally.

If the software development route is pursued, an additional set of activities emerges. Systems designers and programmers provide the flow diagrams and the block diagrams during the detailed design stage. Some modification may be required, however, as the implementation stage progresses. In the implementation stage, coders convert block diagrams into sequences of statements or instructions for the processing (computer) equipment. The development of software is described by the block diagram of Figure 9-4. Some of the danger areas in software development are discussed in Chapter 10.

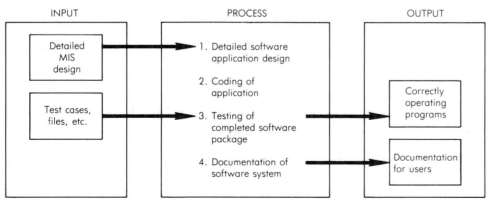

FIGURE 9-4 Preparation of MIS Software

Personnel

Implementation of an MIS offers the company an opportunity to upgrade and promote personnel after training. Jobs may be restructured at higher levels by using the computer to handle routine procedures that were traditionally handled by people.

A personnel planning chart should be prepared showing the number of individuals required in terms of skill, the source (internal and external), and the date they will be required to report to work. Since some computer-related skills are scarce, the plan for acquiring these skills can be critical to the success of the MIS.

Materials

Forms and manuals are the principal materials to be ordered for the MIS. The demand for these must be estimated so that an adequate number may be ordered. The economic order size may be calculated to set the order size and minimize system costs.

Computer supplies such as cards, tapes, printout paper, and storage cabinets should be checked and orders placed as necessary.

DEVELOP FORMS FOR DATA COLLECTION AND INFORMATION DISSEMINATION

A vast amount of detailed data, both external and internal to the company, must be collected for input to the MIS. If control over marketing is to be exercised or sales forecasting is carried out, then somewhere, every day, a salesperson must sit in a room and fill out a form summarizing the day's activities. Obviously, the form ensures that the right information is supplied in a manner that simplifies processing for computer storage. We might ask, "What about a truly modern firm in which the salesperson may plug in a time-sharing terminal and transmit information directly to a computer thousands of miles away? Even in this case, the salesperson must have a form (or format) for guidance.

Forms are required not just for input and output but also for transmitting data at intermediate stages. In a personnel system, input to the computer may consist of all known applicants for all known jobs within a company. The computer may provide sorted output to match jobs and applicants. The personnel recruiting specialist may then have to add a statement of his or her activities —*on a form*, which is attached to the computer output. The entire package is then forwarded to the manager of personnel.

Forms design was discussed at some length in Chapter 8. The implementation phase is the first opportunity to try out the forms in the context of the whole MIS. Also, we see some of the computer printouts for the first time. Since forms are the key user interfaces, this is a very critical step toward the general acceptance of the MIS.

DEVELOP THE FILES

The specifications for the files have been developed in the detailed design stage. In the implementation stage, the actual data must be obtained and recorded for the initial testing and operation of the system. This requires a checklist of data, format of data, storage form and format, and remarks to indicate when the data have been stored. The implementation also requires the development of a procedure for updating each piece of the data and for updating entire sections of the file as required. This collection of data used in routine operations is often called the *master file*.

When data are obtained from the environment—as are economic, competitive, and financial data, or vendor sources—a procedure for obtaining the data may be developed along with the initial acquisition. Responsibility for file maintenance for each file item should also be assigned. For internal data, the generating source or the compiling source (such as marketing) is usually assigned responsibility for file items. The structure of such information is more generalized than that of the master file. This file is often called the *database*, although in practice the master file and database elements are usually stored together.

In the detailed design phase, each item of data for the files is specified and the retrieval methods (indexes) are developed. In the implementation stage, forms must be designed so that the data may be analyzed by the programmers and coders for storage in the computer. Thus, the file name, maximum number of characters required to record each data element, frequency of access, volume of operations on the element, retention characteristics, and updating frequency are examples of relevant information required to translate a specification into a file element. A sample form, not to be taken as ideal or generalized, for recording a file element is shown in Figure 9-5. Although separate forms are often used for recording data before they are stored, Figure 9-5 includes a space for initial values.

The development of files or databases belongs in the conceptual realm of information systems designers and storage and retrieval experts. The translation of specifications for files into computer programs is a function of computer specialists. For our purposes, only an insight into the relation of these specialists' problems to management decision systems is needed. Chapter 4 dealt with database management in more detail.

DATA ELEMENT DESCRIPTION

File Name _____

File Number _____   Date _____

Data Element _____

Field Element _____   Group Label _____

Form _____   Source _____

Maximum Length (Characters/Item Group) _____

Storage Medium _____

Retention Characteristics _____

_____

Update Procedure _____

_____

_____

Initial Value _____

Units _____

FIGURE 9-5 File Form

TEST THE SYSTEM

As each part of the total system is installed, tests should be performed in accordance with the test specifications and procedures described earlier. Tests during the installation stage consist of component tests, subsystem tests, and total system acceptance tests. Components may consist of

1. Equipment, old or new
2. New forms
3. New software programs
4. New data collection methods
5. New work procedures
6. New reporting formats

Components may be tested relatively independently of the system to which they belong. Tests for accuracy, range of inputs, frequency of inputs, usual operating conditions, "human factor" characteristics, and reliability are all of concern. We do not require vast amounts of input data for this, but rather representative elements of data and limiting or unusual data. During component testing, employees are further familarized with the system before the organization switches over to complete dependence on it. Difficulties occurring during component tests may lead to design changes that will bring large benefits when systems tests and operations are carried out.

One point difficult to cover in a general discussion of testing, but a very important and *practical* one, is, "How are the new pieces of equipment, new forms, new procedures, and so on, being tested in an organization where daily operations must be maintained?" This is particularly relevant where substitution of components cannot be made, but the entire new system must be installed, operated in parallel, and then cut in on a given day. It is a test of the ingenuity of the MIS project manager in preventing utter chaos. One possible approach is to plan for new equipment to be in different locations from old equipment and available areas. Sometimes it is possible to have operating personnel, using a few files and tables fitted into the room, handle both old procedures and testing of the new components from their regular work stations. In other cases, adjacent available office space may be utilized for testing, and the physical substitution of the new for the old system may take place in overtime on the night before cutover. The fact that partitions may have to be removed may permit temporary, crowded, side-by-side arrangements until the acceptance testing is complete.

As more components are installed, subsystems may be tested. There is a considerable difference between the testing of a component and the testing of a system. System tests require verification of multiple inputs, complex logic systems, interaction of humans and widely varied equipment, interfacing of systems, and timing aspects of the many parts. If, for example, the programming for the computer fails to work in the system test, costly delays may take place. Often, minor difficulties cropping up require redesign of forms, procedures, work flow, or organizational changes. The training program itself is being tested, because, if the supervisors and operators lose confidence in the system at this point, they may resist further implementation of the new system in subtle ways.

Although complete parallel testing before a target day cutover is perhaps the most difficult to implement, it is sometimes necessary. Consider a bank that must collect and process millions of dollars in checks before shipment to various points in the country for collection. A delay of a day, or even of several hours, can be very expensive in terms of interest forgone. Order processing, payroll operations, project management control, retail operations management, and airline reservation service are other examples in which a break in system operation is extremely undesirable.

CUTOVER

Cutover is the point at which the new component replaces the old component or the new system replaces the old system. This usually involves a good deal of last-minute physical transfer of files, rearrangement of office furniture, and movement of work stations and people. Old forms, old files, and old equipment are suddenly retired.

Despite component and system testing, there are still likely to be "bugs" in the system. One of the chief causes of problems is inadequate training of operating personnel. These people are suddenly thrown into a new situation with new equipment, procedures, and co-workers. If the training has been superficial, mass confusion may result. Having extra supervisory help, with the systems designers on hand, is one way of preventing first-day cutover panic. Design analysts should also be present to iron out "bugs" of all kinds that may arise.

The systems designer may observe the cutover and the smoothing out of system operations over a few weeks with some gratification. If the designer is naïve, he or she will depart believing that the system is installed. The more experienced designer will make a few informal return calls later on; the experienced designer knows that employees often go through the motions of adopting the new system while maintaining secret files in their desks and performing old procedures in parallel with the new. This resistance to change, belief that the old methods were best, or lack of confidence in the new system must be detected and overcome. The systems designer may detect such activities and should report them to the supervisor for corrective action. The supervisor should recognize that improper handling of such cases may make it more difficult to ferret out future instances.

The debugging process associated with the cutover to the new system may extend for several months. Programs may require improvement, forms may need to be changed for more efficient operation, or employees may desire transfer to different jobs within the system. In particular, the operational testing of the system over a period of several months exposes it to a volume and variability of data and conditions that could not be practically achieved in preacceptance testing. Production records such as productive time and nonproductive time give indications of future maintenance requirements and idle-time costs.

DOCUMENT THE SYSTEM

"Documentation" of the MIS means preparation of written descriptions of the scope, purpose, information flow components, and operating procedures of the system. Documentation is not a frill; it is a necessity—for troubleshooting, for replacement of subsystems, for interfacing with other systems, for training new operating personnel, and also for evaluating and upgrading the system.

If the system is properly documented,

1. A new team of operators could be brought in and could learn to operate the MIS on the basis of the documentation available.
2. Designers not familiar with the organization or MIS could, from the documentation, reconstruct the system.
3. A common reference design is available for managers, designers, and programmers concerned with system maintenance.
4. The information systems analyst will have a valuable data source for developing a new MIS, schedules, personnel plans, and costs.

Documenting a Manual MIS

The documentation of a manual information system may consist of the following:

1. A system summary of scope, interfaces with other systems, types of outputs and users, assumptions and constraints for design, and name of design project leader
2. Old and new organization charts and comparison of number and kinds of people before and after the new system is installed
3. Flowcharts and layout charts
4. Desk equipment
5. Forms
6. Output reports and formats
7. Manual data processing procedures
8. Methods for controlling and revising the system—that is, specification of faulty operation and organizational procedures for initiating changes

Documenting a Computer-Based MIS

Documentation of a computer-based MIS is similar to that of a manual system except that all software development, programs, files, input/output formats, and codes should be documented. Of particular importance is the documentation of the master file and the means for entering, processing, and retrieving data.

EVALUATE THE MIS

After the MIS has been operating smoothly for a short period of time, an evaluation of each step in the design and of the final system performance should be made. There is always the pressure to go on to new jobs, but the feedback principle should apply to the work of the MIS as well as to the product. Thousands of dollars are invested in an MIS, and it is good business to measure the value of the results.

Evaluation should not be delayed beyond the time when the systems analysts have completed most of the debugging. The longer the delay, the more difficult it will be for the designer to remember important details.

The evaluation should be made by the customer as well as by the designers. For each step we have covered in this and the last three chapters, the question should be asked, "If we were to start all over again, knowing what we now know, what would we do differently?" The customer may ask, "How does the system now perform and how would we like it to perform?" In addition, even though it is less important than the previous evaluations, the financial specialists should evaluate the project in terms of planned cost versus actual cost of design, implementation, and operation. They should also attempt to identify cost savings and increased profits directly attributable to the MIS.

A clear-cut method for measuring the costs and benefits of a new MIS has not yet been found. We present here a structure that, when adapted to a specific company, will permit partial evaluations.

Structure

The measurement of costs or benefits of an MIS is the measurement of a change or difference between the old and the new. The measurement of change must be related to the basic goals of the MIS, the principal activities that further these goals, or the many minor activities that further these goals. In other words, we may measure the change in the total output of the system or measure the many changes accomplished throughout the system. The former is obviously the most desirable.

What we have is a hierarchy of levels at which we consider measuring costs and benefits. Table 9-1 shows this hierarchy. For a particular MIS, the designer may select the level at which measurement is to take place based upon specific objectives of the MIS. It is probably rare that a measurement of the total system is attempted at the system level. At the system level, judgment of broad concepts might be employed:

1. *System integrity.* How well are the subsystems integrated into the total system without redundancy? How flexible is the system? How easily may the system be expanded?

TABLE 9-1 Measurement Hierarchy

Level	Hierarchy in the MIS	Change That Is Measured
1	Company profit, return on investment	Dollars
2	Company costs, revenues	Dollars
3	Planning	Specificity, quantification, degree to which plans are achieved, time required to produce plans, number of alternative plans made available for consideration, cost
	Control	Degree of control by exception, selection of activities to be controlled, forewarning of activities going beyond acceptable limits, managerial time required for control, automation of control of repetitive situations, cost
4	Decisions	Quality of decisions, frequency of reversal of decisions by superiors in the organization, number of alternatives examined in arriving at decisions, sophistication of "what if" questions permitted, time required for decisions, number of decisions, automation of repetitive decision situations, cost
5	Information	Validity, accuracy, clarity, distribution, frequency, appropriateness of detail for each level of management, timeliness, format, availability on demand, selectivity of content, disposition method, retention time, cost
6	System characteristics	Number of people required, equipment and facilities, response time, frequency of breakdowns, inputs, outputs, number of forms, number of operations, number of storages, sizes and quality of data bank, size and quality of model bank, flexibility, simplicity, degree of automation, scope of business components that are related by the MIS, user satisfaction, error rates, persistent problem areas, ease of maintenance and modification, unplanned-for impact on company performance, savings, cost, etc.

2. *Operating integrity.* How skilled are the people operating the system? What backup is there to prevent system breakdown in the event of loss of key personnel or equipment failure?

3. *Internal integrity.* How well does the system do what it is supposed to do? How valid are system outputs? How secure is the system against human error, manipulation, sabotage, or theft?

4. *Procedural integrity.* How good is the documentation of the system and procedures? Are procedures such that employees are motivated to follow them? How well are procedures followed in practice? What controls ensure that procedures are followed?

TABLE 9-2 MIS Evaluation Form

Page _____
Date _____
No. _____

MIS Project Name _____

Initial costs	1980	1981	1982	Total
1. Project planning	$5,000			$ 5,000
2. Gross design	1,000	$ 2,000		3,000
3. Detailed design		10,000	$23,000	33,000
4. Implementation			7,000	7,000
5. Testing			4,800	4,800
6. Special			600	600
Total initial costs	$6,000	$12,000	$35,400	$53,400
Capital costs				
7. Computer center hardware		$10,300	$33,000	$43,300
8. Facilities		5,000	13,000	18,000
Total capital costs		$15,300	$46,000	$61,300
Annual operating costs				
9. Computer and equipment lease		$ 5,000	$ 24,000	$ 29,000
10. Personnel		47,000	200,000	247,000
11. Overhead and supplies		10,000	20,000	30,000
Total annual operating costs		$62,000	$244,000	$306,000
Benefits				
12. Reduced salary and labor costs			$ 2,000	$ 2,000
13. Reduced inventory costs			97,000	97,000
14. Better strategic decisions (estimated impact)		$50,000	320,000	370,000
15. Freeing up of managerial time (estimated)		5,000	60,000	65,000
Total benefits		$55,000	$479,000	$534,000

Formalization of the Measurement

Once the variables of interest have been identified, a table should be set up to formalize the measurement. Table 9-2 illustrates how this might be done.

CONTROL AND MAINTAIN THE SYSTEM

Control and maintenance of the system are the responsibilities of the line managers. Control of the system means the operation of the system as it was designed to operate. Sometimes operators will develop their own private procedures or will short-circuit procedures designed to provide checks. Often well-intentioned people make unauthorized changes to improve the system, changes that are not approved or documented. Managers themselves may not be factoring into decisions information supplied by the system, such as sales forecast or inventory information, and may be relying on intuition. It is up to management at each level in the organization to provide periodic spotchecks of the system for control purposes.

Maintenance is closely related to control. Maintenance is that ongoing activity that keeps the MIS at the highest levels of effectiveness and efficiency within cost constraints. In other words, maintenance of the MIS is directed toward reducing errors due to design, reducing errors due to environmental changes, and improving the system's scope and services. These activities are sometimes classified as (1) emergency maintenance, (2) routine maintenance, (3) requests for special (one-time) reports, and (4) systems improvements.

Maintenance may be applied to the following entities or activities:

1. Changes in policy statements
2. Changes in reports received by a manager who replaces an outgoing manager
3. Changes in forms
4. Changes in operating systems
5. Changes in procedures
6. Changes in hardware or hardware configuration
7. Software modification or addition
8. System controls and security needs
9. Changes in inputs from the environment

Item 9 requires some amplification. If changes in the environment are not monitored closely, a constant stream of errors may run rampant throughout the MIS. The maintenance team may lose many hours tracking them to their source. Let us look at some areas of change in the environment.

Environmental Change

Governmental Policies, Regulations, and Legislation

Most large companies require specialists or lawyers to keep management appraised of the numerous changes in reporting requirements, compliance requirements, and pressures for change. For example, banks must be aware of new regulations, maximum interest rates, interest rates established through Federal Reserve activities, minimum down payments required on loans and mortgages, and mortgage acceptance rules. Manufacturing companies must be aware of changes in pension rules, financial disclosure, and so on. Health care facilities must be aware of legislation and rulings with regard to state and federal government payments for the elderly, indigent, and so on. In other words, there is a continual flow of rules from government that requires constant updating of the MIS in a company.

Economic Conditions

Changes in general economic conditions play a major role in defining financial information systems. If the system is properly designed, it should meet the needs of all users, not just the accounting and finance departments. General economic conditions dictate corporate policy in several areas, and the ability to internalize these changes is an important part of good systems design. As these changes are only partly predictable, the system should be evaluated periodically to ensure both proper inclusion and measurement of new conditions. Changes in the unemployment rate, both nationally and locally, could affect the direct labor cost and could also affect the timeframe for completion of planned projects. Changes in inflation and interest rates have even more far-reaching impacts. A rise in interest rates may hinder customers attempting to obtain short-term credit to purchase a company's product. The same rise in interest rates may stop a company from expanding plant capacity, stockpiling inventories, or replacing and updating fixed assets. This list is not all inclusive, but it should be noted that periodic systems evaluations will help to ensure that these and similar items are included.

Industry and Competitive Conditions

Changes in industry conditions should be treated in the same manner as changes in economic conditions; however, the timing of reactions to these changes may be more important. The expansion or collapse of a market for a company's products is of such importance that failure to react on a timely basis may mean failure of the business as a whole. Competitive strategies, price policy, hiring, and capital budgeting are but a few of the areas affected by changes in business conditions. New technology, either in production of products or in the creation of alternative products, may affect even the basic concepts that form the corporate objectives.

New standards for measurement such as package sizes or the metric system may have great financial impact. Industry innovations in reporting or gathering data, such as point-of-purchase data collection in retailing and video responses to stock price information in brokerage houses, are other examples. These and the changes cited earlier require anything from routine to major changes in the MIS.

New Technology

The development of computer technology, applications programs, and management techniques has progressed at such a rate as to make farcical the articles of only a few years ago suggesting that total information systems would always be myths. Data communications systems, interactive systems with video displays, tremendous storage capacities, and higher-speed computers are staggering to old-line managers. This new technology is being introduced and used by the flood of accounting and business graduates entering organizations each year. The aggressiveness of computer and software companies in promoting entire systems has also been a major factor. Thus technological change alone requires continual system maintenance.

Internal Problems Related to MIS Maintenance

Several problems can arise in the area of maintenance:

- No plan for maintenance
- No resource allocation for maintenance
- Lack of management understanding, interest, and commitment
- Lack of user understanding and cooperation
- Inadequate documentation
- Lack of qualified personnel

These problems are self-explanatory. They will also be discussed in more detail in Chapter 10. Suffice it to say that the MIS project is not over when the MIS becomes operational. A full third of the work effort and cost remains to be expended under the title of maintenance for the MIS to be truly effective and useful.

Responsibility for Maintenance

Specific responsibility for maintenance should be assigned to a supervisor and team of MIS analysts, programmers, and forms specialists. Fragmentation of responsibility to MIS analysts, the computer experts, and the forms coordinator, without at least a unifying committee, can lead to compounding of MIS maintenance problems. Although many view MIS maintenance as primarily computer program maintenance, it is not. The most important maintenance activities may precede, or not even include, program maintenance.

Initiation of Maintenance Projects

Maintenance activity may be initiated by error reports, a user's change request, a member of the maintenance team, or company management. Usually, specially designed forms for error reports and for change requests must be completed. A barrier to soliciting information on errors or for changes is the detail required on the form. It may be more useful to have a very simple form that calls for only the requested correction or change and a brief statement of the need. Once a maintenance analyst receives such a form, a more detailed documentation may be filled out after an interview.

Planning

Maintenance cannot be performed on a haphazard, informal basis or on a first-come, first-served basis. Four steps are necessary for a good maintenance program:

 1. Log all requests for change. Only written requests should be accepted and included in the log.
 2. Assign priorities to all requests. These will be determined by urgency of the project for the MIS, long-range benefits, time and resources required, and, in some cases, management dictum.
 3. Prepare annual and short-range (usually monthly) plans.
 4. Document maintenance as it occurs. When a project is completed, revise the MIS design manual.

SUMMARY

The implementation of the MIS is the culmination of the design process. We have pointed out the close pre- and postimplementation relationships between design and implementation. We have discussed three major approaches to implementation from the design time standpoint. Finally, we have given a step-by-step procedure for implementation. As we pointed out in the chapters on design, such a procedure is only an approximation of the timing, because there may exist a parallel execution of some steps. Thus, it seems logical to document the system after it has been debugged and is in final form. In practice, however, it is necessary to document the system as installation takes place, so that there will be an up-to-date reference design during the design phase. The final documentation should be a complete, formal, accurate version of the MIS as it exists in operation.

We have given the major implementation steps as

1. Planning the implementation activities
2. Acquiring and laying out facilities and offices
3. Organizing the personnel for implementation
4. Developing procedures for installation and testing
5. Developing the training program for operating personnel
6. Completing the system's software
7. Acquiring required hardware
8. Generating files
9. Designing forms
10. Testing of the entire system
11. Completing cutover to the new system
12. Documenting the system
13. Evaluating the MIS
14. Providing system maintenance (debugging and improving)

In conclusion, we point out that many practitioners believe that the design and implementation of an MIS is always an evolutionary process. There are, however, many advantages to a complete redesign of the MIS despite the difficulties of installing a new system while an old one is in operation. The "big-step" approach permits complete rethinking of the entire system and encourages innovative ideas. Indeed, it *is* the systems approach.

PROBLEMS AND QUESTIONS

1. Case 4, Johnson Enterprises (G) covers the actual decision of which hardware and software items to buy.

2. Column A identifies the four basic methods for installing an MIS when it is complete. In column B, list the characteristics of the situation which would lead management to choose the option in column A.

	A		B
a.	Install the system in a new operation or organization.	a.	_____
b.	Cut off the old MIS and install the new one.	b.	_____
c.	Cut over by segments.	c.	_____
d.	Operate the old MIS and the new one in parallel and cut over.	d.	_____

3. List the 14 major implementation tasks:

4. Order the following implementation tasks by their logical time sequence:

_____ Test the entire system
_____ Cut over to the new system
_____ System maintenance
_____ Acquire and layout facilities
_____ Evaluate the MIS
_____ Complete the system software
_____ Plan implementation activities
_____ Document the system

5. What are four sources of maintenance requirements?

_____
_____
_____
_____

6. Give three reasons for severe problems in the area of MIS maintenance.

_____
_____
_____

7. Group the list of individual tasks under A into the major categories listed under B — the work breakdown structure. Be sure and group the individual tasks *in sequence*.

A — Individual Tasks

1. Define personnel cutover needs
2. Perform staff review
3. Remove old equipment
4. Assign project manager for implementation
5. Construct equipment room
6. Test personnel
7. Prepare program documentation
8. Evaluate personnel test results
9. Submit cost estimates of floor space for management approval
10. Complete phase cutover
11. Order tapes and disks packs
12. Schedule implementation tasks
13. Perform staff review
14. Organize training seminar for users
15. Arrange training facilities
16. Test operating system
17. Have equipment delivered
18. Review implementation plan
19. Prepare program logic diagram
20. Define implementation tasks
21. Schedule implementation tasks
22. Document cutover results
23. Complete system test
24. Determine that equipment is operational
25. Review physical plan with manufacturer
26. Test user equipment
27. Brief departmental personnel on implementation plan
28. Conduct manufacturer's installation and test
29. Interview and select personnel
30. Prepare cost estimates for floor areas
31. Perform staff review
32. Review cutover plan
33. Begin application cutover
34. Code program
35. Announce personnel testing
36. Establish application cutover sequence
37. Establish training sessions for computer personnel
38. Organize orientation meetings
39. Define program processing specifications
40. Develop procedures for implementation
41. Perform staff review
42. Schedule application cutover
43. Prepare system flowchart
44. Test program
45. Confirm equipment delivery date
46. Finalize equipment configuration
47. Keypunch program and desk check
48. Prepare rough layouts and estimates of floor areas
49. Finalize environmental requirements
50. Complete system cutover

B — Work Breakdown Structure

Work Breakdown Structure

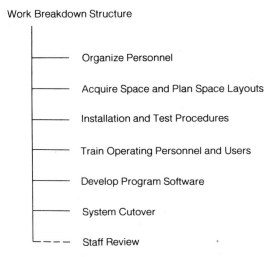

- Organize Personnel
- Acquire Space and Plan Space Layouts
- Installation and Test Procedures
- Train Operating Personnel and Users
- Develop Program Software
- System Cutover
- Staff Review

8. Study Figure 9-A carefully along with the activity description details below.

Activity	Description	Time (weeks) Required
1 – 2	Record layouts prepared	4
2 – 3	Special cards / forms designed	3
3 – 4	Special cards / forms on order	1
2 – 5	System controls defined	2
5 – 6	System flowchart prepared	3
1 – 7	Manual processes defined	2
6 – 8	System flowchart finalized	2
7 – 10	Procedure narratives written	4
4 – 10, 9 – 10	Staff review	1
8 – 9	File design completed	3
8 – 10	Prepare management presentation	1

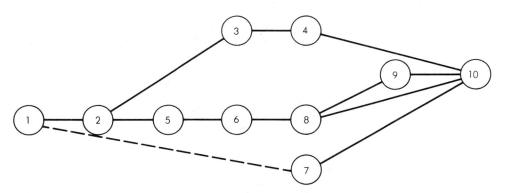

FIGURE 9-A Activity Network for Implementation of an MIS

Critical Path ―――――――――――――――――――――――――

Activities	Critical Activities (X) Weeks to Complete Activity ▰▰
Record layouts prepared ( )	
Special cards/forms designed ( )	
Special cards/forms on order ( )	
System controls defined ( )	
System flowchart prepared ( )	
System flowchart finalized ( )	
Procedure narratives written ( )	
Staff review ( )	
Staff review ( )	
File design completed ( )	
Management presentation ( )	

FIGURE 9-B   Gantt Chart to Portray Implementation Phase Critical Path and Critical Activities

Now complete the Gantt chart for the project (Figure 9-B), identifying the critical path and the critical activities by marking them with (x). Also indicate the scheduling of each activity by drawing in a bar ▰▰ on the chart.

9. Prepare a test specification for testing a portion of an MIS of your own choosing.

10. At present, the Snocan Company, which manufactures 25 products has 103 sales offices throughout the United States with an average of 10 sales representatives per office. Every week, the sales reports in each office are tabulated by a clerk on a rotary calculating machine. The reports divide sales according to sales representative, product, and customer. The reports are mailed to headquarters where they are combined by clerks using calculating machines. The results are then typed and given to marketing research and to management. While top management is studying the reports, marketing research analyzes them and forecasts sales for the next six months. Unfortunately, by the time management receives the reports, they are from three to six weeks old.

A new system has been devised in which daily sales by salesperson, product, and customer are sent over a data communication line from each office to headquarters. A new electronic computer is to be installed to compile and analyze the data and forecast sales. The computer will also handle payroll calculations and replace three clerks in payroll.

The detailed design has been approved by management. The company's system designer is now ready to detail plans for implementation. Nobody in the company has had any experience with computers or computer languages. About

2000 square feet of floor space is available at present for the computer center. The kind of data transmission equipment and the computer have not yet been specified.

Provide the Snocan Company with a thorough set of plans for implementing their new MIS.

SELECTED REFERENCES

AGRESTI, WILLIAM W. "Managing Program Maintenance," *Journal of Systems Management*, February 1982.

BERRY, ELIZABETH. "Prepare for the Future with Updating Systems." *Journal of Systems Management*, February 1982.

CHENEY, PAUL H. "Measuring MIS Project Success." *Proceedings, 9th Annual Conference, American Institute for Decision Sciences*, Chicago, October 19–21, 1977.

GIBSON, CYRUS F., AND RICHARD L. NOLAN. "Organizational Issues in the Stages of EDP Growth." *Data Base*, nos. 2, 3, 4 (1973).

GILCHRIST, BRUCE. "Technological Limitations on MIS Implementation." Paper presented ORSA/TIMS Conference, Colorado Springs, November 1980.

GRIMSBERG, MICHAEL J. "Steps Toward More Effective Implementation of MS and MIS." *Interfaces*, May 1978.

HERZOG, JOHN P. "System Evaluation Technique, Selected References for Users." *Journal of Systems Management*, May 1975.

INGRASSIA, FRANK S. "Combatting the '90% Complete' Syndrome." *Datamation*, January 1978.

KAHN, JAFAR. "How to Tackle the Systems Maintenance Dilemma." *Canadian Datasystems*, March 1975.

KEET, ERNEST E. "Eliminating the Risks of Buying Software." *Infosystems*, February 1978.

KING, JOHN LESLIE, AND EDWARD L. SCHREMS. "Cost Benefit Analysis of Information Systems Development and Operation." *ACM Computing Surveys*, March 1978.

KOOGLER, PAUL, FRANK COLLINS, AND DONALD K. CLANCY. "The New System Arrives." *Journal of Systems Management*, November 1981.

KOTTER, JOHN P., AND LEONARD A. SCHLESINGER. "Strategies for Change." *Harvard Business Review*, March–April 1979.

LUCAS, HENRY C., JR. "Unsuccessful Implementation: The Case of a Computer-Based Order Entry System." *Decision Sciences*, January 1978.

MARTIN, GEORGE N. "EDP Systems Maintenance." *Journal of Systems Management*, September 1979.

MURDICK, ROBERT G. *MIS: Concepts and Design*, Englewood Cliffs, N.J.: Prentice-Hall, 1980.

OSBORN, ROBERT W. "Theories of Productivity Analysis." *Datamation*, September 1981.

PEOPLES, DONALD E. "Measure for Productivity." *Datamation*, May 1978.

SCHROEDER, WILLIAM J., JR. "Economic Evaluation of Computers by Smaller Companies." *Data Management*, October 1979.

SMITH, WILLIAM A., JR., AND ALAN M. WOLF. *Guide for Evaluation of Information Systems*. Atlanta: American Institute of Industrial Engineers, 1974.

SMOLENSKI, ROBERT J. "Test Plan Development." *Journal of Systems Management*, February 1981.

STIMMLER, SAUL. *Data Processing Systems: Their Performance, Evaluation, Measurement, and Improvement*. Trenton, N.J.: Motivational Learning Programs, 1974.

10

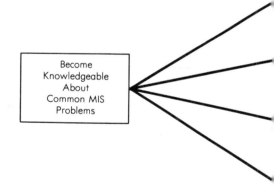

Become
Knowledgeable
About
Common MIS
Problems

Pitfalls in MIS Development

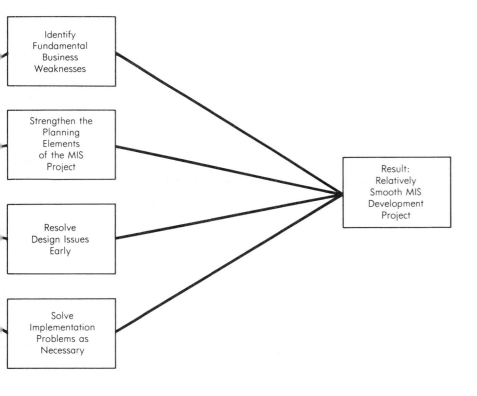

"Nothing can go wrong... go wrong... go wrong..." has become a sad joke among experienced MIS managers and developers. There is a definite perversity in the process of developing both management information systems and programming systems that has given rise to sardonic humor. It seems that, given experienced and talented managers, well-defined plans and contingency plans, ample and gifted implementors, money and time, one is at best able to *minimize* the problems encountered in MIS development. The fatal errors and the extremely costly and time-consuming problems can be avoided. But a continual stream of petty inconveniences and minor problems remains.

In this chapter, we will draw on our own experience and the experience of other MIS professionals to discuss several of the most serious problems you may encounter while constructing your MIS. This is by no means an exhaustive list of what can go awry. In fact, in the MIS context, *there is nothing that cannot go wrong*. However, this discussion will guide you in avoiding the fatal MIS development errors. Then, by good management, you have the framework for solving the smaller problems.

FUNDAMENTAL WEAKNESSES

There are some problems that lurk in the broom closets and front offices of corporations just looking for places to manifest themselves. These are fundamental weaknesses in the firm itself. When the company decides to develop an MIS, these problems correctly recognize fertile soil and jump at the chance to be part of the project.

No Management System to Build Upon [1]

For some reason many managers think that they can patch up a company's shortcomings in basic *management systems* by applying a computerized manage-

[1] Joel E. Ross, *Modern Management and Information Systems* (Reston, Va.: Reston, 1976), p. 23.

ment information system as a band-aid. Unfortunately, this will not work. If good planning and control do not exist within the framework of a good organizational structure, no degree of sophistication with a computer is going to cure the basic ill. The MIS must be built on top of a management system that includes the organizational arrangements, the structure and procedures for adequate planning and control, the clear establishment of objectives, and all the other manifestations of good organization and management.

The lack of managerial and operational applications (as opposed to accounting and clerical applications) is serious, because it implies that the process of management is not being performed well. If we can say (as we must) that information is the raw material of decision making, and if information is not being generated, disseminated, and used for management, then no system—manual or computer—is going to solve the problem.

It is worth repeating that only the manager-user can establish, repair, or modify the management system prior to superimposing the MIS on it. The computer technician cannot do it because of his or her background and training, position in the organization, and perspective of the situation. For some excellent guidance on what the basic management system should be, read Peter Drucker's classic *Management: Tasks, Responsibilities, Practices*.

What Business Are We In?

Not having a crisply stated mission and purpose for the company is a common weakness. This problem evolves from the firm's top management wanting to be (or being comfortable with being) operating managers. Top management focuses on the day-to-day operational problems and abdicates the responsibilities of providing a future for the company. The results are as you would expect. Since it is not terribly clear what business we are in, each major challenge the company must face is a *completely new* challenge and must be analyzed from the ground up. If there was a mission statement, some of these problems could be dealt with routinely as opposed to their being major crises. Let us look at a couple of examples.

IBM is well known for the computers that it manufactures and sells. One might easily conclude that IBM's mission is to build and sell computers. If management took that view, all would go well for a few years until computers and computing product markets followed the hand-held calculator markets (stiff competition and rapidly disappearing margins), and suddenly building and selling computers is the wrong business to be in. IBM is a well-managed company and has avoided this problem. IBM's mission is (approximately) to provide society with solutions to its information processing needs. Under that definition, the computer is only one element in the equation and its demise as a high-profit product becomes normal business evolution, not a management crisis.

Let us take the IBM example one step farther. Given the information processing definition of IBM's business, when IBM is approached to consider a joint venture with an oil company to find oil in Antarctica, it is straightforward for management to decide that oil drilling is not IBM's purpose for being in business. Again, the mission statement helps management in decision making.

Much of the guidance for what the MIS should do rests on a clear idea of what business the firm is in. Many of the constraints on the MIS are derived from knowing what business the company is in and what business it will be in. Without this background information, the MIS may or may not satisfy management needs.

Company Objectives

Written objectives are also often missing in a company. A firm without objectives is much like a company without a statement of mission and purpose—it is a ship without a rudder.

This problem evolved in the same way the previous one did. Top management failed to set objectives for the company. The results are also similar. Everyone in the company is left without the benefit of the guidance that objectives give. For example, clear objectives provide decision-making criteria when problems arise. Without these objectives, not only is each problem a major new challenge, but each time a problem arises, management must generate decision-making criteria *for this case* before it can attack the problem. Let us turn to an example.

Sears has a mission statement (roughly) of being the premier buyer for Middle America. A possible objective would be to provide a thorough inventory management system for the Sears empire. This objective (taken in the context of the Sears mission statement) helps the MIS development team to know the goals and constraints of the system they are building. For example, Rolls Royce cars and top-of-the-line Tiffany jewelry are not going to be inventory items. Home improvement items and financial services are. These are key guidance factors in developing this comprehensive inventory management system for Sears. Without the business objectives, the chances of the MIS satisfying management needs are slight.

Managerial Participation [2]

Of all the reasons for MIS failure, lack of managerial participation probably heads the list. Dozens of studies on hundreds of companies have concluded that the most striking characteristic of the successful company is that MIS development has been viewed as a responsibility of management. This includes both top management and operating line management. The reasonable conclusion that managers must reach is that MIS is too important to be left to the computer technician.

This position is substantiated if one examines the companies that have been successful with computer-based MIS—Weyerhaeuser, IBM, Xerox, Pillsbury,

---

[2] Ibid., pp. 25–26.

and Ford, to name a few. Their success is attributed directly to the fact that manager-users are required to become involved in the design of their own systems. Moreover, the presidents take a personal interest and participate directly in defining what work the computer should do for the company. Nothing less is acceptable when computers are becoming the largest single item of capital budgets and have such a widespread impact on all operating systems of the firm.

There are three good arguments for managerial participation. First, the time has come when the up-to-date manager must bring to the job at least a minimal familiarity with the topic of MIS. Second, from the point of view of the organization, the time is rapidly approaching when a company's information system will become a vital part of its operation just as marketing, operations, and finance are today. Third, it simply makes good sense for managers to become involved, because much better and more effective information systems will be the result of that involvement.

Organization of the MIS Function [3]

Another significant cause of computer failure is the lack of proper organization of the EDP and MIS function. When computers first burst upon the business scene in the late 1950s and early 1960s, the only practical applications were concerned with the automation of clerical work: accounting, payroll, inventory reporting, and similar *financial* jobs. Following the classical organizational principle of assignment of a service activity by *familiarity*, the overwhelming trend at that time was to assign the computer to the controller or the chief accountant. Unfortunately, this is where it has remained in many companies. The result has been a disproportionate emphasis on accounting and related clerical work. This development was a natural one because the computer gave the accountant an added dimension of importance. However, the result has been a reluctance on the part of the financial managers to share the machine with others. Many have forgotten the first rule of staff employees: they exist to serve the line operations.

Fortunately, the trend has reversed itself. More and more academicians and practitioners of business realize that the *information* resource of the company ranks alongside the classical Four M's (money, manpower, materials, and machines and facilities) and deserves vice presidential attention just as the other resources.

The exact location in the organization and the authority granted to the MIS manager is, of course, a function of the type of business the firm is in and how important the information resource is to its operation. In banking, transportation, many service industries, and perhaps to a lesser extent in manufacturing, data processing and MIS pervade all areas of the business.

Alternative assignments of the MIS function are shown in Figure 10-1.

[3] Ibid., pp. 22–23.

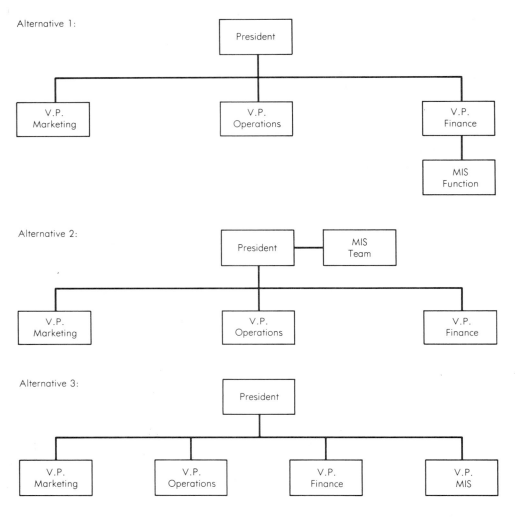

Alternative 1: Not recommended at any time.
Alternative 2: Recommended for early stages of development.
Alternative 3: Recommended for eventual permanent organization.

FIGURE 10-1 Alternative Assignment of MIS Function

Reliance on Consultant or Manufacturer[4]

Some computer manufacturers and some consultants will try to sell the *turnkey* system, one that is designed and debugged and ready for its buyer to push the button or turn the key. Although some complete packages exist (there are several

[4] Ibid., p. 20.

truly excellent offerings), be careful! In most cases, the consultant or manufacturer is concerned more with the machine than with management solutions. Before buying a "solution" from a consultant or manufacturer, be sure that it is the whole solution, that you understand it thoroughly, and that you understand your legal recourse when things do not work the way you expected.

There are other good reasons for going slow in allowing consultants or manufacturers to make your computer and MIS decisions. First, there is a good chance that you will have to spend a great deal of time educating them in the operations of your company before they are in a position to make recommendations. Second, installing the system without substantial preparation is likely to result in some chaos. And third—and this is a general rule—if the buyer does not have the personnel capable of designing the organization's MIS, it is unlikely that it will have the expertise to operate those that were designed and installed by the outsider.

If, despite this advice, you want to use the consultant or manufacturer in a major way, remember these do's and don'ts:

- *Don't* let a technological romance with the computer obscure management's objective of improved operations.
- *Do* take a return-on-investment approach to expenditures.
- *Do* avoid operating in a reactive mode rather than against a master plan.
- *Don't* buy the argument of reduced unit processing costs unless it means lower absolute or total costs.

Communications Gap [5]

It is unlikely that for the foreseeable future the computer technician (EDP manager, systems analyst, programmer, management scientist) will be able to speak the language of management, and managers for the most part are not prepared to speak the language of the computer. The result is a communications gap that sometimes causes a design standoff.

Technicians have little appreciation of the process of management or of the problems of managers. Operation of the machine is their "thing." They measure their performance by how many shifts the computer is running and how much printout or output they can generate. Given the choice, technicians will give the user all the data contained in the system pertaining to the user's problem. Thus the sales manager who asks for the sales performance report is likely to get computer printout in a stack two feet high. What he really wants is an exception report that highlights significant variances from plan.

On the other hand, the manager is not without guilt. Unless he's been to a business school or a good seminar recently, he is not likely to be very knowledgeable about the computer and how it can be used to help him improve his operations. The result is frequently abdication to the computer technician. A

[5] Ibid., pp. 18–19.

phrase that is too often heard by the systems analyst or EDP manager is, "You're the expert. You figure it out!"

But the expert cannot "figure it out." Because of his or her training, interests, desires, and peer pressures, the technician's compulsive tendency is to generate massive databases, install display devices and data communications techniques, and install newer and grander designs—all for the purpose of empire building but not for improved management—and it is probably too much to expect that the computer technician will change.

Characteristically, there are three stages in the development of an MIS, each stage depending on a fragile process of communications. These stages and the typical communication breakdown are shown:

Development Stage	*Typical Communication Breakdown*
• Designer asks user what information is needed.	• User is not accustomed to rigorous self-analysis and cannot adequately express information needs.
• Designer works out a plan and gives it to programmer.	• Designer converts what he *thinks he heard* from the user into flow charts and trappings of systems design, altering information needs in the process.
• Programmer implements system.	• Programmer incorporates his *own ideas and interpretations*, further altering user's needs. Final results frustrate the user, who becomes hostile, or worse, sabotages the system.

The negative impact of this situation on MIS success is great. There simply is no substitute for extensive, honest conversation between the MIS developer and the MIS user.

The People Involved

Whether we are talking about the management team, the MIS specialists, or the people who are doing the company's main work (and will be the MIS users), one criterion is overriding: there is no substitute for competence. The performance of employees (including managers) can be compared as follows:

- Good performers are an *order of magnitude* more productive than average performers. Given tools from the Stone Age and no light to work by, good performers will produce good results. Average performers can be made productive only in the right environment.
- Average performers are *infinitely* more productive than poor performers. In fact, poor performers produce negative work; that is, someone else's time is spent fixing poor performers' messes.

The moral of the preceding paragraph is that you can guarantee success with your MIS if the key management spots, the key MIS roles, and the key user positions are occupied by good performers. The degree to which one relies on average or poor performers in these key places is the degree to which the project will probably fail. If the key managers involved are poor managers, the MIS will almost certainly be a failure. If the key MIS roles are occupied by poor performers, a respectable result is possible only with extra time and extra management involvement. If the key user positions are held by poor performers, more education and selling is required and the user interface to the MIS must be enhanced greatly to increase correct input and to make the output more easily understood.

There is no substitute for competence. Hire only good performers. They are well worth the price.

Review

We have discussed several things that can go wrong when developing an MIS:

1. No management system to build upon
2. No clear definition of mission and purpose
3. No objectives for the company
4. Lack of management participation
5. Misorganization
6. Overreliance on the consultant or manufacturer
7. The communications gap
8. Performance of key people

All these pitfalls are really general weaknesses in the company as a whole. They could (and do) show up anywhere in the firm. Due to the complexities of MIS development projects, these problems are guaranteed to show up quickly and harshly. Information systems are not a solution to any of these problems, only the medium by which they become obvious to the organization. However, these deficiencies in the firm's infrastructure must be corrected before an MIS can truly succeed.

SOFT SPOTS IN PLANNING

A second area where problems often occur, this time more directly related to the MIS under development, is planning. We will look at system and project planning, strategic and detailed planning, and some of the "nonsolutions" to planning problems.

MIS Response to Business Plans

One of the great hazards of MIS planning is the tendency to forget the original purpose of management information systems. Management information systems exist solely to assist line management in executing the main business of the company. Each step the MIS or computer group goes beyond that definition of their role is waste of company resource.

The point just made must be kept in mind as the MIS department responds to the general business plans, both strategic and operating. It is extremely difficult for talented professionals to respond "merely" to the information needs of the main business. There is an almost irresistible temptation to purchase the latest hardware, implement the latest software techniques, try out new ideas, and in general, encourage the MIS function into a life of its own. These desires to do interesting technical things and the corresponding MIS management tendency to build an empire are not acceptable to the larger organization. They represent key friction points between line management and the MIS function. They are also a source of upper management losing faith in the MIS group.

In summary, the purpose of the MIS group is to support line management in the company's main business. As business plans are made and modified, the corresponding MIS plans must be made and changed. Each MIS plan must be a proper response to a business plan.

A System View, a Master Plan [6]

Another cause of computer failure is the lack of a master plan to which hardware development and individual MIS designs can be related. Without such a plan, the result is likely to be a patchwork approach that will result in *islands of mechanization* with little integration between separate systems. In other words, we need a systems approach to MIS development.

This patchwork or piecemeal approach to systems development, which lacks a unifying framework and is without a master plan, has several disadvantages. One of these stems from the unrelated nature of the subsystems developed. Frequently autonomous departments and divisions have developed individualistic systems without regard to the interface of such systems elsewhere in the organization. The result has been an inability to communicate between systems and the incompatibility of subsystems of a like nature throughout the company. A second disadvantage is the cost involved—cost in time, resources, and money.

The reasons for MIS planning are the same as for planning in general: it offsets uncertainty, improves economy of operations, focuses on the objectives, and provides a device for subsequent control of operations. If the patchwork approach is allowed to progress too far, it may be too expensive to start again from scratch and redesign to an integrated master plan. The point of no return may have been passed.

[6]Ibid., p. 21.

One-for-One Conversion [7]

The overwhelming majority (estimates range up to 98 percent) of computer applications are for clerical data processing and paperwork automation, not for managerial decision making. In this type of system (e.g., payroll, inventory accounting, accounts receivable), the computer is used for the most part as a piece of high-speed tabulating equipment. Despite the fact that this "clerical" automation approach yields minimum benefits in terms of information usage for managerial purposes, it remains the most frequent type of application.

The clerical approach may have been justifiable in the past when cost savings through clerical automation was a major objective. However, this approach has been carried about as far as it can go, and the time has come to adopt improved management as an objective.

The worst possible approach to systems design is the one-for-one conversion, which occurs when a technician takes an existing manual or computer system and converts or modifies it without upgrading or changing it. In other words, ledger accounting remains ledger accounting (instead of being upgraded to *financial planning*), order entry remains order entry (instead of being upgraded into *sales analysis*), and production reporting remains production reporting (instead of being upgraded to *production planning and control*). The conversion process provides an excellent opportunity to upgrade an existing clerical system into a *management information system*. So why not take advantage of the opportunity?

One final note remains on converting subsystem for subsystem. Unless the original system was robust, the converted system will be a problem. The element of tremendous speed (computer processing and printing) has been added to a marginally effective procedure. This is a strong argument for doing some systems design and not just converting an existing subsystem.

Setting Project and System Objectives

Setting objectives for projects and systems is not itself a planning activity. However, no meaningful plans can be made until these objectives have at least been roughed in. Conversely, no serious objectives can be set until some of the general planning variables are known. These two activities (setting objectives and planning) are co-requisite.

The pitfall for those developing an MIS is trying to do either of these tasks before the other. The proper way to approach the problem is to decide what kind of system/project is desired (in general terms). In the next breath, ask when it is needed and about how much it can cost. Continue to bounce back and forth between objectives statement and plan response, refining each in turn. This method will allow both objectives and plans to evolve, each synchronized with the other.

[7] Ibid., p. 17.

Facing Constraints

Many people believe that perfect freedom is a good thing and that the fewer constraints, the freer they are. More sober reflection on this problem will probably reverse most adherents' views. Complete freedom from automobile driving restrictions would allow people to drive anywhere on the road and would lead to horrible accidents. Freedom from social restraints leads to anarchy and its attendant woes. Similarly, freedom from constraints on

- Functional definition
- System performance
- System cost
- Development schedules

will lead to enormous MIS problems. Let us turn to some examples.

Implementors of MIS functions like to do creative work. Functions that are dull or repetitive are generally not fun to do, and many implementors will try to get out of doing them, even though they may be crucial to making the system work. On the other hand, these same implementors may be really "turned on" by some new idea and be feverishly creating a completely unnecessary function or an overly elaborate version of a necessary one. Functional constraints are critical to getting the correct MIS implemented.

Performance of the MIS is really a special aspect of the MIS functional description. But it is worth noting that an MIS that produces the right results too late is worse than no MIS at all. An MIS that costs too much to produce the right results on time is also not acceptable. Hence the constraints on system performance are important to the resulting system.

Next is system cost, a topic of no interest to the technicians and of supreme interest to the management team. One set of constraints here is obvious: if the system costs too much, the firm cannot afford it. The other set of constraints is not so readily accepted by management but it is just as real. Some money and time must be invested to get the benefits of the desired MIS. In fact, a lot of money and time must be invested before any payoff occurs. That is the nature of development projects, and it is a meaningful constraint with which the management team must deal.

And, finally, there are constraints on schedules. Again, management is very interested and the technicians really are not overly concerned. The situation is analogous to cost. A system delivered too late may be useless. On the other side of the coin, substantial time must be invested to get any meaningful results.

These examples amply illustrate some real constraints on every MIS development effort. It is essential that both managers and technicians recognize the reality of these constraints and plan accordingly. It is a big plus for the project if those involved also recognize the *value* of these constraints.

Plan to "Sell" the MIS [8]

Most systems designers admit to the unpleasant reality that the toughest part of designing and implementing an MIS is gaining acceptance of the users for whom the system is designed. How many analysts or EDP managers have asked themselves this frustrating question: "Since my system is technically optimum and is obviously going to result in improved performance and more efficient operations, why can't I get the user to accept it and welcome it?"

The fact is that many people will not only resist a new system, but what is worse, they will work around it, continue to use the old system, and in many cases *sabotage* the new system. Yet resistance to MIS is not inherent or automatic. People only resist things that they fear or do not understand.

The first and major step in learning how to overcome resistance to a new MIS is to try and gain some understanding of the *reasons* for resistance. This understanding will give the designer and the manager a new attitude toward resistance and go a long way toward helping to overcome it. Indeed, this understanding and this attitude, if achieved, constitute about the best answer that behavioral science has to offer. After all, resistance to MIS is nothing more than a special case of the general problem of resistance to change.

The wrong approach, of course, is to try to sell an MIS based on its technical superiority. People are just not interested. They are interested only in how the system will affect them and their jobs. Typical reasons for resistance might be illustrated:

Reason	*Illustration*
• Threat to status	• Sales representatives are downgraded below production planners upon installation of production control system.
• Threat to ego	• Manager's job skills become less important due to computer takeover.
• Economic threat	• Clerical personnel fear job loss.
• Insecurity	• Managers may be deprived of personal power or political base due to quantitative measures provided by MIS.
• Loss of autonomy and control	• Production planning and control function is now largely being performed by new MIS.
• Interpersonal relations changed	• Former relationships built up on personal information exchange are changed.

[8] Ibid., pp. 27–28.

These illustrations lead to the conclusion that human acceptance of the computer can be obtained only on the basis of how it affects people personally in their job and the way in which they view it as an instrument of social change in their relationship with others. In other words, consider the social and behavioral aspects rather than the technical ones. Here are some do's and don'ts:

- *Don't* design the system first and then try to force acceptance.
- *Don't* pay lip service to participation in design.
- *Don't* emphasize technical and physical constraints of the system to the exclusion of the social and behavioral.
- *Do* begin in the initial stages to take account of the emergent social system and other behavioral variables affecting acceptance.
- *Do* remember that the MIS you propose to modify is resident in various individual personnel. Involve them in the early stages.

To summarize, sell the MIS to the users through their design participation, suggestions, comments, education, and continual involvement. And, above all, *plan* on this set of activities.

Detailed Planning

We cannot possibly review thoroughly the pitfalls related to this topic. That would be a volume by itself. There is, however, one attitude related to detailed planning that deserves special attention. "Detailed planning is for beginners. I can remember everything I need to do." Most experienced MIS development managers have heard this refrain and cringe every time someone says it. The truth of the matter is that detailed planning is the hallmark of the real professional. The more experienced one becomes, the more clearly we see the need for detailed planning. It is the *only* method that permits one successful MIS project to follow another. All veteran MIS development managers know this and plan in detail for every phase of the project. Do not apologize for the money or time spent laying out good plans—they will pay off many times over.

The Mythical Man-Month [9]

Fred Brooks, an eminent computer expert, wrote *The Mythical Man-Month* about his Operating System/360 programming development experience. Although the work is actually about a very large programming effort and some of the difficulties encountered, it applies just as well to any MIS development activity. It is required reading for the literate MIS manager.

We will consider several of Professor Brooks's points later under the section on programming. But he makes one very important point about planning that

---

[9]Frederick P. Brooks, Jr., *The Mythical Man-Month* (Reading, Mass.: Addison-Wesley, 1975).

requires recognition: people and months are not interchangeable; hence the "man-month" as a unit for measuring the size of a job is a dangerous and deceptive myth.[10] This is a critical fact to be reckoned with in all MIS planning. This same phenomenon has been commented on by other writers who noted the exponential communications requirements as the group grows, hence the drop in productivity per person.

This problem, viewed from any angle, is a planning problem. Once we know about the pitfall, we are expected to plan around it. This means that for projects involving a very few people (less than 5), normal productivity estimates are acceptable. For larger projects (25 to 50), productivity per person may drop 25 to 30 percent due to project complexity and interpersonal communications requirements. On very large projects (hundreds of people), a 50 percent or more productivity drop may be reasonable. The morals are

- Plan for complexity and communications costs.
- Run small projects (rather than large) when possible.

Planning for Maintenance

Few MIS development managers do any planning for maintenance. This seems very peculiar at first blush, especially since maintenance activities may consume a third of the total MIS project budget. There are several reasons for this ostrichlike behavior:

1. The work is generally not as exciting as new MIS development, and few people want to work on maintenance projects, including the managers.
2. Upper management is aghast to find out the cost of continued upgrades to an MIS they thought was complete. No one wants to be the bearer of bad tidings.
3. At least some maintenance activities are done in crisis mode when the MIS malfunctions. This is not pleasant, and people try to avoid it.

These are all good personal reasons for avoiding maintenance work, but management is paid for facing hard problems for the company and solving them. Planning for maintenance is the solution to the reality that maintenance is necessary.

Review

We have covered a number of problems related to planning for MIS development:

1. Misresponse to business plans
2. Need for a systems view and master plan

[10] Ibid., p. 16.

3. One-for-one conversions
4. Setting project and system objectives
5. Facing the reality of constraints
6. "Selling" the MIS
7. Detailed planning
8. The man-month myth
9. Planning for maintenance

Now we will look at problems encountered during the design stage.

DESIGN PROBLEMS

We first covered general weaknesses in the firm and how they affected MIS development. We then looked at problems in MIS planning. Now we are looking at pitfalls during the design phase. Although the problems we will now consider are extremely serious and can sink an MIS project, they are within the control of the MIS manager and are consequently more easily solved.

Consider Alternative Designs

During the early stages of design, as many ideas as possible should be considered. As time passes, the alternatives should dwindle to two or three. And by the time detailed design starts, one conceptual design should have been chosen. The error usually made here is not considering numerous ideas at the outset. This stems from the nature of conceptual design, which demands a benevolent dictator or a very small number of like-minded aristocrats to do the design. Only in this way can you get conceptual integrity of the system. The price you pay is the prejudice of the key designer and his or her inability or unwillingness to consider alternatives.

One possible solution to this problem is for the manager to require the key designer to lay out several alternative designs and explain the positive and negative features of each. The secondary problem here is that the designer can make his or her recommended design look best by creating weak alternatives. This would suggest the need for a different key designer who knows better how to handle positions of responsibility.

Hard Trade-offs

Making difficult decisions is not something that most people want to do. However, many tough choices will face the key designer and the MIS development manager. A problem arises if either or both of these people cannot or will not make a required decision. Although snap decisions are seldom required, after reasonable deliberation, a choice is necessary. For example, if alternative A is chosen, activities J, K, and L must take place. If alternative B is the path taken, tasks X, Y, and Z must be done. Clearly this tree branches out very quickly, and it becomes economically infeasible to pursue multiple branches very far. Hence, irrevocable choices are required.

A trade-off of the type just discussed is the buy-or-make software decision. The ramifications are immense, and the key designer and the manager must trade off one set of problems and benefits for another.

Beware the User Interface!

This is not the same problem as selling the system, although it is related. This is, at least partially, a technical problem. Computer experts soon become trapped in a language of their own—alphabet soup (MVS, IMS, CICS) and regular English words with some altered meaning (assemble, edit, crash). This facilitates conversation among computer experts but completely eliminates meaningful dialogue with the user. And that is the problem.

For example, consider a warehouse operation serving various retail outlets. A truck from the retail store drives up and the driver hands a list of needs to the warehouse attendant. The inventory control MIS is now on the critical path to both these employees' assignments (the user interface has become critically important). The warehouse attendant must "ask" the MIS if item A is in stock. He would like to ask the MIS in spoken English, but this system requires that he type in his request. The computer expert will prefer an interface that is succinct and full of abbreviations:

> F   A, #   (Find out how many of Item A are in stock)

The warehouse attendant wants something he can understand and use, perhaps

TYPE IN NUMBER OF ACTION YOU WANT
1. FIND an item in stock
2. REMOVE an item from stock
3. ADD an item to stock
4. REPORT on inventory status
NUMBER _____   (ITEM _____ , AMOUNT _____)

in which case he enters the number 1. The next display of data will request the item name and the amount of A desired. If the warehouse attendant wants a shortcut, he answers those questions in the parenthetical expression on the first screen.

The warehouse attendant is the deciding factor in the question of user interface. Too often, information systems are implemented to the whims of the specialists, not the needs of the users. A technically and financially excellent system will founder unless it is easy for the user to work with.

The Real World as Acid Test

Very briefly, the reality to be faced here is that most businesses are not research institutions. The MIS is being implemented to support the firm's main line of business, not to extend the state of the art in MIS design. Although it is fun to do new and creative things, the practical need is for an MIS that solves today's real problems. Design systems that are implementable with today's known and tried technology. Leave the state of the art to the universities and research departments of large organizations.

If It Moves, Automate It

Some things could be automated, but good sense tells us not to. For example, we could easily design and implement an application to replace the receptionists in most firms. Visitors/customers would just type in the names of the persons they wanted to see or the subjects they wanted to discuss and the correct persons would be called to come to the lobby and retrieve their visitors. But we can be sure that visitors would very soon dwindle along with the company's revenues. People want and expect human interaction to at least be immediately available when they enter the lobby of a place of business. So although this function could be automated, it would not represent good business judgment.

Another aspect of this problem is overautomation, for example, using a computer terminal in place of a pocket calculator or desk-top adding machine. The overhead and complexity introduced to perform simple arithmetic functions are just not worth it.

The Computer Obsession

Various gods have been worshipped down through the ages, and the computer threatens to become another of the pantheon. An MIS consists of several elements:

- People
- Procedures
- Input forms
- Computer processing
- Reports
- And so on...

Note that the computer is just one of several elements, and probably not the most important (people are). As with other gods, we can trace the worship of the computer to fear of the unknown. The computer is nothing but a tool for people to use in getting their jobs done more effectively and efficiently. The computer seldom makes mistakes (it usually operates *as instructed* but may be operating on bad input or instructions). On the other hand, the computer never makes any original decisions and never has any good ideas.

It is important to keep the computer element of the MIS in perspective. Think of it as a hammer or a screwdriver—very valuable for solving the right problems, useless for solving others. In the final analysis, it is a tool.

Documentation

This problem spans the planning, design, and implementation phases. The dilemma the MIS team faces is how much of their work needs documenting. Documentation can become the great, white tide that buries everything in its path (a real threat in these days of high-speed printers). Certain items must be documented and in considerable detail:

1. All plans (including budgets and schedules)
2. Project and system objectives
3. Specifications of function and performance
4. User interface specifications
5. User instruction and reference manuals (including procedures)
6. Maintenance guidance material

These items are necessary to manage and use an MIS over time. Not documenting these things in detail is a guarantee of failure in some part of the operation of the MIS.

On the other hand, documentation can get out of hand. Programmers are notorious for keeping every computer printout, even though the program no longer resembles its earlier forms. Some managers keep every memo, whether it will likely be relevant to future decisions or not. And, finally, most computer professionals keep mountains of technical journals stacked within arm's reach. This is a safety hazard and a fire trap—the library should keep one or two complete sets. A good rule of thumb for all the overflow documentation just discussed is, if you know exactly what useful work you will do with a document in the next two weeks, keep it; otherwise, throw it out.

Review

The design phase presents us with a whole new set of problems. They include

- Consideration of alternative designs
- Making irrevocable decisions
- User interface importance
- The real-world acid test
- Overautomation
- Worshipping the computer
- Documentation

Now let us turn to the final stage of MIS development: implementation.

IMPLEMENTATION: THE TAR PIT

No scene from prehistory is quite so vivid as that of the mortal struggles of great beasts in the tar pits. In the mind's eye one sees dinosaurs, mammoths, and sabertoothed tigers struggling against the grip of the tar. The fiercer the struggle, the more entangling the tar, and no beast is so strong or so skillful but that he ultimately sinks.[11]

Thus begins Fred Brooks's book on the perversities of developing large software systems. The La Brea tar pits are superb symbolism for the problems of MIS implementation.

Hardware Perspective

We have already discussed the misguided worship of the computer. This problem is most noticeable with the hardware since that is all that can really be seen. Managers proudly show off their computer centers, discussing the amount of disk space they have and the millions of instructions per second the processors will execute and the thousands of square feet occupied by all this hardware. These are all forgivable human antics—we all like to show off our new sports cars. But let us ask the hard question of management: "How should the hardware question be approached?"

The answer is, "Last." In the past, the hardware has been the major purchase, dwarfing software and personnel costs. Today hardware costs are falling rapidly, and in the near future the bulk of the MIS dollar will go to software and services. The hardware will follow the price curve of the pocket calculator, becoming a minor part of the MIS purchase decision. Hence we should start with the really important question: "What management problem(s) do we want to solve?" We then move on to questions about what software is available or can be developed to solve the posed problems. And, last, we ask the question of what hardware must we buy to support our management solutions. This is the proper perspective on MIS hardware.

Software Development

Anything that can go wrong with the MIS as a whole can go wrong in microcosm with the software development. We will not discuss all these again in this context because the analogies are straightforward. Again, we recommend reading *The Mythical Man-Month* before embarking on any nontrivial software development venture.

Another pitfall in software development is both hardware and personnel related. The software must be perfect, without error. The hardware does exactly what it is told; hence, incorrect incantations result in the wrong magic. People

[11]Ibid., p. 4.

are not accustomed to being perfect, and this requirement for perfection is a very difficult adjustment. Only the good performers, as discussed earlier, will adjust and produce excellent work product.

Finally, note Brooks's law:

Adding manpower to a late software project makes it later.[12]

Careful planning, careful contingency planning, and more careful planning is the preventive solution to this omnipresent problem.

Test It and Test It Again

The most common error made with regard to testing is not planning to do enough of it. A good rule of thumb to use in project estimating and planning is

$\frac{1}{3}$ planning and design
$\frac{1}{3}$ implementation
$\frac{1}{3}$ testing

For an MIS project of any reasonable size, this figure for testing is by no means too much. Testing must be done at the function level, the component level, and the system level. Problems will be discovered at each level, and solutions must be found. A good manager will recognize this phenomenon from the start and plan accordingly.

Controlling the MIS Project

Although controlling is one of the four basic management functions, it remains one of the preeminent causes of MIS development project failure. In a chapter entitled Hatching a Catastrophe, Brooks relates the following quotation:

How does a project get to be a year late?... One day at a time.[13]

Although a project can die of too much tracking and reporting, it can equally well die of half-hearted control efforts by management.

Many relatively small events taken together make a project. The MIS manager can take good advantage of this situation by crisply defining the completion criteria for these events and then tracking their successful completion. It is very hard for a project to become late if all relevant parts are completing per schedule and the project had a good initial plan.

[12] Ibid., p. 25.
[13] Ibid., p. 153.

Review

In this final section on the tar pit of MIS implementation, we discussed these problems:

- Hardware perspective
- Software development
- Need for extensive testing
- Controlling the MIS project

The solution to these pitfalls lies entirely in the MIS development manager's hands.

SUMMARY

We have discussed numerous pitfalls in the development of a management information system. The problems were specified, but more important, a tried and workable solution was presented. These are serious problems, but they can be surmounted.

Finally, lest the picture seem too bleak, the following are some famous quotations from the database of acidic wit surrounding the MIS field:

To err is human. To really foul things up takes a computer.

Anything that can go wrong will go wrong in such a way and at such a time that it causes the maximum damage.

—Murphy

I know that you believe you understand what you think I said, but I'm not sure you realize that what you heard is not what I meant.

The eight phases of a successful project:
(1) Uncritical acceptance
(2) Wild enthusiasm
(3) Dejected disillusionment
(4) Total confusion
(5) Escape by the clever
(6) Search for the guilty
(7) Punishment of the innocent
(8) Promotion of the nonparticipants

It works better if you plug it in.

The government is very keen on amassing statistics. They will collect them, add them, raise them to the Nth power, take the cube root and prepare wonderful diagrams. But you must never forget that every one of these figures comes in the first instance from the village watchman, who just puts down what he pleases.

—Sir Josiah Stamp

An expert is a person who avoids the small errors while sweeping on to the grand fallacy.

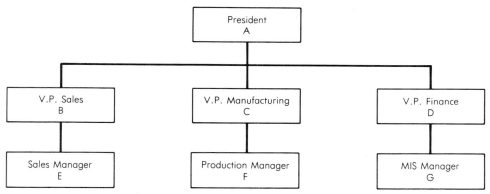

FIGURE 10-A Company XYZ Organization Chart

PROBLEMS AND QUESTIONS

1. List five general weaknesses that may afflict a firm. Why do MIS projects make these weaknesses painfully obvious?

    Weakness   *Why Exposed*

    _____   _____
    _____   _____
    _____   _____
    _____   _____
    _____   _____

2. Figure 10-A is the organization chart for the XYZ Company. Managers E and F need an MIS to more closely coordinate customer demand with company production. Managers A, B, and C are neither for nor against the MIS — they do not care. Manager D measures manager G's performance based on timeliness of financial reports. Manager G is frustrated.

    a. What is the likelihood of E and F getting their MIS?
       _____ Low   _____ Medium   _____ High
    b. What are the problems here?
       _____
       _____

    c. Figure 10-B is a new organization for the XYZ Company. Place the managers in the correct spots.

3. Identify six planning problems that could adversely impact an MIS project.

    _____
    _____
    _____
    _____
    _____
    _____

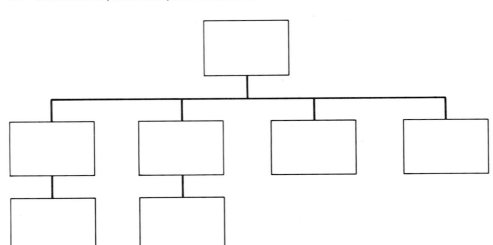

FIGURE 10-B Revised Organization Chart for Company XYZ

4. In column A are some memorable quotations from beginners in the MIS field. Classify the type of problem in column B.

A	*B*

"There is 10 months' worth of work to do. That's one person for 10 months, two people for 5 months, or five people for 2 months."

"The hardware manufacturer says we should buy more hardware because we'll grow into it."

"You technical people handle it. I don't want to be involved."

"If the managers would just quit griping about cost and schedules, we could make a really good system."

5. What are four design pitfalls?

6. What is wrong with the following MIS development plan (assuming it is at the correct level of detail)? Reschedule it as it should be.

Jan. 1 to Feb. 1, plan and design
Feb. 1 to Jun. 1, implement
Jun. 1 to Jul. 1, test and go live

7. What are the four pitfalls to watch for in MIS implementation?

_____

_____

_____

_____

8. The following quotation, in the section entitled "Controlling the MIS Project," is central to all management control activities.

How does a project get to be a year late?

_____

9. Discuss other pitfalls that you have encountered in MIS development.

10. If forced to choose *one* problem that sinks the most MIS projects, which would you choose and why?

SELECTED REFERENCES

AXELSON, CHARLES F. "How to Avoid the Pitfalls of Information Systems Development." *Financial Executive*, April 1976.

BOSTROM, ROBERT P., AND J. STEPHEN HEINEN. "MIS Problems and Failures: A Socio-Technical Perspective." Working Paper MISRC-WP-76-07, Management Information Systems Research Center, University of Minnesota, 1976.

DRUCKER, PETER F. *Management: Tasks, Responsibilities, Practices.* New York: Harper & Row, 1974.

McFARLAN, F. WARREN. "Portfolio Approach to Information Systems." *Harvard Business Review*, September–October 1981.

NOLAN, RICHARD L. "Managing the Crisis in Data Processing." *Harvard Business Review*, March–April 1979.

SCHEWE, CHARLES D., JAMES L. WIEK, AND ROBERT T. DANN. "Marketing the MIS." *Information & Systems*, November 1977.

11

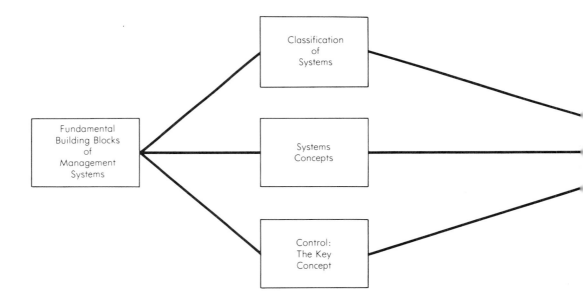

Systems Concepts and Control

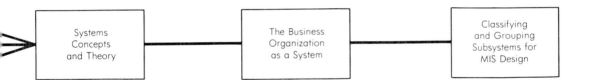

| Systems Concepts and Theory | The Business Organization as a System | Classifying and Grouping Subsystems for MIS Design |

This third part of the text is entitled "Advanced Concepts," and that is exactly how we propose to approach these several subjects. Parts I and II covered the theory and practice of management in relation to management information systems—all from the viewpoint of providing useful information for everyday application in today's business world. The two interrelated topics covered in this chapter, control and systems concepts, are also useful in the real world. However, they go beyond survival in management. They start to show the underpinnings of systems and management control in general. As in any field, a grasp of the advanced topics separates the leaders in the discipline from the bulk of the practitioners.

SYSTEMS CLASSIFICATIONS

Systems fall into a number of categories, and confusion may result if we talk about systems behavior and characteristics without identifying and specifying the kind of system we are talking about.

Conceptual and Empirical

It is especially important to distinguish between systems that are conceptual and those that are empirical. For example, there will be misunderstanding if a person is talking about an information system as a set of concepts, ideas, or characteristics while his listener is envisioning an operational system of people, equipment, and reports. *Conceptual* systems are concerned with theoretical structures, which may or may not have any counterpart in the real world. Conceptual systems are typified by those of science, such as economic theory, non–Euclidean geometry systems, the general system of relativity, or organization theory. Note that conceptual systems for organizations as composed of ideas are distinct from empirical organization systems made up of people.

Conceptual systems, then, are systems of explanation or classification. They may also appear in practical management affairs in the form of plans, accounting system structures, and classifications of policies and procedures.

Empirical systems are generally concrete operational systems made up of people, materials, machines, energy, and other physical things, although electrical, thermal, chemical, information and other such systems involving intangibles also fall into this category. Empirical systems may of course be derived from or based upon conceptual systems and thus represent the conversion of concepts into practice. In advancing the science of MIS, we deal with conceptual systems such as models, but MIS are themselves, in practice, empirical (real-world) systems.

Natural and Manufactured

Natural systems abound in nature. The entire ecology of life is a natural system, and each organism is a unique natural system of its own. The water system of the world, at least before man affected it, was a natural system. Our own solar system is a natural system.

Manufactured systems were formed when people first gathered in groups to live and hunt together. They now appear in infinite variety all about us and extend from the manufacturing system of a company to the system of space exploration. Their objectives likewise vary tremendously. One system may be concerned with national defense; another may be a transportation system. A business organization is a system with many smaller systems included—production, accounting, and so on—as well as others such as communication systems and office layout systems overlaid upon the main economic organization of people.

Social, People-Machine, and Machine

Systems made up of people may be viewed purely as *social* systems, apart from other systems objectives and processes. Business organizations, government agencies, political parties, social clubs, and technical societies are examples of systems that may be so studied. Admittedly, all of these employ objects and artifacts that form physical systems, yet the most relevant aspects may be considered to be organizational structure and human behavior.

Most empirical (as opposed to conceptual) systems fall into the category of *people-machine* systems. It is difficult to think of a system composed only of people who do not utilize equipment of some kind to achieve their goals. Even philosophers write and record. It is possible to think of some small systems that are purely mechanical, but they are usually a part of larger systems involving people.

Pure *machine* systems would have to obtain their own inputs and maintain themselves. The development of a self-healing machine system would bring these systems closer to simulation of living organisms. Such systems would need to adapt to their environment. Although some electrical power generating systems approach self-sufficiency, self-repairing and completely self-sufficient machine systems are still in the category of science fiction.

Open and Closed

An *open* system is one that interacts with its environment. All systems containing living organisms are obviously open systems because they are affected by what is sensed by the organisms. In a more important sense, organizations are usually systems operating within larger systems and are therefore open systems. For example, a company's marketing organization is a system that is a part of the larger system, the entire company. The company in turn is a system within the larger industry system.

The fact that a company interacts with its environment—a larger system—makes that individual company an open system. The open system may be further identified by its individually small influence on its environment and inadequate feedback of information from the environment. As business managers will readily agree, they must somehow manage their companies in great ignorance about the future impact of environmental conditions. The environmental system with which they can best contend is the particular industry system of which they are a part.

Continuing in this direction, then, we note that the industry is part of the national economic system, which in turn is a system within our society. Our society is a system within the world system; the world system is a part of the solar system; and so on into the unknown.

The question of what constitutes a *closed* system is more difficult. A closed system is one that does not interact with its environment. Whatever environment surrounds the closed system does not change, or if it does, a barrier exists between the environment and the system to prevent the system from being affected. Although it is doubtful that closed systems really exist, the concept has important implications. We attempt in research to develop models that are essentially closed systems. When we set up experiments in the laboratory for the study of human behavior, we are attempting to establish a closed system temporarily. The scientist who devises a laboratory system to measure the elasticity of a metal is assuming a closed system so that environmental changes that would affect the results are avoided. Problems in business are sometimes resolved as if a closed system existed to simplify the situation enough so that at least a first approximation can be obtained.

Some authors distinguish further between open systems that are simply influenced passively by the environment and those that react and adapt to the environment. These subclasses are designated as *nonadaptive* and *adaptive* systems.

Permanent and Temporary

Relatively few, if any, people-made systems are *permanent*. However, for practical purposes, systems enduring for a time span that is long relative to the operations of humans in the system may be said to be "permanent." Our economic system, which is gradually changing, is essentially permanent for our plans for the future. At another extreme, the policies of a business organization are "permanent" as far as year-to-year operations are concerned. It is true that major policy changes may be made, but these will then last an indefinite and "long" time relative to the daily activities of employees.

Truly *temporary* systems are designed to last a specified period of time and then dissolve. The television system set up to record and transmit the proceedings of a national political convention is only a temporary system. A small group-research project in the laboratory is a temporary system. Some systems that are temporary are not so by design. A company that is formed and quickly goes bankrupt is an example. Temporary systems are important for the accomplishment of specific tasks in business and for research in science.

Stationary and Nonstationary

A *stationary* system is one whose properties and operations either do not vary significantly or else vary only in repetitive cycles. The automatic factory, the government agency that processes social security payments, the supermarket store operation, the high school, and the ferry system are examples of stationary systems.

An advertising organization, a continental defense system, a research and development laboratory, and a human being are examples of *nonstationary* systems.

Let us compare the stationary system—the automatic factory—with the nonstationary continental defense system. In the automatic factory, system quantities may change with time, and operating levels may vary within certain limits. However, there is a manufacturing cycle that is repeated with relatively little change. Such a system could be very complex, and the cost of failure is high. Failure is not necessarily permanent, though, because the factory could be modified to operate properly. In the case of the continental defense system, the cost is likewise very large. One major difference is that initial failure is apt to rule out the opportunity to revise the system. In nonrepetitive systems, failure in one case does not always lead to successful modification for different cases in the future.

Subsystems and Supersystems

From the preceding discussions, it has become apparent that each system is nested in a larger system. The system in the hierarchy that we are most interested in studying or controlling is usually called "the system." The business firm is viewed as "the system" or the "total system" when focus is on production, distribution of goods, and sources of profit and income.

Smaller systems within the system are called *subsystems*. This distinction has important implications in practice with regard to optimization: people tend to optimize for the good of the (sub)system they are most closely related to rather than the whole system.

Supersystem is a term that has at least two uses. First is "as opposed to subsystem." The University of California school system is a supersystem of UCLA. UCLA is a subsystem of the University of California school system. The second, and perhaps more common usage, is to denote any extremely large and complex system.

Adaptive and Nonadaptive

A system that reacts to its environment in such a way as to improve its functioning, achievement, or probability of survival is called an adaptive system. High-level living organisms such as animals and humans use adaptation in meeting threats of changes in the physical environment or changes in their societies. Evolutional theory is based heavily on the concept of an adaptive system. We note that successful businesses are those that adapt to changes in the environment, while many failures are attributed to businesses that failed to respond in time to external change.

Finally, we may associate energy source, learning and self-modification with adaptation. For example, if computers could attach themselves to a long-term source of energy, "learn" how to modify and heal themselves, and then actually do so, they would become adaptive systems.

Classification of Organizational Systems and of MIS

It is useful to identify the classifications into which organizational systems and MIS fall. We summarize our conclusions as follows:

Organizational System

1. Conceptual, if we are discussing the theory of organization charts or manuals; empirical, if we are discussing the people and their actual relationships and activities.
2. Natural, if we are discussing people as part of the ecology of life on earth; manufactured, if we discuss any other organization of human beings.
3. Social. All people-made groupings of people are social systems whose behavior has been subjected to considerable research.
4. Open. Every social organization is open because it reacts with its unpredictable environment.
5. Permanent, almost, if we consider major political systems and companies that last for centuries. England and Lloyd's of London have existed for centuries. Probably

all organizational systems are temporary and doomed to oblivion in the history of Earth.

6. Nonstationary, in general. Organizational systems tend to adapt to a changing environment in the long run. In the short run, we may treat some of those listed earlier as stationary for convenience in studying them.

7. Subsystems *and* supersystems. The organizational system varies from the small, supervised group in business or government to the complex, social-political-economic group making up a country such as the United States.

8. Adaptive, as already noted.

Management Information System

1. Conceptual, if we are discussing the models or theory of MIS; empirical, if we are referring to a specific system in action.

2. Manufactured. Human information systems are devised by people and are not simply "born."

3. Social *and* people-machine. MIS may be viewed purely from the human aspect, which includes communication/decision making. The MIS in its most sophisticated form includes equipment such as electronic computers and is therefore a human-machine system.

4. Open *and* closed. For simple operational and low-level functional management decision making, the MIS may be "decoupled" from its environment to operate on information stored within the system. Most MISs, however, are utilized for planning and decision making that require important interactions with the business environment.

5. Temporary. MISs are constantly being revised, both formally and informally.

6. Stationary. Once designed, the MIS is supposed to handle certain types of problems on a more or less routine basis and supply information to management according to a specified program.

7. Subsystem *and* supersystem. At the present state-of-the-art, MISs are being designed primarily as subsystems of a potential total business MIS. A total, sophisticated MIS for a large corporation or industry would certainly verge on a supersystem, but this is a potentiality rather than a reality.

8. Nonadaptive. MISs are almost always modified intentionally by an outside force.

SOME SYSTEM CONCEPTS

It is the approach of science to ask, "What are the parts?" It is a requirement for design that we ask, "What are systems composed of?" Here we take a conceptual view of systems to answer this question because the answer has already been given: empirical systems are composed of real-life things. Identification of concepts will be important in the development of system theory, in the design of systems, and in the evaluation of systems. System concepts also provide an introduction to models of systems.

To make these concepts more understandable, we will show their application to a simple, computer-based marketing information system (MARIS). The concept of this marketing information system is shown in Figure 11-1.

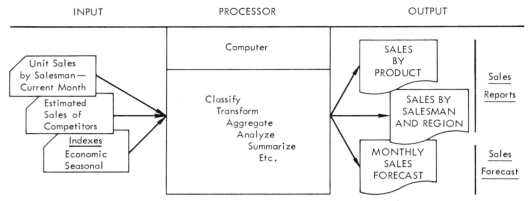

INPUT PROCESSOR OUTPUT

FIGURE 11-1 Inputs and Outputs of a Marketing Information System (MARIS)

Principal System Quantities or Variables

Every system is a processor, according to the definition given earlier. The principal system quantities or variables are representations of amounts of information, energy, or matter that appear as inputs or outputs of the system. In our marketing information system, we have as inputs sales in units by each salesperson for the past month, sales of competitors (estimated), economic conditions, and seasonal indexes. The outputs are sales by product, salesperson, and region, and a forecast for the coming month.

We see first that one of our input variables is sales in units by a particular salesperson. This variable might have been expressed in pounds, gallons, or some other measure such as dollars, but the system designer selected units as the dimension. Similarly, each other input is represented by a name or symbol that has a specified dimension and varies with time.

These input quantities are classified, transformed, aggregated, or analyzed by the computer to yield the desired output variables with values for a particular point in time.

System Parameters

Many quantities that enter into the relationships among the input variables and the output variables are considered constant for a specific period of time or system operational style. In essence, for a fixed set of these values, the system is said to be in a specified "state." These quantities, which determine the state of the system, are called *parameters*. Not entirely jokingly, we might call these parameters " variable constants."

In the MARIS example, it turns out that management scientists who constructed the relationships among the inputs and the outputs included several parameters. One of these is a "fudge" factor to correct the sales forecast in the event that a competitor conducts a special promotion. Normally, this promotion "fudge" factor changes in value from month to month; that is, it is a constant characterizing the no-promotion state. However, it is turned on to a new value once in a while, when one or more competitors increase their promotional level.

Another parameter in the sales forecasting process is the average age of the sales staff. If the average age changes by more than 15 percent, a change in this parameter is called for, and the selling function has changed its "state."

Components

A system's components are simply the various identifiable parts of the system. If a system is large enough so that it is composed of subsystems, and each subsystem is composed of subsystems, eventually we reach some parts that individually are not subsystems. In other words, in a hierarchy of subsystems, the components exist at the lowest level.

In our MARIS system, there are two subsystems: the sales reporting system and the sales forecasting system. The components of the system are telecommunication devices, people, an electric computer, procedure manuals, and reports. These components, except for some of the people, are shared by both systems.

Attributes of Components

Components, because they are objects or people, possess properties or characteristics. These characteristics affect the operation of the system in speed, accuracy, reliability, capacity, and many other ways. Choices must be made in systems design between the use of humans and the use of machines and between various kinds of machines, on the basis of attributes and cost.

Humans, for example, have very limited capacity to absorb information per unit of time compared with machines. However, humans are better than machines in analyzing poorly structured problems. It has been said that people are the most effective control component that can be mass produced by inexperienced labor.

An example of a choice between machines might be the selection of an output device from among a cathode ray tube, an audio system, a mechanical printer, or a plotting device. In the MARIS, the characteristics of the output component are not high speed, but clarity, economy, and relative permanence. Therefore a printer, auxiliary to the computer, is chosen, and the format of the output is a "printed" report, sent to management once a month.

Structure

The structure of a system is the set of relationships among objects and attributes. A description of the way in which the objects and their attributes are connected defines the structure. Levels of relationship may be classified as

First order—functional and dysfunctional relationships caused by natural phenomena or varying attributes.

Second order—symbiosis, the necessary relationship between dissimilar organisms, as for example, plant and parasite.

Third order—synergistic relationships in which attributes of objects reinforce each other to increase or improve system output.

The functional relationships among the people and the equipment form the structure of the MARIS. The organizational hierarchy, the lateral relationships among the people in the system, and the relationship between the computer and the people could be set forth in a block diagram representing the structure of the system.

Dysfunctional relationships among people may be present because of poor system design or personality conflicts among the people. There may be dysfunctional relationships between people and the computer due to humans' inability to perform monotonous, repetitive operations connected with the outputs or inputs of the computer. On the other hand, the computer may fail to operate properly because of rough or careless treatment of punched cards or equipment by humans.

Symbiosis in the MARIS is the necessary relationship between the computer and humans. Each needs the other to accomplish system objectives.

Synergistic effects in the social group making up the system may be achieved by different individuals supplementing each other so that total output is greater than the simple addition of each individual's work.

Process

The total process of a system is the net result of all ongoing activities in converting inputs to outputs. When management and systems designers have established the data that will be available as inputs to an MIS and the information desired for the output, the systems designers have the major project of designing the conversion process.

The total process is actually made up of many small processes. A parallel between a material processing system and an MIS may help to clarify the meaning of a single process. In a certain factory, a worker receives a square of sheet metal, places it in a punch press, and operates the press to produce a formed and perforated piece of metal. This is a single process in the entire production process.

In our marketing information system, the computer flowchart shows the aggregation, by the process of addition, of individual sales reports into total sales. This is a single process among many in the system. The functional relationship between an input and output of a process is called the *transfer function*. This term is commonly used in the design and evaluation of feedback systems.

Boundaries

The concept of boundary of a system makes it possible to focus on a particular system within a hierarchy of systems. The boundary of a system may exist either physically or conceptually. The operational definition of a system in terms of its boundary is

1. List all components that are to make up the system and circumscribe them. Everything within the circumscribed space is called the system, and everything outside is called the environment.
2. List all flows across the boundary. Flows from the environment into the system are inputs; flows from inside the boundary to outside are called outputs.
3. Identify all elements that contribute to the specific goals of the system and include these within the boundary if they are not already included.

We will substitute nested political systems for our marketing information system because the boundaries are easily recognized. Let us start with the city as the smallest system and consider it as part of the county system, which is part of the state system, which in turn is part of the national governmental system.

The boundaries of the city are physical, informational, and legal. The physical boundaries are identified on a map and all physical components of the city system are simply circumscribed on the map. Flows across the physical boundary are inputs from the environment and include flows of people, vehicles, or even animals. Water supply, electrical power, and weather movements are more esoteric examples of inputs. The outputs are of the same type.

The city is an open system that reacts with its environment on the basis of information crossing the boundaries in either direction. The information is usually recorded in newspapers in the city if it is input or outside of the city if it is output. Television, radio, and word of mouth also provide information flow across the boundaries.

The legal boundaries of the city circumscribe all legal or political actions the city may take. The city is limited to action over its inhabitants, its physical system, and people or companies that operate or pass upon its physical system. However, further restrictions limit the legal actions (or components of the legal system) and reserve them for the state or federal systems.

The city is thus composed of several major systems, each of which has fairly well-defined boundaries. What has been said about the city boundaries may be translated to the county system and then to the state as a system.

Characteristics of Systems

For the solution of a given problem there are good systems and poor ones. The poor systems have characteristics that do not fit the requirements of the problem or of the decision makers. Our marketing information system may be a poor system if its sales forecasts are monthly and manufacturing requires weekly

TABLE 11-1 Characteristics of Person-Machine Systems

1. Performance of basic and subsidiary functions
2. Accuracy of performance
3. Speed of performance
4. Cost
5. Reliability
6. Environmental adaptability
7. Maintainability
8. Replaceability by successive models
9. Safety and fail-safe features
10. Producibility (feasibility of manufacture)
11. Optimum materials and process for size of manufacturing run
12. Simplification, standardization, and preferred sizes
13. Weight
14. Size and shape
15. Styling and packaging
16. Compatibility with other systems or auxiliary equipment
17. Modular design
18. Ease of operation (human engineering)
19. Balanced design through trade-offs
20. Ease of transporting and installing
21. Legality
22. Social aspects

forecasts for planning. It may be a poor system if some sales representatives' reports are not included from time to time because of lack of control over reporting.

There are many characteristics of systems that are important for design, production, diagnosis, and evaluation. People-machine systems have a large spectrum of such characteristics, as shown in Table 11-1.

Table 11-1 is useful because it can serve as a checklist for the designer. Each characteristic must be considered in terms of its degree of importance for the system under scrutiny.

CONTROL: THE KEY SYSTEM CONCEPT

Control may be considered the key system concept because it pervades and permeates the whole idea of systems as well as all real-life manifestations of systems. Systems are put together, directly or indirectly, for the purpose of control. For example,

- Governments are created or evolve to prescribe and proscribe types of behavior within their jurisdictions.
- Exhaust systems on automobiles are there to control the flow of exhaust so we are not asphyxiated.
- The cardiovascular system is responsible for controlling the flow of blood and the distribution of oxygen around the body.

So the idea of control is at least part of the "Why" inherent in a system's reason for existence.

Definition of Control

Control means bringing or maintaining

1. the performance of an individual, group, machine, or facility, *or*
2. the characteristics of an individual, group, machine, or facility, *or*
3. the characteristics or value of a variable

within prescribed limits. More specifically, control may be applied to some environmental factor, organizational components, individuals within the organization, functional or specialized activities such as inventory control or product reliability, and mechanical processors such as lathes or elevators. In brief, control means causing events to conform to the desires or plan of the controller.

TABLE 11-2 Examples of Control

Item to Be Controlled	Output or Characteristic	Limits	MIS Report
Salesperson	Weekly sales expense	$53 to $72	Sales expense
Sheet metal department	Applied hours	250 to 300 hours	Attendance or labor hours
Division manager	Profitability of decisions	11.5% minimum ROI after taxes	Earnings statement
Total work force	Years of formal schooling	12 years minimum and 14 years average	Personnel profile summary
Lathe	Tolerance	±0.0015″	Quality control
Capital equipment	Average age	6 to 8 years	Capital equipment summary
Pollution	Investment per year	$0 to $5 million	Impact study

Table 11-2 lists some examples of items to be controlled, such as people, equipment, or effort, and the measure of performance or characteristic that is to be kept within desired limits. The role of the MIS is to inform management whether the limits have been exceeded or are likely to be exceeded. At this point, we may view controlling as (1) setting standards of performance, (2) measuring performance against standards, and (3) taking corrective action to reduce deviations from standards.

Open and Closed Loops

An *open-loop* control system is one with inputs, processes, and outputs that have no connection or information flow from the process or outputs back to the inputs.

FIGURE 11-2 Open-Loop Control System

Figure 11-2 is a simple example. In the open-loop system, the control depends on the inputs and the processes being correct. Nobody gathers data to compare actual sales and actual expenses with quotas and budgets.

In *closed-loop* control systems, information about the process and/or about the outputs is fed back to a controller who adjusts the inputs and system as necessary. Figure 11-3 shows these feedback and control elements applied to sales expenses in Figure 11-2. This concept of feedback is so important that we will give special attention to it.

Information Feedback Systems

An integral part of systems theory is the concept of automatic feedback control. This is particularly important for the study and design of management information systems because the theory and the practice of cybernation (feedback control) underlie all design and application of computers as well as of information systems that utilize them.

The need for feedback control through information is sometimes illustrated by the example of the automobile driver. We accept as a simple, everyday occurrence the complex system of driver, steering wheel, automobile, street, eye, and steering hand. Yet consider the effects of making very slight changes in the system structure by substituting elements and adding time delays. Let the driver

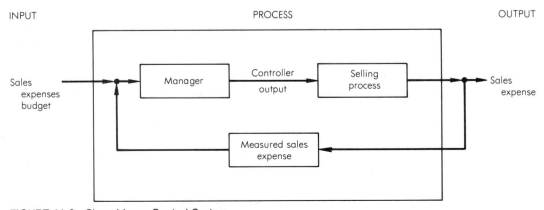

FIGURE 11-3 Closed-Loop Control System

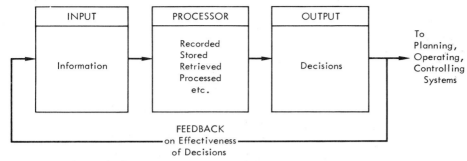

FIGURE 11-4   Information and Decisions — A System

be blindfolded and receive his or her information input from a front-seat companion. It is unlikely that the system output would be acceptable, given the time delay in information transmission plus the distortion caused by an additional input medium provided by the other person.

Consider the much worse situation in which the driver's information input comes from a companion in the back seat facing the rear, who could see only where the vehicle has been and not where it is going. Yet this kind of situation exists in business all the time. Managers do not have a clear view of the road ahead and must depend upon information gathered from a variety of sources with built-in time delays. Their historical accounting information system usually provides them with information on where they have been, not on the course for the future. Information feedback systems, properly designed, offer a tremendous breakthrough in techniques and in the general approach to decision making that will assist the manager in charting a course for the future.

Systems theory and the notion of information feedback are fundamental to the decision-making process and to the design of supporting information systems. Indeed, an MIS can be viewed as a *communication process in which information (input) is recorded, stored and retrieved (processed) for decisions (output) on planning, operating, and controlling.* The concept implied by this definition is shown schematically in Figure 11-4.

The attribute of *information feedback* is essential to an understanding of the self-regulating nature of systems in general and of how this attribute can be applied in a management information system to aid in decision making. To illustrate this point better, we will look at the elements and operation of a system like the one in Figure 11-4. The reader will see how information feedback, as a type of control, is essential to the working of the system.

Input, Processor, Output

Regardless of the complexity of a system, the basic elements are functionally and operationally the same. Table 11-3 illustrates some typical systems with the elements of input, processor, and output. An understanding of these elements and their relationships is essential for proper systems design.

TABLE 11-3   Illustrations of Systems Elements

System	Input	Processor	Output
Data processing	Raw data	Classify, sort, summarize, calculate	Arranged data
Manufacturing	Materials, labor, etc.	Operations	Product
Air conditioning	Electricity	Motor, compressor, etc.	Cooled air
Weapon system	Instructions	Missile, ground support, equipment, personnel, etc.	Target destruction
Computer-based management information system	Information	Computer, people, etc.	Decisions
University	Students	University	Changed students

Input is the start-up component on which the system operates. Table 11-3 illustrates the variety of inputs to systems. Note that in almost all cases, the input to a system is the output from some other system. The input to an MIS is, of course, data or information. *Output,* the result of an operation and the purpose or objective for which the system was designed, is also demonstrated in Table 11-3. (Note, however, that no standard of performance or yardstick has been placed upon these outputs. Performance standard is integral to another system component to be discussed, the control.) The *processor* is the activity that makes possible the transformation of input into output. People, machines, functions, operations, organizations, and combinations of these may act as processors and may be analyzed as such in systems design.

Input, processor, and output are common to *all* systems and are the terms by which all systems are described. Any system may be defined in terms of these elements and their properties. Moreover, they are set in place in fixed positions, which is important for the systems analyst or designer because he or she can work forward or backward in identifying the elements and in solving system problems. For example, the analyst may define the output in some specific value or format (e.g., cost of direct labor hours per product per week) and then proceed to deal with the processor (production control system) and input (shop labor control) to achieve the desired output. Although many design problems may be examined from left to right (considering input first), we shall see that a manager should, in general, consider outputs of the system before the other elements.

The Processor as a Black Box

It would be inadvisable to underrate the complexity of the processor. Illustrations in this chapter are very general and at a high level of coarseness; we should not conclude from this that operations within the processor or "black box" are as simple as depicted. Indeed, the "black box" concept of the system processor reflects a fundamental characteristic of information feedback systems, extreme complexity.

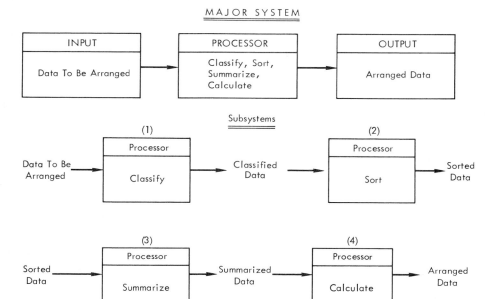

MAJOR SYSTEM

FIGURE 11-5 Subsystems of a Data Processing System

This complexity can be illustrated in a simple way by considering the data processing system of Table 11-3. The "black box" or processor of this system describes the four operations: classify, sort, summarize, and calculate. Figure 11-5 illustrates how, if we wish to think of the details of our system, it might be redesigned and shown as four separate subsystems. So it is with most system processors that at first glance appear to be simpler than they are in reality.[1]

Another reason for complexity in the processor is the difficulty of defining the constraints or boundaries. Where, for example, does the personnel management system start and stop? Does it include the subsystems of training, recruiting, placement, safety, discipline, payroll, labor relations, and scheduling? No doubt top management's view of the system differs from that of a personnel department supervisor, whose definition of the system may include only personnel records. Neither of these views is incorrect; they merely indicate the alternative ways of defining the processor. One of the first tasks of the system designer is to define the boundaries of the system. This places limits on the subsystems to be studied and has the advantages of (1) emphasizing the need for integrating subsystems, (2) concentrating effort in the most profitable areas, and (3) reducing the problem to manageable size.

[1] Consider the shop floor as a processor or "black box," with inputs of material and outputs of product. The shop houses 10 processes, and it is possible to schedule incoming material to these processes in any order and to sell the product at any stage. This planning problem has about 10 million alternatives, and if we assume 1 minute per alternative, it will take us about 19 years working day and night to find the best plan. Yet, with the tools of the computer and linear programming, the best solution can be determined in less than 1 minute.

Control and Feedback

We have previously explained that a system can be defined in terms of the elements and properties of input, processor, and output, and in a strict sense this is so. However, systems are dynamic and changes inevitably occur. Moreover, in a dynamic system it is necessary to review, periodically or continuously, the state of the output to make necessary alterations because of changes in the environment or for other reasons. In the system of the business organization we need to determine whether the product output is profitable and acceptable to the customer; otherwise the system will ultimately come to a standstill. In the air-conditioning system it is necessary to determine whether the output of cooled air oscillates within the range that we, the users, have determined; if it does not, this system will stop operating. The system elements that permit the system to remain in equilibrium are *control* and *feedback*.

A management information system is in all respects an information feedback system that can be defined as a *system measuring changes in output that leads to a decision resulting in action that affects the output.* Information feedback control is a fundamental characteristic of all systems and is essential to the design of a management information system. To illustrate,

1. A thermostat receives information on the temperature and starts the air-conditioning system; this lowers the temperature and the system stops.
2. The output of the direct labor control system is standard labor hours. The information system measures performance and reports deficiencies; this activates a training system that brings performance up to standard.
3. The sales manager receives information that sales are down because competitive prices are lower; he lowers the price of his firm's product, which raises the sales level to normal.

We speak of control and feedback together because they occur together; by definition, the purpose of feedback is control. *Control is defined as the system function that compares output to a predetermined standard. Feedback is the function that provides information on the deviation between output and control standard and delivers this information as input into the process from which the output was derived.* The place of feedback and control may be illustrated as in Figure 11-6.[2]

---

[2] In all systems we are striving to achieve a state of self-regulation. The state of self-regulation through automatic feedback is demonstrated by the classic case of the Watt governor of almost 200 years ago. The engine has a valve that controls its power and hence its speed. The *control* (desired speed) is set on this valve. As the engine turns at increasing speed, with it turn weighted arms, also at an increasing speed. The arms are mounted on pivots so that they are free to rise by centrifugal force as they revolve. The arms operate a valve that admits fuel to the engine so that the valve is closed in proportion as the arms rise and the speed grows. Hence we have a self-regulating automatic feedback control system. The more the machine tends to exceed a given speed (output), the less it is supplied with the energy to do so. Conversely, if it fails to reach the desired speed (the output as set on the control), the governor will regulate the power upward until it does. The input to the machine is adjusted by the output itself, and both settle down to a state of equilibrium.

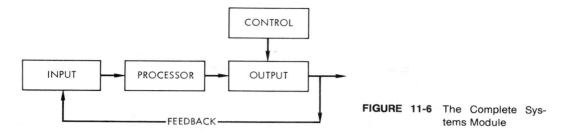

FIGURE 11-6 The Complete Systems Module

The nature of these two all-important components becomes clear if we recall the steps in the control process: (1) setting standards of performance, (2) measuring performance against the standard, and (3) correcting deviations. Because we are considering an information control system, the control element is concerned with comparing output against a predetermined standard. This standard is fundamental to the systems of *management, information,* and *control.* The concept is illustrated in Figure 11-7 for the generalized business system. The *feedback* element is the arrangement for collecting information on the comparison of output to control standard and for delivering this information (measuring performance) as input to the system so that deviations from expected output can be corrected through the management process.

Feedforward Control

Feedforward control is another form of anticipatory control. It takes effect before the anticipated deviation of performance from standard can occur. This requires

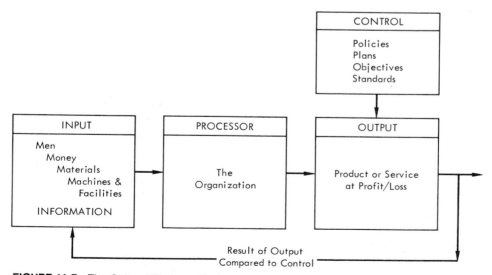

FIGURE 11-7 The General Business System

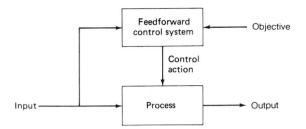

FIGURE 11-8 Feedforward Control System

control of the inputs and/or the process. Figure 11-8 shows a schematic of control of the process to overcome variations in inputs. Figure 11-9 illustrates feedforward control for a cash flow system. Components of the process are shown inside the process block.

An idea of the importance of the MIS for feedforward control can be gleaned from a study of Figure 11-9. The variability and uncertainty to sales, the many process components and their interrelationships, the uncertainty of collections and interest rates, and the periodic change of the objective require a very responsive control system. The computerized MIS will alert management to required inputs and required adjustments of the process of cash flow to have the needed cash on hand at any given date.

Except when noted otherwise, we will use feedback to cover the idea of feedforward. It should be clear that anticipatory control has advantages over reaction to deviations.

THE BUSINESS ORGANIZATION
AS A SYSTEM

It is important to understand how the elements of an organization function as a system because, as in any other system, the organization operates through the medium of information. It is also necessary to understand that because the functions of management are served by an information system, these functions should be considered in the design process. These concepts can be better understood by relating them to the organization as a system, as is done in Figure 11-10.

Because the outputs of the system identify the purpose for which the system exists, we examine the outputs of the business organization. These objectives are multiple, but for the manufacturing firm, they must necessarily include the manufacture and sale of a product at a profit. Later we will examine the subsystems and outputs of the subsystems that contribute to this objective. Note that, as in the management process, if no objective is established, the organization has no stated reason for existing, and therefore no system can be described or designed.

Inputs to the organization include the four classic factors of people, money, materials, and machinery, plus the vital fifth input of information. Again, as we

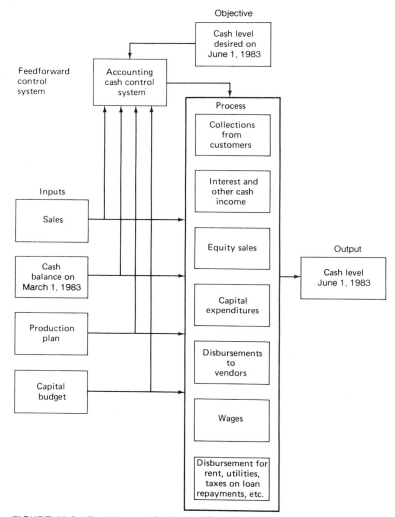

FIGURE 11-9 Feedforward Control of Cash Level

begin to analyze the subsystems of the organization, the inputs will break down into subclassifications (direct labor, indirect labor, and so on).

What controls operate on the output of the organization? There are considerations outside the firm, such as custom, competitive environment, and government regulation, that imply *external control*. These must be considered limitations on the operation of the system, and information measures must be designed to measure output against them. However, for most design purposes, the *internal controls* are more important. Each subsystem has one or more measures of control, and, as in the *central process*, these consist of *standards of performance*

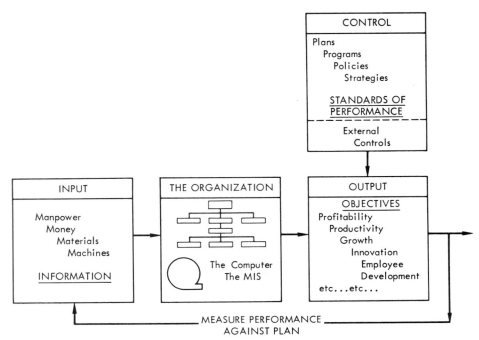

FIGURE 11-10 The Organization as a System

or some other measure of whether the output is within the limits previously established in the *control measures* (standards of performance) that operate on them:

Subsystem	Output	Control
Sales	Sales orders	Quota
Industrial relations	Employee morale	Turnover
Quality control	Quality product	Rejections
Accounts receivable	Collections	Bad debts

The final element of *feedback* is essential for system operation and for self-regulation or correction of deviations. If sales quotas are not met, if labor turnover is high, if bad debts exceed expectations, this information must be fed back into the system as input so that connections can be made. In the ultimate (and perhaps theoretical) management information system, the feedback provides information for system self-correction.

CONTROL AND SYSTEM DESIGN

The elements of a business system may be grouped in different ways to serve as the basis for design of the MIS. Such groupings are used to organize the information subsystems. Let us first consider a classification of information needed to manage the business:

1. *Task*—the job, the function (selling, manufacturing, financing, etc.) represents the *purpose* for which the information is reported
2. *Resource*—the objects or events reported upon are the resources (personnel, equipment, money, etc.) that are being used or acquired
3. *Networks*—flows of information and resources representing a model of the organization; the focus of planning and control
4. *Level*—three levels representing the hierarchy of planning and control in the organization: strategic planning, management control, and operational control
5. *Environment*—the environment in which the firm operates, including information needed to set goals and objectives, information concerning other external environment (suppliers, government, etc.), and other external planning premises

The job of the systems planner is to devise the master classification scheme that best fits his or her particular organization, keeping in mind the need to design a *master plan* that will serve for integration of various additional applications over the near and long term. In most cases a combination of the approaches cited will be sufficient, but *some grand scheme* is necessary if the planning objectives previously detailed are to be achieved.

The emphasis of the MIS, the angle from which the information is viewed, yields the control posture of the system. For example, if the information system is strongly oriented toward the functions (selling, manufacturing, finance) of the firm, the system will support control *primarily* from the functional/task angle. We will be able to tell quickly when the marketing group is not meeting quota. We may well *not* be able to see its environmental cause because the MIS is not oriented to handle that information. Hence we need to design with all the desired elements of control in mind.

The task of selecting the proper classification framework can be described conceptually in Figure 11-11. From the "menu" offered, the designer must select the combination that suits the needs of management. The combination is multidimensional:

1. Two hierarchical classifications of systems (function and decision making)
2. The common tasks/functions among systems
3. Resources to be managed in the transformation process
4. Information and resource flows
5. The environment in which management sets goals and objectives

In addition to these five dimensions, the designer is concerned with additional dimensions of a classification scheme: the common functions and resources among systems in the vertical hierarchy and, finally, informational elements that go to construct integrated subsystems across horizontal boundaries.

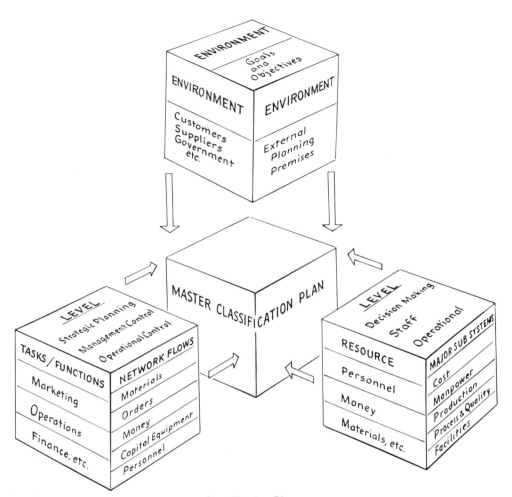

FIGURE 11-11 Elements of a Master Classification Plan

Task or Function

The most logical and the most widespread type of categorization in information systems is organized around the job to be done, the task to be performed, and the use to which the information will be put. Classification in this fashion tends to develop for the same reason that most firms choose it for its basic organization: homogeneity of functions performed. This approach produces a natural subgrouping of work as well as of the information required to plan and control this work. Moreover, this approach permits or encourages integration of subsystems, be-

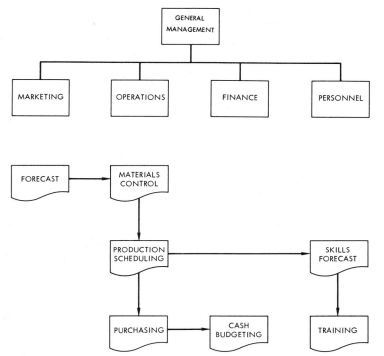

FIGURE 11-12 Horizontal and Vertical Integration of Functions and Resources

cause different functional organizational entities frequently deal with the same resource or with different aspects of the same task. For example, sales orders from the marketing function have an important interface with production control and other subsystems. As already noted, this type of orientation in the information system will provide management with *primarily* functional control tools.

Figure 11-12 illustrates some of the major subsystems classified by task or function in a manufacturing organization. Others are shown in Table 11-4.

Resource

A second and widely used means of classifying information systems is around the resource (people, money, materials, and machines) to be managed. Each resource usually has characteristics peculiar to its description and hence to the information surrounding it. Resources tend to be organized around the functions of the organization: money around treasury department, personnel around personnel department, and raw materials around production. Because of this association there is naturally a great deal of overlap between tasks (functions) and resources.

TABLE 11-4 Selected List of "Task-Oriented, Function-Related" Subsystems

Product Development	Operations	Finance	Personnel
Engineering	Classification	Accounts	Arbitration
Project control	Cataloging	receivable	Classifying
Bill of	Inventory	Accounts payable	Interviewing
material	control	Billing	Placing
Research and	Labor scheduling	Cost accounting	Recruiting
development	and reporting	Cash receipts	Selection
Styling	Manufacturing	Cash budgets	Staffing
	Cutting	Financial planning	Testing
	Welding	General ledger	Services
	Finishing	Plant accounting	
	Etc.	Variance analysis	
	Production	Taxes	
	control	Timekeeping	
	Process control		
	Purchasing		
	Quality control		
	Stores control		
	Scheduling		
	Labor		
	Finished goods		
	Etc.		
	Servicing		
	Maintenance		
	Repair		
	Materials		
	handling		
	Packaging		
	Receiving		
	Shipping		
	Warehousing		

For each major resource, an information system can be constructed with files that contain information in subcategories: the personnel system contains a subsystem entitled Employee Benefits, which in turn has files on Insurance, Savings, Retirement, and so on. Major elements of a resource classification system are illustrated in the accompanying table. Note that several of the *task* subsystems are common to two or more *resource* systems. This makes the point once again that subsystems are seldom mutually exclusive; they are usually multidimensional, with dimensions of (1) hierarchy, (2) task, and (3) resource, each of which has two other dimensions of (4) vertical and (5) horizontal boundaries. Although these multiple dimensions make the information ingredient in the MIS design more complex, they have a very positive effect also—control is now natural along several of the key avenues.

Task / Function Information System

Resource	Purchasing	Inventory Control	Billing	Sched- uling	Job Control	Personnel Adminis- tration
Logistics						
Raw materials	x	x				
Finished goods		x	x	x		
Production				x		
facilities		x				
Physical assets				x	x	
Property and						
equipment	x	x				
Financial				x		
Cash and						
credit	x		x			
Personnel						
Payroll					x	x
Benefits						x

Network Flows

Most existing information systems are organized around either resources or what might be called "task-oriented, function-related" categories, but these classification approaches leave something to be desired. Conceptually, they are static and do not adequately take account of the *dynamic* nature of the business firm. Yet we know that business is a dynamic organism composed of systems that process inputs into useful outputs of products or services. This processing or transformation of resources into outputs is made possible through an information system characterized by two attributes: first, *movement* or *flow* through a complex interconnected system, and second, the *integrative* nature of the information used at multiple points throughout the organization. These characteristics are difficult to achieve in an information system organized by resource or task alone. What is needed is an additional dynamic dimension of *flow*. This concept can be applied to either information or physical resources, and these can be classified into *networks*. The idea of flow gives a greater conceptual grasp of the twin notions of upper management's development of plans and lower management's execution and control of these plans. To say it another way, we want to have operational planning and control systems, and these may be achieved through an analysis of the flow process: its inputs, the transformation processes, its outputs, and the *decision points*.

The subjects of the network flows are the inputs to the organization: people, money, materials, machines, and information. To illustrate how an information system can be built around such a flow network, let us take the *materials* flow. Conceptually (and practically), we can depict a system that plans and controls the acquisition of materials; their subsequent transportation to the factory; their allocation, storage, and production transformation within the factory; and their transportation and distribution and final sale to a customer. We can see that an information system built around such an approach would *integrate* a number of activities that have traditionally been organized and managed by function (marketing, purchasing, etc.) or resource (plant, materials, etc.).

The categories or *networks* we shall mention comprise an arbitrary classification around which the systems designer may begin to construct a master classification plan. Regardless of the extent to which this scheme is utilized, it does provide an excellent sketch of the operation as a *dynamic system* whose total objectives can be achieved through the planning, allocation, and control of flows of inputs that are transformed into outputs.

The *materials network* includes the flow and stocks of all materials, whether raw materials, work in process, or finished goods. An information system using this concept would include all decisions from the point at which acquisition decisions are made until final delivery to a customer. Obviously, a number of other subsystems would need to be architecturally integrated with this flow because of interfaces. By taking the systemic network approach to design of this system, planning and control as well as time and cost considerations could be substantially improved over the traditional functionalism associated with management of materials. To illustrate, consider the traditional system in which a sale triggers a change in the production schedule, which triggers a requisition for replenishment, which triggers a change in purchasing, and so on until the entire system has "geared up" to handle this input stimulus. Under a systems or network approach to materials flow, the initial trigger provided by the sale can stimulate responses all the way through the integrated system with much less delay and at less cost than the traditional organization, which is intent upon optimizing subsystem (department) objectives rather than the system (firm) as a whole.

The flows of *orders* comprise another network. These are not physical objects but rather symbolic representations of what will become arrangements of other resources and the allocation of resources to meet the commitment of the order. Viewed in this light, orders become the catalyst that can provide the decision inputs for optimization of transformation resources.

It is important to design a system to track the *money* network because money is the common language of managing and provides a tool for measuring results against plans. Moreover, money is a medium of exchange that reflects the firm's actions with its total environment, outside and inside. Outside, the money flow interfaces with banks, customers, stockholders, government (tax), labor, suppliers, and the community at large. Inside the firm it is a yardstick to measure resource allocation and control. Focusing on the money flows within and without the organization should improve the integration of subsystems at both these levels, as well as the management of the individual functions, resources, or outside entities.

Other network flows consist of the *personnel network*, the *facilities network*, and the *information network*. The first two of these work in much the same fashion as those just discussed in that they improve decision making, shorten the time involved in decision making, and integrate the organization subsystems for greater economies and efficiencies. The *information network* is in a category by itself; it represents the other flows and provides the linkage that causes them to interact in the manner of a *total system*.

Level of Systems within a Business Firm

Earlier we discussed the impact that the systems approach will have on the function of organizing and the structure of organizations. One major change will probably be the elimination or reduction of the sharp lines of demarcation between existing departments as we know them—purchasing, accounting, sales, manufacturing, engineering. However, one essential feature of organizations will no doubt remain: the managerial hierarchy of planning and control. This hierarchy of management and organizational structure has been described in a number of ways, but almost invariably as having three levels. Some of the ways of structuring this hierarchy have been by layer, task, location, function, and level:

Classification

Layer	Task	Location	Management Function	Level
First	Strategic planning	Management	Management	Top
Second	Management control	Office	Planning and control	Middle
Third	Operational control	Factory and field	Execution	Supervisory

Whatever the combination of classifications we choose to describe the organizational hierarchy, different levels and tasks must be recognized and provided for in systems development and design.

Environment

The classifications we have discussed thus far (task, resource, information flows, levels) have been concerned for the most part with the interaction of subsystems within the firm and information available inside the organization. However, some of the most vital sources of information are external to the firm and concern the external environment in which it operates. Although the satisfaction of the manager's *total* information needs, including those external to the firm, is probably impossible, these needs must nevertheless be taken into account despite the two major difficulties of (1) little control over the environment and (2) inability to design a system to capture this information. A variety of schemes exist for classification of environmental information needs. In general they follow our breakdown of planning premises. These may include

Economic	Technological
Political	Competitive
Social	Market
Demographic	

SUMMARY

The purpose of this chapter is to define more precisely, intensionally, extensionally, and contextually the meaning of "system." In so doing, we have developed various systems classifications, system terms, and system characteristics fundamental to the modeling, design, operation, and evaluation of systems.

We have turned the spotlight on one very key system concept: control. This is proper since control is the reason for having systems, particularly MIS.

The notion of automatic control through information feedback is essential to understanding systems theory and to applying it to management. Control measures changes in output, which in turn leads to decisions resulting in actions that affect the output. This idea is basic to the structure and design of the organization as a system and to the utilization of information as the central catalyst for integrating the many subsystems of the organization.

The components of any system include input, processor, output, control, and feedback. All systems can be explained in these terms, and the interaction between subsystems can be examined as an operation of these components. The management information system (MIS) is the common system that permits the other four resource systems to function as a whole.

Finally, we looked at the very important question of how MIS design affects management's ability to control using that information.

PROBLEMS AND QUESTIONS

1. Identify the eight categories that can be used to specify the characteristics of a system.

_____

_____

_____

_____
_____
_____
_____
_____

2. Choose a system and describe it using the preceding categorization scheme.

_____
_____
_____
_____
_____
_____
_____

3. Match the system classification of column A with the operating system description of column B by using only *one* — the primary — classification.

A *System Classification*	B *Operating System*
1. Conceptual	_____ A business that adapts to changes in environment
2. Empirical	
3. Natural	_____ The oceans and water systems of the world
4. Manufactured	
5. Social	_____ The Republican Party
6. People-machine	_____ The business firm as a "total system"
7. Machine	_____ The manufacturing plant of a business firm
8. Open	
9. Closed	_____ The pilot-airplane combination
10. Permanent	_____ An order processing system designed from empirical data
11. Temporary	
12. Stationary	_____ A sales analysis reflecting customer desires
13. Nonstationary	
14. Subsystem	_____ The theory of business cycles
15. Supersystem	_____ The tool control system of the manufacturing system of the firm
16. Adaptive	
17. Nonadaptive	_____ A business that does not adapt to changes in environment
	_____ A laboratory experiment that assumes no environmental impact on results
	_____ The programmed, automated assembly line
	_____ The temporary MIS that operates until the cutover to the redesigned system
	_____ A machine system that obtains its own inputs and maintains itself
	_____ The economic-political system that can be assumed as fixed for the foreseeable future
	_____ An advertising campaign for a fixed period of time

4. What type of control system is depicted here?

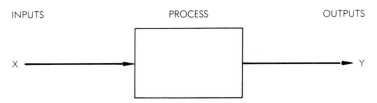

5. What type of control system is depicted here?

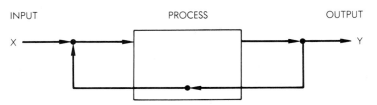

6. For the decisions listed in column A match the measure of change in output in column B.

A Decisions	B Measure of Change in Output
1. Shall I change our credit policy?	_____ Shop loading schedule changes
2. Should we lower labor standards?	_____ Direct labor budget variance
3. Should we raise prices?	_____ Cash budget forecast
4. Where are cost overruns occurring?	_____ Change in warehouse schedule
5. Which items are approaching obsolescence?	_____ Price-volume relationship
6. With whom should I place this order?	_____ Distribution by value analysis
7. How many people do I need for this production job?	_____ Standard cost variances
8. How much should my warehouse budget be?	_____ Vendor performance
9. Will our sales plan be met?	_____ Sales quota control
10. Do we have enough cash for accounts payable?	_____ Level of accounts receivable

7. Match the systems classification of column A with the systems of column B.

A Systems Classification	B System
1. Task	_____ Financial model
	_____ Project planning and control
2. Resource	_____ Technological data

	_____ Operational control system
3. Networks	_____ Personnel administration
	_____ Inventory simulation
4. Level	_____ Strategic planning
	_____ Systems design plan
5. Environment	_____ Economic model
	_____ Cash budget

8. Consider a young person who is charged with managing a room in which duplicating services of several kinds are supplied. People from various offices throughout the plant go to a counter opening out from the room and place orders. Define all elements of the basic system of which the young person is a part. Next, list all systems that link with the person's basic system (consider equipment, materials, costing, etc.).

9. If you grant that every system is a part of a greater system, discuss the meaning and the advantages and disadvantages of "decoupling" a system.

10. If you wished to study the function of business as an institution in society using the systems approach, would you proceed "inside-out" (business, industry, economy, society) or "outside-in" (society, economy, industry, business)? Why?

SELECTED REFERENCES

ATHEY, THOMAS H. *Systematic Systems Approach*. Englewood Cliffs, N.J.: Prentice-Hall, 1982.

CHECKLAND, PETER. *Systems Thinking, Systems Practice*. New York: John Wiley, 1981.

HARTNETT, WILLIAM E. *Systems Approaches, Theories, and Applications*. Dordrecht, Holland: D. Reidel, 1977.

LUCAS, HENRY C., JR., AND JON A. TURNER. "A Corporate Strategy for the Control of Information Processing." *Sloan Management Review*, Spring 1982.

MELCHER, ARLYN J., ed. *General Systems and Organization Theory: Methodological Aspects*. Kent, Ohio: Kent State University Press, 1975.

MERCHANT, KENNETH A. "The Control Function of Management." *Sloan Management Review*, Summer 1982.

MOCK, THEODORE J., AND HUGH D. GROVE. *Measurement, Accounting, and Organizational Information*. New York: John Wiley, 1979.

MURDICK, ROBERT G. *MIS: Concepts and Design*. Englewood Cliffs, N.J.: Prentice-Hall, 1980.

NEWMAN, WILLIAM H. *Constructive Control*. Englewood Cliffs, N.J.: Prentice-Hall, 1975.

PUTT, ARLENE M. *General Systems Theory Applied to Nursing*. Boston: Little, Brown, 1978.

SAFIUDDIN, MOHAMMED. "Systems Analysis, Part 2," *Machine Design*, January 25, 1973.

SCHODERBECK, CHARLES G., PETER P. SCHODERBEK, AND ASTERIOS G. KEFALIS. *Management Systems: Conceptual Considerations*. Dallas: Business Publications, 1980.

STASCH, STANLEY F. *Systems Analysis for Marketing Planning and Control*. Glenview, Ill.: Scott, Foresman, 1972.

WEINBERG, GERALD M. *An Introduction to General Systems Thinking*. New York: John Wiley, 1975.

12

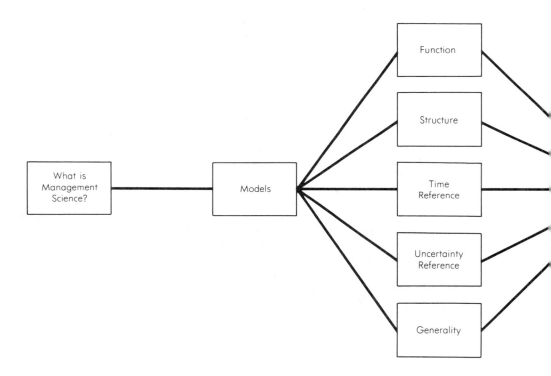

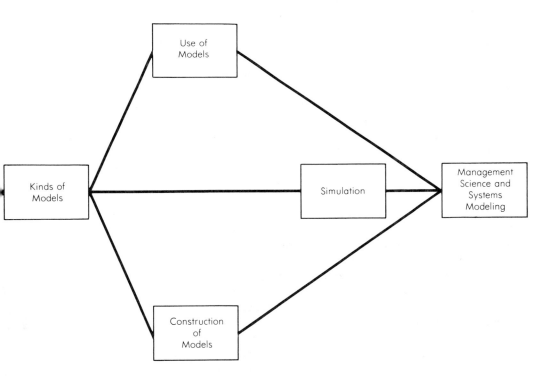

"Operations research," "management science," "modeling," or just "scientific method"—all represent pretty much the same process. That process, which we shall call management science, is a sophisticated aid to practical decision making, directed toward the solution of broad business problems by means of specialized techniques. The application of management science to MIS represents a tremendous advance over the disorganized collection of information and management by experience based on "feel." Management science requires managers to define their problems and assumptions carefully, usually in terms that may be quantified and measured, so that they may achieve better problem definition. When it is applied to the design of organizational and operating systems for problem solving, management science utilizes a considerable volume of people's knowledge of many related sciences. Therefore, problem-solving systems may be designed that are more effective and more efficient for the organization as a whole.

The techniques of management science are also incorporated *in* the system. Basically, these techniques, employed in conjunction with modern computers, provide "programmed" decision making for the solution of many subproblems in the system. Optimum solutions to such subproblems may be obtained in minutes. This contrasts to rule-of-thumb, intuitive, and approximate solutions on which decision makers were forced to rely in the past. Without the computational power of the computer, management science techniques usually could not be applied within the time span of realistic operational requirements. Thus the computer and management science combine to free humans from repetitive decision making, so that they may concentrate on more complex, novel, and ill-constructed problems as well as on "nonprogrammed" decision making.

The dysfunctional aspects of the increased application of management science are twofold. The first is the failure of the systems designer to recognize that his or her models of systems and problems will always be abstractions of the real world. Qualitative factors and human judgments must find a place in all higher-level decisions. Mathematically derived solutions must be checked against intuition and variances must be accounted for. Failure to do this may result in absurd and costly decisions. The second drawback to the introduction of management science techniques is organizational resistance to change. This resistance is further complicated when the management scientist fails to communicate with managers-users in terms that the manager understands.

We have brought out in general terms the role that management science plays in designing decision rules for programmed decisions and in helping managers make nonprogrammed decisions in the person-machine mode. It is now necessary to explore in more detail the nature of management science and its applications to MIS design.

WHAT IS MANAGEMENT SCIENCE?

Management science is simply a scientific approach to the solution of operational problems. It is concerned with providing management with *decision aids* or *decision rules* derived from

1. A total system orientation
2. Scientific methods of investigation
3. Models of reality, generally based on quantitative measurements and techniques

In previous chapters, we have presented the systems approach. The systematic approach to problem solving parallels the generally accepted steps of management science (operations research). These steps consist of

Problem Solving	*Management Science*
1. Observation	1. Search for problems
2. Statement of a problem	2. Statement of a problem
3. Collection of data	3. Collection of data
4. Development of hypotheses for solution of the problem	4. Development and testing of a model representing the problem solution
5. Evaluation of the alternative hypotheses	5. Manipulation of the model to determine the outcomes of various input conditions

Subsequent to the problem-solving process of developing feasible alternatives is the decision process, in which the parallelism continues:

Decision Making and Action	*Management Science*
1. Selection of best alternative	1. Selection of the best course of action
2. Implementation of best alternative	2. Implementation of the solution
3. Review of results	3. Control of the model by maintaining a check on its validity as time goes by

We now look at the third characteristic of management science—modeling. Since the time when cave dwellers drew symbols and pictures on the walls of caves, people have utilized "models" to represent aspects of their environment. It is only recently that scientists in many disciplines have discovered that the term *model* applies to what they have been doing all along. It now appears that most scientific conversations start with a mention of a model. The field of MIS is no exception; models are a necessity for both study and design of MIS. Because models are so important, we need to know what they are, what their characteristics are, and how they help us.

WHAT ARE MODELS?

We can solve both simple and complex problems of the practical world if we concentrate on some *portion* or some *key features* instead of on every detail of real life. This approximation or *abstraction* of reality, which we may construct in various forms, is called a *model*. Models do not, and cannot, represent every aspect of reality because of the innumerable and changing characteristics of the real world to be represented. If we wished to study the flow of material through a factory, we might construct a scaled diagram on paper showing the factory floor, position of equipment, tools, and workers. It would not be necessary to give such details as the color of the machines, the heights of the workers, or the temperature of the building. In other words, models deal with the relevant variables, and often only the relevant variables that have a major impact on the decision situation.

Many forms of models exist, and the particular form selected depends upon the purpose. Generally, models may be used to define or describe something such as an MIS; to assist with analysis of a system; to specify relationships and processes; or to present a situation in symbolic terms that may be manipulated to derive predictions. This last purpose, to provide a prediction system that can be manipulated to aid a decision maker, is perhaps the most important attribute of models.

Models provide two very important benefits that are closely related but distinct. The first is economy in representation and inquiry. It is cheaper, for instance, to represent a factory layout or an MIS visually in a diagram than it is to construct either one. It is also cheaper to try out modifications of such systems by rearrangements on paper. Second, models permit us to analyze and experiment with complex situations to a degree that would be impossible by constructing the actual system and its environment. For example, the experimental firing of an Apollo lunar vehicle may cost tens of millions of dollars and require months of preparation. If the lunar flight and the systems are simulated by a model, the application of large computers permits the simulation of many flights under various conditions. By simulation, information may be obtained in a few minutes that could not be obtained in generations of time or with billions of dollars of expenditure if the life-sized system were used for experimentation.

KINDS OF MODELS

Models may be divided into five different classes. The characteristics of a particular model may then be represented by a term from each class. Thus a manager might ask a management scientist in her marketing organization to construct a model for the selling and logistics system of a new shoe-cleaning product. The management scientist might then ask, "Shall we make that a symbolic, dynamic, probabilistic, and general model, or should we try to keep costs under $10,000 and construct an iconic, static, deterministic, and specialized model?" When put as a single question, this may seem facetious; in practice the answer to this question must be evolved in the discussion.

It is apparent that a few terms must be defined to describe classes of models, simply for economy of expression. It is also desirable to know what options exist when we are about to embark upon the construction of models. Models may be classified in five ways:

Class I — Function

Type	Characteristics	Examples
1. Descriptive	Descriptive models simply provide a "picture" of a situation and do not predict or recommend.	a. Organization chart b. Plant layout diagram c. Block diagram representing the structure of each chapter of this book
2. Predictive	Predictive models indicate that "if *this* occurs, then *that* will follow." They relate dependent and independent variables and permit trying out "what if" questions.	a. $BE = \dfrac{F}{1-v}$, which says that if fixed costs (F) are given and variable costs as a fraction of sales (v) are known, then break-even sales (BE) are predicted (deterministically) b. $S(t) = aS(t-1) + (1-a)S(t-2)$, which says that predicted sales for period t depend on sales for the previous two periods
3. Normative	Normative models are those that provide the "best" answer to a problem. They provide recommended courses of action.	a. Advertising budget model b. Economic lot size model c. Marketing mix model

Class II — Structure

Type	Characteristics	Examples
1. Iconic	Iconic models retain some of the physical characteristics of the things they represent.	a. Scaled three-dimensional mockup of a factory layout b. Blueprints of a warehouse c. Scale model of next year's automobile

Type	Characteristics	Examples
2. Analog	Analog models are those for which there is a substitution of components or processes to provide a parallel with what is being modeled.	An analog computer in which components and circuits parallel marketing institutions and facilities and processes so that by varying electrical inputs, the electrical outputs provide an analog simulation of the marketing system outputs
3. Symbolic	Symbolic models use symbols to describe the real world.	a. $R = a[\ln(A)] + b$, which says in symbols that sales response (R) equals a constant times the natural log of advertising expenditure (A), plus another constant b. $TC = PC + CC + IC$, which says in symbols that total inventory cost (TC) equals purchase cost (PC) plus carrying cost (CC) plus item cost (IC)

Class III — Time Reference

Type	Characteristics	Examples
1. Static	Static models do not account for changes over time.	a. Organization chart b. $E = P_1 S_1 + P_2 S_2$, which states that the expected profit (E) equals the probability (P_1) of the occurrence of payoff (S_1) multiplied by the value of the payoff (S_1), plus the probability (P_2) of payoff (S_2) multiplied by the value of (S_2)
2. Dynamic	Dynamic models have time as an independent variable.	$dS/dt = rA(t)(m - S)/M - \lambda S$, which gives the change in sales rate as a function of a response constant r, advertising rate as a function of time $A(t)$, sales saturation (M), sales rate (S), and sales decay constant (λ)

Class IV — Uncertainty Reference

Type	Characteristics	Examples
1. Deterministic	For a specific set of input values, there is a uniquely determined output that represents the solution of a model under conditions of *certainty*.	Profit = revenue − costs

Type	Characteristics	Examples
2. Probabilistic	Probabilistic models involve probability distributions for inputs or processes and provide a range of values of at least one output variable with a probability associated with each value. These models assist with decisions made under conditions of *risk*.	a. Actuarial tables that give the probability of death as a function of age b. Return on investment is simulated by using a probability distribution for each of the various costs and revenues with values selected by the Monte Carlo (random) technique; ROI appears in graph form as return in dollars versus probability of the various dollar returns.
3. Game	Game theory models attempt to develop optimum solutions in the face of complete ignorance or *uncertainty*. Games against nature and games of competition are subclassifications.	Two gasoline stations are adjacent to each other. One owner wonders: "Shall I raise or lower my price? If I raise mine, my competitor may raise or lower his. If I lower mine, he may raise or lower his. I know the gain or loss in any situation, but once each of us sets the price, we must keep it for the week. We can't collude."

Class V — Generality

Type	Characteristics	Examples
1. General	General models for business are models that have applications in several functional areas of business.	a. Linear programming algorithm for all functional areas b. Waiting-line model — applications appear in production, marketing, and personnel
2. Specialized	Specialized models are those that have application to a unique problem only.	a. Sales response as a function of advertising may be based on a unique set of equations b. The probabilistic bidding model has a single application to one functional area

The foregoing classification provides a structure for the understanding of models; specific descriptions of elementary forms of general models will shed more light on their use in business applications. In Figure 12-1, therefore, we show the objectives of some selected models, usually in a specific application. It is necessary to introduce definitions of terms in Figure 12-1 so that a pictorial description of the situation and the mathematical representation may be made meaningful, to some degree at least. We admit that only an impression of the nature of models is given by the figure; only through the detailed derivation of a model can the student gain a complete insight.

What does all of the preceding mean to the student of MIS? First, information systems should solve as many problems as possible on a routine

Model	Objective	Nomenclature for Relevant Variables	Pictorial Representation	Mathematical Representation of the System
Inventory Model	Find Economic Order Quantity by trade-off of carrying costs and ordering costs so as to minimize the system cost.	Q = size of order K = carrying costs S = ordering costs D = estimated annual demand TC = total system cost	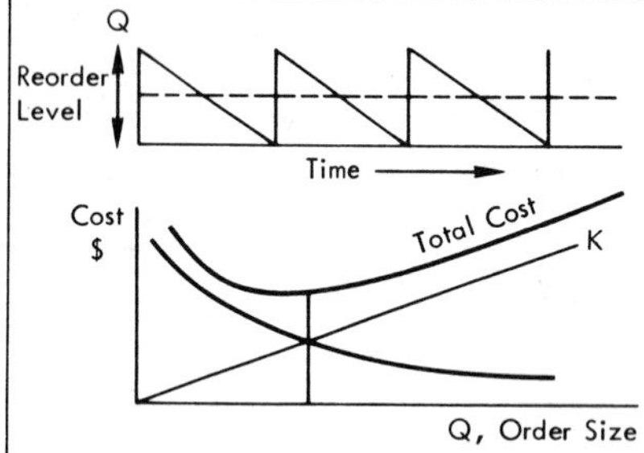 Reorder Level, Q, Time; Cost $\$$, Total Cost, K, Q, Order Size	$TC = (Q/2) \cdot K + (D/Q) \cdot S$
Progress Model	Find time, cost, or price per unit after declines due to experience gained.	K = cost of first unit N = N-th unit produced ϕ = fraction of initial cost required to produce a unit after any doubling of production C_N = cost to produce N-th unit	Cost per Unit $\$$, Number of Units Produced	$C_n = KN^{(\log \phi/\log 2)}$
Waiting-Line Model	Find the average length of a waiting line, the average waiting time, or the optimum number of service facilities.	Poisson arrival rate with exponentially distributed service times for a single service facility. λ = average number of arrivals/period μ = average number of service completions/period C_w = cost per period for a person or unit waiting C_f = service facility cost for one unit TC = total system cost	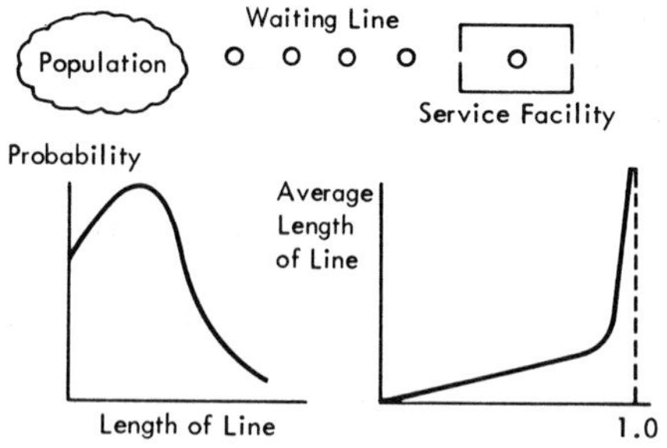 Population, Waiting Line, Service Facility; Probability, Average Length of Line, Length of Line, 1.0	Average number of units in system $= \lambda/(\mu - \lambda)$ Average time a unit waits in the system $= 1/(\mu - \lambda)$ Service rate for minimum cost; $\min = \lambda + \sqrt{\lambda\, C_w/C_f}$

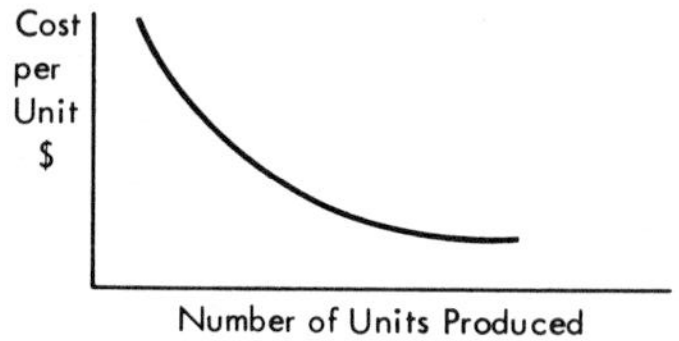

FIGURE 12-1 Illustrations of Models

Model	Objective	Nomenclature for Relevant Variables	Pictorial Representation	Mathematical Representation of the System
Markov Process Model	Find the share of the market held by each company if the probabilities of brand switching by the customers can be estimated.	S_{11} = share of market for brand 1 in period 1 S_{21} = share of market for brand 2 in period 1 S_{12}, S_{22}, similarly P_{11} = probability that a customer who bought brand 1 in period 1 will buy brand 1 in the next period P_{12} = probability of switch from brand 1 to brand 2 P_{21}, P_{22}, similarly	(state diagram with states 1 and 2, transitions P_{11}, P_{12}, P_{21}, P_{22}) where $P_{11} + P_{12} = 1$ $P_{21} + P_{22} = 1$	$$\begin{pmatrix} S_{12} \\ S_{22} \end{pmatrix} = \begin{pmatrix} P_{11} & P_{12} \\ P_{21} & P_{22} \end{pmatrix} \begin{pmatrix} S_{11} \\ S_{21} \end{pmatrix}$$ $$= \begin{pmatrix} P_{11} S_{11} + P_{12} S_{21} \\ P_{21} S_{11} + P_{22} S_{21} \end{pmatrix}$$
Expected-Value Model	Determine the course of action that will yield the greatest expected gain.	☐ Decision point ○ Random event in the world p_i = probability that a particular event occurs a_i = gain or loss resulting from outcome of random event EV = expected value of a course of action	(decision tree) Alternative 1: $P_1 = .2$, $a_1 = -\$20$; $P_2 = .8$, $a_2 = \$100$ Alternative 2: $P_3 = .6$, $a_3 = \$50$; $P_4 = .4$, $a = \$60$	EV (alternative 1) = $P_1 a_1 + P_2 a_2 = .2(-20) + .8(100)$ EV (alternative 2) = $P_3 a_3 + P_4 a_4 = .6(50) + .4(60)$

FIGURE 12-1 (continued)

Model	Objective	Nomenclature for Relevant Variables	Pictorial Representation	Mathematical Representation of the System
Forecasting Model	Estimate short-term demand by a smoothing of past data and extrapolating.	A = arbitrary smoothing weight S_t = actual sales during period t $\bar{S}_{t-1}$ = former forecast of sales for period t $\bar{S}_t$ = forecast of sales		$\bar{S}_t = A\,S_t + (1 - A)\,\bar{S}_{t-1}$ $0 < A < 1$
Linear Programming Model	Optimize a linear function with linear constraints. In particular, maximize profit from production of two products when a limited number of hours, per period of time, is available on each of two machines used.	**Product / Profit per unit / Hours Required Machine 1 / Machine 2** P_1 — $8 — 4 — 3 P_2 — $7 — 2 — 4 Machine hours available — 40 — 48 Z = profit x = number of units of P_1 y = number of units of P_2		Maximize $Z = \$8\,x + \$7\,y$ subject to $4x + 3y = 40$ $2x + 5y = 30$
Games-of-Conflict Model	For two competitors each of whom adopts his own set of strategies and knows the payoff for any pair of one of his strategies and one of his competitor's, find the strategy each should adopt.	A = firm A B = firm B i = one of A's strategies j = one of B's strategies a_{ij} = amount B pays A for the pair of strategies i and j		Given $\lVert a_{ij} \rVert$ find a payoff, if it exists, as determined by $\max_{i}\left(\min_{j} a_{ij}\right) = \min_{j}\left(\max_{i} a_{ij}\right)$ (Find a number that is lowest in its row and highest in its column)

FIGURE 12-1 (continued)

392

Model	Objective	Nomenclature for Relevant Variables	Pictorial Representation	Mathematical Representation of the System
Network Planning Models— Critical Path Method (CPM) or Program Evaluation Review Technique (PERT)	Schedule a project and control it by maintaining surveillance on time and costs. Find critical (longest) time path in the planning network and slack times for events outside the critical path.	$\bigcirc$ Event ⟶ Activities 1 – 2 Mold frame — 4 hours 1 – 3 Cut axle — 2 hours 2 – 3 Machine the frame — 6 hours 3 – 4 Insert axle — 1 hour 2 – 4 Get motor from warehouse — 8 hours 4 – 5 Install motor — 2 hours t = time of activity between event i and event j, when it exists		Find the maximum $\sum_{i,j} t_{ij}$ subject to the given order and time constraints of the activities

FIGURE 12-1 (continued)

393

basis. The computer and the application of models make possible much routine problem solving to relieve management. Second, the solutions from models may supply valuable information to aid managers in solving problems. Managers must evaluate the amount of aid that a particular type of model can supply, as well as the associated cost. A probabilistic dynamic prediction model may be very helpful, but it may cost $100,000 to develop and utilize for a year. On the other hand, a deterministic model may be reasonably helpful and cost only $10,000 to develop and process on the computer for a year. In some instances, development of a complex model of a firm's operations may be necessary for survival because of modeling being carried out by competitors. Modeling has become an extremely potent tool in the hands of those who know how to use it in MIS.

USE OF MODELS FOR ANALYSIS
OF SYSTEMS CHARACTERISTICS

There are a number of questions that we would like to ask about a system, regardless of whether it is an inventory, financial, operating, or information system. These questions relate to the efficiency of the system, the "state" of the system, the amount of feedback, the stability of the system, its speed of response to changes in input, and the effect of transient inputs to the systems. The answers to these questions assist us in evaluating current systems or in evaluating alternatives for a system being designed.

Certain types of iconic models combined with their mathematical counterparts are particularly helpful in making such analyses. Some of these appear in Figure 12-1 and will be apparent from the descriptions. There is a large body of knowledge dealing with the manipulation of these models by mathematical means, which is beyond the scope of this book. From the management viewpoint, it is enough to know that such models exist. Here we present an introduction to some of them.

Block Diagram and "Black Box"
Concept

A block diagram usually consists of a network of blocks linked by lines with arrowheads. The blocks are labeled to indicate the processing performed. The lines indicate the order of processing as well as inputs and outputs as labeled. Such a format is consistent with the pictorial and mathematical development of engineered control systems (servomechanism theory). A conceptual model of this type, modeling in gross terms an entire business operation, is shown in Figure 12-2. Only the information processing is indicated in this figure.

The inverse or dual model uses blocks to designate information and the network of lines to designate processing. Some authors use mixed versions of the basic block diagram and its dual form to present concepts, but mixed diagrams may render quantitative analysis more difficult.

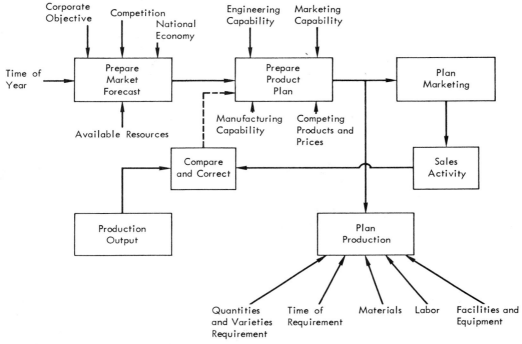

FIGURE 12-2 Gross Model of a Business Information Processing System

To present an overview of modeling with block diagrams and parallel quantitative methods, we will first expand on the nature of block diagrams and then indicate briefly the nature of the quantitative, analytical, parallel analysis. The reader is directed to texts on servomechanisms for an in-depth treatment.

Basic Module

Regardless of the complexity of the block diagram model, the basic modules are the same. Each module consists of one or more inputs, a processor that acts upon the inputs, and one or more outputs. In information systems, both inputs and outputs are either raw data or information, depending on the purpose of the input or output.

The *input* is the start-up source in an information system block or operational system block. Figure 12-3 shows both operational (physical) and informational inputs. In Figure 12-2 one or more inputs may also be identified for each block. The *processor* is the activity that transforms input into a new form called *output*. People, machines, decision procedures, organizations, or even environmental phenomena may act as processors. If we refer again to the basic module of Figure 12-3, we see that the activity of selling performed by a salesperson results in a physical movement of a product. It also results in a conversion of information about ownership and location of the product from input to output.

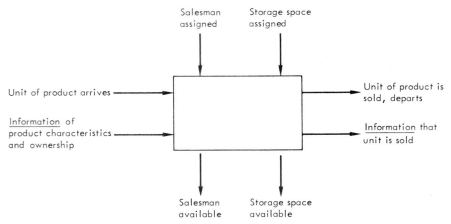

FIGURE 12-3 Basic Module for Operation and Information Processing, Showing Both Physical Inputs and Outputs and Information Inputs and Outputs

If the activity in a processor is well defined so that we describe in detail how the input is converted to the output, we have a good model. Unfortunately, a number of activities must usually be grouped together in a single processor because they are so numerous, complexly interrelated, or not determinable. Such a processor block is usually referred to as a "black box," because we cannot see what goes on inside the block (in a conceptual sense). We try to observe in an empirical situation what happens to inputs when the "black box" activity takes effect. We hope that we may develop from such data a predictive model for the basic module in which the processor activity can be described by means of a mathematical *transfer function.* Figure 12-4 shows a black box representation of the complete manufacturing operation for a single run of a new complex product. If we consider the input of person-days, the number of units of output per day will tend to increase. This relationship or transfer function assumes one form of the several well-known manufacturing progress functions or "learning curves."

How do we know what operation is performed on the input? In manufactured systems, we design the system by specifying what transformation of the

Transfer function = manufacturing progress function

FIGURE 12-4 Black Box Model

input is to be made. We do this also when we construct the model of the system, but this does not mean that the system will actually work that way when it is finally designed and put into operation. It becomes necessary to measure or observe how the input is being affected to verify our design.

If we are called upon to analyze a system that has been in operation for some time, again we must observe how the input is being changed by the process. We hope that there is a stable enough relationship between input and output so that we can develop a prediction (transfer) function. The black box representing the system process must not vary with time, or, if it does, it must vary in a way that is possible for us to determine.

The fundamental block is just the starting point for specification or analysis of systems. Inputs or outputs may be broken down into their components and analyzed. Blocks in series or in parallel may be combined by mathematical methods. When there is feedback, the determination of the effect of the transfer function is further complicated.

Feedback and Control

Business systems are dynamic because changes with time in such systems are inevitable. For a dynamic system, it is necessary to review either periodically or continuously the nature of the output to adjust the system for changes in its own operation or changes in the environment. In a business system we need to observe whether the output of products is profitable and acceptable to the customer; otherwise the system will come to a standstill. In Chapter 11, we discussed information feedback systems and control in some detail. We will not repeat that material here. The reader should study the numerous examples of models that were covered.

State-Descriptive Models of Systems

Most phenomena in the world change continuously with time, but many situations represent discrete changes. Some illustrations of both types of change are

Events That Change Continuously with Time	*Events That Represent Discrete Changes with Time*
1. Age of individual employees	1. Number of owners of Fords, of Chevrolets, of Plymouths
2. Experience of a manager	2. Number of units in inventory
3. Obsolescence of a product	3. Number of machines in the shop
4. Utilization of electrical power	4. Number of employees
5. System operation time of an MIS	5. Waiting line or no waiting line at a store's checkout register
6. Hours of computer time employed by an MIS	6. Market position ranking of three firms in an industry

There are several very useful modeling approaches to representing the important problems in which elements fall into discrete "states" or classes. Even continuous-time variables may be classified into intervals, each interval designated as a "state," and a state description of all variables treated as a discrete case. Because we often wish to hold some quantities *constant with time to represent a particular state*, we call these quantities *parameters* of the model. A simple but common model involves the evaluation of the present value (V) of a future stream of n annual revenues (R_k) for the value of money (r). The rate of return (r) is the parameter that describes possible states of the business system:

$$V = \sum_{k=1}^{n} R_k/(1 + r)^k$$

A "state" is thus a particular system condition. In the case just cited, a particular system condition might be $r = 12$ percent. A state of a system may vary with time in some known manner, or the state of a system may be under the control of management. For example, in an inventory system, management might wish to avoid the stockout state and therefore design a system with a buffer stock, making such a state extremely unlikely.

Some commonly employed models of system states and transitions from state to state are Markov models, matrix models, and tree diagrams. An example of each appears in Figure 12-1. Because business operating systems and information systems are constantly undergoing state changes, preferably under the partial control of management, modeling systems by state-descriptive methods is very useful. Obviously, the systems designer must have a thorough knowledge of management science to perform such modeling. Managers do not require such depth of knowledge, but they should be aware of the existence of these techniques. The following sections are designed to provide this brief introduction.

Markov Process State Descriptions

A special case, the Markov process in simple pictorial form, will illustrate the application of state-descriptive models. Consider two lily pads floating on the water. A frog sits on one of them and contemplates leaping. The state of this system is described by the frog on the lily pad, and thus one of two states is possible depending upon which lily pad the frog is on (Figure 12-5). The transfer functions are probabilities. We define p_{12} as the probability that if the frog is on pad 1, he will leap from pad 1 to pad 2. Also p_{22} is the probability that if the frog is on pad 2, he will be on pad 2 at the next time interval. If there are n states, there are n transfer functions (probabilities) for each state to represent the probabilities for changing from a given state to any of the n states in the next time period. (This includes the no-change transition case.)

An example of a two-state system is an inventory system. It has two states: goods in inventory and stockout. If the period of time is one week, the probabilities of state changes relative to the current state are the transfer functions.

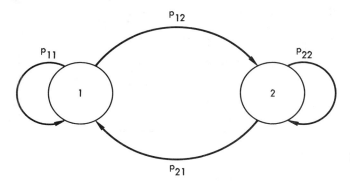

FIGURE 12-5 Two-State Markov Model

A more complex system is the organization of a company or institution. In state 1, let us say, there are a number of individuals, each with a special skill. In the next time period, the list of skills present has probably changed, owing to loss or gain of personnel or substitution of people by leaves and additions. The transfer functions are the transition probabilities, as before.

Matrix State Descriptions

Matrices may also be used to describe systems that change from one state to another. For example, if there are three competing firms in an industry, a state of a firm may be identified as its rank in the market. The matrix shows the probabilities of changes of state from one time period to another (Figure 12-6(a)).

Another matrix representation of systems states and state transitions is that for the balance sheet of a firm (Figure 12-6(b)). There are, of course, an

Probabilities of changing from
one state to another at a later period of time

To state (market position)

		1	2	3
From state (market position)	1	.70	.20	.10
	2	.20	.70	.10
	3	.10	.10	.80

(a)

FIGURE 12-6 Matrix State Description Models

Probabilities of changing states
To specified values

	Assets	Liabilities	Net Worth
Assets	P_{11}	0	0
Liabilities	0	P_{22}	0
Net Worth	0	0	P_{33}

From specified values

(b)

FIGURE 12-6 (continued)

infinite number of possible states, but a few conceivable cases could be listed. A matrix may then be prepared for this limited number of states so that the sum of the p_{1j}'s equals unity, and similarly with the p_{2j}'s and p_{3j}'s.

Tree Diagrams

Tree diagram models are useful for showing sequential changes of states for a very limited number of states and transitions combined. They have the added advantage that decisions can be worked into them. Figure 12-7(a) shows an elementary model and Figure 12-7(b) a stochastic and decision model. The probabilities of transition from any given state to possible next states are shown on the branches.

SIMULATION

Another powerful application of modeling is the numerical simulation of a system process. A simulation is carried out by specifying a set of starting conditions and a set of rules for the system action. Numerical values are then calculated for the change in the system due to a random input of the exogenous variables. The new state of the system becomes the starting point for another "pass." Simulation is a very valuable technique because (1) it provides for testing of explicit models, those that can be stated in a complete "formula" fashion, and (2) it makes possible the solution of implicit or "chain" types of models whose analytic solution may not even be possible. Figure 12-8 shows pictorially the latter case. The model is composed of parts, each depending on the results of the previous part.

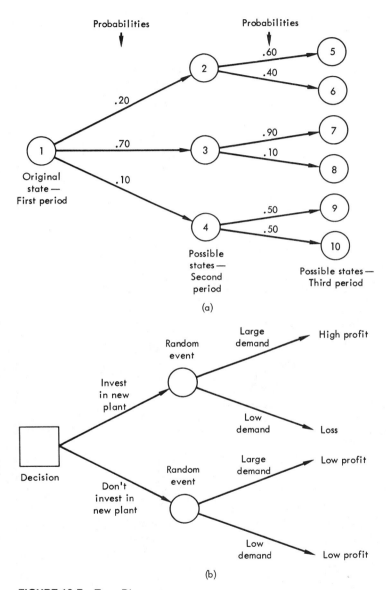

Probabilities

Probabilities

.60

.40

.20

.90

.70

.10

.10

.50

.50

1
Original
state —
First period

2

3

4

5

6

7

8

9

10

Possible
states —
Second
period

Possible states —
Third period

(a)

Large
demand

High profit

Random
event

Invest
in new
plant

Low
demand

Loss

Decision

Large
demand

Low profit

Random
event

Don't
invest in
new plant

Low
demand

Low profit

(b)

FIGURE 12-7 Tree Diagrams

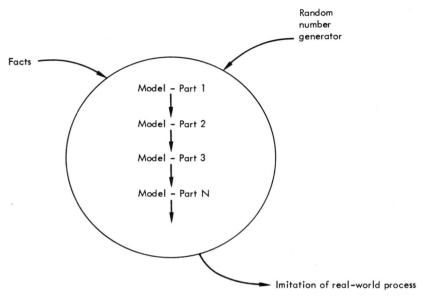

FIGURE 12-8 Simulation

We will attempt to present an explanation of a simulation of an inventory system without lengthy development of many details. The purpose is to give the reader the flavor of the technique rather than a treatise on how to do it.

The following "facts" are given:

1. The objective is to study an inventory system to determine probability distributions for the size of the inventory and for the size of shortages (stockouts), to aid management in evaluating inventory policies.

2. The procurement level is 4 units. This is a parameter, because it is held constant for this simulation, but it could be changed for another simulation of the system. It is also under the control of management. Thus, when inventory drops to 4 units, an order is placed.

3. The size of the order placed each time, the procurement quantity, is 12 units. This is also a parameter under the control of management.

4. There are two exogenous input variables, variables not under the control of management. These are demand and lead time. The demand is simply the number of units to be withdrawn from inventory in a time period, and this obviously fluctuates.

   The lead time is the number of periods of time from placing an order to receiving the goods that replenish the inventory. This also obviously fluctuates.

5. A cumulative probability function or graph links probability values to demand values. This may be constructed from historical data or from a theoretical basis.

   A cumulative probability function or graph links probability values to lead time values. This may be constructed similarly to that for demand.

6. A cycle consists of the number of periods from placing an order to the placing of the next order and is determined therefore by the time it takes the inventory level to drop to 4 units.

7. Assume that the initial stock is 4 units.

TABLE 12-1 Inventory System Simulation

(A) Cycle	(B) Period	(C) Initial Stock	(D) Lead Time	(E) Demand	(F) Final Stock	(G) Units on Hand	(H) Units Short
1	1	4	4	0	4	4	0
	2	4		2	2	2	0
	3	2		1	1	1	0
	4	1		0	13	1	0
	5	13		5	8	13	0
	6	8		2	6	8	0
	7	6		3	3	6	0
2	1	3	2	0	3	3	0
	2	3		4	0	3	1
3	1	0	5	1	10	0	1
	2	10		2	8	10	0
	3	8		2	6	8	0 etc.

Now we set up a table, Table 12-1, to represent the system. Because initial stock is 4 units, we must place an order for 12 more units, according to management policy given under "facts" 2 and 3 above. To find the lead time, we utilize a table of random numbers to give us a number from 0 to 100 and convert it to a probability index by dividing by 100. Suppose that the number drawn were 72; this becomes a probability of .72. Corresponding to this probability, we obtain from the graph mentioned in "fact" 5 a value of the lead time as 4. This is entered in column D of Table 12-1.

We now obtain a value of demand by the same process, and this value turns out to be zero. We enter this in column E. Because no units were demanded in this period and no units arrived, final stock remains at 4, the number of units on hand for the period is 4, and there is no shortage.

The simulation is continued in this manner until period 4, when 12 units arrive at the end of the period. Table 12-1 shows the computations into a portion of the third cycle. In practice, *several hundred cycles* would be carried out. The necessity for an electronic computer in such work is apparent. The results in columns G and H permit management to determine average inventories, average stockouts, and costs associated with each. Probability distributions for inventory size and shortage amounts may also be obtained.

CONSTRUCTION OF MODELS

The construction of models often depends upon recognizing a problem and then finding a matching technique for its solution. The danger in this method is that analysts may find themselves looking for problems to match their techniques instead of vice versa. A general procedure for constructing a model, especially in complex situations, is as follows:

1. Identify and formulate the manager's decision problem in writing.
2. Identify the constants, parameters, and variables involved. Define them verbally and then introduce symbols to represent each one.
3. Select the variables that appear to be most influential so that the model may be kept as simple as possible. Distinguish between those that are controllable by the manager and those that are not.
4. State verbal relationships among the variables, based upon known principles, specially gathered data, intuition, and reflection. Make assumptions or predictions concerning the behavior of the noncontrollable variables.
5. Construct the model by combining all relationships into a system of symbolic relationships.
6. Perform symbolic manipulations (such as solving systems of equations, differentiating, or making statistical analyses).
7. Derive solutions from the model.
8. Test the model by making predictions from it and checking against real-world data.
9. Revise the model as necessary.

Let us see how we might develop a useful model for forecasting the sales of an ongoing retail establishment. One of the most intuitively appealing ways to proceed is to assume that last year's sales will be related to this year's sales (directly). We will follow that line of reasoning.

First Form of the Model

We need to find out what the (direct) relationship is between last year's sales and this year's sales. To do this we take the first n weeks of *actual* sales for this year and look up the corresponding n weeks of actual sales for last year. We form a ratio of these two numbers, which represents the expected direct relation between last year's sales and this year's sales. Our first model then becomes

$$CSE = \frac{C(n)}{P(n)}(P)$$

where

$$
\begin{aligned}
CSE &= \text{current year's sales estimate} \\
C(n) &= \text{current year's sales actuals through week } n \\
P(n) &= \text{previous year's sales actuals through week } n \\
P &= \text{previous year's sales actuals (whole year)}
\end{aligned}
$$

Second Form of the Model

We will no doubt lose some of our old customers and, hence, some of our revenue as compared with last year. We introduce an attrition factor A ($A < 1.00$). This yields a second form of our model:

$$CSE = A\left[\frac{C(n)}{P(n)}\right]P$$

Final Form of the Model

Just as we are very likely to lose some customers, we will also gain some new customers. We believe we will have a 10 percent rise in the number of new customers as compared with last year. New customers, on the average, have spent $250 a year. This brings us to the final form of our model:

$$CSE = A\left[\frac{C(n)}{P(n)}\right]P + 1.1(N)(\$250)$$

where

$$N = \text{the number of new customers last year}$$

As can be seen, models do not give "final answers" to simple problems. Models are constructed to give management a reasonable grasp on an uncertain future.

SUMMARY

In the early history of technology, new inventions were developed by constructing a device and then tinkering with it until it worked. As science advanced, it became possible to work out on paper in advance the design of a new device. Actual construction of impractical and costly devices could be avoided and more nearly optimum devices designed by application of scientific knowledge.

In the complex world of business, we have seen managers blunder and firms fail because of deficient understanding of the operation of businesses. "Trial" was often followed by "error," and errors often proved to be disastrous. The development of modeling signals the beginning of science in business. Experimentation on models is a tremendous advance over betting the company on every real-world experiment.

We have defined the purpose and nature of models in this chapter. The classifications of models by function, structure, time reference, uncertainty reference, and generality have afforded insights into their nature. We have provided in Figure 12-1 simplified presentations of some models, including their goals, schematic representations, and mathematical representations.

Models are used not only for decision problems, but for analysis and evaluation of complete systems. System efficiency, system response, and system simplification may be studied by means of system modeling. Many valuable techniques for the study of business operational and information systems may be drawn from the literature on servomechanisms and engineered control systems.

Finally, we have attempted to provide guidelines for the construction of models. Because of the limited scope of the coverage of management science in this book, we gave only a general approach and a single example. The construction of models requires a highly specialized business talent/mathematical specialist to produce the final result. Managers can perform a most important part of modeling by verbalizing the problem, constraints, and qualitative relationships. From the point of view of MIS, the most significant aspect of modeling is its use to provide programmed decision making and information aids to management decision makers.

PROBLEMS AND QUESTIONS

1. In column A are the steps to systematic problem solving. Provide the parallels to management science in column B.

A (Problem Solving)	B (Management Science)
1. Observation	_____
2. Statement of a problem	_____
3. Collection of data	_____
4. Development of hypotheses for solution of the problem	_____
5. Evaluation of the alternative hypotheses	_____

2. Continue the preceding exercise into the decision-making process.

A (Decision Making and Action)	B (Management Science)
1. Selection of best alternative	_____
2. Implementation of best alternative	_____
3. Review of results	_____

3. Match the types of models in column A with examples of column B.

A Types of Models	B Example
1. Descriptive	_____ Mathematical equation
2. Predictive	_____ Break-even analysis
3. Normative	_____ Waiting line
4. Iconic	_____ Organization chart
5. Symbolic	_____ Scale model
6. Deterministic	_____ Marketing mix model
7. General	_____ Profit = revenue − costs

4. Match the system or component of column A with the type of model in column B.

A System or Component	B Type of Model
1. Factory floor with machine	_____ Game theory model
2. Credit clerks making repetitive decisions regarding granting of credit	_____ Economic lot size
3. People functioning as an organization	_____ Organizational chart
4. Trucks delivering to random demands of customers	_____ Flow diagram
5. MIS showing cash flow from production of a new factory	_____ Simulation
6. Brand switching by consumers	_____ Balance sheet
7. Testing of MIS before it is put into operation	_____ Monte Carlo simulation
8. Computation of how much to produce in a given lot size	_____ Decision table
9. Probability of death as a function of age	_____ Layout on grid paper
10. Businessman asking himself whether to raise prices in view of competitor's action	_____ Markov model
11. Toll booth at a turnpike entrance	_____ Actuarial tables
12. Financial condition of a firm at a discrete point in time	_____ Waiting-line model

5. Describe briefly how management science might be applied in a specific company for the following problems:

   a. Systems evaluation
   b. Detailed system design
   c. Information flow design
   d. Economics of design
   e. Implementation of a system

6. A bank has a drive-in teller system. Long lines form on Fridays, when people cash paychecks. On other days, the lines are rarely longer than five cars, even when there are only one or two tellers. Develop possible variables and objectives. Then develop a verbalized model.

7. a. The circle with the number 1 in it is a lily pad with a frog sitting on it. The circle with the number 2 in it is an unoccupied lily pad. The p_{ij} are probabilities that the frog will or will not jump.

   1. What is the probability that the frog will jump to lily pad 2? _____
   2. What is the probability that the frog will not move? _____

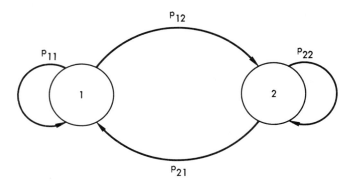

Two-State Markov Model

b. The circle with the number 1 in it is the state of having plenty of item A in stock. The circle with the number 2 in it is the stockout condition (for A).

1. What is the probability of item A being in stock? _____

2. What is the probability of item A running out of stock? _____

8. An example of each type of model is given in the text for the classification system of models; name a different example of a model for each class.

9. Give an example of a business problem that lends itself to simulation, both because of complexity and because of the economics of obtaining a solution.

10. Why is it difficult to model consumer behavior? Organizational behavior? Long-range plans?

SELECTED REFERENCES

DAVIS, ROSCO K., AND PATRICK G. McKEOWN. *Quantitative Models for Management.* Boston: Kent, 1981.

KRAJEWSKI, LEE J., AND HOWARD E. THOMPSON. *Management Science: Quantitative Methods in Context.* New York: John Wiley, 1981.

LARRACEY, SUSAN A. "Hospital Planning for Cost-Effectiveness." *Management Accounting*, July 1982.

MÜLLER - MERBACH, HEINER. "Phases or Components?" *Interfaces*, February 1982.

MURDICK, ROBERT G. *MIS: Concepts and Design.* Englewood Cliffs, N.J.: Prentice-Hall, 1980.

TANEJA, NAWAI, K. *Airline Planning: Corporate, Financial, and Marketing.* Lexington, Mass.: D. C. Heath, 1982.

TERSINE, RICHARD J., AND EDWARD T. GRASSO. "Models: A Structure for Managerial Decision Making." *Industrial Management*, March–April 1979.

WORTHLEY, STEPHEN, G. "Managing Information Through Banks." *Management Accounting*, August 1982.

International Medical Instruments, Inc.

In late 1983, Robert F. Dobrynski, M.D., president of International Medical Instruments, Inc., called an emergency meeting of the executive committee. He was furious over the cancellation of a $60,000 order from a large soon-to-be-opened municipal hospital in Chicago. Among those reasons that were given for cancellation were late delivery dates, the large number of substitutions, and the fact that over 30 percent of the items had been marked "back-ordered" or "out of stock."

Dr. Dobrynski termed the loss of the order a "fiasco" and blamed it on a breakdown in the order processing system. He stated that the majority of the items were either in stock or expected shortly from production or outside suppliers.

After cooling down, Dr. Dobrynski concluded the meeting with the comment, "Some heads are going to roll if this happens again. We've got to clean up the order processing system and those others related to it, even if we have to get rid of that new computer and return to our old card system. Incidentally, I want full cooperation from everyone in helping Frank Bemis [the controller] install management information systems throughout the company."

The normal output from an executive committee meeting was an updated quarterly sales plan. The committee met monthly and was composed of

> R. F. Dobrynski, M.D., president and treasurer
> James Blackwell, Ph.D., director of research and engineering
> Frank Bemis, C.P.A., controller
> Solomon Katz, vice president of marketing
> John Rogers, vice president of manufacturing

Robert Dobrynski

After Robert Dobrynski was graduated from medical school in 1956, his interests quickly turned to research and medical administration rather than medical practice. He founded the company in 1959 to provide a source of high-quality, dependable, medically related research and diagnostic equipment. Over the intervening years he maintained that same basic product strategy but became more businessman than medical doctor. He was particularly frustrated that increasing sales accompanied by increasing size and complexity had made the management of the firm so difficult and time consuming.

Dr. Dobrynski saw his problems as threefold. First, he felt that he was unable to set a long-term course of action because of outside events (customers, markets, technology, economy, etc.) over which he had no control. Second, he could not get his directors and vice presidents to act as a team. "Synergism" was his favorite managerial expression, but he was unable to achieve integration between people and operations. Third, he felt that the work force was unwilling to perform because of lack of motivation. He was particularly annoyed that policies and plans were not always adhered to.

Dr. Dobrynski had attended a three-day manufacturers' seminar on computers in late 1982 and had returned with enthusiasm for MIS. For about a month he took an active hand in planning for the design and installation of management information systems, but more pressing matters had diverted his attention. Shortly thereafter he delegated the entire operation to Frank Bemis. Although Dr. Dobrynski retained the title of president and treasurer, the majority of the work in the treasurer's department was supervised by Bemis.

Frank Bemis

Frank Bemis was first employed by the company in 1959 as a bookkeeper. Through attendance at evening college classes he passed the C.P.A. examination in 1968. After an abortive effort to begin his own accounting firm, he returned to the company in 1972 and in 1980 was appointed controller. Frank was a walking encyclopedia of company financial information, and he was familiar with every facet of operations. He frequently stated that accounting information was the backbone of the company and that his procedures were to be strictly followed at all costs. His primary concern was the cost variance report, and he tended to view the preparation of this report as his objective rather than the utilization of the report to reduce costs. Because he was so quick to produce financial data, other department heads tended to be slack in this regard.

Jim Blackwell

Jim Blackwell was co-founder of the company along with Dr. Dobrynski. He received his Ph.D. from M.I.T. in 1957 and shortly thereafter began the association that led to the company's founding. Blackwell, an introvert and by nature quiet and withdrawn, was interested solely in the more esoteric aspects of his engineering task. Consequently, much of the success of the company could be attributed to his excellent design talent.

Sol Katz

Sol Katz had been the number one district sales manager and before that the number one salesman. He was sometimes described as a "born salesman." Although Katz did have an excellent talent for the sales management function, he admitted to deficiencies in the headquarters functions of research, advertising, and the duties associated with warehousing and inventory.

Katz had very recently taken over the job of vice president of marketing, having been promoted from head of the New York district. He therefore felt that the loss of the $60,000 order and the performance of the order processing system wasn't entirely his fault. Moreover, in view of his short tenure at the Stoughton, Massachusetts, headquarters, he felt he could be somewhat more critical of company operations than other executives.

John Rogers

John Rogers was an industrial engineer who had come to the company upon graduation from college in 1975. He was promoted to vice president in 1980. Hard work was his most noticeable attribute. He could be found either on the shop floor or in this office overlooking the shop floor from 7 : 00 A.M. to 7 : 00 P.M. It was a common practice for Rogers to join a production crew to demonstrate an unfamiliar method or procedure.

COMPANY BACKGROUND

International Medical Instruments (IMI) had been founded in 1959 in Stoughton, Massachusetts, by a small group of physicians and engineers. These men had a great deal of interest in the research and development of hospital and laboratory equipment and enjoyed a personal relationship dating back to college and medical school days. Except for Dr. Dobrynski and Mr. Blackwell, the original founders had retired, but remained stockholders. The original objective of the firm was to develop research and laboratory equipment, to produce the most modern microscopes available, and in general to improve significantly the quality of the laboratory research devices available to clinics, laboratories, hospitals, and universities.

During the first decade of its existence, the company enjoyed growth and prosperity, owing in large measure to the uniqueness of its products and the absence of significant competition. However, beginning in the early 1970s, competition grew as additional firms entered the industry. Among these were Beckman Optical Equipment Corporation, Littman Medical Supply Company, Perkins and Elmer Laboratory Equipment Company, and Bausch & Lomb Optical Company.

In 1979 the company acquired (through an exchange of stock) the Medical Science Instrument Corporation of Stoughton, Massachusetts, whose principal products were disposable laboratory and hospital supplies.

The operations of that company were subsequently merged into those of the parent company and the combined operation utilized the same manufacturing facility, sales force, and other resources. The acquisition of this company also gave IMI additional product lines as well as additional engineering and research capability.

Growth in sales continued on an upward trend throughout the history of the company and by 1983 had reached a level of over $17 million. Despite this sales growth, there was not a corresponding growth in profits. Indeed, earnings after taxes had declined from a level of over $1 million ($2.50 to $3.00 per share) in the late 1970s to about $600,000 by 1983 ($1.00 per share after "dilution" by stock dividends). This decline was termed "alarming" by Dr. Dobrynski, who blamed eroding profits on the inability to control costs. Profit planning existed in the company, but it was a major source of frustration for Dr. Dobrynski. Sales forecasts were made annually and updated monthly. Generally, these forecasts were met. However, it was in the area of cost control that the need for improvement was evident. When costs exceeded plan, as they often did, it was practically impossible to trace the variance to specific products or departments. Inventory control was a constant headache.

The company had four basic sources of revenue:

1. The established line of electron microscopes and standard inventory products such as electroencephalographs, blood reagent equipment, and flame photometers. This was the basic product line that the company emphasized and it yielded the majority of revenue.

2. The high-volume laboratory supplies that have a high demand owing to their disposable features (syringes, laboratory glasswares, specimen containers, etc.). This was the basic product line of the acquired Medical Science Instrument Corporation.
    Since the acquisition of that company this basic product line, laboratory supplies, had suffered significantly in sales and profits. Two reasons were given. First, sales volume was not large enough to offset the cost of small production runs, the proliferation of unprofitable products, the ready availability of the products elsewhere, and the fact that this type of product was foreign to the market strategy of IMI. Slowly but perceptibly the company began to purchase these items from outside vendors for resale rather than manufacture them. It was almost impossible to make a profit under these circumstances. In 1983 the line was viewed as a convenience to customers rather than a major product line.

3. The sale of spare and replacement parts to existing customers. This market will continue to grow in proportion to the sale of major equipment.

4. The design and manufacture of specially engineered products in response to requests from customers. This source had been rising at a rate of approximately 20 percent annually in recent years. Profits realized on these units are presumed to be substantially lower than on production line products and spare or replacement parts; therefore, marketing efforts are not concentrated on products of this type.

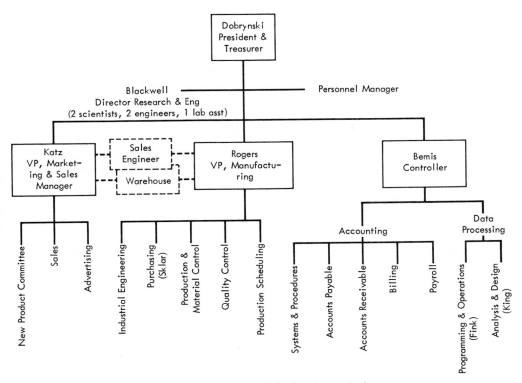

EXHIBIT 1-1   Organization Chart — International Medical Instruments, Inc.

Replacement parts are expected to be profitable despite the difficulty of forecasting any level of sales. Unfortunately, adequate records of prior sales of parent equipment were not maintained.

Although no formal organization chart or position descriptions existed, the general organizational and reporting relationships are as shown in Exhibit 1-1.

DATA PROCESSING DEPARTMENT

This group had only recently been formed. Prior to 1982 it had been called the Accounting Machines Group. The new name presumably was granted to indicate a higher degree of status and responsibility upon the recent installation of an IBM computer system. Prior to that time the department had made the usual progression from unit record equipment to electronic accounting machine systems.

Although for organizational purposes the department was assigned to Frank Bemis, the controller, he was largely unconcerned with the operation of the computer center except for the accounting applications of the accounts payable, general ledger, and accounts receivable. Indeed, except for one or two abortive attempts at sophisticated inventory control and sales analysis systems, the accounting applications made up the overwhelming usage of the old and the new computer hardware.

Immediately after the executive committee meeting when the president threatened that "some heads might roll," Frank Bemis felt that he was in a dilemma. On the one hand, he could feel the increasing operational pressures that demanded better information systems; on the other, he was uncomfortable in the knowledge that neither he nor Otto Fink (data processing manager) had the requisite background to oversee the design of these systems. Otto Fink had earned his job and title through diligent programming and operating efforts, but he knew little of the managerial decision-making needs of the company.

Bemis solved his problem, at least in the short run, by reorganizing the Data Processing Department. He placed himself at the head of the department and split the operation into two sections: Programming and Operating and Analysis and Design.

As head of the Analysis and Design section, Bemis chose Bill King, a recently recruited young man who had just received his M.B.A. degree from a local Boston university. Although Bill King had no previous computer experience of an operational nature, he had taken several computer courses in college and had attended a short course on the IBM computer system just installed. Moreover, Bemis concluded that King's general management background and his exposure to the company through his financial analysis experience would qualify him to take charge of companywide management information systems. Accordingly, Bemis transferred King to the job with instructions to "come up with a master plan in about five or six weeks."

King's Preliminary Study

King had already organized in his mind a tentative plan for the design and implementation of high-priority systems. He decided that he needed more operational details, so he scheduled appointments with various department heads and supervisors throughout the company. In preparation for these interviews he planned to observe operations and carefully review the documentation of systems and procedures in each department. After commencing his review, he was shocked to discover that documentation was either nonexistent or badly out of date. Procedures manuals were not updated, and system descriptions and flowcharts did not exist for most systems.

Of particular concern to King was the fact that forms for initiating action were generally nonexistent, not used, or obsolete. Communications were often made by phone and followed up by handwritten memos without copies to all interested parties. Rarely were tickler files or follow-up files maintained on these memos or on other informal communications.

Marketing

Marketing was organized into three departments: Sales, Advertising, and Market Research. The last department was not really staffed but consisted of an interdepartmental "new products" committee whose job it was to discover and evaluate new product opportunities and follow up on design and sales. The Sales Department was also responsible for customer order processing. This function operated against the finished goods warehouse inventory, the special order section of manufacturing (for special customer's orders), and the resale warehouse inventory stocked from outside purchases. Sales also maintained a credit check activity and finished goods inventory records so that the sales force could keep fully advised on product availability and relay product demand shifts quickly to Manufacturing. Warehousing was a department reporting to the sales manager for standard inventory (manufactured) items and to purchasing for disposable laboratory supplies and resale items.

Sol Katz was the vice president of marketing and also the general sales manager. The sales force was comprised of 68 salaried sales representatives in the sales districts at Miami, St. Louis, San Francisco, New Orleans, and New York. The company also uses its research and development center at Stoughton, Massachusetts, and the main manufacturing plant to good advantage in the sales effort. Prospective customers visiting these locations gain a better appreciation of the products and are better able to verify for themselves their quality. Very often, purchasing agents, pathologists, clinical laboratory technicians, and pharmacologists visit the factory and the R & D center for the purpose of investigating innovative technology in the field of medical or medically related research devices. Moreover, ideas for new products are frequently obtained from these visitors.

Since its founding, the company had maintained a policy of building superior products. Stringent quality controls were maintained, and this aspect was widely advertised in trade and professional journals. Although a substantial advertising budget (3 percent of gross sales) was utilized, effectiveness of this advertising was open to question.

Sales of replacement parts, a growing source of revenue, were normally handled by a telephone call or on a mail-out basis as the customer needed the part. This portion of total sales was beginning to increase as the age and number of units in use increased. The company generally viewed this source of sales as a convenience to customers rather than as a primary profit item. Because there was no catalog or standardized inventory listing of these replacement parts, sales of these items caused considerable inconvenience and cost in terms of time necessary to process and locate the order. The number of parts stocked was about 1200.

Another growing segment of sales was that of custom-designed units, manufactured to meet the particular needs and specifications of research institutions and other customers needing one-of-a-kind products. The company had not generally been able to ascertain development and production costs on items of this nature and as a result did not devote active sales effort to their marketing. Distribution of such units was handled by the sales engineer from the production plant at Stoughton. It was believed by some managers that custom-designed units could represent a significant portion of total revenue, but the absence of development and design costs, in particular, made this a difficult fact to prove.

Growth patterns in sales, inventory, orders, and type of customers can be summarized as follows:

Historical and Estimated Growth

	Actual			Est.
	1970	*1980*	*1983*	*1988*
Sales ($ millions)	$ 1.2	$ 9.7	$ 17.8	$ 35.0
Suppliers	84	198	250	350
Purchase orders	185	560	920	1700
(average monthly)				
Customers				
Hospitals			1232	2000
Schools and universities			437	500
Supply warehouses and wholesale			86	100
Independent labs			427	1600
Government (federal and other)			26	40
Items (sale)				
Standard inventory products	34	46	68	100
Laboratory supplies		962	852	500
Replacement parts			Unknown	
Custom-engineered		540	620	2000
Sales breakdown ($ millions)				
Standard inventory products			11.6	
Laboratory supplies			4.7	
Replacement parts			.3	
Custom-engineered			1.2	

Sales to hospitals, universities, and independent laboratories and clinics were made at list price less the usual time discount. Sales to supply warehouses and wholesale firms were made at list price less 40 percent on laboratory supplies. There were few occasions to sell standard inventory products through this outlet, and it was not the policy of the company to do so.

KING'S INVESTIGATION

Bill King decided to start his investigation by having an informal discussion with Katz. He made no formal appointment, and he did not prepare a structured plan for an interview.

After King introduced himself to Katz and explained the purpose of his visit, Katz, without further prompting, launched into his analysis:

"Listen, kid, I'm all for you and Frank Bemis and your problems with the computer. And I don't blame Dobrynski for losing his cool about the lost order. How can we improve sales and profits with information systems that perform like our order processing did? Some system!

"You ask me about my problems and what information needs I have for solving them. Well, some of my problems can't be helped by the computer and some can. It can't get me a higher advertising budget, it can't get me a better sales training program, and it can't get my sales force off the dime so they can uncover more customers. On the other hand, let me tell you how it can help.

"First, you can give me a sales analysis system so I can find out who our customers are, where they are located, and which ones are profitable. This applies likewise to inventory analysis. How many items are moving? Which are profitable? Which items and lines should be dropped? And which should be given sales effort? I think we should stop selling to wholesalers or raise the price to them. I'm not sure that pricing at 40 percent off list is making us a dime. Besides, why can't we get those customers for ourselves?

"And what about our inventory control system? I think we could cut our inventory and at the same time improve customer service with proper inventory management. Let me add also that improvement of that system would also give us a catalog we could trust. You won't believe this but I had to 'borrow'—physically borrow—stock from two of our good customers this month to satisfy a high-priority sales demand that the warehouse said was out of stock. And while we're on warehousing, let me put in a complaint about that operation. It's in my area of responsibility, but their performance is getting embarrassing to our selling effort because of delays. The order pickers sometimes have to go to two or more locations to find stock, and then it sits around the warehouse waiting for the necessary paperwork.

"Incidentally, before you do any final implementation of any management information systems, you might want to check back with me. I am now engaged in a rather comprehensive research effort to determine both the size and composition of our future sales. We aren't getting our share of industry sales in a growth industry. I think both our product mix and our customer mix is not only going to grow, but it is going to change. These changes might affect the nature of your computer systems.

"Another comment. When you get around to investigating production control, I wish you could help the Sales Department get some information on a customer's order. From what we know of production, once a customer's order enters the manufacturing stream it's lost as far as identification and progress reporting is concerned. What do I say to a customer who wants a progress report? Or how do I find an item that gets set aside halfway through production and is forgotten?

"O.K. This will give you an idea of our problems. If I were you I would begin with order processing. This is our major bottleneck and there's no excuse for the paperwork delays we are having. I know that order processing is my responsibility, but we've been putting out so many brushfires lately and answering so many customer complaints that the Marketing Department hasn't had time to revise the system."

Following this conversation with Sol Katz, Bill King began his investigation of the order processing subsystem. In his view this system was a logical starting point because it was not only causing immediate problems but it also interacted with so many additional subsystems in the company.

His initial step in the analysis of the order processing system was to try to unravel the "fiasco" on the $60,000 order from the Chicago hospital. After a day or two he was able to piece together the causes. He reviewed these in his mind:

1. The system was not organized to handle a large, out of the ordinary, "crash" order. The total paperwork time devoted to the Chicago order was 18 working days. This appeared to be the normal processing time, and the emergency nature of this large order did not give it any special attention.

2. The order had arrived in standard purchasing order form and the order-entry clerk had made a substantial number of errors in transcribing the information to the sales order form. Numerous stock numbers and descriptions required clarification on the order, but subsequent editing did not correct the mistakes.

3. The errors on the sales order form that was prepared by the order-entry group were not subsequently checked by the warehouse. Any discrepancies or unclear items were marked "back-ordered" or "not in stock," whereas later checks showed that many of the items were in stock. Additionally, storage in the warehouse was in disarray and some items couldn't be located even though they were in stock.

4. The customer was a municipal hospital and therefore was entitled to the government discount. Not only was the discount not computed, but the order processing system wasted four days getting credit approval because no credit file was available. To make matters worse, the items were shipped to the downtown city office that prepared the purchase order, not to the hospital.

5. In terms of dollar value, about one-third of the items on the order were in production, but there was no procedure to inform a customer of delivery estimates on items that were not in finished goods inventory.

6. A number of the out-of-stock items were filled with acceptable substitutes, but prices were not changed on the customer's invoice.

It took Bill King two weeks to complete his preliminary study. After two weeks he was able to write the following descriptions:

Order Processing

Orders are received by mail and phone at the Stoughton plant (90,000 per year) by the *order-entry group*. Both salesreps and customers initiate orders by telephone, telegram, or mail. Orders are sometimes delivered by customers and salesreps at the plant. Regardless of the source, the order-entry group prepares a sales order form from the information received. Each order is stamped with the time of receipt and is entered in the sales order log. The purpose of this log is to determine the elapsed time between order receipt and shipment. A similar shipment log is maintained in shipping so that elapsed time can be determined at any time on any order or combination of orders.

After preparation, a number of editing operations are performed on the sales order form. First, it is given a credit check, utilizing the customer credit file. Second, the order is edited for clarification of item groups ordered, quantities, stock number, price, and customer account number. For this purpose the order is

Sales Dept, Order-Entry Group	June 13, 1983	Copy to: Warehouse, Purchasing
SUBJECT: Order Processing Procedure (Edit Procedure)		

Purpose:	Detail the procedure to be followed in editing a Sales Order prior to submission to the warehouse.
Scope:	This procedure applies to all sections and departs involved in the order processing, warehousing, EDP, billing, and accounts receivable functions.
Form:	Sales Order Form (IMI S-23-83)
Responsibility:	ACTION
Sales Order Edit Clerk	1. Receive all orders from the Order-Entry Group
	2. Edit all orders for presence, completeness, and organization the following entries:
	1. Credit--compare credit against Customer Credit File for:
	(a) Credit limitation compared with total value of order.
	(b) Credit limitation compared with total value of order and accounts receivable outstanding.
	3. If credit limitation is exceeded or questionable, refer the sales order to the Sales Department.
	4. etc. etc. etc. etc.

EXHIBIT 1-2 Procedure for Order Processing

CODE

	Product Code	REQUIREMENT
99	Manufacturer	00 is assigned to the item if manufactured by International Medical Instruments, Inc. Other codes 01–99 are assigned to manufacturers (vendors) of resale items.
999	Product class (and location)	Codes 00–50 assigned to IMI product lines manufactured by company. Codes 51–99 assigned to resale items. The third digit of the code indicates one of nine storage locations in the warehouse.
1234 . . . 90	Manufacturer's description and stock number	This ten-digit number is assigned by the manufacturer. For IMI products the assignment is: XXXXX (IMICO), XX (Product Class), and XXX (stock number of the item within the product class).
9	Special code	For product line.
999	Product number	Number assigned to product within the product line 001–999.
9		This last digit is reserved for future classification use.
	Customer Code	
XXXX	First four letters of customer's name abbreviated	Example: General Hospital Supply (GHSU).
XX	Chronological customer number with first letter of name	Example: GHSU76 identify General Hospital Supply as the 76th Customer in the G's.
X	Customer Code	Nine classes of customers ranging from 0 (hospitals) to 9 (government).
XXXXXXX	Customer number	First five numbers identifies zip code. Sixth number is "sold to" or "bill to" code and seventh number of "ship to" code.
X	Reserved	Presently unused but reserved for future classification and use.

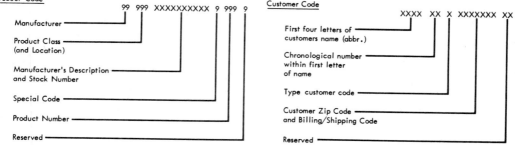

EXHIBIT 1-3 Organization of Product / Customer Codes

compared against the company catalog, price list, and customer list. A third check involves the billing and shipping addresses. These are verified by comparing them with the master customer file.

Because so many delays and errors in order processing had been traced to the edit procedure, Marketing had taken the trouble to write a detailed procedure (Exhibit 1-2) for that operation. An additional purpose of the procedure was to test it for the proposed automation of order processing. In conjunction with the proposed procedure, a new product/customer code system had been devised. Exhibit 1-3 reflects the organization of the code.

After editing, the sales order form is forwarded to the warehouse. Here the order is passed to the inventory clerk, who reduces the perpetual inventory record balance. If an item is out of stock, the ordered item is marked "BO" (for back-ordered). The sales order then goes to Data Processing, where a copy of it is made. This copy is sent back to the warehouse, where it is filed in the warehouse sales order file pending return of the sales order from Data Processing.

The Data Processing Department keypunches detail cards and merges them with the customer master record cards to produce the six-part customer's invoice. This is done by sorting, collating, listing, and tabulating on the IBM computer system. Upon completion of the six-part customer's invoice (shipping order) it is distributed—the original is sent to the Accounting Department. The first copy is for the salesrep; the second copy is for the customer; and the third copy is for the order follow-up section. The fourth copy serves as a delivery receipt, and the fifth copy as a shipping label. The format of the customer's invoice (shipping order) is shown in Exhibit 1-4. Copies, 3, 4, and 5 are sent to the warehouse.

In addition to the preparation of the customer's invoice, the Data Processing Department is responsible for preparing two daily reports: (1) the back order production request for items to be produced in manufacturing and (2) the back order purchase request for items to be purchased. The former goes to Production Control and the latter to Purchasing. Copies of both go to the warehouse and to the order follow-up group.

Standard computer center controls have existed for some time for the EAM operations. Otto Fink has made no plans for additional controls for the forthcoming conversion of manual systems and design of new ones. The warehouse "order picker" selects the item(s) ordered and delivers the items and the order to Shipping. The top invoice copy is detached and is placed in an envelope marked "invoices inside" and the envelope is stapled behind the invoice set. The date, time, and routing are stamped on the top shipping copy and a bill of lading is typed. The third copy of the invoice (shipping order) is sent to *order follow-up*. The price is blanked out on this copy.

In the order follow-up section the invoices are separated into two batches: (1) completed orders, which are filed in the closed-order file, and (2) incomplete orders, which are filed sequentially by order number in the open-order file.

Back-ordered goods are sent to the warehouse, from Receiving if inside the company as a result of the back order purchase request or from Manufacturing if

INTERNATIONAL   MEDICAL   INSTRUMENTS,   INC.

68 Broad Street

Stoughton, Massachusetts   Tel: (202) 624-7564

Customer No. ————————————

Date ————————————

Invoice No. ————————————

Salesman ————————————

Quantity		Description	Unit Price	Total	Shipping Costs	Total
B/O	Ship'd					

SHIP TO:

IMI S-23-83   CUSTOMER COPY

EXHIBIT 1-4   Customer's Invoice and Shipping Order

manufactured in the company's manufacturing facilities as a result of the back order production request. When merchandise arrives from either source, it is checked against purchase orders, purchase requests, and manufacturing requests, and the warehouse receiving clerk notifies the order follow-up section. The open-order file is then searched by a follow-up clerk, and a new sales order is prepared for the back-ordered items. This order is processed the same as a new completely filled order.

In addition to preparing a new order for the back-ordered items, the old back order is placed in the closed-order file if the items completely fill the back order. If not, the open-order file copy is appropriately annotated with information concerning receipt of the partial order.

Purchasing

Requisitions are received in Purchasing from four sources. The first of these is the warehouse where stock records and inventory control of "stock" or "outside purchased" material is maintained. The second source is from Manufacturing and Materials Control, where stock records and inventory control of raw materials for manufactured items are maintained. Third, R & D and Engineering may order equipment, instruments, and supplies. Fourth, each department places orders for office supplies.

Requisitions are received in Purchasing by a clerk who arranges them by general category of buyer specialization and distributes them to the buyers. After editing the requisitions for correctness and completeness, the buyers refer to a manual vendor's historical file that is maintained by part number, price, and vendor information. If the last purchase for a specific item was more than six months ago, the buyer contacts one or more suppliers to verify price and delivery date. In most cases the delivery date agreed upon is within the safety stock level (30 days) of raw materials and stock items for resale. If the item exceeds $1000, three bids are obtained. After the buyer selects a vendor he indicates the necessary information on the requisition, which is then passed to a typist for the creation of a purchase order. In general, there is one purchase order prepared for each requisition. After the buyer edits and signs the purchase order, copies go to a clerk for mailing to the vendor, filing of a copy with the requisition in an open-order file for follow-up, a copy to the warehouse, and a copy to materials control in Manufacturing.

Upon receipt of the material by Receiving, the material is inspected and sent to Manufacturing and Materials Control or the warehouse, depending on the nature of the items (for manufacturing or for stock resale). Receiving prepares a receiving report, attaches the vendor shipping documents, and sends copies of these forms to Purchasing for closing of the open-order file and to Accounts Receivable for payment. Purchasing also uses this form to update the vendor performance history. The basic system is shown in Exhibit 1-5.

Bill King's preliminary analysis of the purchasing function indicated a number of potentially dangerous problems. First, materials were coming in late. A quick review of three months' prior receipts (taken from the monthly materials inspection report) indicated that of 1920 requisitions, 20 percent had been received late, 12 percent had either shortages or overages, and 4 percent of shipments had to be rejected in whole or in part because of quality inspections. Moreover, there was a constant backlog of requisitions that had not yet been converted to purchase orders. The average time between the receipt of a requisition and the preparation of a purchase order was 13 days.

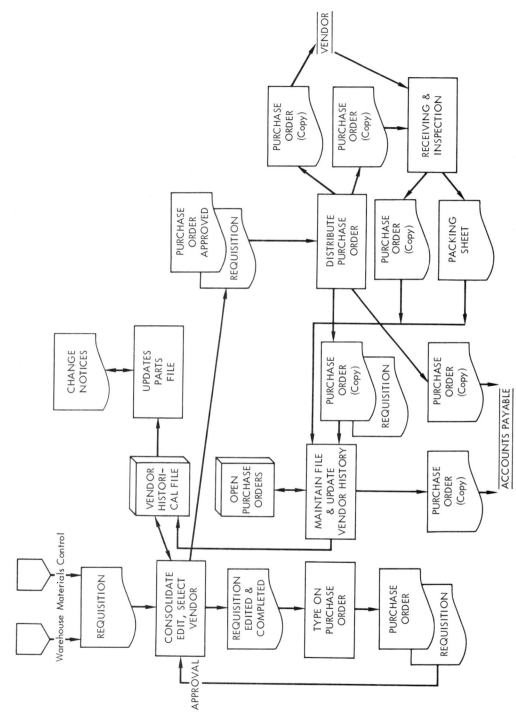

EXHIBIT 1-5 Purchasing System

424

A quick survey of purchasing operations for the previous month yielded the following statistics:

1. Some 724 requisitions resulted in 832 purchase orders valued at $560,000.
2. Over half the purchase orders were valued at less than $50.
3. More than 15 percent of the items were ordered more than once per month and about half of these were ordered weekly.

Al Sklar, the purchasing manager, attributed his problem to "understaffing." He constantly reminded Bill King that "we can't get the work out with the people we've got." He also concluded that his work would be made much easier if requisitions were better prepared before they reached Purchasing and if people would stop requesting emergency purchases that interrupted the routine of his department.

Sklar's annual budget was $145,000, of which $111,000 went to pay the salaries of himself, three buyers, and three clerical personnel.

Al Sklar reported to John Rogers, vice president of manufacturing and operations. In a brief interview with Rogers, Bill King elicited the following summary about the problems in Purchasing:

"Of course, they have problems in Purchasing. But it's not all their fault. We've got to get after the fundamental causes and I see these as three.

"First, we have lousy inventory control. If we could set good inventory levels and order quantities, we wouldn't be preparing the nickel and dime requisitions so frequently and requisitions could be consolidated.

"Next, there's the Engineering bill of materials. In a complex business such as ours with constantly changing products and technical specifications, it's almost impossible to establish adequate materials forecasting and control. This results in a lot of nonroutine and emergency requisitioning.

"Then there's the way we are organized. I'm in charge of manufacturing and naturally am in the best position to manage the raw materials inventory. But what do I know about the stock items that we purchase for resale? Maybe we should give that to Marketing for forming a separate operation of some kind.

"Finally, the main problem as I see it is that those purchasing guys are so busy in the nit-picking paperwork of order preparation and follow-up that they don't have time to do their sourcing job of seeking competitive bids, researching new materials, and seeking new sources."

The record descriptions of requisition, buyer's historical file, and purchase order are shown in Exhibit 1-6.

Despite what Sklar and Rogers had said, Bill King had a different view of the problems in purchasing. In a memorandum documenting what he had learned of the system, he summarized his feelings on the objectives of any redesigned purchasing system:

1. Maintenance of an easily referenced vendor history file
2. Evaluation of both vendors and buyers
3. Reduction of clerical effort
4. Ability to handle a variety of types of purchase orders

EXHIBIT 1-6 Record Descriptions Purchasing Inputs / Files / Outputs

Requisition	Buyer's Historical File	Purchase Order
1. Date	1. Part / assembly number	1. Date
2. Part number / assembly	2. Part description	2. Ship to
3. Part description	3. ID number of vendor	3. Terms of payment
4. Quantity desired	Name	4. Date delivery
5. Date required	Address	desired
6. Manufacturing or	4. Last price and date	5. Quantity
stock	of last price	6. Description
	5. Quantity discounts	7. Price
	6. Delivery time	8. Traffic routing
	7. Dates ordered	
	Items 3 through 7	
	are repeated for	
	second vendor.	
	Items 3 through 7	
	are repeated for	
	third vendor.	

MANUFACTURING AND MATERIAL CONTROL

The revised quarterly sales plan, received each month from the executive committee, provides the basic input from which Manufacturing and Materials Control plans and schedules the production portion of International Medical Instruments, Inc. Manufacturing and Materials Control works closely with Marketing and Warehousing to monitor the level of finished-goods inventory. They also work with Research and Engineering in maintaining files of product specifications and the Engineering bill of materials system. The major job in this department is translating the revised quarterly sales plan into a production schedule and determining what raw materials must be brought into inventories in order to support this schedule. Some 1860 components and parts make up the 68 items of equipment produced. Of these 1860 parts about 80 percent are purchased for direct assembly while the remaining components are manufactured from raw materials at the Stoughton plant. Additionally, the company manufactures about 250 items of disposable laboratory supplies and purchases for resale another 250 to 300. Manufacturing is not concerned with the resale items.

The company has one manufacturing plant. This facility, at Stoughton, where all products are manufactured and assembled, is a modern production plant of 185,000 square feet. It could readily be increased to 225,000 square feet if demand for products created the need for additional capacity. A three-line capacity was built into the plant in anticipation of future manufacturing requirements, but only one line has been equipped and used.

The process of producing a piece of laboratory equipment is primarily a job shop-type process. Parts are produced in three manufacturing shops and sent to shop stores in the assembly shop where purchased material is sent. There the assembly of the equipment takes place. Because of the sophisticated nature of the equipment and the large number of parts involved, there is a scheduling difficulty involved in assuring that the right number of parts are ready for assembly at the same time.

Except for custom-designed units, almost all the company's products are manufactured for inventory. The procedure of manufacturing for inventory has been the subject of constant debate between Marketing and Manufacturing personnel. Because of the high cost of the items and the inability to forecast sales accurately, the Manufacturing group hesitated to produce for a finished goods inventory that might never sell; but the sales force wanted the full line of products on hand for immediate delivery to customers.

Inventory was categorized as follows:

1. Shop stores—parts that had been purchased for production of standard products.
2. Work-in-process inventory—material and labor already expended against pre-planned and project stock
3. Finished goods inventory—completed standard products ready for sale or in fulfillment of customer orders
   Note: General and administrative expenses were recorded and applied to inventory production costs.

Costs of producing standard products were recorded on a material-cost card and a payroll report. Each of these forms was prepared daily (i.e., materials drawn from stock and the transaction were recorded by the stock clerk on a material-cost card). Labor hours were recorded on the payroll report by the Accounting Department as the time cards were collected each day.

When a particular unit or lot of units was completed, the total costs were computed and then compared with historical cost data that had been collected in the past for the production of the same units.

Production problems and production cost data problems arose when custom-designed units entered into the production process. The manufacture of custom-designed units, specially produced rather than produced for inventory, caused production and assembly difficulties because their utilization of engineering, supervisory, and production personnel talents interrupted the producing-for-inventory process. Not only did these custom-designed and manufactured products require the services of various personnel normally involved in the standard production process, but they also caused an interruption of the use of production line equipment, machinery, and materials. Quite often the costs of producing the custom units were in part unrecorded or charged against products manufactured for inventory. Basically, cost data were to be recorded in the same manner as standard inventory products, but because of the uncertainty and inaccuracy of machine time, personnel hours, and material allocation, it was difficult to determine the accuracy of the production costs of special or custom units under the current system.

In discussing the problems of Manufacturing and Material Control with John Rogers, it appeared to Bill King that the difficulties lay not in production scheduling and control but in the materials subsystems. Both of these (engineering bill of materials and material status system) were being increasingly questioned. It was felt that a major redesign might be necessary because neither system was adequately doing the job. Problems were attributed to increasing product complexity. This, in turn, increased purchasing lead time. Moreover, the system was beginning to stagger under an increasing manufacturing volume. Accordingly, Bill King decided to place his initial emphasis on the material subsystems. Both were punched-card systems that had not been converted to the new IBM computer system.

ENGINEERING BILL OF MATERIALS

The original system had been designed in 1977 by Jim Blackwell, director of Research and Engineering, and his department controlled its operation. The design and operation was largely unchanged from the EAM "batch" system of 1977.

When a new product is developed or an existing one changed significantly, the material parts requirements are exploded into "engineering bills of materials." These are entered into the system by keypunching the list of parts, assemblies, and raw materials which make up the item to be produced. The format of the list shows what items, subassemblies, and components are assembled to create the next higher level of product assembly:

Item Number	Item Name	Item Number of Next Higher Level
Subitem Number	Subitem Name	Quantity Required
″ ″	″ ″	″ ″
″ ″	″ ″	″ ″
etc.	etc.	etc.
etc.	etc.	etc.

Modifications are entered through an engineering change notice (ECN). This document is used to make changes on some item in the bill of materials master file. These are also keypunched and used as input to a computer file maintenance run, which updates that master file and also prints a detailed listing of the ECN list—a list of items entered through the ECN process. Updating is accomplished approximately once a month except when a new product or major modification is introduced.

The major purpose of the bill of materials master file is to provide manufacturing with the parts requirements for any production run or for any product engineering change. Therefore, parts requirements listings are initiated by two sources:

1. A sales plan (schedule of items being ordered for production):

   Item Name   Item Number   Quantity Desired   Data Desired

2. Product engineering change:

   Item Name   Item Number   Revision Code

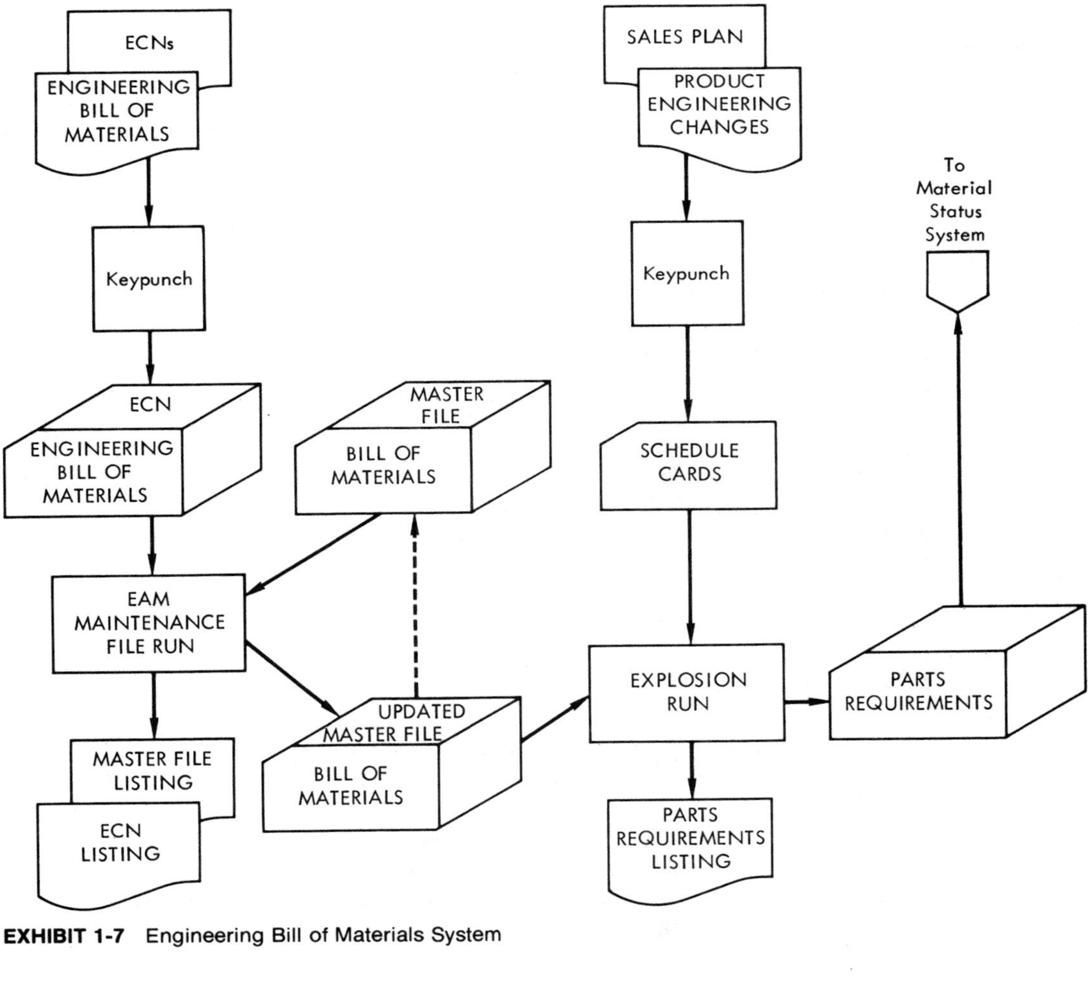

EXHIBIT 1-7 Engineering Bill of Materials System

The output of the system is the parts requirements list; those parts needed to produce the sales plan. The output is generated from the master bill of materials file by selecting those items to be produced and multiplying the unit parts requirements by the quantities of items on the sales plan. Hence,

Part Number	Part Name	Source Assembly Number	Quantity
''	''	''	''
''	''	''	''
etc.	etc.	etc.	etc.

A flowchart of the system is shown in Exhibit 1-7.

MATERIAL STATUS SYSTEM

The two main purposes of this system are to generate an unordered requirements listing for input to the purchasing system and to provide a materials status and history report for use as follow-up and status information.

Each week, and more frequently in pressing situations, a computer parts requirement run is made to develop the new or changed parts requirements that have developed from the bill of materials system. This run uses the parts requirements file of the bill of materials system and material status file to create a purchase requirements list. This list is then used by the material-ordering section to prepare requisitions for purchasing.

In addition to the requisitions for purchasing, material-ordering personnel also manually prepare a material order card that is subsequently keypunched for purposes of preparing material status cards. These are used as input to the daily computer material status run. This run merges the status cards with the materials status file to produce the updated material status file and the materials status and history report. The file, and hence the report, is changed also from these events:

1. Release of purchase order to vendor
2. Receipt of materials in Receiving
3. Material passed into the stockroom from inspection

The computer requirements run is made weekly to develop the new or changed parts requirements that have been developed from the bill of materials system.

A flowchart of the system is shown in Exhibit 1-8.

After completing the initial survey of the material status system, Bill King made an appointment to see John Rogers, vice president of manufacturing and operations. He wanted to get the views of Rogers concerning any problems that

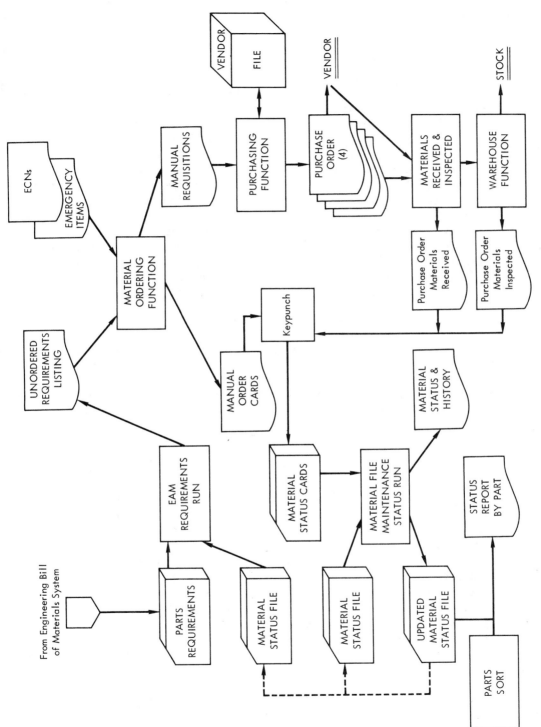

EXHIBIT 1-8 Materials Status System

431

existed in the materials status system. As usual, Rogers was candid and somewhat blunt.

"Sure, we've got problems and I can tell you that most of them result from operations over in Engineering. How the hell can I keep any kind of production line going when those guys change their minds so often on engineering specifications? Remember that an engineering change has a multiplier effect: on parts requirements, on purchasing, and on production. I say keep the changes down.

"I'm not trying to duck the blame, either. In Materials Control we have been remiss in not setting order quantities—or to put it another way, we don't always have the material on the production floor when it's needed. Did you ever see a line close down for lack of a two-dollar part? I say let's invest in more raw materials inventory so the materials tail won't be wagging the production dog."

Bill King thanked Rogers and promised to investigate his suggestions. However, he did not agree with Rogers that the entire problem lay with Engineering and Materials Control. Instead of identifying the specific problem and its causes, he decided to start with objectives and work from there. He therefore wrote down the following objectives for the materials status system:

1. Identify and order long lead-time items in the early stages of requirements determination.
2. Reduce existing clerical work load by paperwork automation to the extent practicable.
3. Provide a system of quick, accurate follow-up and status reporting.
4. Provide whatever controls are needed to ensure that all required items are ordered; conversely, ensure that items are not duplicated.

BILL KING'S APPROACH

After conducting the foregoing interviews and performing his preliminary analysis, Bill King was at a loss on how to proceed with Bemis's instruction to "come up with a master plan in four or five weeks." He was not only becoming more confused by the day but was beginning to be overwhelmed by the magnitude of the tasks involved.

King's conviction, as he had been taught in business school, was that management information systems should be designed for decision making. Yet everyone in International Medical Instruments, Inc., seemed to focus attention on the clerical nature of data processing—keeping the records. Moreover, there seemed to be little concern with production planning and control, a function that absorbed over half of the sales dollar.

King concluded that for the immediate future he should concentrate on two aspects of the overall problem:

1. *Order processing.* Because this system had been the one that was blamed for the loss of the $60,000 order, and because Dobrynski had ordered a review of it, the obvious first choice for redesign was this system. Frank Bemis was unwilling, or

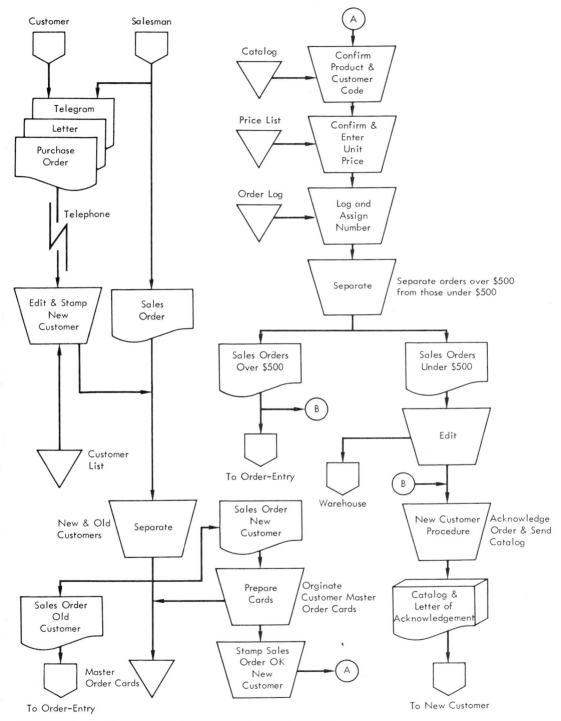

EXHIBIT 1-9 Revised Order Processing System (New Customer)

433

EXHIBIT 1-10 Master Plan of Overall Information Flow

Major Application	Responsible Department	Other System Inputs	Outputs to Other Systems
Order entry	Sales	Customer orders	Open orders
Open orders	Sales	Order entry	Marketing
		Customer file	analysis
		Finished goods	Shipping and
		inventory	invoicing
			Finished goods
			Inventory
			Customer file
Customer file	Sales	Open orders	Open orders
		Accounts	Shipping and
		receivable	invoicing
Sales analysis	Sales	Open orders	Sales analysis
		Shipping and	reports
		invoicing	Demand forecast
			Production
			scheduling
Shipping and	Sales	Customer file	Accounts
invoicing		Open orders	receivable
		Finished goods	Sales analysis
		inventory	Customer invoice
Finished goods	Sales	Open orders	Open orders
inventory	Controller	Transactions	Shipping and
	Manufacturing	Accounts payable	invoicing
		Production	Production
		schedule and	schedule and
		inventory status	inventory status
Engineering bill	Manufacturing	Parts list	Shop floor
of materials		Shop floor control	control
		Production	Production
		schedule and	schedule and
		inventory status	inventory status
Production	Manufacturing	Production	Production
schedule and		schedule	schedule
inventory status		Finished goods	Finished goods
		inventory	inventory
		Bill of materials	Bill of materials
		Shop floor control	Shop floor control
		Purchasing and	Purchasing and
		receiving	receiving
Purchasing and	Manufacturing	Production	Production
receiving		schedule and	schedule and
		inventory status	inventory status
			Accounts payable
Shop floor control	Manufacturing	Bill of materials	Personnel and
		Production	payroll
		schedule	Shop paper
		Shop paper	
Accounts payable	Controller	Purchasing and	General ledger
		receiving	Finished goods
			inventory

Note: This plan does not show information reports or inputs and outputs to systems, but rather the information flow between systems.

unable, to give King any guidance. His concluding comment was, "You've got the ball, now run with it. Don't bother me with details."

King decided that because the entire problem had been precipitated by new customer orders he should concentrate on the processing of orders for new customers. A second consideration would be the dollar amount of the orders. He decided on his own authority that the credit check of new customers would be eliminated or minimized for orders less than $500. In addition, *all* new customers should receive a letter of acknowledgment accompanied by a company catalog.

For purposes of discussion and review he constructed the flowchart shown in Exhibit 1-9.

2. *Master plan.* No attempt had been made to design according to any master plan. Consequently, the company had a number of unrelated mechanized subsystems that had "grown up" over the years. Privately, King labeled these a "patchwork" approach or "islands of mechanization." He began work on the master plan with misgivings. He suspected that the implementation of such a plan would take years, and he doubted that the company would want to allocate the resources to it. Nevertheless, he prepared the preliminary outline of Exhibit 1-10 for presentation to Frank Bemis.

PROBLEMS AND QUESTIONS

1. From the facts given in the case, identify the major problems facing the company.
2. Identify company strategy, objectives, and policies.
3. Does organizational synergism exist in the company? Illustrate with specific examples.
4. If there is a lack of synergism (functional integration), detail how management information systems could help achieve it.
5. Comment on the organization of the company as reflected by the organization chart.
6. Draw an organization chart that reflects your organizational recommendations.
7. Evaluate the organization of the data processing function.
8. Given the personalities and managerial philosophies of the executive committee, how would you go about establishing a climate for MIS? What are your chances of success?
9. Who is responsible for lack of procedures? Are they necessary? Why?
10. What effect will the expected growth in sales and product-customer mix have on systems design?
11. Does the company really need an engineering bill of materials system?
12. Evaluate the proposed master plan. Revise, if necessary, in accordance with your recommendations.
13. What specific information systems might you design for the primary use of the president in his role as chief operating officer and chief executive?
14. For a recommended finished goods inventory control system, provide a general systems concept; a narrative description; a flowchart.
15. Do the same for an inventory control system for resale items that are not manufactured at company facilities.
16. List the major shortcomings of the existing order processing system.

17. Evaluate King's proposed order-entry system.

18. King identified five breakdowns of the order processing system that resulted in the loss of a large order. How could these errors be made despite the system? How could the system be redesigned to overcome these shortcomings?

19. Each system needs an objective and a measure of progress toward achievement of the objective (e.g., reduction in backorders, elapsed time to process an order). For these systems, list objective and measurement of objective performance:

System	Objective	Measure
Order processing		
Purchasing		
Production control		
Material status		
Accounts receivable		

20. What is the main purpose of the sales order? The customer's invoice (shipping order)? The material status report? What are the information inputs and outputs to these documents?

21. For the order-entry system, draw a flowchart and write a procedure that will achieve two objectives: (a) all orders over $5000 will be given special attention, and (b) government and wholesale customers are given the special discount.

22. List five decision rules that should be incorporated into these systems: order processing, purchasing, production control. For each decision indicate the information required, the information sources, and the techniques of documentation to be used in making each decision. Assume that you are a systems analyst who is gathering data for systems redesign. Use this format:

Decision	Information Required	Information Source	Documentation
	Order Entry		
Where should the order be shipped?	Billing address Shipping address	Order-entry personnel	Sales order form layout Procedure for processing order

23. Assume that you are analyzing the warehousing function for possible redesign of the information system. Prepare an interview plan including (a) objectives of the interview, (b) individuals to be interviewed, (c) specific questions to be asked.

24. Give a listing of all inputs and outputs of the order processing system for *each department*.

25. Evaluate the customer and product codes of the company. Redesign if necessary. Consider the needs of the company in answering.

26. Design a form for the purchasing function; the billing function.

27. Prepare an *integrated* flowchart of the entire order processing system. Include order-entry, warehousing, data processing, shipping, order follow-up, and billing.

28. Design an improved shipping order that would be used under an automated order-entry system. Indicate number of copies and distribution. Identify an area of operations that has a potential for automation of source records for this system.

29. Evaluate the system of controls in the company with regard to both the data processing center and the various systems involved.

30. Outline an implementation plan for redesign of the order processing system. Include work breakdown structure and timetable.

31. For the _____ system,

   a. Draw existing system flowchart.
   b. State the system objective(s).
   c. List information needs.
   d. List information sources.
   e. Supply additional information needed for adequate design.
   f. Show how company profitability can be improved by the system.
   g. List the indicated controls.
   h. Indicate the file design.
   i. Give a statement of the system problem.
   j. Show how the existing clerical or manual system could be upgraded for better decision making.
   k. Design the output form.
   l. Illustrate a decision rule to be built into the system.
   m. Draw a systems flowchart of the revised system.
   n. List the system constraints.
   o. Describe any changes that are recommended for
      Procedures
      Equipment
      Personnel
      Facilities

32. Prepare a data gathering plan that Bill King could use for his investigation of order processing. Include an interview plan.

Development of an MIS for Field Office Managers of the Northwestern Insurance Company

The Northwestern Insurance Company currently has 50 full-line field offices located throughout the United States, each consisting of service units that perform processing and administrative services for producers (agents) in the geographical area served by the field office. Although the exact composition varies from location to location, most field offices have separate service units for processing transactions relating to life and accident insurance, fire and marine insurance (e.g., homeowner and business coverage of losses from fire, theft, rain, and windstorm), other casualty insurance (including worker's compensation, public liability, burglary, plate glass, multiperil commercial, and auto fleet coverage), automobile insurance, and fidelity and surety insurance. In addition to the primary service units, each field office normally has an accounting unit.

ADMINISTRATIVE AND POLICY-RELATED PROCESSING OPERATIONS

The primary service units provide processing services to the agent in the field. Each service unit processes four basic types of transactions: new policy applications, policy changes, policy renewals, and claim registrations. Transactions in the field offices arise from correspondence received from the home office, from the producer-agent, and, in some cases, directly from the policyholder.

All incoming mail is transferred in bulk to a record desk. A clerk sorts the mail by unit (e.g., fire, other casualty, automobile). The incoming documents are matched with any existing file records pertaining to each transaction. Although the principal policy records are maintained in the home office, the field offices also keep extensive manual records, some of which duplicate the home office files.

Northwestern Insurance Company is a fictitious name. This case study is based on the operations of a large multiline insurance company, with a few minor modifications. It is adapted from "The Development of a Management Information System for Field Office Managers of the Northwestern Insurance Co.," a paper presented by William C. House at the 1969 TIMS meeting in Atlanta, Georgia. By permission of the author.

Once transaction documents have been matched with appropriate file records, the resulting package is forwarded to the proper service unit for further processing. At the conclusion of processing, existing documents are refiled or otherwise disposed of. New documents created provide the basis for extending or changing coverage to new and old policyholders.

The accounting unit is not directly involved in the major flows of paperwork through the field office, and so it does not ordinarily have direct contact with producers in the field. However, it does perform some important processing functions, including the collection of premiums, reporting of premiums received to the home office, and payroll and expense accounting for the field office.

MANAGEMENT INFORMATION REQUIREMENTS FOR THE FIELD OFFICE MANAGER

The performance of each field office manager is judged by how well he or she meets certain basic objectives in the areas of service, personnel, and expenses. These objectives are largely determined by the home office administrators who are responsible for supervising field office operations. Examples of objectives for each performance area are

Service

Volume of unfinished business (e.g., no more than two days' work left undone at the end of the week)
Quantity of work done (e.g., number of transactions processed per day)
Quality of work done (e.g., no more than 5 percent errors)

Personnel

Available hours for each service unit (i.e., number of person-hours available to perform work)
Earned hours for each service unit (i.e., standard processing times for each type of transaction, multiplied by number of transactions processed)
Number of employees hired
Turnover rate—by office, by service unit, by salary grade, by position code

Expense

Actual costs: provisional budget costs
Actual costs: budget costs (adjusted for volume changes)
Cost per hour (by field office)

The field office manager needs information relating to service, personnel, and expense performance within 10 days after the end of the (usually monthly) reporting period, so it can be determined if any service unit is failing to meet one or more of the basic objectives and corrective action can be taken before serious deterioration occurs. Determining the basic causes and sources of inadequate performance often requires quickly accessible and detailed information on the performance of particular service units and of specific individuals within these units. In addition, all basic performance information should be provided to the field office manager in one package at one time instead of in several reports issued at different time intervals, as is now the case.

In the service area, timely information is needed on the rate at which work is coming into the unit and the speed with which it is being processed. If a unit is falling behind in its work, the field office manager needs to take corrective action quickly, to avoid a serious bottleneck. For such purposes, a two-week reporting period would be much better than a monthly one, and weekly reports on the volume of unfinished business by unit would be even more valuable.

To utilize data concerning service levels and work backlogs most effectively, the manager needs to know the size of the work load and the number of people available to handle it. If a peak volume period is being experienced and the office is understaffed, the manager may have to consider the use of overtime, of contract services, of transferring some work to another office, or of hiring and training additional employees. In making such decisions, the manager needs to know probable service requirements by line of business, since some lines are more difficult to handle than others or require specialized training to handle, and by type of transaction (e.g., new business, policy changes, renewals, and claims), because some types of transactions require more employee processing time than others. Therefore, a forecast of service requirements 60 to 90 days in advance would be extremely helpful in determining staffing and training requirements.

To project future requirements, the manager needs past data on the number of new policies, number of endorsements (changes), number of renewals, and number of claims for each service unit for comparable periods. If a relationship could be established between new policies issued and probable number of changes, claims, and renewals that could be expected in each period per 100 or 1000 policies issued, a complete work load forecast could be developed simply by predicting the amount of new business. The estimated number of new policies, changes, renewals, claims, and premium payments developed from past experience and considered judgment about the future could be exploded into volume requirements for service to be performed by the various service units.

These volume requirements could then serve as the basis for establishing the size and composition of the work force needed to meet expected volumes, in terms of hours and experience required. Work load requirements in hours would indicate the amount of work required for each service unit for each type of work (e.g., rating, typing, duplicating), and such information could then be used to decide the best way of meeting work load requirements (e.g., increasing or decreasing the existing work force, using overtime, employing contract services, shifting some of the work load to other offices, or finding ways to improve present unit productivity).

To decide how to meet these estimated work load requirements most efficiently and economically, the field office manager needs an up-to-date picture of the status of his or her current work force. In particular, the manager needs to know the amount of lost time being experienced, because of absences owing to illness and other causes, and the personnel losses of each service unit because of turnover. A realistic forecast of the lost time each service unit is likely to experience during the next three months would help to determine the probable number of available hours obtainable from the existing work force. By matching available hours with required hours forecast, the manager could determine in advance if he or she is overstaffed or understaffed in terms of work load requirements for the coming quarter.

If an increase in service is forecast and the manager is understaffed to meet such an increase, a number of alternatives is open. If he or she is willing to pay the training costs entailed and can afford to wait until the end of a normal training period, the manager can increase the existing work force. For temporary work load peaks, the use of overtime or contract services may be considered. The manager may find it economical to transfer some of the peak load to other field offices that have idle time, at a cost per hour less than other feasible alternatives. In some cases, improving the productivity of the existing work force may be the best solution. Fewer people may be able to do the work required if they are placed in the right positions and are paid large enough salaries. To choose wisely from among these alternatives, the manager must be provided with the cost per hour involved in each alternative.

In essence, the manager must decide whether the projected work load can be performed with the staff available at a reasonable cost. If the manager cannot get the work out with the available staff, other alternatives must be considered. In most cases the least costly alternative will be selected, but not at an unreasonable sacrifice in terms of service provided. Some balance must be maintained, because it is possible to meet service objectives satisfactorily at an unreasonable cost, or to provide inadequate service at satisfactory costs. In the dynamic situation, the office manager must make continual and rapid adjustments to keep the entire office operating at a satisfactory level. Timely and complete information about all aspects of service, personnel, and expense performance is essential if the manager is to make sound and effective decisions.

SERVICE REPORTING

Each field office has the objective of providing 24-hour service on new business and claim registrations and 48-hour service on policy changes. Objectives for renewal service are more flexible, because renewal processing can be accelerated or delayed in many cases without ill effects.

Service reports are prepared manually for each week of a month and are transmitted by mail to the home office once a month. Each field office reports the current status of 55 different processing activities on its service reports. Thus, 2750 transactions (i.e., 55 × 50) must be processed monthly for all field offices. These reports, normally received by the home office within 7 to 10 days after the end of the reporting period, are used to evaluate the service status of each field office, and the transaction counts in the reports are also used as basic inputs for expense reporting.

At present, field office managers do not, in many cases, receive information on deteriorating service quickly enough to prevent work load bottlenecks. Although the manager is informed of the amount of unfinished business in the various service units, he or she is given no idea of the volume or composition of the service requirements to anticipate for the next quarter or the cost of maintaining or changing desired service levels.

PERSONNEL REPORTING

Each field office maintains basic personnel files on clerical employees. However, the home office also maintains personnel files, and each field office is responsible for advising the home office of changes in the clerical work force, so that companywide statistical information can be compiled and payroll information maintained for the preparation of tax withholding information.

Three basic input documents—the personnel employment authorization, the personnel change slip, and the absence report—are used to collect data on personnel changes. Owing to a lag in the forwarding and posting of change slips, the home office personnel file is normally at least 10 days out of date.

Transactions affecting the personnel file occur at irregular intervals, but they are substantial in number over the entire working year. On an annual basis, the total volume of typical personnel transactions might be estimated as follows:

Transaction Type	Number of Transactions
Salary changes	18,000
Absences	38,000
Personnel time off	1,000
Name changes	2,000
Annual updating	16,000
	75,000

Assuming 300 working days in a year, there would be an average of 250 (i.e., 75,000/300) personnel updating transactions per day for all field offices. And assuming 6 service units per field office, there would be 300 transactions (6 × 50) each time the number of available hours is calculated for all service units in the company.

The time lag in updating personnel files makes it difficult to produce personnel information such as turnover statistics, average salaries, and so on, in time to be of the greatest potential value to users. High turnover rates and high costs of recruiting and training clerical personnel make it imperative that managers select the best qualified people with the greatest potential for long tenure; but the present reporting system does not provide information as to what age, education, and experience groups are producing the best results and in which areas recruiting efforts should be concentrated. Also lacking is sound, factual information on the causes of turnover in a particular service unit (e.g., salary inequities, specific job-related dissatisfaction, unit morale problems) that the manager could use to select, train, and motivate individuals so as to achieve higher levels of unit efficiency.

EXPENSE REPORTING

Expense performance in the field offices is measured through the use of a provisional (planned) and earned budget system that includes both fixed and variable budget items. Fixed cost items include stenographic services, telephone operations, mail handling, and so on; variable cost items include such activities as the screening, rating, coding, typing, duplicating, and disassembly of various types of insurance policies. "Earned hours" are calculated by multiplying the number of transactions processed by the budgeted time rates in the provisional budget. For all field offices, a maximum of 2750 transactions would be involved for each reporting period.

In preparing the provisional budget, the field office manager estimates the volume of each type of activity, the time rate required to process each activity, and employee salaries (including increase programs) for the coming year. The number of hours needed by each office to handle the expected work load is obtained by multiplying the time rate by the number of items to be processed for each activity and then summing the expected activity times. The dollar costs of providing the necessary clerical hours, and the estimated cost per hour for each service unit and for the total office, can then be developed. The completed provisional budget shows planned hours and planned costs for each service unit in the field office.

Comparisons between actual expense performance and budgeted expense levels are presented in monthly and quarterly performance reports. Available hours and earned hours for each service unit and for the total office are shown in the monthly report on a current-month and year-to-date basis. Available hours are the person-hours actually worked by each unit (i.e., gross hours minus vacation time, time lost to illness, and other miscellaneous causes). Earned hours are calculated as previously described.

The monthly expense reports come out approximately 20 days after the close of the month being reported. Quarterly expense reports are not available until approximately 45 days after the end of the reporting period. As a result, many supervisors are currently figuring productivity ratios by hand from work counts. By the time reports arrive from the home office, the unit supervisors already know the results. Although this practice gives the supervisor information more quickly than would otherwise be possible, it is time consuming, costly, and cumbersome. Also, the lag between the receipt of information on service status and corresponding information about expense performance means that the office manager does not have a complete picture of service unit status at a given instant of time and cannot make completely informed decisions about work load scheduling, hiring new employees, using overtime, employing contract services, and so on at the time when such decisions must be made.

Monthly and quarterly expense reports are needed by field office managers much sooner after the end of the reporting period so they can make better informed decisions about alternative ways of providing clerical service. Under the present reporting system, information is frequently received too late to be of real value in controlling expense levels, and the manager cannot determine from the information received what actions should be taken to correct present performance. The system does not relate expenses to expected volumes and does not indicate to the manager how to plan to achieve best results. Finally, there is no way at present of coordinating expense performance with service results, nor does the manager know the economic resources that must be used to improve service, personnel, and expense performance.

DESIGN OF AN INFORMATION SYSTEM TO MEET MANAGEMENT INFORMATION REQUIREMENTS

At the present time, policyholder records and many other administrative records are maintained in the home office, although some duplicate records are kept by the field offices. Most of the inputs for creating new records and updating those existing in the home office come from the field offices. A large amount of performance data is forwarded to the home office through the use of mail and telegraph services. In addition, two-way data and voice communication channels rapidly transmit data collected for policy record creation and policy updating to the home office data center for batch processing at appropriate times, and inquiries from the field offices about the status of an individual policy are answered promptly on a real-time basis by means of the same network.

The home office maintains four basic but separate files pertinent to performance reporting: policyholder, service, personnel, and expense files. Each file requires a separate processing run. Consideration is being given to consolidation of service, personnel, and expense data into one centralized file. Input devices used to transmit messages to the central computer center could be utilized to input office service, personnel, and expense performance data. A second alternative being considered is the use of two regional processing centers, one in the eastern and the other in the western United States, to divide the total data processing load.

Another important issue is the frequency of reporting. At the present time, the bulk of reporting is done on a monthly basis, with an average time lag of 20 to 30 days from the end of the reporting period to the receipt of desired management reports by field office managers. This time lag is caused by delays in forwarding data to the home office; in processing data, owing to the occurrence of transaction volume peaks at the end of each month; and in consolidating data, items that are obtained from several different processing runs on different computer systems into a single performance report.

More frequent reporting, on a bimonthly, weekly, or even daily basis, is feasible but will probably require integration of existing files, a greater degree of compatibility between existing computers, and expansion of the on-line processing capability now largely restricted to certain classes of policyholder records. For example, if transactions for the service, personnel, and expense areas were processed for all 50 field offices on a daily basis, the estimated number of transactions to be processed would be as follows:

Service	2750
Personnel updating	250
Personnel available hours	300
Expense	2750

Assuming 300 working days in a year, 1,815,000 transactions (i.e, 6050 × 300) would be handled annually by the consolidated system. On a monthly basis (corresponding to the present reporting period), 72,600 transactions (i.e., 6050 × 12) are processed. Thus, daily updating would necessitate about a 30-fold increase in the number of transaction processed.

The field offices are now processing approximately 20,000,000 policy-related transactions per year. The number is expected to increase at a rate of at least 5 percent annually as new policyholders are added and the coverage of existing policyholders is increased to meet changing needs. Office performance transactions can also be expected to increase at approximately the same rate as new employees are added, as the scope of performance reporting is increased, and as new field offices are created to handle the ever-expanding increase in volume of business.

Expansion of business volume will also increase the number of data calculations that must be performed by existing processing equipment. Consideration is being given to development of simulation models in conjunction with existing computers, which would allow field office managers to develop their own forecasts and to test alternative methods of meeting service requirements before making decisions.

PROBLEMS AND QUESTIONS

1. Sketch a recommended computer hardware configuration for the company.
2. Design a conceptual data flow along the lines of Figure 3-28. Include flowcharts of major data flows.
3. Would your configuration of question 1 and your data flow of question 2 change the organization structure or the number of field offices? If so, recommend a reorganization.
4. Does file duplication exist? How would you reduce it? Be specific.
5. What would you recommend with regard to the growing number of files and the need for storage capacity?
6. Are files, data elements, and information sources duplicated? Show the conceptual design of a company data bank that would reduce this duplication.
7. What applications, if any, justify the real time concept?
8. Could modeling / simulation be utilized beneficially? How?
9. Give a list of subsystems that you would recommend be included in a master plan for MIS.
10. For each of the four major subsystems — policy data, personnel data, service data, and administrative data — provide the following:

Subsystem	Objectives	Constraints	Info Needs
Policy			
Personnel			
Service			
Administrative			

Subsystem	Info Sources	Info Inputs	Info Outputs
Policy			
Personnel			
Service			
Administrative			

Case 3 | IMI Staff Assignment

Bill King, you will recall from Case 1, has been hired by International Medical Instruments to develop a management information system for the company. He has been quite successful in providing systems to support IMI's management team in their various activities. He has been promoted to director of MIS and reports directly to the president of IMI, Robert Dobrynski.

Dobrynski has watched King for quite some time now. He believes that King has a lot of ability. Bill King's contributions to the firm consistently have a widespread and very positive impact. Dobrynski has given King the following staff assignment:

> *Distinguish problem solving and decision making and tell me how you go about each of these activities (step-by-step analysis).*

Bill has completed his staff work and submitted the following paper to Mr. Dobrynski.

BILL KING'S REPORT

We will distinguish between problem solving and decision making. Problem solving, in its essential form, is the *seeking of answers to a question.* Decision making is the *cutting off* of further consideration of the problem, the elimination of all alternatives but one; it is a commitment to action. Let us turn first to problems and problem solving.

A problem is a deviation between *that which is* (or is anticipated) and *that which is desired*, or between *that which is known* and that which is *desired to be known.* Note that problems may exist and not be recognized. In fact, too often managers remain unaware of problems until a crisis is reached or affairs have gone beyond the point of no return. Recognizing that a problem exists or impends is one of a manager's most important and often overlooked responsibilities.

Step 1 of Problem Solving:
RECOGNIZE THE PROBLEM

We live in a very complex world replete with opportunities for improvement. When interpreted for the business environment, these opportunities are problems to be solved. Since there are and will always be more problems to solve than a firm has resources to cover, a business endeavor must choose which problem(s) it will work on.

Step 2 of Problem Solving:
CHOOSE THE PROBLEM TO BE SOLVED

Having recognized a problem and chosen to solve it still leaves us miles from the solution. We must now formulate the problem as precisely as possible. It has been said that a problem well defined is a problem half-solved. In complex business situations, verbalization, discussion, and reflection can do much to refine a problem, leading to its formulation and thereby ultimately contributing to its solution. It is also true that some problems are never solved because they are not formulated correctly. The right answer to the wrong problem may be more damaging than no solution at all.

Formulation requires these key items:

1. Elements—the factors that are relevant to describing the various states and the relationships among the factors. Company resources and competition are examples.
2. Present state—for example, the company has had 10 percent sales decline for three years.
3. Desired state—steadily increasing sales and profits.
4. Constraints—diversification must be accomplished internally rather than through acquisition, for example.
5. Criteria the solution must meet—an example is "Sales must increase by 5 percent each year."

Step 3 of Problem Solving:
FORMULATE THE PROBLEM

Formulating the problem can be extremely difficult, and multiple techniques are available for accomplishing it. A highly recommended method is to start with a corporate mission statement that tells us what business we're in: then follow this with the objectives we are trying to achieve in the various areas of our business. Given clear objectives, the problem can now be stated as a deviation from one of our goals. This is an excellent technique for putting the problem in the proper perspective and also for regularly verifying our objectives/direction.

> Step 4 of Problem Solving:
> APPLY SPECIFIC TECHNIQUE(S) TO PROBLEM

Steps 4 and onward come down to the application of the various known techniques of problem solving. The pragmatic approach to problem solving in business firms, which has proved effective throughout the years, is clarified by means of the model in Exhibit 3-1. The general approach is "handling" the

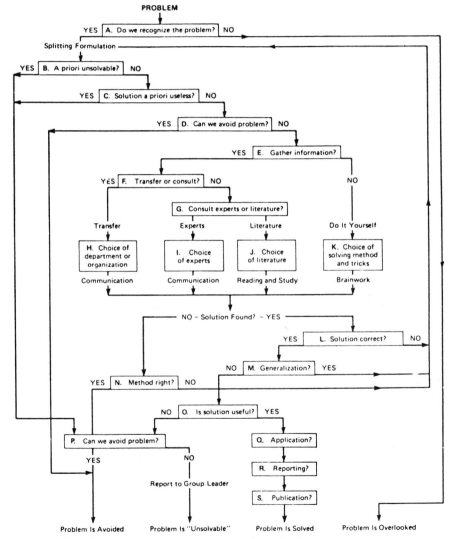

EXHIBIT 3-1 Problem-Solving Decisions in an Organization

Source: Ir. A. H. Boerdijk, "Step-by-Step Guide to Problem-Solving Decisions," reprinted from *Product Engineering.* Copyright 1963 by McGraw-Hill, Inc.

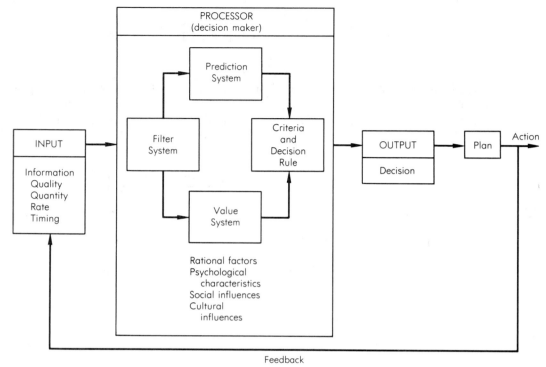

EXHIBIT 3-2   Management and the Decision System

problem to avoid the intellectual process of creating an original solution except as a last resort. This is because it is simply more economical to bypass the problem, find someone who has solved similar problems (an expert), or find a published solution.[1]

Now let us turn to decision making. We will avoid the theoretical byways such as the psychological processes of the manager's mind or the electrochemical reactions in the decision maker's brain. Rather we will pursue the gross, workaday aspects of deciding.

Consider Exhibit 3-2 depicting a decision system. The information received as input can have various attributes. *Quality* of information covers such things as accuracy and relevance. With regard to *quantity*, human beings can only retain and use small amounts of information under the normal time restrictions of business situations. Further, people are sensitive to the *rate* and *timing* of information arrival. Information presented too soon is forgotten; too late, and it becomes irrelevant.

---

[1] There are many books that will give us leads on where to go for more detailed information on specific types of problem solving. A particularly good volume is *Conceptual Blockbusting* by James L. Adams (New York: W. W. Norton, 1976).

Our manager (processor, decision maker) receives the information with all its imperfections and adds some of his own. He applies a set of "filters" built from rational factors, personality characteristics, social biases, and cultural influences. He then consults his value system and experience. The decision criteria and the decision rule are laid over all the above. The result is the same as when we face the ice-cream counter: alternatives are eliminated, we choose one solution, we commit ourselves to that action plan.[2]

In summary, we noted that problem solving is the seeking of answers to a question. Decision making is choosing one solution and committing to the implied action. There are some initial steps to problem solving that apply to all problems. Following that, a variety of specific techniques can be applied depending on the nature of the problem. Decision making, as do all systems, has input, a processor, and output. The input comes in varied quality and quantity. The manager, acting as processor, brings his or her experience and values to bear on the information at hand. The decision rule and criteria are applied. A commitment to act on one solution results. That decision is the output.

FOLLOW-UP

Robert Dobrynski is happy with Bill King's paper on problem solving and decision making. But, like most executives, he wants to ask some questions:
"Pick a problem you are familiar with, Bill, and

1. List the elements of the problem.
2. Describe the present state of the situation.
3. Describe the desired state of the situation.
4. List the constraints.
5. Develop criteria for solutions.
6. Suggest several possible solutions.

After you take me through a problem in detail, I'm sure I will understand the process better.
"Select a repetitive problem and show me how its solution could be programmed (solved by computer).
"Help me through the steps of deciding to replace my old refrigerator."

---

[2] For additional discussion on the topic of decision making, see *People, Profits, and Productivity* by Joel Ross (Reston, Va.: Reston, 1981).

BACKGROUND MATERIAL

Tim Johnson is a dynamic young businessman. In 1975, he started a machine shop that makes special parts of any type that anyone is willing to pay for. When he first started, he had a steady flow of work, but he wanted to expand; hence he developed a policy of taking all jobs on a first-come, first-served basis. By 1980, Johnson's machine shop work was backlogged four weeks consistently, and he had reached capacity within his space constraints. By 1982, the backlog was four months, and some customers were going elsewhere rather than wait for delivery.

Johnson has 11 machinists working full time and some overtime. All work is done on a cash basis. Bills are paid by check when they come due. Inventory control consists of buying raw materials and tools when the stock "looks low" or the supplies run out. Payroll consists of collecting everyone's time cards Thursday afternoon. Thursday night Jack Johnson, Tim's father, does the payroll and writes the paychecks by hand.

In 1980, Tim bought the hardware store next door. Sales to the general public are for cash. Credit is given to some builders on a 2, 10 net 30 basis. Bills are paid by check as they come due. Payroll is handled the same way as at the machine shop (17 employees). Inventory control is the usual manual system: a card is kept on each part stocked. Purchases are added by hand, and sales are deducted by hand. A reorder point has been identified for most items. It takes a clerk full time plus overtime to handle this.

Last month, the key plumbing service firm in town came up for sale. There are 24 employees. Two of them sell replacement parts to the general public. This is done from a window in the stock room that these same two employees manage (inventory system comparable to the hardware store). There is one salesman who specializes in schools, hospitals, and so on in the area. Another calls on the large businesses. Yet another deals with individual contractors who are building houses and apartments. There is a fleet of 10 trucks, each regularly used by a journeyman plumber. Although the goal is to have an apprentice plumber assigned to each of the experienced plumbers, there are currently only 8 in training. One badly overworked secretary serves as receptionist, dispatcher, and bookkeeper (payroll, accounts receivable, accounts payable, general ledger, etc.). Payroll is calculated differently for each job classification. The owner has, in the past, worked at whatever was most critical that day (sales, plumbing, ordering parts, helping the secretary).

Tim wants to buy the plumbing firm. But his dad is getting tired of spending Thursday nights doing payrolls by hand and weekends paying bills and figuring taxes. He is strongly in favor of helping Tim expand, but he sees that management control cannot be maintained without some change in the way the firm does business. Computers are common in accounting firms such as Jack Johnson's, and lately, more and more of his co-workers have small computers at home. Jack believes Johnson Enterprises could make good use of a small computer, both as an accounting device and as an aid to management decision making as Johnson Enterprises expands (rather than relying entirely on Tim's intuition). Tim is not particularly interested in the details. In fact, he suspects his father really wants the computer to play with. He recognizes the evolving strains on management decision-making capacity, he wants to expand, and he needs his father's backing.

JOHNSON ENTERPRISES (A)

Tim Johnson and his father have debated for some time the question of automating a portion of their work. They have concluded that they want a small computer or a set of small computers. Large computers take special facilities and a specialized staff to function properly. Renting time on someone else's computer introduces a degree of vulnerability that neither Tim nor Jack finds acceptable (payroll could be late, computing costs are out of their control, and so on). Small computers have their share of problems, but the headaches are at least outweighed by the benefits.

Jack has agreed to do all the analysis and planning involved with introducing automated management information systems into Johnson Enterprises. He first pursues the following problems:

1. For each of the three businesses (machine shop, hardware store, plumbing service firm), draw a flowchart showing how they currently handle payroll, inventory control, accounts receivable, and accounts payable.
2. Highlight the similarities and differences in these systems.
3. What advantages/disadvantages will there be to automating these systems versus continued manual operation?

JOHNSON ENTERPRISES (B)

Jack has talked to some knowledgeable people and has concluded that his database decisions can have a profound impact on both the initial and operational costs of his computer system. He has decided that he should make an effort to define his database system correctly.

Jack wants to have a sales analysis MIS to apply to the plumbing service firm when they buy it. He would like to measure the productivity of the two stockroom employees in two ways: (1) revenue generated and (2) selling hours versus general stockroom work (selling adds revenue, putting things on shelves is overhead). Jack would like to measure the three field sales representatives against an "opportunity" quota, which he is not sure yet how to describe.

The following tasks must be completed to define the database for this MIS:

1. List all data items required to
   a. Determine revenue generated by each stockroom employee.
   b. Determine selling hours and general stockroom work for each stockroom employee.
2. What pieces of data must Jack have to set the sales quotas fairly for the three field sales representatives?
3. What data items must each salesrep report for Jack to be able effectively to measure performance?

JOHNSON ENTERPRISES (C)

There are immediate benefits to be derived from automated systems for

1. Inventory control
2. Payroll
3. Accounts receivable
4. Accounts payable

Although these areas are the obvious, quick payoff systems that should be implemented first, Jack would like to look ahead and discover what additional capabilities he will want to have in the future.

1. Assuming that the plumbing business is purchased, what opportunities for automated problem solving/decision making (other than the four just listed) present themselves? How about a scheduling rule for the machine shop to optimize machine utilization? to optimize machinist time? to optimize overall profits?
2. Draw the flowcharts for the new subsystems you have suggested.

JOHNSON ENTERPRISES (D)

One thing has been bothering Jack. As he has worked on the various pieces he intends to automate, he has had a nagging feeling that there is no master plan. Finally, he can stand it no longer. He stops work on the various pieces and tries to draw the "system view."

1. Assume that payroll, inventory control, accounts payable and receivable, and sales analysis are the five subsystems that make up the whole Johnson Enterprises

management information system. Draw a system overview that shows the relationships among these subsystems.

Jack also needs to lay out a rough plan for implementing the system he has in mind.

2. Make a high-level plan for this set of projects. Be sure to include a statement of objectives, a work breakdown, interdependencies, schedules, skills required, other resources required, and budgets.

JOHNSON ENTERPRISES (E)

Jack is quite sure he will end up buying some standard applications from the computer manufacturer or a software house (for example, payroll, inventory control, accounts payable and receivable). He knows, however, that he will have to create his own MIS for sales analysis. He breaks down the task as follows (consider only the stockroom employees):

1. Review the objectives as stated in Johnson Enterprises (B).
2. What constraints exist or should be imposed on this system?
3. Where will the required inputs come from?
4. What outputs are desired?
5. Roughly, what would the system flowchart look like?

JOHNSON ENTERPRISES (F)

It is now necessary to design the sales analysis system in detail:

1. Exactly which inputs will come from which sources in what formats?
2. Exactly what do the outputs look like?
3. Exactly what data will be stored in the database?
4. What type of storage media will the data reside on?

Draw the detailed system flowchart.

JOHNSON ENTERPRISES (G)

Jack will soon start the implementation phase of his sales analysis project. He will be implementing the programs in BASIC. He also must acquire the hardware and packaged programs he needs.

1. Based on the first three columns of the following table being all of the manufacturers that Jack is seriously considering, choose the "best" computer system for Johnson Enterprises and explain your choice. Now add your choice of current hardware offerings and repeat the exercise.

Feature / Computer from	Vendor A	Vendor B	Vendor C	Your Choice of Current Hardware Offerings
User memory	512K	1,024K	512K	
Display				
Black / White	Yes	Yes	Yes	
Color	No	Yes	Yes	
External	Diskette	Diskette	Diskette	
storage	Disk	Disk		
Printers	Yes	Yes	Yes	
Data com-				
munications	Yes	Yes	Yes	
Optional I / O	None	Cassette jack	Wide variety	
Graphics	Extensive	None	Business graphs only	
Programming				
languages	BASIC, etc.	BASIC, etc.	BASIC, etc.	
Documentation	20 manuals	2 manuals	100 manuals	
Support	Dealer train.	Dealer train.	None	
Maintenance	Dealer	Dealer	On-site	
Warranty	90 days (hwr)	90 days	90 days	
Vendor				
reputation	Excellent	Good	Good	
Avg. system				
price	$500 – $2000	$1500	$1500	

2. If these same vendors are the only ones Jack is considering for software package purchases, which packages should he buy and why? Assume that they all offer similar packages at similar prices.

Package	Yes	No	Reason
Spreadsheet	____	____	_____
Letter writing	____	____	_____
Text editing	____	____	_____
Stock market	____	____	_____
General ledger	____	____	_____
Accounts receivable	____	____	_____
Accounts payable	____	____	_____
Inventory control	____	____	_____
Games	____	____	_____
Time manager	____	____	_____

Index

N